THE RISE OF SCRIPTURE

To Father Columba Stewart
In appreciation for your
great work,

Sincerely

Father Paul Tarazi

The Rise of Scripture

Paul Nadim Tarazi

OCABS PRESS
ST PAUL, MINNESOTA 55124
2017

In Loving Memory of
Widad Dides Tarazi, my mother
and
Jamal Tarazi, my father
who
Like Enoch before them
"Walked with God"
and
Showed me the path

THE RISE OF SCRIPTURE

ISBN 1-60191-038-X

Other Books by the Author

I Thessalonians: A Commentary
Galatians: A Commentary

The Old Testament: An Introduction

Volume 1: Historical Traditions, revised edition
Volume 2: Prophetic Traditions
Volume 3: Psalms and Wisdom

The New Testament: An Introduction

Volume 1: Paul and Mark
Volume 2: Luke and Acts
Volume 3: Johannine Writings
Volume 4: Matthew and the Canon

The Chrysostom Bible

Genesis: A Commentary
Philippians: A Commentary
Romans: A Commentary
Colossians & Philemon: A Commentary
1 Corinthians: A Commentary
Ezekiel: A Commentary
Joshua: A Commentary
2 Corinthians: A Commentary
Isaiah: A Commentary
Jeremiah: A Commentary
Hebrews: A Commentary
The Pastorals: A Commentary

Land and Covenant

The Rise of Scripture

ISBN 1-60191-038-X

Published by OCABS Press, St. Paul, Minnesota.
Printed in the United States of America.

Books are available through OCABS Press at special discounts
for bulk purchases in the United States by academic institutions,
churches, and other organizations. For more information please
email OCABS Press at press@ocabs.org.

Abbreviations

Books by the Author

1 Thess   *I Thessalonians: A Commentary,* Crestwood, NY: St. Vladimir's Seminary Press, 1982

Gal   *Galatians: A Commentary,* Crestwood, NY: St. Vladimir's Seminary Press, 1994

OTI₁   *The Old Testament: An Introduction, Volume 1: Historical Traditions,* revised edition, Crestwood, NY: St. Vladimir's Seminary Press, 2003

OTI₂   *The Old Testament: An Introduction, Volume 2: Prophetic Traditions,* Crestwood, NY: St. Vladimir's Seminary Press, 1994

OTI₃   *The Old Testament: An Introduction, Volume 3: Psalms and Wisdom,* Crestwood, NY: St. Vladimir's Seminary Press, 1996

NTI₁   *The New Testament: An Introduction, Volume 1: Paul and Mark,* Crestwood, NY: St. Vladimir's Seminary Press, 1999

NTI₂   *The New Testament: An Introduction, Volume 2: Luke and Acts,* Crestwood, NY: St. Vladimir's Seminary Press, 2001

NTI₃   *The New Testament: An Introduction, Volume 3: Johannine Writings,* Crestwood, NY: St. Vladimir's Seminary Press, 2004

NTI₄   *The New Testament: An Introduction, Volume 4: Matthew and the Canon,* St. Paul, MN: OCABS Press, 2009

C-Gen   *Genesis: A Commentary.* The Chrysostom Bible. St. Paul, MN: OCABS Press, 2009

C-Phil   *Philippians: A Commentary.* The Chrysostom Bible. St. Paul, MN: OCABS Press, 2009

C-Rom   *Romans: A Commentary.* The Chrysostom Bible. St. Paul, MN: OCABS Press, 2010

C-Col   *Colossians & Philemon: A Commentary.* The Chrysostom Bible. St. Paul, MN: OCABS Press, 2010

C-1Cor   *1 Corinthians: A Commentary.* The Chrysostom Bible. St. Paul, MN: OCABS Press, 2011

C-Ezek   *Ezekiel: A Commentary.* The Chrysostom Bible. St. Paul, MN: OCABS Press, 2012

C-Josh   *Joshua: A Commentary.* The Chrysostom Bible. St. Paul, MN: OCABS Press, 2013

C-2Cor   *2 Corinthians: A Commentary.* The Chrysostom Bible. St. Paul, MN: OCABS Press, 2013

C-Is   *Isaiah: A Commentary.* The Chrysostom Bible. St. Paul, MN: OCABS Press, 2013

C-Jer   *Jeremiah: A Commentary.* The Chrysostom Bible. St. Paul, MN: OCABS Press, 2013

C-Heb   *Hebrews: A Commentary.* The Chrysostom Bible. St. Paul, MN: OCABS Press, 2014

C-Pas   *The Pastorals: A Commentary.* The Chrysostom Bible. St. Paul, MN: OCABS Press, 2016

LAC   *Land and Covenant,* St. Paul, MN: OCABS Press, 2009

Abbreviations

Books of the Old Testament*

Gen	Genesis	Job	Job	Hab	Habakkuk
Ex	Exodus	Ps	Psalms	Zeph	Zephaniah
Lev	Leviticus	Prov	Proverbs	Hag	Haggai
Num	Numbers	Eccl	Ecclesiastes	Zech	Zechariah
Deut	Deuteronomy	Song	Song of Solomon	Mal	Malachi
Josh	Joshua	Is	Isaiah	Tob	Tobit
Judg	Judges	Jer	Jeremiah	Jdt	Judith
Ruth	Ruth	Lam	Lamentations	Wis	Wisdom
1	1 Samuel	Ezek	Ezekiel	Sir	Sirach (Ecclesiasticus)
Sam	2 Samuel	Dan	Daniel	Bar	Baruch
2	1 Kings	Hos	Hosea	1 Esd	1 Esdras
Sam	2 Kings	Joel	Joel	2 Esd	2 Esdras
1 Kg	1 Chronicles	Am	Amos	1 Macc	1 Maccabees
2 Kg	2 Chronicles	Ob	Obadiah	2 Macc	2 Maccabees
1 Chr	Ezra	Jon	Jonah	3 Macc	3 Maccabees
2 Chr	Nehemiah	Mic	Micah	4 Macc	4 Maccabees
Ezra	Esther	Nah	Nahum		
Neh					
Esth					

Books of the New Testament

Mt	Matthew	Eph	Ephesians	Heb	Hebrews
Mk	Mark	Phil	Philippians	Jas	James
Lk	Luke	Col	Colossians	1 Pet	1 Peter
Jn	John	1 Thess	1 Thessalonians	2 Pet	2 Peter
Acts	Acts	2 Thess	2 Thessalonians	1 Jn	1 John
Rom	Romans	1 Tim	1 Timothy	2 Jn	2 John
1 Cor	1 Corinthians	2 Tim	2 Timothy	3 Jn	3 John
2 Cor	2 Corinthians	Titus	Titus	Jude	Jude
Gal	Galatians	Philem	Philemon	Rev	Revelation

*Following the larger canon known as the Septuagint.

Contents

Part Four
Post New Testament

Dedication

The dedication of this book, the epitome of a lifetime submission to the scriptural text, is in thanksgiving to the Almighty Scriptural God for my parents, Widad and Jamal. Whatever goodness and paternal care my hearers have perceived in me throughout the past forty-five years of teaching is due to my parents. Their framed pictures grace my bedroom: they still rock me to sleep and even to power-nap, and I awaken at their loving gaze. My father Jamal was the reason behind my capturing what the Ezekelian God is all about: a humanly speaking impossible combination of an unflinchingly firm hand and a soft, very soft, heart. They say, perfection is not of this world, yet at this stage in my life when the Bible, God's words, have become literally an open book for me, I can say that, in his life, my father was as close to perfection as can be. At his death, a neighbor said of him: "Very probably not everyone that met Jamal Tarazi said good things of him, but I, personally, never, ever heard anyone who knew him say negative things about him." That is only understandable in the light of Jesus' reply to the man who called him "Good Teacher": "Why do you call me good? No one is good but God alone." (Mk 10:18) My father partook of the Eucharist four times a year and, yet, he never did so without asking, besides my mother, each of his little children—and I say 'little' because he was shy of 38 years of age when he was granted his first child—and individually so, "Forgive me!" Of my mother, my very intelligent and beautiful mother, her true being is etched in my memory in the following story. In the Roman Catholic Christian Lasallian Brothers French School I attended in Beirut, Lebanon, there was no such thing as breaks or vacations, including summer vacations. We had always homework to do. One year, during Easter break, I kept playing and postponing study until 7 PM of the last day. I came to my mother and confessed my wrongdoing in tears. Without any word of reproach and, not even expressing astonishment so as not to hurt my feelings, she simply said: "We have time; we can do it." And she sat next to me and, with a Herculean willpower—her French was at best imperfect—she went over with me all the subjects I had to master for the tests on the first day of school after the break. We did as much as we could until 11 PM. Then she woke me up at 3 AM and we continued until I had to leave for school. Thereafter, she never hinted at, let alone mentioned, that episode in her conversations with me. She just simply did it!

Widad and Jamal are with me at every Eucharist when I commune, always after having asked their forgiveness as well as God's. Besides God, they are my "genesis" and that is why I dedicated to their memory my book "Land and Covenant," where I discuss in detail the Book of Genesis and the will of God for their homeland, Palestine, as well as my first book, a commentary on Paul's First Letter to the Thessalonians.

The feeling of thanksgiving that prompted this dedication is not without pain. It is indeed agonizing for me that neither of my parents witnessed, let alone read, any of my books. They both died at an early age. My father passed in April 1970, at the age of 70, six months shy of the start of my teaching at St John of Damascus School of Theology at Balamand, Lebanon, an event he had been so much looking forward to. My mother died on January 6, 1977—the Feast of Theophany—at the age of 61, again a few months shy of her planned visit to the USA where I was about to start my teaching at St Vladimir's Seminary. Neither was granted to see the fruit of their labor in and through me. But again "glory to God in and for all things." They are especially on my mind and in my prayers each year on the Sundays of Thomas and of the Samaritan Woman, both part of the Paschal cycle. On the former I hear the Lord saying to Thomas: "Have you believed because you have seen me? Blessed are those who have not seen and yet believe." (Jn 20:29) On the latter I hear the same Lord say to his disciples: "For here the saying holds true, 'One sows and another reaps.' I sent you to reap that for which you did not labor; others have labored, and you have entered into their labor." (Jn 4:37-38)

One can say that both my mother and my father were honorary Thessalonians of whom the Apostle wrote: "We give thanks to God always for you all, constantly mentioning you in our prayers, remembering before our God and Father your work of *faith* and labor of *love* and steadfastness of *hope* in our Lord Jesus Christ." (1 Thess 1:2-3) At any rate they both lived by the Apostle's directive: "For through the Spirit, by *faith*, we wait for the *hope* of righteousness. For in Christ Jesus neither circumcision nor uncircumcision is of any avail, but *faith* working through *love*." (Gal 5:5-6) In the way they implemented their faith in a life of selfless love, I have no doubt that their hope is now realized.

Paul Nadim Tarazi
October 2, 2017
The seventy-fourth anniversary of the day my mother gave
birth to me

Foreword

All People of the Book—Jews, Muslims, and Christians alike—share the conviction that their own religious communities possess the highest and best understanding of Holy Writ. These great world religions express themselves in nominal and sociological categories (orthodox, conservative, reformist, reconstructionist, catholic, protestant, church, denomination, confession, sect, etc.) and are led by religious authorities that assume hegemonic advantage over matters of canon and interpretation. As self-appointed bastions of scriptural defense and preservation, many religious communities find creative ways of accommodating themselves to scripture, to the effect that the Bible becomes just another in-group identity marker and a tool for collective self-justification. Even some Protestant denominations standing in the tradition of sola scriptura manage to water down scripture by recasting biblical characters as shining examples to be emulated rather than mirrors of our inglorious selves, a phenomenon psychologists call projection. Other religious communities apparently believe scripture somehow affirms holiness by dint of simply reading it. By avoiding real engagement with the biblical text, we escape confrontation with its demands and avoid any encounter with the real paradox of biblical understanding, that—contrary to parochial belief—scripture privileges none save those (non-existent ones) who would submit fully in obedience to it. As the nineteenth-century Danish Lutheran philosopher Søren Kierkegaard once remarked about the Bible, ". . . the minute we come to understand [it], we are obliged to act accordingly." This no-win paradox lies at the center of Fr. Paul Nadim Tarazi's *The Rise of Scripture*. This book—the product of Fr. Paul's lifetime of dedication to the study and living out of scripture—provokes radical insights concerning what it means to know and understand the Bible.

As a student of Fr. Paul Tarazi for over thirty years now, I am patient zero for my own students who have become infected by thinking biblically. At first they are puzzled to hear me lament how reading the Older Testament ruined my life, but over the course of the semester they begin to recognize scripture's sharp critique of humanity and its institutions, including royal and priestly leadership, fortified cities, chariots of iron, the cult, and, by extension, the ego-self. In coming to understand the Hebrew Bible as the most scathing collective and personal self-examination ever produced, scripture becomes painfully transformative—albeit liberating—at the expense of the autonomy of the former self. After all, being created in *imago Dei* implies that one is not actually God; similarly, the flipside of the great "I Am" is a resounding "You're not!" Even the patient and longsuffering Job is abandoned by his friends for being "righteous in his own eyes" (Job 32:1), necessitating four chapters' worth of intense and direct divine chastisement and character realignment.

It is no small task leading today's young people through scripture in a way that erodes and dethrones the ideal of autonomous and self-sufficient individualism that they have been culturally conditioned to affirm. I sometimes wonder if exposing them (along with my own children) to the divergent mode of thinking embodied in scripture might somehow cripple them for gaining an edge in our highly competitive, shamefully egocentric, and insatiably greedy consumerist society. To be sure, this mode of existence is not only antithetical to living the truly good life, but is the mirror opposite of living scripturally, "For what shall it profit a man if he shall gain the whole world and lose his own soul?" (Matt 16:26 // Mark 8:36 // Luke 9:25). The psalmist's existential, open-ended question, "What is man that Thou art mindful of him, a son of man [i.e., mortal] that Thou carest for him?" (Ps 8:4), is reflected throughout the whole of scripture—not in this part or that, not in any particular source or genre, form or school, but lies there naked and unobscured on the surface level of the text; thus, lay people who read the Bible over and over again acquire an understanding of what it means scripturally to be human in ways that most biblical scholars do not, compelling and facilitating obedience to its teaching.

Accounting for *how* this scathing, self-critical amalgam of texts came about is somewhat more elusive. Prior to reading this book, my own approach has been to see the Bible as a response to the sixth-century BCE destruction of Jerusalem's palace-temple complex and its related deportations. The natural question "What went wrong?" was answered by an expanded Deuteronomistic definition of idolatry in which misplaced trust had not only been invested in religious idols, but also in Judah's royal and priestly leadership, its fortified cities, chariots of iron, and in all of Israel's temples and shrines. Fr. Paul Tarazi's explanation is more radical, more intriguing, and seems more plausibly situated in a later historical context. His overall thesis is that the Bible, in the form that it has come down to us, represents a fourth-century BCE Aramean defensive literary assault upon Hellenistic thought, culture, and institutions, the plan of which depended upon critical self-deprecation within its own narrative world. In other words, the targets of prophetic critique mentioned earlier—leadership, cities, armaments, religious institutions, etc.—are all exposed as illusory and self-defeating bulwarks of human achievement when viewed within the scriptural vision of humankind in relation to the God of scripture. According to this book, the dominant paradigm for that relationship is shepherdism, which for many ancient cultures represented the most natural social relationship imaginable. Such a model is the great leveler that restores the dignity and true state of created humanity, binding human beings together in the barren wilderness of authentic human existence in obedience to, and under the care of the ultimate Shepherd, the God of Scripture.

The term "shepherd" (*ro'eh*) is not the only analogy that biblical writers applied to God. It is not even the most ubiquitous one, especially in light of how many times the word "king" (*melek*) is used. But the pastoral model would have been much more familiar to ancient readers and hearers, who would have experienced far more interaction with shepherds than with kings. Besides, one can hardly imagine that the words of Psalm 23, "The Lord is my shepherd; I shall not want / he makes me to lie down in green pastures / he leads me beside the still waters / he restores my soul," would convey the same set of comforting assurances coming from an ancient Near Eastern monarch. One should also be careful not to discount the strength, bravery, and cunning of a shepherd, whose leadership in the untamed wilderness meant life or death for his sheep; thus, there were good shepherds and bad, depending upon how well they led, protected, and provided for their respective "flocks." In ancient cultures, where honor was valued and shame despised, social groups themselves were judged on the basis of their leaders. The model of shepherdism would have been understood by all cultures of the ancient world—including the occupying Hellenists. For the writers of scripture, affirming shepherdism as a model for living was hardly a new idea. Affirming the world between the two great rivers (Mesopotamia) as it actually was— and in many ways still is—the biblical writers launched a powerfully defiant literary assault upon the arrogant and ethnocentric urban culture of the Greeks, which necessarily included the denigration of biblical Israel's own self-aggrandizing ways.

Already one can imagine raised eyebrows at the implications the book's thesis that the biblical narrative represents a fourth-century, anti-hellenistic literary assault, an assertion that implicitly challenges the historicity of the biblical narrative. To be sure, having co-directed and supervised a massive Iron Age site for nearly two decades, I can say with confidence that what is known of the actual history of Syria/Palestine and the narrative world of the Bible seldom overlap. The names of biblical places, kings, and things were sometimes taken from the world in which the writers lived, lending an air of historicity to the story. The sagas of many ancient cultures mention actual persons, places, and things, but it hardly means the stories in which they are set are historical. People simply have greater visceral investment in their own living myths. One should realize that the Bible is not history in the sense that we moderns understand it, for doing so shifts the focus away from engaging with the enduring power of the teaching for which it was intended. One has only to compare the stories of the conquest of Canaan in the books of Joshua and Judges to see an example of two very different versions of the emergence of Israel in the land, neither of which is actually historical in the sense we moderns expect. Critical reading reveals that ancient writers were always up to something else, and that readers should never impose their own presuppositions upon the text. What one does learn from the conquest narratives is that obedience to the God of scripture, the Shepherd, is the only option for authentic human existence.

This scriptural "something else" returns us to the paradox mentioned above. How is it possible for a person, a community, or a nation to live scripturally—that is, to exist in a state of constant self-negation, especially when the world seems to be all about self-aggrandizement, winning, and the acquisition of wealth and power? I recently visited an Orthodox church in St. Paul, MN, which occupies a very old, formerly Methodist church building in one of the city's earliest neighborhoods. There above the front door, I saw a newly placed sign which bore an unsettlingly ironic quote from Jeremiah 7:4: "Do not trust in lying words saying, 'The temple of the Lord, the temple of the Lord, the temple of the Lord are these.'" What shockingly unexpected words to find above a place of worship! What could they mean? And how is it most readers fail to notice such plain and timeless words of scripture, dismissing them out of hand by relegating them to some distant, irrelevant past? I leave it to the reader to pause a moment to think about these questions, for wisdom—ever paradoxical and open to the infinite—is never adequately explicated in finite terms. But for those who have ears to hear, suddenly scripture comes alive. Understood in light of the Older Testament, the New Testament begins to make sense in ways it may not have done before. Orthodox and Roman Catholic readers of the Bible are admonished that the Older Testament must be read through the lens of the New, but what is often overlooked is the fact that the New Testament is wholly unintelligible without the Hebrew Bible. Ultimately, it is about the circumcision of the heart by acting accordingly, submitting fully to the teaching of scripture in avoiding self-righteousness and extending the justice (*mišpat*) and mercy (*ḥesed*) of the one true Shepherd. The principle is especially apparent in the words of Jesus, which almost every biblical scholar deems authentic on the basis of the criterion of dissimilarity with the early church: "Why do you call me good? There is none good, but God alone" (Matt 19:17 // Mark 10:18 // Luke 18:19). By contrast, I have rarely heard a homily on the parable of the Pharisee and the tax-collector in which the homilist did not come off sounding like the Pharisee by the end of the sermon, calling to mind the words of Golda Meir, "Don't be so humble; you aren't that great."

In the end, scripture is not creedal, nor something to be possessed by a religious community. Its teaching is the life that sustains it, as well as the standard by which it will be judged. But as Fr. Paul Tarazi affirms in this volume, the teaching in itself counts for nothing if it is not lived out, actualized in the life of the reader or hearer. He writes:

> The primary intent of scripture is to lead the hearers to the path of righteousness and have them *walk* on that path by listening and submitting to scripture's instruction. The bottom line in and from the scriptural perspective is not so much hearing the Law as it is doing its commands.

Tarazi also points out the secondary relationship of teaching to actually walking the path of righteousness (to Paul, running the race) in the words of Jesus in the Sermon on the Mount:

> For truly, I say to you, till heaven and earth pass away, not an iota, not a dot, will pass from the law until all is accomplished. Whoever then relaxes one of the least of these commandments

and teaches men so, shall be called least in the kingdom of heaven; but he who does them and teaches them shall be called great in the kingdom of heaven. For I tell you, unless your righteousness exceeds that of the scribes and Pharisees, you will never enter the kingdom of heaven. (Mt 5:18-20)

To be sure, writings that originated in cultures more than two millennia ago and roughly six to seven thousand miles away, can be expected to contain practices and ways of thinking not readily available to us. Those who assert that early representatives of their Holy Tradition selected the canon and handed down control over its proper interpretation to their in-group successors fail to recognize that the original selection process itself was inaugurated by the power and influence of its witness to truth. Again, Fr. Paul's observation that ultimately humans do not judge scripture, rather it judges us, comes to the fore. Thus, in the end, this monograph is based less upon some parochial idea of *how* Scripture should be read, but *that* it be read and that it be done. "Obey my voice, and I will be your God, and you shall be my people; and walk in all the way that I command you, that it may be well with you" (Jer 7:23). May scripture continue to ruin our present lives in order that we may live them more fully.

Nicolae Roddy
Creighton University

Part One

What triggered the writing of scripture

1
The Beginning

In mid third century B.C. the socio-political situation for the people living in the major cities along the Euphrates was very grim. The tight grip the Seleucids had over the region for decades appeared stronger than ever. In order to fathom the impact of such a state of affairs in the minds of the upper class living in that area, one has to remember the value of those cities over the preceding millennia before Southeast Europe, whence originated the Seleucids, was not yet on the map of civilization or, at least, definitely not at the same level of civilization as the cities in the area between the Tigris and the Euphrates. So the elite and the leadership in the cities of Aram Naharayim—the "Aramite" or "Aramean" region between the Two Rivers—not only felt subjugated, but also humiliated as well.

The people of that region were the descendants of the Akkadians of old via the Assyrians and Babylonians, all of whom were of Semitic stock, and they had every right to be proud of their remote ancestors. The Sumerians, definitely from a non-Semitic stock, were early settlers in Southern Mesopotamia and by the fourth millennium B.C. established an advanced civilization around the city of Ur.[1] They produced a substantial amount of literature in their language, using cuneiform writing, which they were first to develop. The success of their script was so overwhelming that soon neighboring groups adopted it for their own use. One of those groups were the Semitic-speaking Akkadians who resided to the north of Sumer, in mid-Mesopotamia. Around 2300 B.C. the Akkadian dynasty overpowered Sumer and, as a result, Akkadian supplanted Sumerian as the primary language of Mesopotamia. The Akkadian language would continue to be spoken for the next

---

[1] At that time Ur was at the mouth of the Euphrates, on the shore of the Arabian/Persian Gulf.

two millennia and evolve into its later forms, Babylonian and Assyrian. What is amazing, however, is that the Akkadians preserved Sumerian as a parallel language. Not only was there bilingualism, whereby important texts were preserved in both languages, but also Akkadian language itself was influenced by Sumerian on a vast gamut: convergence in matter of phonology, morphology, and syntax as well as lexical borrowing. Moreover, Sumerian continued to be used as a sacred, ceremonial, literary, and scientific language in Mesopotamia until the 1st century A.D. This unprecedented feat made for a peaceful symbiosis between the Semite Akkadians and their non-Semite counterparts, the Sumerians, and reflected a worldview quite different from our own today that revolves around ethnic nationalism. Their worldview encompassed different groups united in a bond dictated by geophysical neighborliness and thus geography, regardless even of language. Akkadian remained the lingua franca of the region throughout the Babylonian and Assyrian hegemonies, heirs of the ancient Akkadians.[2]

This tradition of practicality, if not outright tolerance, survived through two millennia as evidenced in the stance taken in the middle of the 8th century B.C. by the Neo-Assyrian emperor Tiglath Pileser III whose language was Akkadian. He surpassed his forebears the Akkadians. Whereas these co-opted Sumerian, he decided to make of Aramaic, the language of the conquered Aram,[3] the official language of his realm. To be sure, Aramaic was alphabetical and thus more amenable for

---

[2] Another example of mutual "acceptance" so-to-speak between Indo-Aryans and Semites of the region between the Two Rivers can be seen in that the Indo-Aryan [Hurrian] Hittites and the Semite Amurru/Amorites ruled that same region at different periods. These two had even a relation at one point. An interesting aspect of such relation was the discovery of Hittite literature that allowed us to better understand the covenant "language" of scripture: it is not a "deal" between two equals but a "condition" imposed by a master/monarch/conqueror on his conquered vassal.

[3] This area comprised the city-states of Arpad, Hamath, and Damascus, which lie at the western rim of the Syrian Desert.

correspondence in a vast empire. Still, it was a daring move by all accounts, reflecting the millennia long mentality of that part of the world, namely, that the human connection is more geographical than ethnic. Humans who share the same earth are her children and thus siblings, regardless of the color of their skin or their physical traits. We shall see later in detail how that view impacted all of scripture. Suffice it to say here that, *in the scriptural Hebrew*,[4] *'adam* (man) is the grammatically masculine noun of its counterpart *'adamah* (ground), a grammatically feminine noun. The corollary is that the human being is either the child or the husband of the ground he lives on. This view is clearly reflected in the description of the human being in Genesis 2:

> then the Lord God formed man (*ha'adam; the* human being) of dust from the ground (*ha'adamah*) (v.7)

> The Lord God took the man (*ha'adam*) and put him in the garden of Eden to till it (her) and keep it (her). (v.15)[5]

This mentality of the region is further corroborated in the welcome the Semite population gave the Indo-Aryan Medo-Persian Cyrus I when he liberated them from the oppression of the Semite Neo-Babylonian kings.[6] The Babylonians did not consider the Medo-Persians as "foreigners," thus following the attitude of their forebears the Akkadians toward the Sumerians who had moved to Southern Mesopotamia from across the Tigris, that is, from the same area whence came Cyrus and his followers. This understanding of what happened again finds

---

[4] I shall defend later in more detail my thesis that Hebrew is a concocted Semitic language.

[5] Virtually no translation, including Arabic, reflects the original where *gan* (garden) is a masculine noun whereas the complement pronouns after each of the verbs "till" and "keep" are grammatically feminine and thus cannot refer except to the *'adamah* (ground) mentioned earlier in Gen 1:7. It is thus the ground of the garden that the man is instructed to till and keep.

[6] Actually, the Persian administration of their empire—delegation of power to the governors of the different geographical districts/satrapies—was hailed as beneficial for its citizens. Alexander of Macedon himself seems to have been an admirer of Cyrus and his policies.

support in scripture itself from two different angles. On the one hand, Cyrus is referred to by name twice in a row in a passage presenting him as liberator, assigned by none other than the Lord of Israel, in terminology reserved to the monarchs of Israel and Judah:

> Thus says the Lord, your Redeemer, who formed you from the womb: "I am the Lord, who made all things, who stretched out the heavens alone, who spread out the earth–Who was with me?– who frustrates the omens of liars, and makes fools of diviners; who turns wise men back, and makes their knowledge foolish; who confirms the word of his servant, and performs the counsel of his messengers; who says of Jerusalem, 'She shall be inhabited,' and of the cities of Judah, 'They shall be built, and I will raise up their ruins'; who says to the deep, 'Be dry, I will dry up your rivers'; who says of Cyrus, 'He is my shepherd, and he shall fulfil all my purpose'; saying of Jerusalem, 'She shall be built,' and of the temple, 'Your foundation shall be laid.'" Thus says the Lord to his anointed, to Cyrus, whose right hand I have grasped, to subdue nations before him and ungird the loins of kings, to open doors before him that gates may not be closed: "I will go before you and level the mountains, I will break in pieces the doors of bronze and cut asunder the bars of iron, I will give you the treasures of darkness and the hoards in secret places, that you may know that it is I, the Lord, the God of Israel, who call you by your name." (Is 44:24-45:3)

On the other hand, and only a few verses later, Isaiah declares that the liberation of the Babylonian populace was wrought from under the yoke of its own major gods, Bel and Nebo: "Bel bows down, Nebo stoops, their idols are on beasts and cattle; these things you carry are loaded as burdens on weary beasts. They stoop, they bow down together, they cannot save the burden, but themselves go into captivity." (46:1-2) This thought finds echo in the teaching of Jeremiah: "Babylon is taken, Bel is put to shame, Merodach is dismayed. Her images are put to shame, her idols are dismayed" (50:2b); "And I will punish Bel in Babylon, and take out of his mouth what he has swallowed.

The nations shall no longer flow to him; the wall of Babylon has fallen." (51:44)[7]

Another indication that ancient societies were bound by geography rather than ethnicity[8] is that while the Persian empire acted beneficently toward the Semite Babylonians, its expansionist policy reached not only to the westernmost parts of Asia Minor (Turkey) but also tried to swell across the Aegean into Thrace, Macedonia, and Greece, an area as Indo-Aryan as Persia. To be sure, the Persian forces were plagued by defeat after defeat, yet the people of the Two Rivers region were not very affected by those far away wars.

In the 4th century, however, the tide changed with Alexander of Macedon. Following the expansionist pattern of the Persians, he started by overtaking Thrace and Greece; he then crossed the Aegean in the opposite direction to conquer the entire turf of the Persian empire, and even went beyond into India. Three factors heightened the jolt of such expansionism to an unprecedented level:

1. Whereas the Persians were seen as "liberators," the Macedonians were perceived as total "subjugators." The Persians were "locals" just as the Sumerians before them. The Macedonians were far away strangers and thus invaders.

2. Alexander imposed Greek, a totally unknown language to the area, as a new lingua franca to

---

[7] See further the ironical twist in the "Letter of Jeremiah," following the Book of Lamentations in the LXX: "Why then must any one think that they are gods, or call them gods? Besides, even the Chaldeans themselves dishonor them; for when they see a dumb man, who cannot speak, they bring him and pray Bel that the man may speak, as though Bel were able to understand." (1:40-41) See as well the extensive satire against the same Bel in "Bel and the Dragon" (LXX Dan 14). The Letter of Jeremiah is found only in the LXX. Hebrew Daniel has only 12 chapters; chapters 13 and 14 of Daniel are found only in the LXX.

[8] This is the rule rather the exception as can be seen not only in the Peloponnesian Wars between Sparta and Athens, but also, in more recent times, in the Napoleonic Campaigns and in the two World Wars.

replace the Semitic Aramaic that was indigenous to the Two Rivers region.

3. Alexander established Babylon, one of the main historical centers of the region, as his new capital,[9] driving the final nail in the coffin. He actually forced his companions to "settle" by marrying locals in order to create an irreversible merger between Greeks and Babylonians as well as Persians, thus literally "invading" the multi-millenial domain of the Two Rivers and Grecizing it.[10] Put otherwise, not only was the turf of the residents of Akkad literally invaded for good, but their multi-millennial "world"— including their lingua franca—was forever robbed from them. It would have been more tolerable for them to be "shipped off" to—exiled in—Greece or Macedonia. In other words, they were "exiled" on their own turf.

Any hope for this new "world" to be ephemeral was soon shattered by the realization that Alexander was definitely here to stay. After his death the entire area was divided between his successors, the Seleucids in the Fertile Crescent and the Ptolemies in Egypt. By the mid-3rd century B.C. these two dynasties were so well established that it looked as though they would remain forever. In human terms, there was no hope in sight of overthrowing the enemy by sheer force, à la Iliad. This consummate *Greek* epic of machoism was the literature the inhabitants of the Two Rivers region had to read and hear and learn in a language imposed upon them.

---

[9] Whereas in Egypt he established a new city, Alexandria, after the Greek model, here in the Two Rivers region he put the Greek stamp on a millennial local center.
[10] His co-adjutants, who wanted to return to their "home," were unhappy, a fact which, according to many, may have precipitated his early "demise" at the very young age of 33.

The erudite leaders of the region, "barbarians" in the eyes of the Greeks, conceived and executed what no one had ever conceived before them: they created an anti-epic aimed at not only disarming their invaders, but also at disempowering them by voiding their superiority from within, or as in modern sport and fighting techniques, by using the opponent's power against himself. Besides being colossal—larger than twice the size of the Iliad and Odyssey combined[11]—and to overwhelm the enemy at his own game, so to speak, the anti-epic they conceived and executed was ultimately intended to be in the enemy's language itself.[12] In order to bring the arrogant oppressor to his knees, they used the pen as a sword.[13]

The scriptural language they created—and thus it never existed before as language—is an amalgam from the different Semitic languages of the area. The purpose was to avoid imposing one language over the others. By the same token, they avoided Aramaic, the previous lingua franca of the area, for the same reason that they relegated Greek to a secondary status.[14]

---

[11] There are 593,493 words in the Old Testament (the shorter Hebrew canon) versus Iliad—155,150 words; Iliad and Odyssey together—269,183 words.

[12] The effect is similar to that of a non-native, the like of Gibran Kahlil Gibran, excelling in the language of his host, and yet writing in Arabic in New York. A similar effect would be if an American Indian would win a prestigious prize in literature for something he wrote in English.

[13] Their disciple Paul will follow suit by even borrowing the Iliad's "shield of Achilles" to describe the panoply of God: "Finally, be strong in the Lord and in the strength of his might. Put on the whole armor of God, that you may be able to stand against the wiles of the devil. For we are not contending against flesh and blood, but against the principalities, against the powers, against the world rulers of this present darkness, against the spiritual hosts of wickedness in the heavenly places. Therefore take the whole armor of God, that you may be able to withstand in the evil day, and having done all, to stand. Stand therefore, having girded your loins with truth, and having put on the breastplate of righteousness, and having shod your feet with the equipment of the gospel of peace; besides all these, taking the shield of faith, with which you can quench all the flaming darts of the evil one. And take the helmet of salvation, and the sword of the Spirit, which is the word of God." (Eph 6:10-17)

[14] The authors' mastery of Aramaic is evident in Daniel 2:4-7:28 that is scripted in Aramaic, whereas the beginning and remainder of the Book is in scriptural Hebrew. The intention, as I shall indicate later, is not to allow their own people to boast over

They wrote the original in a language akin to Aramaic, their "barbarian" lingua franca, and then they themselves translated it into Greek, thus reminding the oppressor that he had always to make the extra effort to *submit* to the original.[15] Such is outspokenly stated in the Preamble to Sirach:

> [The Prologue of the Wisdom of Jesus the Son of Sirach.] Whereas many great teachings have been given to us through the law and the prophets and the others that followed them, on account of which we should praise Israel for instruction and wisdom; and since it is necessary not only that the readers themselves should acquire understanding but also that those who love learning should be able to help the outsiders by both speaking and writing, my grandfather Jesus, after devoting himself especially to the reading of the law and the prophets and the other books of our fathers, and after acquiring considerable proficiency in them, was himself also led to write something pertaining to instruction and wisdom, in order that, by becoming conversant with this also, those who love learning should make even greater progress in living according to the law.
>
> You are urged therefore to read with good will and attention, and to be indulgent in cases where, despite our diligent labor in translating, we may seem to have rendered some phrases imperfectly. For what was originally expressed in Hebrew does not have exactly the same sense when translated into another language. Not only this work, but even the law itself, the prophecies, and the rest of the books differ not a little as originally expressed.
>
> When I came to Egypt in the thirty-eighth year of the reign of Euergetes and stayed for some time, I found opportunity for no little instruction. It seemed highly necessary that I should myself devote some pains and labor to the translation of the following book, using in that period of time great watchfulness and skill in order to complete and publish the book for those living abroad

---

the Greeks, given the basic thesis of scripture itself, that is, the scriptural Israel is no better—actually it is worse than—the scriptural "nations."

[15] As in the case of the two giants Origen and Jerome.

who wished to gain learning, being prepared in character to live according to the law.

This intent is reflected in the "miraculous" story of the LXX translation found in the Letter of Aristeas.[16] Notice that both works, the LXX and the translation of Sirach, were commissioned by the ruling Ptolemy in Alexandria, Alexander's city.

The scriptural authors conceived their lengthy story, repeated ad nauseam in so many different ways and in each of the three parts of scripture (Law, Prophets, and Ketubim), as a literary *mashal*.[17] Still, their story needed to be "realistic," i.e., relate to real life, and not just be appealing entertainment. In real life everything comes at a price, especially if it is about fighting against an established "world power." Since the authors themselves did not have the actual capacity to overthrow the seemingly all-powerful enemy, it would have been preposterous for them to present themselves in the story either as helpless martyrs—such could not have changed the odds on the ground and, worse, would have made their compatriots more helplessly despondent—or as almighty—which would have sounded understandably ludicrous to their companions on the ground. They had to "come up" with at least an all-powerful, if not even more powerful, champion *gibbor* (mighty warrior) who would resist and eventually subdue the all-powerful enemy, just like Achilles in the Iliad. However, even Achilles had an inherent weakness—his heel—that proved to be his downfall and potentially that of his colleagues, were it not for the ingenuity of Ulysses. Yet, even the victorious Ulysses had to undergo ten years of perilous wandering through the "wilderness" of the

---

[16] A legendary account of the translation of the Old Testament into Greek, commissioned by Ptolemy II Philadelphus (third century B.C.) at the urging of his librarian. This legend is intended to canonize the value of the Septuagint (LXX) translation by purporting that seventy two men (6 from each of the twelve tribes) "miraculously" accomplished the task in seventy two days. Hence the Latin name *septuaginta* that means "seventy," a round figure for 72.

[17] See my comments on Ezekiel and Ps 78 in *OTI₁* 22-25 and *C-Ezek* 209-11.

Mediterranean Sea on top of the ten years of the Trojan War before he could reach the "rest" of his home. Still, all along, he was protected by his patron Athena, the goddess of wisdom, who finally led him home safely when she appeared to him in the form of a shepherd.

The real dilemma was how to thwart the expansive literature of the victor invader whose upper hand the scriptural authors were planning to undermine in order to give hope to their contemporaries, real hope and not one in either the "heavens above" or in an uncertain future. Such hope had to be "sure" hope, on the ground people were living on, or else it is no hope at all. Moreover, the opponent was majestically powerful with its "philosophy"—Alexander was Aristotle's pupil—as well as with its epic literature, both unique and uniquely compelling at that time. Add to this their historic as well as historical victories (Marathon, Salamis) against the mighty Persians, the "relatives" of the authors—not to mention Alexander's himself.

The invader's literature, philosophical as well as epic, was rooted in and smacked of superiority (Greek versus barbarian) and thus entitlement. The scriptural authors, mentally and more so practically, could not afford such a stand. Moreover, they would have been deemed delusional had they not acknowledged that the invader was, humanly speaking, fully justified in his entitlement. He had an "identity," a "self," whereas they had none, again humanly—i.e., de facto—speaking. Even their pantheon was subjugated to the Olympian gods and goddesses.

In view of the proven helplessness of the "gods" that were held in esteem for millennia and in whose honor gigantic temples were erected, the solution to this dilemma would have been to opt for the way of Plato who demythologized the Greek Pantheon and conceived in its stead a "world of ideas" whereby the assumed god and the humans were bonded through the same fabric: the divine *logos* and the human "soul" were "ideal" eternal entities. However, in reality, such ideas were as much a mental human fabrication as the deities.[18] In either case, the solution would have been Hellenic, and thus would have been a capitulation to the terms of the Macedonian Alexander. Put otherwise, the "Barbarian" Mesopotamians would have had to submit to the "Greek" will and ways. The authors, themselves city dwellers just as, if not more so, than the Greeks, opted rather, against all odds, to create their epic in the realism embedded in a totally different kind of reality which has been in their backyard, actually front yard, all along, i.e., the Syrian Desert/wilderness, a land mass that stretched southward into the Arabian Desert, forming a unique feature in the then known "civilized-literary" world. This desert/wilderness was not only inhabited, but actually reflected a full symbiosis between human and animal, and with the vegetation that supported both. And in Genesis we hear: "And God said, 'Behold, I have given you every plant yielding seed which is upon the face of all the earth, and every tree with seed in its fruit; you shall have them for food. And to every beast of the earth, and to every bird of the air, and to everything that creeps on the earth, everything that has the breath of life, I have given every green plant for food.' And it was so." (Gen 1:29-30)

That "living" wilderness which survived thousands of invaders from the surrounding Fertile Crescent and beyond was still there as it always has been, without the artificiality of (urban) civilization. It was a society of shepherdism and oases. The oases functioned as caravan stops, mini-cities as it were, which proved essential for the traffic of commerce across the desert instead of around it, thus saving precious time for trade that is the backbone of global life. For any incredulous person, Tadmor/Palmyra has stood and will stand as proof that a full-fledged "city" can not only survive but also blossom into a full-fledged kingdom and civilization with its own language and history, *literally* in the middle of the wilderness, at the heart of the Syrian Desert, as its geographical capital.

---

[18] In this sense, Buddhism and Platonism are akin.

But if the scriptural proposition is an invitation to shepherd-like life, then the corollary entails a condemnation of (urban) civilization, which is a quintessential staple of Greek life. Ironically, (urban) civilization is also, and more so, a staple of the Two Rivers region that extends back for millennia, well before Greece and Macedonia were on the world map, so to speak. Put otherwise, the authors' critique of the invader entailed a price that had to be paid by themselves and their people as well, namely, that they would be subject to the same critique as their opponent. This, in my estimation, is precisely the most sui generis feature of the scriptural literature: its promotors were cast as *anti-heroes* under constant unflinching criticism of their way/s of life. This is readily noticeable by any first time hearer/reader of scripture. Scripture is not so much a toned down self-critique as it is a flagrant self-criticism, if not an outright self-condemnation.[19] Paul fully captured this message of the Old Testament. Not only does he equate the wise Greek and the foolish Barbarian,[20] but also, and more openly so, the "Jew" knowledgeable of the Law and the Gentile non-privy to it. The latter case is more forceful since, after having said "What then? Are we Jews any better off? No, not at all; for I have already charged that all men, both Jews and Greeks, are under the power of sin (Rom 3:9)," he immediately quotes a long series

---

[19] As I shall detail later, it is precisely this not so classically "human" feature of scripture that was generation after generation misheard and thus misconstrued first by the Jewish leaders, starting with Paul's times, down to our own times, and then by the church theologians starting with Justin the Philosopher through Irenaeus through Origen and Alexandria down to our own times. The classic common denominator is that the subject matter is by definition *worthwhile* to be spoken of. This is bluntly in disharmony with Gen 6:5-7 and Ezek 20:1-39. The classic example of someone who truly believed that he was a necessary ingredient in the divine scheme of things is the "great" Elijah who was condemned to early retirement and replaced with Elisha and whose mistake Paul refused to repeat in Rom 11:1-5.

[20] "I am under obligation both to Greeks and to barbarians, both to the wise and to the foolish" (Rom 1:14); "Here there cannot be Greek and Jew, circumcised and uncircumcised, barbarian, Scythian, slave, free man, but Christ is all, and in all." (Col 3:11)

of scriptural passages that specifically apply to the scriptural Israelites and not outsiders:

> ...as it is written: "None is righteous, no, not one; no one understands, no one seeks for God. All have turned aside, together they have gone wrong; no one does good, not even one." "Their throat is an open grave, they use their tongues to deceive." "The venom of asps is under their lips." "Their mouth is full of curses and bitterness." "Their feet are swift to shed blood, in their paths are ruin and misery, and the way of peace they do not know." "There is no fear of God before their eyes." (3:10-18)

Paul concludes, "Now we know that *whatever the law says it speaks to those who are under the law (en tō nomō*; in [within the realm of] the law), so that every mouth may be stopped, and the whole world may be held accountable to God." (3:19). The quintessential passages that refer to the "chosen" ones as anti-heroes *generation after generation* are in the preamble of Psalm 78 and in the introductory remarks in Ezekiel:

> A Maskil of Asaph. Give ear, O my people, to my teaching; incline your ears to the words of my mouth! I will open my mouth in a parable; I will utter dark sayings from of old, things that we have heard and known, that our fathers have told us. We will not hide them from their children, but tell to the coming generation the glorious deeds of the Lord, and his might, and the wonders which he has wrought. He established a testimony in Jacob, and appointed a law in Israel, which he commanded our fathers to teach to their children; that the next generation might know them, the children yet unborn, and arise and tell them to their children, so that they should set their hope in God, and not forget the works of God, but keep his commandments; and *that they should not be like their fathers, a stubborn and rebellious generation, a generation whose heart was not steadfast, whose spirit was not faithful to God.* (Ps 78:1-8)

> And he said to me, "Son of man, I send you to the people of Israel, to a nation of rebels, who have rebelled against me; *they and their fathers have transgressed against me to this very day."* (Ezek 2:3)

The antithesis of rebelliousness is obedience. Obedience is by definition unconditional.[21] In scripture, unconditional obedience is tantamount to total submission, as reflected in the phraseology of Deuteronomy:

> This day the Lord your God commands you to do these statutes and ordinances; you shall therefore be careful to do them with all your heart and with all your soul. (26:16)

> "Cursed be he who does not confirm the words of this law by doing them." And all the people shall say, "Amen." (27:26)

> If you are not careful *to do all the words of this law which are written in this book*, that you may fear this glorious and awful name, the Lord your God, then the Lord will bring on you and your offspring extraordinary afflictions, afflictions severe and lasting, and sicknesses grievous and lasting. And he will bring upon you again all the diseases of Egypt, which you were afraid of; and they shall cleave to you. Every sickness also, and every affliction which is not recorded in the book of this law, the Lord will bring upon you, until you are destroyed. Whereas you were as the stars of heaven for multitude, you shall be left few in number; because you did not obey the voice of the Lord your God. And as the Lord took delight in doing you good and multiplying you, so the Lord will take delight in bringing ruin upon you and destroying you; and you shall be plucked off the land which you are entering to take possession of it. And the Lord will scatter you among all peoples, from one end of the earth to the other; and there you shall serve other gods, of wood and stone, which neither you nor your fathers have known. And among these nations you shall find no ease, and there shall be no rest for the sole of your foot; but the Lord will give you there a trembling heart, and failing eyes, and a languishing soul; your life shall hang in doubt before you; night and day you shall be in dread, and have no assurance of your life. In the morning you shall say, "Would it were evening!" and at evening you shall say, "Would it were morning!" because of the dread which your heart shall fear, and the sights which

---

[21] We often hear in our contemporary world that one is to submit only to oneself, which is oxymoronic. In the army, for instance, a junior obeys while a senior, by definition, does not obey; he issues orders and directives.

your eyes shall see. And the Lord will bring you back in ships to Egypt, a journey which I promised that you should never make again; and there you shall offer yourselves for sale to your enemies as male and female slaves, but no man will buy you. (28:58-68)

This corresponds to another staple of scripture, which is unbearable and thus unacceptable to the classical "human" mind, be it ancient or modern: whenever the scriptural God "liberates" us, he does not change our status of "slaves," but takes us under his wings *as slaves* and makes us *his* slaves.[22] Notice how the scriptural God insists that his people are his slaves. Although the liberating God introduces himself as "the Lord your God, who brought you out of the land of Egypt, out of the house of bondage (*bet 'abadim*, literally 'house of slaves'; Ex 20:2),[23] he unequivocally states: "For to me the people of Israel are servants (*'abadim*; slaves), they are my servants (*'abaday*; my slaves) whom I brought forth out of the land of Egypt: I am the Lord your God." (Lev 25:55)[24] Paul will repeat this in Romans:

What then? Are we to sin because we are not under law but under grace? By no means! Do you not know that if you yield yourselves to any one as obedient slaves, you are slaves of the one whom you obey, either of sin, which leads to death, or of obedience, which leads to righteousness? But thanks be to God, that you who were once slaves of sin have become obedient from the heart to the standard of teaching to which you were committed, and, having been set free from sin, have become slaves of righteousness. I am speaking in human terms, because of your natural limitations. For just as you once yielded your members to impurity and to greater and greater iniquity, so now yield your members to righteousness for sanctification. When you were slaves of sin, you

---

[22] The translation of *'ebed* and *doulos* into "servant" is, to say the least, an outright distortion of the scriptural teaching. One may choose to be servant, while a slave does not choose his status. If one is looking for a new "identity" and thus definition of oneself, one had better not appeal to scripture; one will be sorely disappointed, if not crushed.

[23] See also Ex 13:3, 14; Deut 5:6; 6:12; 7:8; 8:14; 13:5, 10.

[24] See also Deut 32:36, 43.

were free in regard to righteousness. But then what return did you get from the things of which you are now ashamed? The end of those things is death. But now that you have been set free from sin and *have become slaves of God* (*doulōthentes tō Theō*; having been enslaved to/by God), the return you get is sanctification and its end, eternal life. For the wages of sin is death, but the free gift of God is eternal life in Christ Jesus our Lord. (6:15-23)

But how would leading a life patterned after that extant in the wilderness be a "solution" to the dilemma of disobedience? The question is not merely academic since the scriptural story of Israel in the wilderness after their redemption across the Sea of Reeds is one of continual infraction of God's will. Furthermore, we hear repeatedly that those same Hebrews were shepherds while sojourning in Egypt.[25] So, assuming that my thesis is correct, scripture itself seems to contradict the fact that it could present itself as a viable solution, and the entire matter would seem to be no more than a catch-22 situation.

However, the catch-22 situation applies solely because we are accustomed to either reading the scriptural story as a description of actual facts rather than a parable (*mashal*) or, worse, due to our anthropocentric view of all realities, consider a situation whereby we have no say, let alone control, an impossibility. The reason for the impossibility is that we cannot—or rather obstinately refuse to—fathom a reality where being an outright "slave" is more beneficial than being a willing "servant." Put otherwise, after the manner of the scriptural Adam, we value our freedom of choice—that is to say, our *control* over our destiny—over and above life itself. This is the Iliad and Odyssey approach to reality, an approach that scripture aimed at counteracting, since the question remains, "Better for whom?" The answer is obvious: better for the one who ends up as oppressor. Being an oppressor was the fate of Alexander and *all* his predecessors on the historical scene, whether Indo-Aryan

---

25 Gen 46:32, 34; 47:3.

or Semite, since any human being ultimately acts as Adam.[26] The supposedly ultimate solution for a humanity, where each individual is in control of his destiny, was proposed by Plato and has controlled our worldview due to its appeal to our ego. Plato conceived of an unprovable premise, the human soul whose existence extends beyond death, which allows each and every one of us to have a supposedly ultimate say, even against our oppressor.[27] Notice that both the Iliad-Odyssey and Platonic "solutions" to the human "dilemma" are Greek in origin, whereas scripture was conceived as an anti-Hellene proposition.

So what is the scriptural proposition all about, and why is it not a catch-22 solution? The paradigm that the scriptural authors are proposing is shepherdism. In shepherdism, the "societal" unit is the flock. There can be few or many sheep in the flock, but there can be only *one* shepherd. When applying the paradigm to us humans, we, being many, cannot be but the sheep, not the shepherds. We are unwilling to accept this paradigm since it literally contradicts our propensity to individualism. Sheep are beings without choice when it comes to their destiny. An individual sheep does not exercise the option of being or not being a member of a flock; *by definition* a sheep is part of a flock.[28] Put otherwise, a flock can be and,

---

[26] Both male and female human beings are subsumed into *ha'adam* and thus *'adam*-ic: "Then God said, 'Let us make man (*'adam*) in our image, after our likeness; and let *them* have dominion over the fish of the sea, and over the birds of the air, and over the cattle, and over all the earth, and over every creeping thing that creeps upon the earth.' So God created man (*ha'adam*) in his own image, in the image of God he created *him*; male and female he created *them*." (Gen 1:26-27) The "him" is due to the fact that *'adam* is a masculine noun in Hebrew.

[27] Such a view is nowhere to be found in scripture; it was endorsed by the Christian intelligentsia that was thoroughly Greek minded; even Jesus Christ ended up in their "theology" as the Platonic eternal *logos*. In scripture, the *nephesh*, rendered as soul, is nothing else save the breath(ing) reflecting our being alive versus our being dead at its ceasing. Consequently, the "soul" in scripture is functional: it reflects or indicates life, but is in no way the basis of existence. The view of an immortal, if not outright eternal, soul has become common currency to the extent that the Jews are not impervious to it.

[28] The reality of this matter is reflected in the English language where the same noun "sheep" refers indiscriminately to the individual animal as well as the entire flock.

actually is, regardless whether an individual sheep is part of it or not, whereas an individual sheep simply *is not* unless as one of the flock.[29] Consequently when a sheep wanders on its own, it is bound to extinction.[30] Without a shepherd there is no flock. It is precisely this reality that justifies as well as explains the extreme harshness with which scripture handles the shepherds of Israel. A paradigmatic example of this is Ezekiel 34 where one hears that the only valid shepherd of the people is God himself and, only exceptionally, *one individual* of his choice may be shepherd.

That the paradigm of shepherdism was paramount on the authors' mind in view of the scriptural society they were promoting finds an incontrovertible proof in the language they used to describe the societal units of the scriptural Israel. Not only do they refer to God as shepherd and to the people as flock, but also they view the progeny of each of the twelve sons of Jacob/Israel as tribe. What is compelling in this regard is that the original for "tribe" is *šebeṭ* that strictly refers to the staff a shepherd holds to lead his flock. It is, to say the least, utterly strange to refer to a given group of human beings as "staff." However, the oddity can be explained by the fact that a flock is defined by its shepherd, and not vice versa. Actually, the existence itself of the flock hangs on the flock's submission to the shepherd's staff. Put otherwise, the "being" of the flock is dependent on the staff and thus is reflective of the latter. Functionally, and thus realistically, the shepherd's staff is proof that there is a flock. This intimate relation between staff and flock can be seen in the earliest scriptural occurrences of *šebeṭ*

---

[29] It would be ludicrous—except for philosophers who can afford the luxury to fathom the impossible as possible—to assume that, at one point, one can encounter a wandering individual sheep in the wilderness, unless it is in the vicinity of a flock or an oasis.

[30] Such matter of fact is detectable in the phrase "A wandering (*'obed*) Aramean was my father" (Deut 26:5) the meaning of *'obed* being "perishing, unto perdition, unto extinction."

where, within a few verses, that same noun refers to a tribe and a staff:

> Then Jacob called his sons, and said, "Gather yourselves together, that I may tell you what shall befall you in days to come. Assemble and hear, O sons of Jacob, and hearken to Israel your father ... Judah, your brothers shall praise you; your hand shall be on the neck of your enemies; your father's sons shall bow down before you. Judah is a lion's whelp; from the prey, my son, you have gone up. He stooped down, he couched as a lion, and as a lioness; who dares rouse him up? The scepter (*šebeṭ*; staff) shall not depart from Judah, nor the *ruler's staff* (*meḥoqeq*; ruler [as instrument]) from between his feet, until he comes to whom it belongs; and to him shall be the obedience of the peoples ... Dan shall judge his people as one of the tribes (*šibṭe*)[31] of Israel ... All these are the twelve tribes (*šibṭe*) of Israel; and this is what their father said to them as he blessed them, blessing each with the blessing suitable to him. (Gen 49:1-2, 8-10, 16, 28)

Before proceeding to discuss the further implications of shepherdism as viable parabolic paradigm, let me dispel any misconceptions concerning choosing an animal, and one without any option of controlling its own destiny to boot, as a stand-in for the human being. One of the most influential Greek writers is Aesop, whose fables have been emulated as well as translated in many languages. No one seems to worry or question, for example, that the hare and the tortoise are stand-in characters for human beings. Were it not so, Aesop's fables would lose their permanent value. In a similar way fables appear in scripture as valuable teaching material, even to the point that vegetation is used as a stand-in for humans:

> And all the citizens of Shechem came together, and all Bethmillo, and they went and made Abimelech king, by the oak of the pillar at Shechem. When it was told to Jotham, he went and stood on the top of Mount Gerizim, and cried aloud and said to them, "Listen to me, you men of Shechem, that God may listen to you.

---

[31] This is the form *šebaṭim*, the plural of *šebeṭ*, takes when it is followed by a noun complement.

The trees once went forth to anoint a king over them; and they said to the olive tree, 'Reign over us.' But the olive tree said to them, 'Shall I leave my fatness, by which gods and men are honored, and go to sway over the trees?' And the trees said to the fig tree, 'Come you, and reign over us.' But the fig tree said to them, 'Shall I leave my sweetness and my good fruit, and go to sway over the trees?' And the trees said to the vine, 'Come you, and reign over us.' But the vine said to them, 'Shall I leave my wine which cheers gods and men, and go to sway over the trees?' Then all the trees said to the bramble, 'Come you, and reign over us.' And the bramble said to the trees, 'If in good faith you are anointing me king over you, then come and take refuge in my shade; but if not, let fire come out of the bramble and devour the cedars of Lebanon.' "Now therefore, if you acted in good faith and honor when you made Abimelech king, and if you have dealt well with Jerubbaal and his house, and have done to him as his deeds deserved—for my father fought for you, and risked his life, and rescued you from the hand of Midian; and you have risen up against my father's house this day, and have slain his sons, seventy men on one stone, and have made Abimelech, the son of his maidservant, king over the citizens of Shechem, because he is your kinsman—if you then have acted in good faith and honor with Jerubbaal and with his house this day, then rejoice in Abimelech, and let him also rejoice in you; but if not, let fire come out from Abimelech, and devour the citizens of Shechem, and Bethmillo; and let fire come out from the citizens of Shechem, and from Bethmillo, and devour Abimelech." (Jdg 9:6-20)

Even in the New Testament parabolic teaching obviously aimed at human beings one hears often of animals and vegetation. The most compelling example is found in Luke 15 where we hear *one* parable—"So he told them this parable" (v.3)—rendered in three different versions; the "item" around which the story revolves is, in turn, a sheep, a coin, and a human being. All three "items" in the stories are not valued intrinsically; since they play a similar role in each of the three parallel stories, their value lies in their "function" in those stories, which is the same: each is "lost and found."

When applying this rule to shepherdism as a paradigm for teaching, it is how the sheep "functions" in that setting, which encapsulates the example to be followed by the human addressee. Just as the hare and the tortoise *as described in the fable*—and not any given hare or tortoise—are the models to avoid or follow, so also it is the sheep *of the Syrian Wilderness*—and not any sheep elsewhere—that constitutes the point of reference in the scriptural teaching. In other parts of the world where "grazing pastures" encompass brooks, if not rivers, and green hills and the like, wandering sheep can possibly "survive" and flocks can be substantial in numbers. In the wilderness the reality is quite different. Besides making survival an impossibility in the case of a wandering sheep, the scarcity of water imposes a limit on the size of a flock tended by one shepherd. So the flock formed a tight-knit entity with the shepherd and his household that functioned as a family where the father had absolute authority.[32] In Hebrew, such absolute authority is transparent in the noun by which a family was designated: *bet 'ab*, house(hold) of the father. In other words, the house members were defined by the father, not vice versa. In the same vein, a flock was posited as a living entity by its one shepherd. The shepherd can live without some individual sheep; however, an individual sheep acting "independently" is *by definition* doomed to extinction. The parable Nathan resorted to in order to teach David a lesson is a perfect example that combines this reality with animals functioning as stand-ins for humans:

> And the Lord sent Nathan to David. He came to him, and said to him, "There were two men in a certain city, the one rich and the other poor. The rich man had very many flocks and herds; but the poor man had nothing but one little ewe lamb, which he had bought. *And he brought it up, and it grew up with him and with his children; it used to eat of his morsel, and drink from his cup, and lie in his bosom, and it was like a daughter to him.* Now there came a traveler to the rich man, and he was unwilling to take one of his own flock

---

[32] Just as was the case in a Roman household.

or herd to prepare for the wayfarer who had come to him, *but he took the poor man's lamb, and prepared it for the man who had come to him.*" Then David's anger was greatly kindled against the man; and he said to Nathan, "As the Lord lives, the man who has done this deserves to die; and he shall restore the lamb fourfold, because he did this thing, and because he had no pity." Nathan said to David, "You are the man. Thus says the Lord, the God of Israel, 'I anointed you king over Israel, and I delivered you out of the hand of Saul; and I gave you your master's house, and your master's wives into your bosom, and gave you the house of Israel and of Judah; and if this were too little, I would add to you as much more.' Why have you despised the word of the Lord, to do what is evil in his sight? *You have smitten Uriah the Hittite with the sword, and have taken his wife to be your wife, and have slain him with the sword of the Ammonites.* Now therefore the sword shall never depart from your house, because you have despised me, and have taken the wife of Uriah the Hittite to be your wife." Thus says the Lord, 'Behold, I will raise up evil against you out of your own house; and I will take your wives before your eyes, and give them to your neighbor, and he shall lie with your wives in the sight of this sun. For you did it secretly; but I will do this thing before all Israel, and before the sun.'" David said to Nathan, "I have sinned against the Lord." And Nathan said to David, "The Lord also has put away your sin; you shall not die. Nevertheless, because by this deed you have utterly scorned the Lord, the child that is born to you shall die." (2 Sam 12:1-14)

Obviously the story is hyperbolic in that the poor man is said to have only one ewe-lamb. Still, the story reflects the "family" relation between humans and sheep, which relation is a trademark of Syrian Desert flocks.

Another essential aspect concerning the flock is that the individual sheep is not aware of the reality that binds it to the shepherd. The fate of a wandering individual sheep ends in extinction, the scriptural "perdition" (*apōleia*). In other words, the so-called "freedom of choice," the *liberum arbitrium*, which is virtually sacrosanct in theological as well as philosophical pursuits, is actually a non-issue in shepherdism since the choice itself is literally "immaterial," that is, not even a subject matter. Put succinctly, a disobedient (wandering) sheep is simply *'obed* (bound to non-existence) regardless of its non-awareness of this fact, and such a fate is noticed by the humans who witness this fact of life. Thus the realism of the parabolic teaching around shepherdism does not need extra comment, let alone theological debate. It is simply overwhelmingly "true," that is, factual within the realm of the paradigm. Hence the immediacy, if not outright urgency, of the scriptural message. A case in point is the statement heard at the outset of Isaiah: "Hear, O heavens, and give ear, O earth; for the Lord has spoken: 'Sons have I reared and brought up, but they have rebelled against me. The ox knows its owner, and the ass its master's crib; but Israel does not know, my people does not understand.'" (1:2-3) For the original hearer, this statement *is* an indictment in no need of further comment, let alone lengthy commentaries.[33]

The corollary to this is that what is for the good of the sheep has nothing to do with what the sheep may do, but lies in the will of the shepherd who alone knows what is best for his sheep. The sheep does not know where the oases lie in the wilderness. Consequently, the will of the shepherd is obviously to be obeyed and not first weighed for its value, which would be impossible for a sheep in the wilderness. The will of the scriptural God is presented within this context at the start of the scriptural story. Just as a sheep *cannot* be a shepherd, the human being formed *according to scripture* by the Lord God from the dust of the ground *cannot* possibly be "divine," pace Plato and Plotinus and Alexandrian theology.

---

[33] Lengthy erudite commentaries actually void the scriptural message of one of its basic features, the urgency for it to be heeded "lest I come and smite the land with a curse" (Mal 4:6). See the appeal "For he is our God, and we are the people of his pasture, and the sheep of his hand. O that *today* you would hearken to his voice! Harden not your hearts, as at Meribah, as on the day at Massah in the wilderness" (Ps 95:7-8). See also Jesus' summons "Go and do likewise" (Lk 10:37) to the lawyer who asked him "Teacher, what shall I do to inherit eternal life?" (v.25).

Adam is faced with a *command* that is basically unacceptable to any reasonable human being: "You may freely eat of every tree of the garden; but of *the tree of the knowledge of good and evil* you shall not eat, for in the day that you eat of it you shall die." (Gen 2:16-17) In order to continue living, Adam is strictly forbidden to entertain any understanding of the good and the evil—which is precisely one of the basic purposes of the Greek *philosophia*. Indeed, the infraction of God's command will result in Adam's being prohibited to *continue eating* from the tree of life:

> Then the Lord God said, "Behold, the man has become like one of us, knowing good and evil; and now, lest he put forth his hand and take also of the tree of life, and eat, and live for ever"— therefore the Lord God sent him forth from the garden of Eden, to till the ground from which he was taken. He drove out the man; and at the east of the garden of Eden he placed the cherubim, and a flaming sword which turned every way, *to guard the way to the tree of life*. (3:22-24)

Eve was tempted by the serpent who is only apparently "more subtle (*'arum*; crafty) than any other wild creature" (Gen 3:1). In Job one learns that Eve was fooled since such "subtlety" is reserved solely to God himself:

> As for me, I would seek God, and to God would I commit my cause; who does great things and unsearchable, marvelous things without number: he gives rain upon the earth and sends waters upon the fields; he sets on high those who are lowly, and those who mourn are lifted to safety. He frustrates the devices of the *crafty (*'arumim*)*, so that their hands achieve no success. He takes the wise in *their own craftiness (*'ormam*)*; and the schemes of the wily are brought to a quick end. (Job 5:8-13)[34]

---

[34] The interconnectedness between the temptation of Eve into falling for "human" wisdom and the teaching of the Book of Job was magisterially captured by Paul in his letters to the inhabitants of Corinth, the capital of Roman Greece (Province Achaia), which letters are aimed at belittling Greek wisdom. At the beginning of the Corinthian correspondence, his critique of Greek wisdom culminates in his quoting Job 5:13a (He takes the wise in their own craftiness) in 1 Cor 3:19b (For it is written, "He catches the wise in their craftiness [*panourgia*]"); see on this matter *C-1Cor* 81-2. And toward the end of this same correspondence he refers to Eve's being beguiled by

Later one further learns that it is precisely the exclusiveness of God's subtlety that reveals human "craftiness" as specious:

> But you are doing away with the fear of God, and hindering meditation before God. For your iniquity teaches your mouth, and you choose the tongue of the *crafty* (*'arumim*) (15:4-5)[35]

The solution to the dilemma lies in "the fear of God" that is, in scripture, the beginning (*re'šit*) of "true" knowledge (*da'at*; Prov 1:7).[36] More importantly for our case, the punishment for having preferred human wisdom—that is, Greek wisdom according to 1 Corinthians 1—over the divine command was an exile away from the life provided by a tree located exclusively in the garden that the Lord God himself planted (Gen 2:8; 3:24). A garden that only God plants and containing, besides plants (*śiaḥ*; shrubs) and herbs (*'eśeb*; grass) (2:5), a few trees "pleasant to the sight and good for food"[37] (v.9) is clearly an oasis. This oasis, surrounded by the Euphrates, the Tigris, and two rivers that water Havilah at the east of Egypt,[38] that is, in Southern Arabia, and Cush, covering the area of Ancient Egypt and Ethiopia (2:10-14), would obviously be located in the Syrian-Arabian Wilderness, which is topographically one entity.

Greek Philosophy as Entrapment

The scriptural anti-Greek partiality is detectable at the outset of the scriptural narrative. The denigration of Greek Philosophy, especially as championed by Plato—the teacher of Aristotle,

---

the serpent: "But I am afraid that as the serpent deceived Eve by his cunning (*panourgia*)." (2 Cor 11:3)

[35] The word play in the original in Genesis 2-3 is compellingly unmissable. Both Adam and Eve realized they were "naked" (*'arummim*) upon their eating from the fruit of the tree of the knowledge of the good and the evil, and made themselves aprons from fig leaves (3:7) to cover the nakedness they were not ashamed of earlier (2:25). Shame in scripture is an expression of divine punishment (passim in the Prophets).

[36] *re'šit* is the same noun found in Gen 1:1 and *da'at* is the same noun found in Gen 2:17.

[37] Surely a reference to the date palm trees.

[38] The land of the Ishmaelites (Gen 25:16-18) and Amalekites (1 Sam 15:7).

Alexander's tutor—as beguiling and unfruitful craftiness is evident in the wordplay found in the original. Right before the introduction of the "crafty" serpent we hear this seemingly unwarranted statement: "And the man and his wife were both naked (*'arummim*, plural of *'arom*), and were not ashamed." (Gen 2:25) Shame is a—if not *the*—ultimate scriptural punishment, shy of death itself.[39] And being stripped naked before the eyes of the multitude and especially the opponents is *the* sign of utter shame:

> "Behold, I will press you down in your place, as a cart full of sheaves presses down. Flight shall perish from the swift, and the strong shall not retain his strength, nor shall the mighty save his life; he who handles the bow shall not stand, and he who is swift of foot shall not save himself, nor shall he who rides the horse save his life; and he who is stout of heart among the mighty shall flee away naked in that day," says the Lord. (Am 2:13-16)

> For this I will lament and wail; I will go stripped and naked; I will make lamentation like the jackals, and mourning like the ostriches. For her wound is incurable; and it has come to Judah, it has reached to the gate of my people, to Jerusalem. Tell it not in Gath, weep not at all; in Bethleaphrah roll yourselves in the dust. Pass on your way, inhabitants of Shaphir, in nakedness and shame; the inhabitants of Zaanan do not come forth; the wailing of Bethezel shall take away from you its standing place. (Mic 1:8-11)

> Behold, I am against you, says the Lord of hosts, and will lift up your skirts over your face; and I will let nations look on your nakedness and kingdoms on your shame (Nah 3:5)

Consequently the original nakedness of the man and his wife was natural and not an expression of punishment.

This scenario will change with the introduction of the serpent that is "more *'arum* (crafty; subtle) than any other wild creature that the Lord God had made" (Gen 3:1). The intended close connection between Genesis 2:25 and 3:1 is evident in that the

---

[39] See, e.g., Ex 32:25; 2 Sam 13:13; 19:3; Job 8:22; Ps 4:2; 6:10; 25:2-3.

plural *'arummim* (naked) has the same sound as *'arum* (crafty; subtle) whose plural is *'arumim*. In scriptural Hebrew, the sounds *o* and *u* are supported by the same consonant ו (*waw*) that is transliterated as *w* whenever it retains its original value as consonant, and as *o* or *u* whenever its value is vocalic.[40] The result is that both *'arom* (naked) and *'arum* (crafty; subtle) look exactly the same in the original: ערום (*'rwm* in transliteration). Consequently, the intentional linkage between the two adjectives in the original is readily detectable, and thus the word interplay is much more compelling than in any translation. In order to capture the ingenuity of the original, a more "subtle (crafty)"[41] rendering of the original would be to translate the scriptural *'arum* (subtle, crafty) of Genesis 3:1 into the English "smooth (slick)" that reflects cunning and slyness as well as the smoothness of nakedness. The choice of the serpent fits perfectly the scenario because its skin is smooth (slick) as well as "naked" in the sense that it is not covered by hair or fur. Thus the serpent was beguiling precisely because it appeared similar in its "nakedness" to the humans when compared to the other animals that are covered with a layer of fur or thick hair. The humans are more prone to relate to it and, by extension, to be more easily duped by it through the medium of an engaging "dialogue" à la Plato. We were taught to assume that the Socratic dialogue method is an "equal opportunity" among those who have the impression that they are "engaged." In fact, it is ultimately Socrates who is authoritatively expounding his viewpoint that ends up being the "lesson," the "teaching." The serpent, a stand-in for Plato,[42] only seems to be engaging Eve, whereas, in reality it is "leading" her—ultimately out of the garden. On the other hand, the unilateral command of God to Adam and, by extension, to Eve is rooted is his care for them

---

[40] The same rule applies to the consonant י (*yod*) that is transliterated as *y* whenever it retains its original value as consonant, and as *i* or *e* whenever its value is vocalic.

[41] Pun intended.

[42] Later I shall show how the Philistines function as a stand-in for Alexander's Macedonians and how Goliath is a stand-in for Alexander himself.

whose aim is to have them enjoy their stay in the garden. This understanding finds corroboration in that Eve is mentioned only twice in the Pauline letters and, in both cases, in conjunction with her having been "deceived" by the serpent (2 Cor 11:3; 1 Tim 2:14). More *à propos* is the fact that the invitation not to follow in the footsteps of Eve is addressed to the church in Corinth, the capital of the Roman province Achaia, covering ancient Greece whose main center was Athens, Plato's city. Moreover, it is precisely in that same chapter (2 Cor 11) that we encounter a high incidence of the Greek root *phron—* used with a negative connotation (vv.16 [twice], 19 [twice], 23), which is precisely the root that the LXX used to render *'arum* (subtle) in Genesis 3:1a: "Now the serpent was more subtle (*phronimōtatos*) than any other wild creature that the Lord God had made."

2

The Language of the Old Testament

Christian as well as Jewish theological premises distorted the original parabolic intent of scripture by historicizing its events and individualizing its personalities. Such distortion affected the handling of the scriptural language. We have all been programmed to refer to it as "Hebrew" and assume, without any compelling proof, that such language predated scripture. Dealing with the language of scripture suffered from the same abuse that the scriptural "events" and "personalities" did at the hands of "archeologists" who looked for archeological remains in the Syrian Wilderness with the view of evidencing their literalistic view of scripture. Dubbing the script on ceramic shards or pieces of stone as "Hebrew" is at best preposterous. Such is evidenced in the reference to that language in scholarly circles as "Old Semitic," "Phoenician," "Proto-Sinaitic," and the like. Semitic languages were very akin to one another to the extent that a good number of scholars of Ugaritic consider that language to be the closest to Arabic. To give the example of modern languages such as Germanic, Romance, and even Scandinavian and Slavic, does not do justice to the matter given that Semitic languages were and still are much more closely related. Besides, in as extensive a literature as the Old Testament is, one encounters the same language throughout without any sign of a development between the different individual books that would warrant speaking of "Archaic Biblical Hebrew" having assumedly flourished between the 10th and 8th centuries B.C., "Standard or Classical Biblical Hebrew" (8th to 6th centuries), and "Late Biblical Hebrew" (5th to 3rd centuries). The fallacy of the matter lies in the qualification of that "language" as "Biblical" and thus *as found in scripture*. If so, then it is the least to say superlatively strange that the only reference to that language as Hebrew is found in the very late date—by unanimous admission—of the Book of Sirach and, to boot, in the preamble that is exclusive to the Greek text, even if one assumes an original Hebrew as the preamble itself does:[1]

> Wherefore let me intreat you to read it with favour and attention, and to pardon us, wherein we may seem to come short of some words, which we have laboured to interpret. For the same things uttered *in Hebrew (Hebraisti)*, and translated into another tongue, have not the same force in them: and not only these things, but the law itself, and the prophets, and the rest of the books, have no small difference, when they are spoken in their own language.

The author of the preamble is clearly referring to the scriptural language as Hebrew, and not to a previously known language by that name. My view is borne out in that the language that was spoken during the so-called "Late Biblical Hebrew" period as well as at the height of the so-called "Standard or Classical Biblical Hebrew" period, is qualified as "Judean" or Judahite":

> Then Eliakim the son of Hilkiah, and Shebnah, and Joah, said to the Rabshakeh, "Pray, speak to your servants *in the Aramaic language* ('*aramit*; LXX *Syristi*; Vulgate *syriace*; KJV in the Syrian language), for we understand it; do not speak to us *in the language of Judah* (*yehudit*; Greek *Ioudaisti*; Vulgate *iudaice*; KJV in the Jews' language) within the hearing of the people who are on the wall." But the Rabshakeh said to them, "Has my master sent me to speak these words to your master and to you, and not to the men sitting on the wall, who are doomed with you to eat their own dung and to drink their own urine?" Then the Rabshakeh stood and called out in a loud voice in the language of Judah (*yehudit*; Greek *Ioudaisti*; Vulgate *iudaice*; KJV in the Jews' language): "Hear the word of the great king, the king of Assyria!" (2 Kg 18:26-28)

> Then Eliakim, Shebna, and Joah said to the Rabshakeh, "Pray, speak to your servants *in Aramaic* ('*aramit*; LXX *Syristi*; Vulgate

---

[1] The preamble's reference to an original Hebrew is simply a literary device to invite the hearers to take seriously the fact that the LXX is only a translation that cannot supersede the original but is always to be subordinate to it.

syriace; KJV in the Syrian language), for we understand it; do not speak to us *in the language of Judah* (*yehudit*; Greek *Ioudaisti*; Vulgate *iudaice*; KJV in the Jews' language) within the hearing of the people who are on the wall." But the Rabshakeh said, "Has my master sent me to speak these words to your master and to you, and not to the men sitting on the wall, who are doomed with you to eat their own dung and drink their own urine?" Then the Rabshakeh stood and called out in a loud voice *in the language of Judah* (*yehudit*; Greek *Ioudaisti*; Vulgate *iudaice*; KJV in the Jews' language): "Hear the words of the great king, the king of Assyria!" (Is 36:11-13)

And they shouted it with a loud voice *in the language of Judah* (*yehudit*; Greek *Ioudaisti*; Vulgate *iudaice*; KJV in the Jews' speech) to the people of Jerusalem who were upon the wall, to frighten and terrify them, in order that they might take the city. (2 Chr 32:18)

... and half of their children spoke *the language of Ashdod* (*'ašdodit*; Greek *Azōtisti*; Vulgate *azotice*; KJV in the speech of Ashdod), and they could not speak *the language of Judah* (*yehudit*; Greek *Ioudaisti*; Vulgate *iudaice*; KJV in the Jews' language), but the language (*lašon*) of each people. (Neh 13:24)

Notice how in the last passage the "Judean" is treated as the "Ashdodite," a language of a nation or a geographical area.[2] In view of that, it becomes important for our case that, in Isaiah, the same "the Jews' language" (36:11 and 13) is referred to earlier as "the language of Canaan": "In that day shall five cities in the land of Egypt speak *the language of Canaan* (*šephat* [from *šaphah* literally "lip"] *kena'an*; *tē glōssē tē Khananitidi*; Vulgate *lingua Chanaan*; KJV the language of Canaan) and swear to the Lord of hosts; one shall be called, The city of destruction." (Is 19:18 KJV) It would behoove us to discuss more in detail this instance in order to show how it sheds light on my overall thesis.

The more common noun for "language" in scripture is *lašon* that refers to a spoken language as well as the tongue, the organ

---

[2] My readers are reminded that, in scripture, those two realities overlap as is clear from Genesis 10; see on this matter my comments on that chapter.

that, together with the lips, is essential to the uttering of words. One can therefore understand why, in the Semitic languages, we encounter either "tongue" or "lip" as tantamount to "language." This linguistic feature is reflected early on in scripture where, in the two chapters dealing with the nations of the earth, one encounters both terms sequentially: *lašon* (tongue) in Genesis 10 (vv.5, 20, 31) and *šaphah* (lip) in chapter 11 (vv.1, 6, 7 [twice], 9). A closer look at the original will soon betray that this "allocation" is intentional. The author used the first noun in a setting of plurality (ch.10); each nation had "naturally" its own tongue[3] as is evident in the use of both the singular and the plural forms:

> From these the coastland peoples spread. These are the sons of Japheth in their lands, each with his own language (*lašon*), by their families, in their nations. (Gen 10:5)

> These are the sons of Ham, by their families, their languages (*lešonot*), their lands, and their nations (v.20)

> These are the sons of Shem, by their families, their languages (*lešonot*), their lands, and their nations. (v.31)

In order to underscore the decision humans took to *unite* "unnaturally," that is, against the will of God (ch.11), under the umbrella of "*one language*" (*šaphah 'eḥat*; vv.1 and 6) the author uses the other noun and always in the *singular*:

> Now the whole earth had one *language* and few words. (Gen 11:1)

> And the Lord said, "Behold, they are one people, and they have all one *language*; and this is only the beginning of what they will do; and nothing that they propose to do will now be impossible for them. Come, let us go down, and there confuse their *language*, that they may not understand one another's *speech* (*šaphah*)." (vv.6-7)

---

[3] See the text of Nehemiah quoted above.

> Therefore its name was called Babel, because there the Lord
> confused the *language* of all the earth; and from there the Lord
> scattered them abroad over the face of all the earth (v.9)

However, and much more importantly, the wording of Genesis
11 looks ahead to Isaiah 19 where God will unite, in accordance
with his will, the different nations under the aegis of one
language which, as I shall show, is the "scriptural language,"
that is to say, the scriptural message.

It is striking that the use of *saphah* to refer to "language" in the
Old Testament is restricted exclusively to Genesis 11 and Isaiah
19. However, the question we need to deal with is, How does
Isaiah 19 refer to Genesis 11 and how does it propose to correct
the mistake of arrogance perpetrated in the latter? In his oracle
concerning Egypt Isaiah brings into the picture, seemingly out
of the blue sky, Assyria and, to boot, no less than six times in the
last three verses, in conjunction with the rehabilitation of the
repentant Egypt into God's good graces:

> In that day the Egyptians will be like women, and tremble with
> fear before the hand which the Lord of hosts shakes over them.
> And the land of Judah will become a terror to the Egyptians;
> every one to whom it is mentioned will fear because of the
> purpose which the Lord of hosts has purposed against them. In
> that day there will be five cities in the land of Egypt which speak
> *the language of Canaan (sephat kena'an)* and swear allegiance to the
> Lord of hosts. One of these will be called the City of the Sun. In
> that day there will be an altar to the Lord in the midst of the land
> of Egypt, and a pillar to the Lord at its border. It will be a sign
> and a witness to the Lord of hosts in the land of Egypt; when they
> cry to the Lord because of oppressors he will send them a savior,
> and will defend and deliver them. And the Lord will make himself
> known to the Egyptians; and the Egyptians will know the Lord in
> that day and worship with sacrifice and burnt offering, and they
> will make vows to the Lord and perform them. And the Lord will
> smite Egypt, smiting and healing, and they will return to the
> Lord, and he will heed their supplications and heal them. In that
> day there will be a highway from Egypt to Assyria (*'assur*), and the
> Assyrian (*'assur*) will come into Egypt, and the Egyptian into

Assyria (*'aššur*), and the Egyptians will worship with the Assyrians (*'aššur*). In that day Israel will be the third with Egypt and Assyria (*'aššur*), a blessing in the midst of the earth, whom the Lord of hosts has blessed, saying, "Blessed be Egypt my people, and Assyria (*'aššur*) the work of my hands, and Israel my heritage." (Is 19:1-25)

The inclusion of Assyria with Egypt is to be explained in that Assyria was the land of exile of Israel because the latter did not follow the Law promulgated to them in the wilderness after they were saved from their lengthy exile of four hundred thirty years in Egypt (Ex 12:40), which Law was intended to protect and preserve them in the land of the promise, Canaan. The two exiles, in Egypt and in Assyria (Mesopotamia), are intertwined in scripture as being functionally equivalent, as is repeatedly evident in Hosea:

Ephraim[4] is like a dove, silly and without sense, calling to Egypt, going to Assyria. (7:11)

They shall not remain in the land of the Lord; but Ephraim shall return to Egypt, and they shall eat unclean food in Assyria. (9:3)

For behold, they are going to Assyria; Egypt shall gather them, Memphis shall bury them. Nettles shall possess their precious things of silver; thorns shall be in their tents. (9:6)

They shall return to the land of Egypt, and Assyria shall be their king, because they have refused to return to me (11:5)

They shall go after the Lord, he will roar like a lion; yea, he will roar, and his sons shall come trembling from the west; they shall come trembling like birds from Egypt, and like doves from the land of Assyria; and I will return them to their homes, says the Lord. (11:10-11)

Ephraim herds the wind, and pursues the east wind all day long; they multiply falsehood and violence; they make a bargain with Assyria, and oil is carried to Egypt. (12:1)

---

[4] In the Prophets Ephraim is tantamount to the northern Kingdom of Israel that ended exiled in Assyria (2 Kg 17).

Even the two exoduses from Egypt and Mesopotamia are spoken of in parallel terms in Ezekiel:

> I will bring you out from the peoples and gather you out of the countries where you are scattered, with a mighty hand and an outstretched arm, and with wrath poured out; and I will bring you into the wilderness of the peoples, and there I will enter into judgment with you face to face. As I entered into judgment with your fathers in the wilderness of the land of Egypt, so I will enter into judgment with you, says the Lord God. (20:34-36)

Egypt's change of heart is clearly the result of its submission to the Lord and his teaching, the upshot of which will be the true worship rendered to him.[5] And the teaching is none other than that of the Law as one can gather from the reference to the "five cities"—an oblique intimation to the five books of the Law—that will learn to "speak the language of Canaan" brought to them by Judah and originated in the "wilderness" upon the exodus from Egypt. Although that teaching was entrusted to Judah and Israel, still it was to reach ultimately all nations as Isaiah himself established early on:

> The word which Isaiah the son of Amoz saw concerning Judah and Jerusalem. It shall come to pass in the latter days that the mountain of the house of the Lord shall be established as the highest of the mountains, and shall be raised above the hills; and all the nations shall flow to it, and many peoples shall come, and say: "Come, let us go up to the mountain of the Lord, to the house of the God of Jacob; that he may teach us his ways and that we may walk in his paths." For out of Zion shall go forth the law, and the word of the Lord from Jerusalem. He shall judge between the nations, and shall decide for many peoples; and they shall beat their swords into plowshares, and their spears into pruning hooks; nation shall not lift up sword against nation, neither shall they learn war any more. O house of Jacob, come, let us walk in the light of the Lord. (2:1-5)

---

[5] Assyria's submission is obviously assumed. For the unconvinced hearer this will be made clear in the Book of Jonah.

It is important to point out at this juncture that the inclusion of Assyria is made in a way as to point out its union with Egypt through a "highway," which cannot possibly refer except to the Syrian Wilderness that covers the area of the "scriptural" Canaan where the "scriptural" Judah and Israel are said to have resided.[6] The most convincing as well as plausible conclusion is that the "language (śaphah) of Canaan" is none other than the "language (śaphah)" concocted by the scriptural authors, assumedly on behalf of the scriptural God whose "language (śaphah)" brought about the unity of all nations that their "one language" of Genesis 11 was not able to realize. It thus stands to reason to take the sui generis scriptural phrase "language of Canaan" as equivalent to the equally sui generis scriptural "Hebrew" (*Ebraisti*) of the Prologue to Sirach. Since there is no literary as well as epigraphical evidence for a self-standing "Hebrew" language, Sirach coined that appellation to reflect the scriptural "shepherd" forefathers who are referred to as "Hebrews" (*'abarim*; "crossers"), that is to say, itinerant shepherds "crossing" back and forth through the Syrian Wilderness as shepherds do after the manner of their progenitor who was introduced early on as "Abram *the* Hebrew" (*'abram ha'ibri*; Gen 14:13) soon after his introduction as "shepherd" (13:6-9).

The scriptural authors concocted a novel Semitic language that is a cross of the different Semitic languages extant at that time in order to correspond to their novel deity unlike any other in the Ancient Near Eastern world. Whereas all these "existed" by "standing out" in monumental statues of stone sitting or standing in temples erected in stone for that purpose, the scriptural deity "revealed" itself in the scriptural stories laid down in writing in a concocted language as though he, in his uniqueness, conceived his equally unique language, making himself equivalent to the Law inscribed in words of that

---

[6] I shall deal later with the equation between that wilderness and the scriptural "land of Canaan."

language. Put otherwise, instead of the humans going to him in his temple, he "comes" to them "incarnate," not as an eternal Platonic "word," but in the actual words of scripture. He was the Law and the Law was he, to know the Law is to know him, as accurately described by the Apostle in Romans where he fully equates between the Jew's "boasting of God" and "boasting of the Law":

> Behold, thou art called a Jew, and restest in the law, and makest *thy boast of God* (*kavkhasai en Theō*), And knowest *his* will, and approvest the things that are more excellent, being instructed out of the law; And art confident that thou thyself art a guide of the blind, a light of them which are in darkness, An instructor of the foolish, a teacher of babes, which hast the form of knowledge and of the truth in the law. Thou therefore which teachest another, teachest thou not thyself? thou that preachest a man should not steal, dost thou steal? Thou that sayest a man should not commit adultery, dost thou commit adultery? thou that abhorrest idols, dost thou commit sacrilege? Thou that makest *thy boast of the law* (*en nomō kavkhasai*), through breaking the law dishonourest thou God? (Rom 2:17-23 KJV)

In other words, there is no scriptural God before, after, or outside the actual words of scripture in the language in which its stories were conceived by the authors. Scripture projects God or rather pours him into the ears of the listeners or, as in the words of the Book of Psalms, "God is enthroned on the praises of Israel" (Ps 22:3b). Thus the listeners to scripture do not "find" God; rather he "meets" them *in* the scriptural stories worded in the concocted *scriptural* Hebrew. A (real; Rom 2:28) Jew learns Hebrew by learning the Old Testament just as a (real) Muslim learns the Qur'an-ic Arabic. The scriptural language *becomes* their language. Otherwise, God remains a deity of stone, albeit electronic, and his "heaviness" (*kabod*; glory) residing in *his* cloud becomes a mere mental iCloud.

Still, if the scriptural God is no stone, he is no flesh either just as our fleshly mind is, but he is *ruaḥ se'arah* (a mighty wind) that shatters and scatters man-made mental conceptions as well as

man-made statues and temples in spite of what Plato and
Origen presumed. At least, the latter acknowledged his
agreement with what I am saying since he, the consummate
Greco-Roman, forced himself to learn Hebrew. Unfortunately,
instead of putting this learning to submit simply to the scriptural
stories in Hebrew, he "concocted" his own "god" by
theologizing (*theologein*), that is, "uttering" him "out (of his own
mind)" instead of hearing God's "utterances" and simply
repeating them—reading them aloud—to the others as the
inimitable John Chrysostom did:

> It were indeed meet for us not at all to require the aid of the
> written Word, but to exhibit a life so pure, that the grace of the
> Spirit should be instead of books to our souls, and that as these
> are inscribed with ink, even so should our hearts be with the
> Spirit. But, since we have utterly put away from us this grace,
> come, let us at any rate embrace the second best course. For that
> the former was better, God hath made manifest, both by His
> words, and by His doings. Since unto Noah, and unto Abraham,
> and unto his offspring, and unto Job, and unto Moses too, He
> discoursed not by writings, but Himself by Himself, finding their
> mind pure. But after the whole people of the Hebrews had fallen
> into the very pit of wickedness, then and thereafter was a written
> word, and tables, and the admonition which is given by these.
> And this one may perceive was the case, not of the saints in the
> Old Testament only, but also of those in the New. For neither to
> the apostles did God give anything in writing, but instead of
> written words, He promised that He would give them the grace
> of the Spirit: for "He," saith our Lord, "shall bring all things to
> your remembrance." And that thou mayest learn that this was far
> better, hear what He saith by the Prophet: "I will make a new
> covenant with you, putting my laws into their mind, and in their
> heart I will write them," and, "they shall be all taught of God."
> And Paul too, pointing out the same superiority, said, that they
> had received a law "not in tables of stone, but in fleshy tables of
> the heart." But since in process of time they made shipwreck,
> some with regard to doctrines, others as to life and manners, there
> was again need that they should be put in remembrance by the
> written word. Reflect then how great an evil it is for us, who ought

to live so purely as not even to need written words, but to yield up our hearts, as books, to the Spirit; now that we have lost that honor, and are come to have need of these, to fail again in duly employing even this second remedy. For if it be a blame to stand in need of written words, and not to have brought down on ourselves the grace of the Spirit; consider how heavy the charge of not choosing to profit even after this assistance, but rather treating what is written with neglect, as if it were cast forth without purpose, and at random, and so bringing down upon ourselves our punishment with increase. But that no such effect may ensue, let us give strict heed unto the things that are written; and let us learn how the Old Law was given on the one hand, how on the other the New Covenant.[7]

Even when Chrysostom, who lived after Nicaea, submitted to the established theological lingo concerning the "essential" invisibility of God,[8] he always resorted to scripture to explain scripture as he did in his commentary on the first chapters of Isaiah.[9] In his comments on the opening verses of ch.6, Chrysostom does not delve, as often theologians do, into a fruitless discussion about "Isaiah's vision of God." Rather he captures the meaning of the text by reading it functionally, i.e., according to its intention:

"I saw the Lord seated." Christ has indeed said, "No one has seen God at any time. The only-begotten Son, who is in the bosom of the Father, has explained him." … How then can Isaiah claim to have seen the Lord? … After all, no one has observed bare divinity in its pure essence except the only-begotten. Isaiah, on the other hand, claimed to have seen his power. It is impossible to see God in and of himself. Isaiah saw God in an assumed form, one as much lowered as Isaiah's weakness was elevated. That neither he nor anybody else has seen bare divinity is made very clear by what they claim. For example, Isaiah says, "I saw the Lord

---

[7] Homily I on the Gospel of St. Matthew in P. Schaff, ed., *The Nicene and Post-Nicene Fathers* (Grand Rapids, 1st Series, x 1978).

[8] See later my comments on that misconstruction of the scriptural intent in *Absenteeism versus Divine Invisibility*, pp.87-94.

[9] He is the one who coined the phrase "scripture is its own interpreter" in that same commentary on Isaiah.

seated." But God does not sit. He does not have a bodily form. Not only does he say "Seated," but "Seated on a throne." … Therefore, why does he now appear seated on a throne among the Seraphim? He is imitating a human custom because his message is to humans. For he is about to carry out a decision that involves great matters and the whole world, but which also concerns Jerusalem. For it was the custom of their judges not to work in secret but while seated on high platforms with curtains drawn while everyone stood. God, in imitation of these things, places the Seraphim about him, sits on a high throne, and pronounces his verdict from there. I will try to make this point from another prophet so that you will not regard my analysis with suspicion but understand that this really is God's way of revealing himself…[10] we can, as I said, deal with the question at hand accurately and explain the genre of each text. Therefore, why did he say, "I saw the Lord seated?" Sitting on a throne is always a symbol of judgment, as David said, "You have sat on the throne to judge righteously." … His precise language makes it clear that he is not talking about a chair … To sit on the throne is to judge.[11]

Concocted Languages

Most probably the majority of my readers will raise their eyebrows at my proposition that scriptural Hebrew was a concocted language rather than an already existing one. In support of my theory I should like to point out two phenomena of concocted languages closer to our own times, Yiddish and Esperanto.

Since the end of the first millennium A.D. Yiddish has been a common language used by the Ashkenazi (European) Jews. It originated in Poland and its base is Germanic infused with Hebrew and Aramaic and also, to some extent, the Slavic languages. Its alphabet is based on the Hebrew script of the Old Testament. The first evidence of use dates from the twelfth

---

[10] Chrysostom then proceeds to speak of the similar setting of Dan 7:9-11.
[11] Duane A. Garrett, *An Analysis of the Hermeneutics of John Chrysostom's Commentary on Isaiah 1-8 With An English Translation.* The Edwin Mellen Press, 1992, pp.123-5.

century. Nowadays it is a common language among Hasidic Jewish communities.[12]

By far more interesting is the case of the much more recent Esperanto. It also originated in Poland. It was conceived as a full-fledged language in a book entitled "Unua Libro" (1887) by the Polish-Jewish ophthalmologist L. L. Zamenhof. The name of the language derives from the author's pseudonym "Doktoro Esperanto" and means "one who hopes." In creating the language, Zamenhof had three goals quoted here:

1. To render the study of the language so easy as to make its acquisition mere play to the learner.

2. To enable the learner to make direct use of his knowledge with persons of any nationality, whether the language be universally accepted or not; in other words, the language is to be directly a means of international communication.

3. To find some means of overcoming the natural indifference of mankind, and disposing them, in the quickest manner possible, and en masse, to learn and use the proposed language as a living one, and not only in last extremities, and with the key at hand.[13]

Its worldwide acceptance can be gleaned from the following major milestones[14] in its bicentennial history:

- The first World Congress of Esperanto was organized in France in 1905, followed by congresses held in various countries every year

---

12 For more detailed information see https://en.wikipedia. org /wiki / Yiddish.
13 For more detailed information see https://en.wikipedia. org /wiki / Esperanto.
14 These milestones were taken directly from https://en.wikipedia .org/wiki/ Esperanto, which I would recommend for interested readers.

thereafter, with the exception of the years of the world wars.

- Esperanto was recommended by the French Academy of Sciences in 1921 and recognized by UNESCO in 1954, which recommended in 1985 that international non-governmental organizations use Esperanto.

- Esperanto is currently the language of instruction of the International Academy of Sciences in San Marino, established in 1983.

- Esperanto was the 32nd language accepted as adhering to the "Common European Framework of Reference for Languages" in 2007.

- On 22 February 2012, "Google Translate" added Esperanto as its 64th language.

- On 28 May 2015, the language learning platform "Duolingo" launched an Esperanto course for English speakers. By January 2017, over 710,000 users had signed up, with approximately 30 users completing the course every day.

- The World Esperanto Association has more than 5,500 members in 120 countries.

- Finally, since Esperanto is seen by many of its speakers as an alternative or addition to the growing use of English throughout the world as lingua franca, its function recalls that of the scriptural Hebrew concerning Alexander's Greek as lingua franca of its time.

Semitic Languages

Anyone even slightly familiar with Semitic languages will immediately realize that all Platonic jargon is a non sequitur since it is not factually supported. None of the four nouns— existence, essence, person, being—which we routinely use to explain man and God is to be "genuinely" found in those languages. Their counterparts from the original Greek or Latin are found, but only because the translators of Plato, Aristotle and later European philosophers had to use words or terms that would render to some extent the meaning of the original. Even modern languages use such an approach. For instance, "cardiology" in English, French, Spanish, and even Latin is a transliteration from the Greek (καρδία *kardia*, "heart" and λόγια *logia*, "[words, and thus] study"). But even then, it is the original, and not its rendering, that dictates the meaning.[15]

Let me begin by pointing out the conundrum of what we refer to as "existence." The issue is complicated by our usual equation, if not outright confluence, between "existence" and "essence." Add to this the equation between "person" and "being" and the understanding of both in terms of "singularity" or "defining feature." Notice that all the preceding terminology is founded on Platonic style philosophy that left its indelible imprint on common theological vocabulary across all denominations.

When looking at the original language of the Old Testament, we are aware that it is not just written in Hebrew, but it is written in "its own Hebrew," much in the same way medieval English literature is written "in its own English."[16] Still, language is much more complex than morphology and lexicography; it is also, if not primarily, grammar and phraseology. These are especially important when dealing with

---

[15] That explains the importance, if not necessity, of "lexica" at the end of books dealing with specialized material or subjects, even for readers fluent in the original language.

[16] There are, of course, affinities between them but they are not the same "language."

literature and not simply street language or slang. In order to understand the Old Testament, one must be either fluent in *its* language or be earnestly willing to be introduced to it or guided through it. Of the three monotheistic religions, only Islam has taken this matter into serious consideration. No one expects Muslim Indonesians to know Arabic, but their imams *must* know it very well since it is the language of the Qur'an. Most Orthodox Christian clergy, educators, and laypeople do not bother with the original Hebrew, especially if they are conversant with Septuagint Greek.[17] Yet even Greek speaking students have to be introduced to classical Greek, and Greek seminarians have to master the scriptural Greek of the LXX.[18] In any case, if Hebrew was not important, why did Origen and Jerome take the trouble of learning it, and learning it very well, to boot?

Linguistically speaking, Hebrew has no word for the Greek *ousia* (being, essence) and the Latin *essentia*. Both *ousia* and *essentia* are nouns reflecting the verb "to be" (Greek *einai*; Latin *esse*), and thus assume the use of such verb in the "present" tense. Hebrew, however, has no equivalent for the "present" tense, nor any other grammatical tense for that matter. Its two main conjugations, as is the case in all Semitic languages, are built not on the basis of time, but rather from the perspective of the action, which can be either already consummated or in the

---

[17] They consider the Greek of LXX to be the original scripture language of both the Old and New Testaments.
[18] I recall how a visiting Greek Professor of Old Testament at the Balamand Orthodox School of Theology in Lebanon, teaching in English, spent a good half hour explaining to the Arabic speaking seminarians that the scriptural *psykhē* is to be understood against the original Hebrew *nepheš* and not Plato's "(eternal) soul" (*psykhē*). Little was he aware that the Arabic *naph(a)s* had the same connotation as the Hebrew, and the students did not need the extensive explanation. Their Greek counterparts, however, would need such an explanation since some of them, having been stamped by classical Christian theology and its view of the "human soul," would end up equating the "scriptural" *nepheš* with the "theological" soul.

process of taking place.[19] Consequently, the "present" tense of the verb "to be" is rendered through a nominal sentence where the subject matter (noun) is immediately followed by either another noun or an adjective describing its status or an adverb indicating its location. Nominal sentences—without the verb "to be"—are a staple of both Greek and Latin languages[20] where the addition of "is" to link the "subject" and the "predicate" is optional, and thus unnecessary for the meaning of the statement. Stating that someone or something *is* or *exists* is as oxymoronic as stating that someone or something *is not* or *does not exist*. In the first case, why stress the existence of someone or something you are speaking of, and conversely why try to deny the existence of someone or something after having assumed their existence through the mere fact of mentioning them? Also in Semitic languages there are no uppercase letters; consequently there are no "proper" names or nouns. It is only from the context of a passage that the hearer or reader is able to figure out whether an actual person is intended, or a function, or possibly both, in case of wordplay.[21]

An aside is in order here to explain a rampant misunderstanding of the meaning of the term "existence." Both the Greek verb *existēmi* and the Latin *existo* literally mean "stand out from the norm" and thus "be egregious" when compared to others who just "stand" in the sense of being present at the time of a gathering. Consequently, "exist" has a meaning only in a functional comparison and not in either a biological sense or in

---

[19] This approach to verbal conjugation is more realistic since one cannot speak of an action *before* its start (past tense), nor can one vouchsafe that an action will *for sure* take place (future tense).

[20] Nominal sentences are still heard in Slavic languages.

[21] Two examples will clarify my point. Let's say a young man just won the soccer state championship and his father greets him with "Oh my victor (victorious one)"; if the young man's name is Victor, then the greeting "Oh my Victor" has a double connotation. The same applies in the case of an elderly sick mother who is visited by her caring daughter whom she addresses as "Oh my hope (in life)"; if the daughter's name is Hope, then the connotation is even more forceful: "Oh my Hope!" However, in both cases, even a stranger who does not know the names of the children will still get the same basic message.

a philosophical sense of "to be or not to be." It bears repeating that, in Semitic languages, the verb "to be" is *immaterial*—it has no intrinsic "matter" or "existence."[22] Technically speaking, in a classroom only the teacher "stands out," whereas the students are "immaterial" since the class would still "be" in the sense of "take place" whether one of them is present or absent.[23] The actual value of "is" lies solely in the phrase "there is," that is, one has to be *somewhere*; one cannot possibly be nowhere.[24]

I should like here to expand on how "to be," or what we refer to as "(essential) existence," does *not* "exist" in Semitic languages. Early on in the history of nascent Islam the Arab philosophers and religious intelligentsia translated the works of Plato and Aristotle into Arabic. The importance of this for the West is that Ancient Greek philosophy entered the European scene via the medium of the Arabic translations. The rendering of "existence" into Arabic was done through the infinitive—or more precisely the infinitival noun (infinitive functioning as noun)—*wujud* (pronounced *wujood*) of the verb *wajada* (find), to the effect that "the existence" would be *'al-wujud*, which literally means "the (being) found." Consequently, the passive participle of the verb "find"[25] would correspond to "being there" in the phrase "are you there?" In this phrase "are" does not have the value of a being's essence, but rather is reflective of whether the person is, at that specific moment, in a given place. The Arabic would sound as a literal rendering of the slangy inquiry "you

---

[22] Pun intended.

[23] Only some of the students do sincerely believe that the class would not be the same in their absence and yet they say "I missed *my* class." How could one miss "his" class? A teacher never misses "his" class; in his absence "the" class simply does not take place. In the same vein, an absent parishioner does not affect the liturgical service, whereas if the pastor suddenly takes ill just before the service, there will be no liturgy unless there is a second pastor. Even the phrase "liturgy has been cancelled" does not make sense for how can one speak of a liturgy that did not take place?

[24] The police, for instance, keep looking for a suspect until that person is found; they do not debate whether that person "is" or "is not." Even if an informer made up that person, the immediate reaction of the police is to look *somewhere* for that "reality" which has been implanted in their mind.

[25] In Arabic *mawjud* (pronounced *mawjood*) simply means "found."

there?" without the verb "to be" which does not exist—is not (nowhere) to be found—in the present tense. The slangy "you there" would be a perfect Semitic style nominal sentence. Notice further in the preceding sentence that "exist" is practically the full equivalent of "is to be found somewhere" and has nothing to do with philosophical "essential" existence.[26]

In scripture it is the Semitic language that has the upper hand, a premise that classical theology across the board has a hard time accepting. Indeed how could the supposedly superior language of the Indo-Aryan world that stamped, if not created, artificial theological lingo be subordinate to a "barbarian" language that has no vowels as alphabetical letters? And yet, in scripture, God speaks precisely in such a language.

---

[26] So one can, or rather should make the effort to, understand my frustration in my high school Arabic philosophy classes where I was forced to bend the grammatical as well as logical Arabic language rules to accommodate a Greek term that does not "exist" in Arabic.

3

The Scriptural Deity

In the Ancient Near East the only person who stood out, and thus de facto "existed," was the monarch. The king was the one who uttered prayers to the deity on and in behalf of the people as well as himself, as witnessed in the story of Solomon in conjunction with the dedication of the temple.[1] That is also why the Book of Psalms is commonly known as the "Book of the Psalms of the King (and Prophet) David." More importantly for our discussion is that monarchs, as well as their deities, had to "stand out" in representative statues so that the common people, the children of a deity, so to speak, would be always reminded that they are issued from that deity in the same vein as the monarch is "the son of (God) the deity." Oxymoronically, in his palace only the king "stands out" while "sitting" on the throne. Yet in the temple the same king has to be "standing" before the "seated" deity in order for him, the king, to "stand out" in the eyes of his people. In other words, the people are irrelevant in the gathering, it is only the deity, by definition, and its locum tenens, by appointment, that are relevant. This societal feature has remained down to our days whereby laic human history is divided into "reigns" or "presidencies," and religious human history is depicted through a succession of "papacies" (papal reigns) or "patriarchates" (patriarchal reigns) or "episcopacies" (episcopal reigns).

Contrariwise, shepherdism does not require the artificial superstructure of temple/palace and thus existence in the sense of standing out or being egregious. In shepherd society the patriarch is the elder and his authority is unquestioned. At his demise, another patriarch—usually his eldest son—takes over. Consequently, there is no need for an artificial authority that

---

[1] See how Solomon prays for himself (1 Kg 8:22-29), then for the people (vv.30-40), and finally requests God's blessing over them (vv.52-61).

requires an imposed egregiousness.[2] The fluidity of shepherd society was by necessity not linked to a shrine; its life was regulated by the instruction/voice of the elder that was passed on from elder to elder.[3] The elder functioned as a "deity."[4] However, it was his teaching/instruction that was important and sufficient; there was no need for his actual presence. In a similar way, the scriptural God, the universalized El, circumvented the institutionalized/genealogical temple priesthood and spoke directly to the shepherd forefathers in Genesis, and then opted for prophets, chosen randomly for the occasion, so to speak, who carried the content of God's "voice" in every generation. In other words, God was "living" (*ḥay*) and continued to speak through the prophets raised for the occasion:[5]

> Thus says the Lord of hosts, the God of Israel: "Add your burnt offerings to your sacrifices, and eat the flesh. For in the day that I brought them out of the land of Egypt, I did not speak to your fathers or command them concerning burnt offerings and sacrifices. But this command I gave them, 'Obey my voice, and I will be your God, and you shall be my people; and walk in all the way that I command you, that it may be well with you.'" But they did not obey or incline their ear, but walked in their own counsels and the stubbornness of their evil hearts, and went backward and not forward. From the day that your fathers came out of the land

---

[2] Such as in a society where both the deity and its representative, the monarch, are conceived as seniors/elders, unnaturally, of course, since the monarch could be younger than his subjects.

[3] Similarly, among the American Indians, the elder or shaman ruled.

[4] This tradition was preserved in the urban civilizations in the forms of "council of the elders" or "senate," that is, "council of the senators (seniors)."

[5] Later Jesus will be portrayed as an ad hoc prophet: "He who receives you receives me, and he who receives me receives him who sent me. He who receives a prophet because he is a prophet shall receive a prophet's reward, and he who receives a righteous man because he is a righteous man shall receive a righteous man's reward." (Mat 10:40-41) And the crowds said, "This is the prophet Jesus from Nazareth of Galilee." (Mat 21:11) King Herod heard of it; for Jesus' name had become known. Some said, "John the baptizer has been raised from the dead; that is why these powers are at work in him." But others said, "It is Elijah." And others said, "It is a prophet, like one of the prophets of old." (Mar 6:14-15/Lk 9:7-9)

of Egypt to this day, I have persistently sent all my servants the prophets to them, day after day; yet they did not listen to me, or incline their ear, but stiffened their neck. They did worse than their fathers. So you shall speak all these words to them, but they will not listen to you. You shall call to them, but they will not answer you. And you shall say to them, 'This is the nation that did not obey the voice of the Lord their God, and did not accept discipline; truth has perished; it is cut off from their lips.' Cut off your hair and cast it away; raise a lamentation on the bare heights, for the Lord has rejected and forsaken the generation of his wrath. For the sons of Judah have done evil in my sight, says the Lord; they have set their abominations in the house which is called by my name, to defile it. And they have built the high place of Topheth, which is in the valley of the son of Hinnom, to burn their sons and their daughters in the fire; which I did not command, nor did it come into my mind." (Jer 7:21-31)

Surely the Lord God does nothing, without revealing his secret to his servants the prophets (Am 3:7)

Be not like your fathers, to whom the former prophets cried out, 'Thus says the Lord of hosts, Return from your evil ways and from your evil deeds." But they did not hear or heed me, says the Lord. Your fathers, where are they? And the prophets, do they live for ever? But my words and my statutes, which I commanded my servants the prophets, did they not overtake your fathers? So they repented and said, As the Lord of hosts purposed to deal with us for our ways and deeds, so has he dealt with us." (Zech 1:4-6)

"When Jerusalem was inhabited and in prosperity, with her cities round about her, and the South and the lowland were inhabited, were not these the words which the Lord proclaimed by the former prophets?" And the word of the Lord came to Zechariah, saying, "Thus says the Lord of hosts, Render true judgments, show kindness and mercy each to his brother, do not oppress the widow, the fatherless, the sojourner, or the poor; and let none of you devise evil against his brother in your heart." But they refused to hearken, and turned a stubborn shoulder, and stopped their ears that they might not hear. They made their hearts like adamant lest they should hear the law and the words which the

Lord of hosts had sent by his Spirit through the former prophets. Therefore great wrath came from the Lord of hosts. "As I called, and they would not hear, so they called, and I would not hear," says the Lord of hosts, "and I scattered them with a whirlwind among all the nations which they had not known. Thus the land they left was desolate, so that no one went to and fro, and the pleasant land was made desolate." (7:7-14)

Let your hands be strong, you who in these days have been hearing these words from the mouth of the prophets (8:9)

Of course, God's "servants the prophets" are those whose words have been consigned in scripture.[6] In other words, the voice of God as patriarch resounded in each generation through the leaders who *repeated* his words, and not commented on them. Hence his words are put in the mouth of Jeremiah (Jer 1:9), who later consigned them to writing (ch.36), and are received by Ezekiel as divine words in an already written scroll from God (Ezek 2:9-10). In the case of Jesus, anyone who listens to him listens to the one who sent him. That is why, as Chrysostom underscored, Jesus' words were consigned as a writ:

Now Jesus did many other signs in the presence of the disciples, which are not written (*gegrammena*) *in this book.* (Jn 20:30)

This is the disciple who is bearing witness to these things, and who has written (*ho grapsas*) these things;[7] and we know that his testimony is true. But there are also many other things which Jesus did; were every one of them to be written (*graphētai*), I suppose that the world itself could not contain the books that would be written (*graphomena*). (21:24-25)[8]

Since the scriptural God—a sheik-like Bedouin—resides in a movable tent, he is in no need of a "residence."[9] Moreover, he issues his directives in the wilderness, then he "absents" himself

---

[6] Similarly in the New Testament whenever Paul speaks of "apostles," he is actually referring to himself whose words were scripturalized.

[7] See also "I Tertius, the writer (*ho grapsas*) of this letter, greet you in the Lord" (Rom 16:22).

[8] All the Greek terms are from the same root as *graphē* (scripture).

[9] See my discussion of *God as Shepherd*, pp.143-50.

"for a while" to see if his children will abide by his directives as though he were present, and children beware, since he *is* coming back. Notice how the Pauline school, that captured the scriptural mind, put the matter:

> Therefore, my beloved, as you have always obeyed, so now, not only as in my presence but much more in my absence, work out your own salvation with fear and trembling; for God is at work in you, both to will and to work for his good pleasure. (Phil 2:12-13)

> This is the third time I am coming to you. Any charge must be sustained by the evidence of two or three witnesses. I warned those who sinned before and all the others, and I warn them now while absent, as I did when present on my second visit, that if I come again I will not spare them -- since you desire proof that Christ is speaking in me. He is not weak in dealing with you, but is powerful in you. For he was crucified in weakness, but lives by the power of God. For we are weak in him, but in dealing with you we shall live with him by the power of God. Examine yourselves, to see whether you are holding to your faith. Test yourselves. Do you not realize that Jesus Christ is in (among) you? -- unless indeed you fail to meet the test! I hope you will find out that we have not failed. But we pray God that you may not do wrong -- not that we may appear to have met the test, but that you may do what is right, though we may seem to have failed. For we cannot do anything against the truth, but only for the truth. For we are glad when we are weak and you are strong. What we pray for is your improvement. I write this while I am away from you, in order that when I come I may not have to be severe in my use of the authority which the Lord has given me for building up and not for tearing down. Finally, brethren, farewell. Mend your ways, heed my appeal, agree with one another, live in peace, and the God of love and peace will be with you. (2 Cor 13:1-11)[10]

Following God is tantamount to hearing his voice,[11] and it is the Law promulgated through his voice that *is* God. Yet, even when he promulgates his law, he cannot be "seen" and is de

---

[10] Read my *C-2Cor* 223-30.
[11] The Middle Eastern shepherd walks *ahead* of his flock that follows his voice.

facto "absent." In other words, he does not *exist*, in the sense of standing out, like the other gods. While the other gods, the idols, "are silver and gold, the work of men's hands. They have mouths, but do not speak; eyes, but do not see. They have ears, but do not hear; noses, but do not smell. They have hands, but do not feel; feet, but do not walk" (Ps 115:4-7a), because they are "made after their makers" (v.8a), the scriptural deity is not to be fathomed in that way. Although he has no mouth, eyes, ears, nose, hands, or feet, he nevertheless speaks, sees, hears, smells, feels, and walks, and above all he "does wonders." If he is said to have a "city," that city is Zion "on high" and patterned, as we shall see, after Tadmor, the oasis at the heart of the Syrian wilderness. Tadmor,[12] like the heavenly Zion, will survive the collapse of Jerusalem, the "city of David." The connection between Tadmor and Zion is borne out in the original Hebrew. Although an oasis without protective walls, the Semitic *tadmor* means "she[13] prevails by destroying the aggressor" and thus should be rendered as "the indomitable." The Hebrew *ṣiyyon* (Zion) is from the root *ṣiy(y)* whose meaning is "wilderness." If one considers that the Hebrew consonants *y(od)* and *w(aw)* sometimes behave as an interchangeable pair, then *ṣiyyon* could have been chosen because it also points toward the root *ṣiw(w)* whence we have the verb *ṣiwweh* ([to] command) and the noun *miṣwah* (commandment) that are connected to the Law promulgated on a high mountain in the wilderness. This feature explains why, although Zion and Jerusalem appear to be equated in Isaiah 2:2-5 as referring to the high mountain of the *torah* (instructional teaching) for both Israel and the nations,[14] it is only because the earthly Jerusalem has been renewed into the heavenly Zion in the "wilderness" of the exile:

---

[12] Built by Solomon (2 Chr 8:4), the builder of Jerusalem (v.1).

[13] In Hebrew the noun *'ir* (city) is of the grammatically feminine gender.

[14] It shall come to pass in the latter days that the mountain of the house of the Lord shall be established as the highest of the mountains, and shall be raised above the hills; and all the nations shall flow to it, and many peoples shall come, and say: "Come, let us go up to the mountain of the Lord, to the house of the God of Jacob;

Hear the word of the Lord, you rulers of Sodom! Give ear to the teaching of our God, you people of Gomorrah! … "Come now, let us reason together, says the Lord: though your sins are like scarlet, they shall be as white as snow; though they are red like crimson, they shall become like wool. If you are willing and obedient, you shall eat the good of the land; But if you refuse and rebel, you shall be devoured by the sword; for the mouth of the Lord has spoken." How the faithful city has become a harlot, she that was full of justice! Righteousness lodged in her, but now murderers. Your silver has become dross, your wine mixed with water. Your princes are rebels and companions of thieves. Every one loves a bribe and runs after gifts. They do not defend the fatherless, and the widow's cause does not come to them. Therefore the Lord says, the Lord of hosts, the Mighty One of Israel: "Ah, I will vent my wrath on my enemies, and avenge myself on my foes. I will turn my hand against you and will smelt away your dross as with lye and remove all your alloy. And I will restore your judges as at the first, and your counselors as at the beginning. Afterward you shall be called the city of righteousness, the faithful city." Zion shall be redeemed by justice, and those in her who repent, by righteousness. But rebels and sinners shall be destroyed together, and those who forsake the Lord shall be consumed. For you shall be ashamed of the oaks in which you delighted; and you shall blush for the gardens which you have chosen. For you shall be like an oak whose leaf withers, and like a garden without water. And the strong shall become tow, and his work a spark, and both of them shall burn together, with none to quench them. (Is 1:10, 18-31)[15]

Absenteeism versus Divine Invisibility

It is from that perspective that one should dismiss even the patristic philosophical premise of a divine entity that is "unseen" or "invisible" (*aoratos*; Col 1:15; 1 Tim 1:17) because it is *essentially* "not see-able":

that he may teach us his ways and that we may walk in his paths." For out of Zion shall go forth the law, and the word of the Lord from Jerusalem. (Is 2:2-3)
[15] Notice the total absence of a mention of Jerusalem.

I charge you to keep the commandment unstained and free from reproach until the appearing of our Lord Jesus Christ; and this will be made manifest at the proper time by the blessed and only Sovereign, the King of kings and Lord of lords, who alone has immortality and dwells in unapproachable light, *whom no man has ever seen or can see.* To him be honor and eternal dominion. Amen. (1 Tim 6:14-16)

God's invisibility in scripture is tantamount to his *voluntary* absence and is no way to be construed in terms of a philosophical *essential* quality or feature. This is, linguistically, an impossibility. *In scripture* God is not only a given, but an essential component of, if not the outright main agent in, the scriptural story. In order to test our resolve to follow his commandments, he repeatedly plays the role of the absentee landlord, so to speak. The most pertinent example of this is the parable in Luke 12:42-48. "Playing the role" should be taken at face value since the original meaning of the Greek *prosōpon* and the Latin *persona* refers to the mask that an actor donned to play a role on the stage.[16] Unfortunately, theology made of *prosōpon* an actual "person." The original connotation is evident in the Septuagint's opting for *prosōpon* to render the original Hebrew *panim* whose meaning is "face," and thus how someone *appears* when facing the others. Any deity is the judge of its subjects, and the scriptural God is the judge par excellence. This is clear in Psalm 82 where God judges all other deities:

A Psalm of Asaph. God has taken his place in the divine council; in the midst of the gods he holds judgment: "How long will you judge unjustly and show partiality to the wicked? [Selah] Give justice to the weak and the fatherless; maintain the right of the afflicted and the destitute. Rescue the weak and the needy; deliver them from the hand of the wicked." They have neither knowledge nor understanding, they walk about in darkness; all the foundations of the earth are shaken. I say, "You are gods, sons of the Most High, all of you; nevertheless, you shall die like men,

---

[16] This understanding is reflected in our English "persona," connoting the character of a "person."

and fall like any prince." Arise, O God, judge the earth; for to thee belong all the nations!

The connotation of a judging presence linked to *panim* is corroborated in that the Hebrew for the adverb "before" or the adverbial phrase "in front of" is either *liphne* (to the face of) or *le'ene* (to the eyes of). That is to say, being "before" is practically equivalent to being "in the presence of" and, more specifically, "standing before" or "being under scrutiny." This, in turn, explains why the two most common Hebrew nouns for "ire" or "wrath" are *ḥemah* (heat) and, more so, *'aph* (nose). The nose is more pertinent for our discussion since it is the prominent feature of the face that can appear as "(nostrils) fuming (with heat)" in the classic graphic depiction of divine ire. Thus the "face" of God connotes his presence *as judge* since that same face can turn into a "nose" at any given moment if what the divine "eyes" see is unsatisfactory. Given this ambivalence pertaining to the presence of a judge, an absence on his part carries with it a sense of relief among those who would otherwise be standing before the judgment seat. The absence of God as the master who is away is not to be construed in negative terms as though he does not care for us. To the contrary, God recedes *on purpose* to the background *as an expression of his mercy*, and sends us his emissaries and representatives whose mission is to remind us of his will. This allows us extra time to repent of our unsatisfactory behavior so that, whenever he does comes back or becomes present, we would be found as righteously innocent as Christ. That is why, at the *beginning* of his first letter Peter writes:

> Therefore gird up your minds, be sober, set your hope fully upon the grace that is coming to you at the revelation of Jesus Christ. As obedient children, do not be conformed to the passions of your former ignorance, but as he who called you is holy, be holy yourselves in all your conduct; since it is written, "You shall be holy, for I am holy." *And if you invoke as Father him who judges each one impartially according to his deeds, conduct yourselves with fear throughout the time of your exile.* You know that you were ransomed from the futile ways inherited from your fathers, not with perishable things

such as silver or gold, but with the precious blood of Christ, like
that of a lamb without blemish (*amōmou*) or spot (*aspilou*). He was
destined before the foundation of the world *but was made manifest
at the end of the times for your sake.* Through him you have confidence
in God, who raised him from the dead and gave him glory, so
that your faith and hope are in God. (1 Pet 1:13-21)

At the closing of his second letter, and thus bracketing his entire
message, Peter concludes with the warning:

Since all these things are thus to be dissolved, what sort of persons
ought you to be in lives of holiness and godliness, *waiting for* and
hastening *the coming of the day of God*, because of which the heavens
will be kindled and dissolved, and *the elements will melt with fire!* But
according to his promise we wait for new heavens and a new
earth *in which righteousness dwells.* Therefore, beloved, *since you wait
for these*, be zealous to be found by him without spot (*aspiloi*) or
blemish (*amōmētoi*),[17] and at peace. And *count the forbearance of our
Lord as salvation.* (2 Pet 3:11-15a)

It is no wonder then that, immediately thereafter, Peter
recommends:

And count the forbearance of our Lord as salvation. So also our
beloved brother Paul wrote to you according to the wisdom given
him, speaking of this as he does in all his letters. There are some
things in them hard to understand, which the ignorant and
unstable twist to their own destruction, as they do the other
scriptures. (vv.15b-16)

This understanding of awaiting righteously is emphasized in
Paul's letter to the bishop (*episkopos*) Timothy: "I charge you to
keep (*tērein*) the commandment unstained (*aspilon*) and free from
reproach until the appearing of our Lord Jesus Christ." (1 Tim
6:14) His teaching finds resonance in a passage from the letter
of James, Paul's nemesis:[18] "If any one thinks he is religious, and
does not bridle his tongue but deceives his heart, this man's

---

[17] The pair *aspilos* and *amōmos/ētos* occurs only in these two instances in the New
Testament.
[18] It is noteworthy that this letter is addressed "to the twelves tribes in the Dispersion
(*diaspora*)" (1:1), that is to say, to all the Jews who live among Paul's Gentiles.

religion is vain. Religion that is pure and undefiled *before God and the Father* is this: to visit (*episkeptesthai*; from the same root as *episkopos*) orphans and widows in their affliction, and to keep (*tērein*) oneself unstained (*aspilon*) from the world." (1:26-27) Both Paul and James are at one in underscoring that the ultimate test on judgment day is the care for the needy neighbor. This message will be immortalized in Matthew (25:31-46), the last book of the New Testament to be written by the Pauline school.

By delving into the vain discussion of divine invisibility and making of it a conundrum to be solved through the incarnation, theology practically voided the urgency of the gospel message: God absents himself for a while in order to test our resolve to abide by his will *while he is absent*. This is precisely his touch of grace since his "presence" may well reveal itself as a (fuming) nose rather than as a face, i.e., a well-meaning countenance. This is why his emissary Paul, who is not the judge but merely the teacher of the divine law, warns the Philippians to emulate Christ, the consummate divine emissary and teacher, in his consummate obedience to his God and Father:

> So if there is any encouragement in Christ, any incentive of love, any participation in the Spirit, any affection and sympathy, complete my joy by being of the same mind, having the same love, being in full accord and of one mind. Do nothing from selfishness or conceit, but in humility count others better than yourselves. Let each of you look not only to his own interests, but also to the interests of others. Have this mind among yourselves, which is yours in Christ Jesus, who, though he was in the form of God, did not count equality with God a thing to be grasped, but emptied himself, taking the form of a servant (*doulou*; slave), being born in the likeness of men. And being found in human form he humbled himself and *became obedient* unto death, even death on a cross. Therefore God has highly exalted him and bestowed on him the name which is above every name, that at the name of Jesus every knee should bow, in heaven and on earth and under the earth, and every tongue confess that Jesus Christ is Lord, to the glory of God the Father. Therefore, my beloved, as *you have always obeyed*, so now, not only as *in my presence* but *much more in my*

absence, work out your own salvation with fear and trembling; for God is at work in you, both to will and to work for his good pleasure. (Phil 2:1-13)

The gospel is an invitation to the Gentiles to obediently follow God's law *already handed down* in the Old Testament (Rom 1:1-2) and entrusted to Israel (3:2). In both Colossians and 1 Timothy, one hears of the "invisible, unseen" (*aoratos*) God after having heard the gospel word (*logos*) that revolves around doing God's will, which is to be merciful to the needy others just as God himself behaves toward us.[19] The Gentile intelligentsia that "turned to Christ" revamped that gospel message using the philosophical lingo of Plato, Aristotle, Philo, Justin the Philosopher, Origen, Plotinus, and the like, and twisted it into a mental discourse, something that was strictly forbidden by Paul. He purposely uses terminology woven around the root *logos* to describe the cunning perversion of the gospel word: "I am astonished that you are so quickly deserting him who called you in the grace of Christ and turning to a different gospel—not that there is another gospel, but there are some who trouble you and want to pervert the gospel of Christ." (Gal 1:6-7)

In Colossians Paul writes, "And so, from the day we heard of it, we have not ceased to pray for you, asking that you may be filled with *the knowledge of his will* in all spiritual wisdom and understanding, *to lead a life worthy of the Lord, fully pleasing to him, bearing fruit in every good work* and increasing in the knowledge of God."[20] (1:9-10) Then he proceeds to write in the following chapters:

> For I want you to know how greatly I strive for you, and for those at Laodicea, and for all who have not seen my face, *that their hearts may be encouraged as they are knit together in love*, to have all the riches

---

[19] See especially Rom 5:1-11. See also the Matthean parable of the unmerciful servant (Mt 18:23-35).

[20] As I pointed out in *C-Col* 40-42 "the knowledge of God" is a shortened formula for "the knowledge of God's will" (v.9) and does in no way refer to an intellectual knowledge, which would amount to human (Greek) wisdom that is openly criticized in 1 Cor 1-3.

of assured understanding and the knowledge of God's mystery, of Christ, in whom are hid all the treasures of wisdom and knowledge. I say this in order that no one may delude (*paralogizetai*; speaks in a manner to skirt the true gospel word)[21] you with beguiling speech (*pithanologia*). (2:1-4)

In these *you once walked*, when *you lived in them*. But now put them all away: anger, wrath, malice, slander, and foul talk (*aiskhrologian*) from your mouth. (3:7-8)

He follows a similar strategy in 1 Timothy:

As I urged you when I was going to Macedonia, remain at Ephesus that you may charge certain persons not to teach any different doctrine, nor to occupy themselves with myths and endless genealogies (*genealogiais*) which promote speculations rather than the divine training that is in faith; whereas *the aim of our charge is love* that issues from a pure heart and a good conscience and sincere faith. Certain persons by swerving from these have wandered away into vain discussion (*mataiologian*), desiring to be teachers of the law, without understanding either what they are saying or the things about which they make assertions. (1:3-7)

I desire then that in every place the men should pray, lifting holy hands without anger or quarreling (*dialogismou*) ... (2:8)

Deacons likewise must be serious, not double-tongued (*dilogous*), not addicted to much wine, not greedy for gain ... (3:8)

Now the Spirit expressly says that in later times some will depart from the faith by giving heed to deceitful spirits and doctrines of demons, through the pretensions of liars (*psevdologōn*) whose consciences are seared ... (4:1-2)

If any one teaches otherwise and does not agree with the sound words of our Lord Jesus Christ and the teaching which accords

---

[21] Notice the use of the same preposition *para* twice in a row in Galatians to describe the perversion of the gospel he is preaching: "But even if we, or an angel from heaven, should preach to you a gospel contrary to (*para*) that which we preached to you, let him be accursed. As we have said before, so now I say again, If any one is preaching to you a gospel contrary to (*para*) that which you received, let him be accursed." (1:8-9)

with godliness, he is puffed up with conceit, he knows nothing; he
has a morbid craving for controversy and for disputes about
words (*logomakhias*), which produce envy, dissension, slander, base
suspicions … (6:3-4)

Unfortunately, and to the detriment of us all, the development
of classical theology in all its different trends and traditions more
often than not fell precisely in—and is still captive to—this trap
of beguiling speech (*pithanologia*), foul talk (*aiskhrologian*), vain
discussion (*mataiologian*), quarreling (*dialogismou*), disputes about
words (*logomakhias*), and, worst of all, endless genealogies
(*genealogiais*) of the names of those who supposedly upheld from
generation to generation the so-called "living tradition." This
was done in overt contravention of the caveat at the start of
Psalm 78: "Give ear, O my people, to my teaching; incline your
ears to the words of my mouth!" Although scripture is utterly
concerned with God's will, theology has made of it a
complicated treatise *about* (the mystery of) God, so much so that
by the time the common believers are able to fathom it, they are
without enough energy and time to fulfill the Lord's command
to care for any and all needy brethren "for whom Christ died"
(1 Cor 8:11b).

Elohim and Yahweh

Dealing with the topic "the scriptural deity" cannot be complete
without a discussion as to how and why that deity came about
to be known throughout scripture under two "names": *'elohim*
(Greek [*ho*] *Theos*; God) and *yahweh* (Greek [*ho*] *kyrios*; the Lord).
Keeping with my overall thesis that scripture was devised to
warn its primary addressees against any kind of arrogance by
belittling them and to undermine the conqueror's infatuation
with its own power, the authors used two major deities of the
Semitic pantheon to express the two faces of their sole and thus
universal scriptural deity.

The choice of El (*'el*) could not be avoided since he had no
equal: he, "the kind, the compassionate," the creator of

creators," was "the god and father of all deities and humans."[22]
Two important facets that played a central role in the scriptural
story dictated the choice of Baal. On the one hand, he
corresponded to Zeus, the supreme deity of the Greeks. Zeus
was the leader of the Olympian gods who revolted against their
parents, the Titans. Baal acceded to the status of a full-fledged
deity when his father El granted him a mountain on which he
would build his temple. He supplanted his father as leader with
the support of his sister and consort Anat, just as Zeus needed
the support of his siblings. On the other hand, and more
importantly, Baal's domain was the thunder and thus included
the rain that secured life on earth, especially in the wilderness
devoid of major rivers. The functional parallelism between
yahweh (the Lord) and Baal is at its clearest in their showdown
depicted in Hosea:

> Therefore I will take back my grain in its time, and my wine in
> its season; and I will take away my wool and my flax, which were
> to cover her nakedness. Now I will uncover her lewdness in the
> sight of her lovers, and no one shall rescue her out of my hand.
> And I will put an end to all her mirth, her feasts, her new moons,
> her sabbaths, and all her appointed feasts. And I will lay waste
> her vines and her fig trees, of which she said, "These are my hire,
> which my lovers have given me." I will make them a forest, and
> the beasts of the field shall devour them. And I will punish her for
> the feast days of the *Baals* when she burned incense to them and
> decked herself with her ring and jewelry, and went after her
> lovers, and forgot me, says *the Lord*. (2:9-13)

In scripture *yahweh* and Baal, a stand-in for Alexander's Zeus,
are vying to "lord it"[23] over the scriptural nations as well as over

---

[22] From the Ugaritic "Baal Cycle."

[23] This "lordship" is unmistakably reflected in the Greek rendering of *yahweh* as *ho
kyrios* (the Lord; the master) who rules over his "slaves" (Hebrew *'abadim* plural of *'ebed*
[slave]). This in turn influenced the Jewish tradition of reading aloud *yahweh* as *'adonai*
(my lord; my master). That *yahweh* is viewed as *'adon* just as Baal is, is at its clearest in
Joshua: "Behold, the ark of the covenant of the Lord (*'adon*) of all the earth is to pass
over before you into the Jordan. Now therefore take twelve men from the tribes of
Israel, from each tribe a man. And when the soles of the feet of the priests who bear

the scriptural Israel. This antagonism between these two deities is established right from the start of Israel's life in the scriptural earth of Canaan and in no uncertain terms by none other than *yahweh* (the Lord) himself whose "law" was read aloud to the hearing of *all* the inhabitants of Canaan:

> Then Joshua built an altar in Mount Ebal to the Lord, the God of Israel, as Moses the servant of the Lord had commanded the people of Israel, as it is written in the book of the law of Moses, "an altar of unhewn stones, upon which no man has lifted an iron tool"; and they offered on it burnt offerings to the Lord, and sacrificed peace offerings. And there, in the presence of the people of Israel, he wrote upon the stones a copy of the law of Moses, which he had written. And all Israel, sojourner as well as homeborn, with their elders and officers and their judges, stood on opposite sides of the ark before the Levitical priests who carried the ark of the covenant of the Lord, half of them in front of Mount Gerizim and half of them in front of Mount Ebal, as Moses the servant of the Lord had commanded at the first, that they should bless the people of Israel. And afterward he read all the words of the law, the blessing and the curse, according to all that is written in the book of the law. There was not a word of all that Moses commanded which Joshua did not read before all the assembly of Israel, and the women, and the little ones, and the sojourners who lived among them. (Josh 8:30-35)

> When Joshua dismissed the people, the people of Israel went each to his inheritance to take possession of the land. And the people served the Lord all the days of Joshua, and all the days of the elders who outlived Joshua, who had seen all the great work which the Lord had done for Israel. And Joshua the son of Nun, the servant of the Lord, died at the age of one hundred and ten years. And they buried him within the bounds of his inheritance in Timnathheres, in the hill country of Ephraim, north of the mountain of Gaash. And all that generation also were gathered to their fathers; and there arose another generation after them, who did not know the Lord or the work which he had done for

---

the ark of the Lord (*yahweh*), the Lord (*'adon*) of all the earth, shall rest in the waters of the Jordan, the waters of the Jordan shall be stopped from flowing, and the waters coming down from above shall stand in one heap." (Josh 3:11-13)

Israel. And the people of Israel did what was evil in the sight of the Lord and served the Baals; and they forsook the Lord, the God of their fathers, who had brought them out of the land of Egypt; they went after other gods, from among the gods of the peoples who were round about them, and bowed down to them; and they provoked the Lord to anger. They forsook the Lord, and served the Baals and the Ashtaroth. So the anger of the Lord was kindled against Israel, and he gave them over to plunderers, who plundered them; and he sold them into the power of their enemies round about, so that they could no longer withstand their enemies. Whenever they marched out, the hand of the Lord was against them for evil, as the Lord had warned, and as the Lord had sworn to them; and they were in sore straits. Then the Lord raised up judges, who saved them out of the power of those who plundered them. And yet they did not listen to their judges; for they played the harlot after other gods and bowed down to them; they soon turned aside from the way in which their fathers had walked, who had obeyed the commandments of the Lord, and they did not do so. Whenever the Lord raised up judges for them, the Lord was with the judge, and he saved them from the hand of their enemies all the days of the judge; for the Lord was moved to pity by their groaning because of those who afflicted and oppressed them. But whenever the judge died, they turned back and behaved worse than their fathers, going after other gods, serving them and bowing down to them; they did not drop any of their practices or their stubborn ways. So the anger of the Lord was kindled against Israel; and he said, "Because this people have transgressed my covenant which I commanded their fathers, and have not obeyed my voice, I will not henceforth drive out before them any of the nations that Joshua left when he died, that by them I may test Israel, whether they will take care to walk in the way of the Lord as their fathers did, or not." So the Lord left those nations, not driving them out at once, and he did not give them into the power of Joshua. (Jdg 2:6-23)

However, although they both act as "masters" and "lords" of their subjects, there is a far cry between Zeus and *yahweh*. The Greeks ended up viewing themselves as superior to the surrounding nations that were dubbed "barbarians." Put otherwise, the superiority of the victorious Greek gods over the foreign deities entailed the superiority of their followers over the subjects of the vanquished deities. In the case of *yahweh* and the scriptural Israel, there was no room whatsoever for such arrogance. The rationale—reflected in the conjunction "for" (*ki*)—behind the strict ban against submission to the deities of the nations (Deut 7:1-5) is the following:

> For (*ki*) you are a people holy to the Lord your God; the Lord your God has chosen you to be a people for his own possession, out of all the peoples that are on the face of the earth. It was not because you were more in number than any other people that the Lord set his love upon you and chose you, *for you were the fewest of all peoples*; but it is because the Lord loves you, and *is keeping the oath which he swore to your fathers*, that the Lord has brought you out with a mighty hand, and redeemed you from the house of bondage, from the hand of Pharaoh king of Egypt. (Deut 7:6-8)

Bona fide salvation, so to speak, of the Israelites does not translate into superiority. Rather it levels the playing field between them and the strangers or the foreigners (*gerim*):

> You shall not wrong a stranger or oppress him, for you were strangers in the land of Egypt. (Ex 22:21)

> You shall not oppress a stranger; you know the heart of a stranger, for you were strangers in the land of Egypt. (23:9)

> The stranger who sojourns with you shall be to you as the native among you, and you shall love him as yourself; for you were strangers in the land of Egypt: I am the Lord your God. (Lev 19:34)

> The land shall not be sold in perpetuity, for the land is mine; for you are strangers and sojourners with me. (25:23)

And the Israelites better beware since their "savior" from the house of bondage (Deut 7:8) proceeds to say:

> Know therefore that the Lord your God is God, the faithful God who keeps covenant and steadfast love with those who love him and keep his commandments, to a thousand generations, and requites to their face those who hate him, by destroying them; he will not be slack with him who hates him, he will requite him to

his face. You shall therefore be careful to do the commandment, and the statutes, and the ordinances, which I command you this day. (Deut 7:9-11)

So, in spite of his Baal-ic and Zeus-like features, the scriptural *yahweh*'s concern is not localized and or aimed only at the welfare of his own constituency abiding around his "holy mountain" Jerusalem, which corresponds to Baal's holy mountain Hermon and Zeus' Mount Olympus. His concern embraces the "strangers" and "barbarians" as well and in an equal manner. Actually the strictness embodied in his statutes is aimed specifically at Israel since the Law was first addressed to them (Ex 19:20-25; 21:1; Deut 5:1) and thus was entrusted to them (Josh 23:2; 24:1-2; Rom 3:2). In other words, first and foremost it is Israel who is accountable to follow the Law that dictates the equal handling of the outsiders. In this regard *yahweh* acts in a way consistent with the universal fatherhood of El over all nations that inhabit his world. Thus, the scriptural *yahweh* "behaves" similarly to the Semitic El rather than to Baal or Zeus. Put otherwise, the scriptural *yahweh* is "conditioned" by the scriptural *'elohim*; that is to say, it is *'elohim* who has the upper hand in the scriptural divine twosome. This functional subordination of *yahweh* to *'elohim* is borne out in the phraseology and structure of the following passage from Deuteronomy:

When the Lord your God brings you into the land which you are entering to take possession of it, and clears away many nations before you, the Hittites, the Girgashites, the Amorites, the Canaanites, the Perizzites, the Hivites, and the Jebusites, seven nations greater and mightier than yourselves, and when the Lord your God gives them over to you, and you defeat them; then you must utterly destroy them; you shall make no covenant with them, and show no mercy to them. You shall not make marriages with them, giving your daughters to their sons or taking their daughters for your sons. For they would turn away your sons from following me, to serve other gods; then the anger of the Lord would be kindled against you, and he would destroy you quickly. But thus shall you deal with them: you shall break down their altars, and dash in pieces their pillars, and hew down their

Asherim, and burn their graven images with fire. For you are a people holy to the Lord your God; the Lord your God has chosen you to be a people for his own possession, out of all the peoples that are on the face of the earth. It was not because you were more in number than any other people that the Lord set his love upon you and chose you, for you were the fewest of all peoples; but it is because the Lord loves you, and is keeping the oath which he swore to your fathers, that the Lord has brought you out with a mighty hand, and redeemed you from the house of bondage, from the hand of Pharaoh king of Egypt. Know therefore that the Lord your God (he) is God, the faithful God who keeps covenant and steadfast love with those who love him and keep his commandments, to a thousand generations, and requites to their face those who hate him, by destroying them; he will not be slack with him who hates him, he will requite him to his face. You shall therefore be careful to do the commandment, and the statutes, and the ordinances, which I command you this day. (7:1-11)

It is immediately noticeable that (1) the Lord (*yahweh*) is systematically qualified as *your* God (*'elohim*) except in conjunction with the salvation out of Egypt (vv.7-8) where one hears simply "the Lord" (*yahweh*), and (2) that salvation has nothing to do with Israel, but is carried out simply because of the oath previously sworn to the fathers. Thus, the re-issuance of the Law before the entrance into the earth of the promise repeats in its own way what we heard in the earlier Book of Exodus:

But the Lord (*yahweh*) said to Moses, "Now you shall see what I will do to Pharaoh; for with a strong hand he will send them out, yea, with a strong hand he will drive them out of his land." And God (*'elohim*) said to Moses, "I am the Lord (*yahweh*). I appeared to Abraham, to Isaac, and to Jacob, as God Almighty (*'el šadday*), but by my name the Lord (*yahweh*) I did not make myself known to them. I also established my covenant with them, to give them the land of Canaan, the land in which they dwelt as sojourners. Moreover I have heard the groaning of the people of Israel whom the Egyptians hold in bondage and I have remembered my covenant." (Ex 6:1-5)

When untainted by later theological surmises relating to the "godhead," the unbiased hearer gets the distinct impression that *yahweh* is more specifically connected with "the law (of the land)," just as are Baal and Zeus. That is to say, *yahweh* acts as a local deity would; his interest is his own defined realm. The "strangers" are within his purview only to the extent to which they happen to reside in that defined realm. Otherwise, they are viewed as outsiders and enemies. On the other hand, *'elohim* acts more universally and his concern is more encompassing in that (1) it covers a much larger expanse of territory rather than specifically "the earth of the promise" and (2) it deals directly with all nations residing in that area, each within its own territory. Hence the specific reference to the "fathers" in conjunction with him rather than with *yahweh*. This makes sense only in scripture where the story of those "fathers," to whom reference is made in both Exodus and Deuteronomy, is found in the Book of Genesis that covers a period of human (hi)story predating the exodus and the issuance of the Law, both specific to Israel. The "contrast" between *'elohim* and *yahweh* is at clearest when one compares the way in which the same addresses himself to Abram/Abraham, on the one hand, where one hears the first instance of "God Almighty" in Genesis, and to Moses, on the other hand, where we have the only occurrence of that same phrase in the rest of the Old Testament with the exception of Ezekiel 10:5.[24] In order to allow my readers to follow my argument I should like to quote the lengthy passage in Genesis for them to compare it visually with that of Exodus quoted above:

> When Abram was ninety-nine years old the Lord appeared to Abram, and said to him, "I am God Almighty; walk before me, and be blameless. And I will make my covenant between me and you, and will multiply you exceedingly." Then Abram fell on his face; and God said to him, "Behold, my covenant is with you, and you shall be the father of a multitude of nations. No longer shall

---

[24] And the sound of the wings of the cherubim was heard as far as the outer court, like the voice of God Almighty when he speaks.

your name be Abram, but your name shall be Abraham; for I
have made you the father of a multitude of nations. I will make
you exceedingly fruitful; and I will make nations of you, and kings
shall come forth from you. And I will establish my covenant
between me and you and your descendants after you throughout
their generations for an everlasting covenant, to be God to you
and to your descendants after you. And I will give to you, and to
your descendants after you, the land of your sojournings, all the
land of Canaan, for an everlasting possession; and I will be their
God." And God said to Abraham, "As for you, you shall keep my
covenant, you and your descendants after you throughout their
generations. This is my covenant, which you shall keep, between
me and you and your descendants after you: Every male among
you shall be circumcised. You shall be circumcised in the flesh of
your foreskins, and it shall be a sign of the covenant between me
and you. He that is eight days old among you shall be
circumcised; every male throughout your generations, whether
born in your house, or bought with your money from any
foreigner who is not of your offspring, both he that is born in your
house and he that is bought with your money, shall be
circumcised. So shall my covenant be in your flesh an everlasting
covenant. Any uncircumcised male who is not circumcised in the
flesh of his foreskin shall be cut off from his people; he has broken
my covenant." And God said to Abraham, "As for Sarai your
wife, you shall not call her name Sarai, but Sarah shall be her
name. I will bless her, and moreover I will give you a son by her;
I will bless her, and she shall be a mother of nations; kings of
peoples shall come from her." Then Abraham fell on his face and
laughed, and said to himself, "Shall a child be born to a man who
is a hundred years old? Shall Sarah, who is ninety years old, bear
a child?" And Abraham said to God, "O that Ishmael might live
in thy sight!" God said, "No, but Sarah your wife shall bear you
a son, and you shall call his name Isaac. I will establish my
covenant with him as an everlasting covenant for his descendants
after him. As for Ishmael, I have heard you; behold, I will bless
him and make him fruitful and multiply him exceedingly; he shall
be the father of twelve princes, and I will make him a great
nation. But I will establish my covenant with Isaac, whom Sarah
shall bear to you at this season next year." When he had finished
talking with him, God went up from Abraham. Then Abraham

took Ishmael his son and all the slaves born in his house or bought with his money, every male among the men of Abraham's house, and he circumcised the flesh of their foreskins that very day, as God had said to him. Abraham was ninety-nine years old when he was circumcised in the flesh of his foreskin. And Ishmael his son was thirteen years old when he was circumcised in the flesh of his foreskin. That very day Abraham and his son Ishmael were circumcised; and all the men of his house, those born in the house and those bought with money from a foreigner, were circumcised with him. (Gen 17:1-27)

Notice that, although it is the Lord who appears to Abram, yet—just as we heard in Exodus—he introduces himself to him as God, which God takes over the rest of the chapter where the Lord is not to be encountered even once! Moreover, it is under the aegis of "God" that Abram is made into Abraham, the father of many nations, and Sarai into Sarah, the mother of many nations, through the medium of circumcision that was a widespread tradition among those same nations (Jer 9:25-26). The authors' intentionality is unmissable: it is the universal God who controls the general scene of Genesis where not only the progeny of the supposedly sidelined Ishmael is given special attention with the names of his "twelve" sons (Gen 25:12-16) but also and more importantly, that of the supposedly renegade Esau is given extensive and detailed attention in a lengthy chapter (35) of forty three verses. Even Egypt, under divine wrath in Exodus, shares with Israel the blessings secured by Joseph who saved both from the curse of famine.

Even more. Abram, the forefather of Israel, does not appear on the scene until the end of chapter 11 and, to boot, in the progeny of Terah who is the tenth descendant in a long series of sons of extended life spans to Shem, one of three sons of Noah. In turn, Noah is the tenth descendant to Adam in a long series of sons of similar extended life spans. Put otherwise, in scripture, Abram entered the historical scene 11,536 years after Adam. Until Abram's time the scriptural deity was busy with the entire earth's humanity and its "nations." Looking more

closely at Genesis 1-11 even a first time hearer will not miss the
fact that *yahweh 'elohim* is introduced only in chapter 2 while it is
'elohim who rules uncontested in chapter 1 that deals with the
"progeny" (*toledot*) of the "heavens and the earth," that is, of the
entire universe, and is satisfied to the fullest with the way
matters stand between human, animal and vegetation (1:29-30).
One can clearly detect that the contrast we find between *'elohim*
and *yahweh* in Genesis and Exodus is retrojected to the times of
the origins. Not only is the *yahweh* of Genesis defined as *'elohim*,
that is, in comparison with the *'elohim* of Genesis 1:1-2:3, but
also this *yahweh 'elohim*'s first verbal dealing with "the human
being" (*ha'adam*) is a matter of a command to be heeded (2:16-
17), a presaging of the Law: he commands the human being
(v.16) as he will command Moses. The upper handedness of
'elohim over *yahweh* is sealed at the end of chapter 4 where, after
a long series of *yahweh 'elohim* (Gen 2:4-3:24) and even of simply
yahweh (no less than ten times in Gen 4), Elohim himself, who
has been totally sidelined since Genesis 2:3, reappears out of the
blue in 4:25 to "appoint" a new "seed" of humanity: "And
Adam knew his wife again, and she bore a son and called his
name Seth, for she said, 'God has appointed for me another
child instead of Abel, for Cain slew him.'" (Gen 4:25).[25] *'elohim*'s
sudden introduction is, to say the least, striking when one
considers that (1) the phraseology of that verse parallels that of
4:1 where Eve refers to the Lord as the agent of her birth
giving[26] and (2) in the immediately following verse 26 *yahweh* is
referred to on his own in the rest of chapter 4: "To Seth also a
son was born, and he called his name Enosh. At that time men
began to call upon the name of the Lord (*yahweh*)." (Gen 4:26)
It as though the authors intended to convey to the hearers that
it is *'elohim* who controls the entire first scriptural literary unit,
i.e., the *toledot* of the heavens and the earth—before the *toledot* of
Adam (5:1-6:8), the very distant forefather of Abram. It is

---

[25] See later my detailed comments on Gen 4:25-26.
[26] Now Adam knew Eve his wife, and she conceived and bore Cain, saying, "I have
gotten a man with the help of the Lord."

Elohim who "rules" uncontested in that original and abiding setting of all life on our planet, whereas his alter scriptural persona, *yahweh*, acts simply in *'elohim*'s shadow, as it were. Elohim's absolute rule is at its clearest in Psalm 82 that speaks of his judging the other deities and where his appellation *yahweh*—that is otherwise omnipresent in the Book of Psalms— is totally absent. It furthermore stands to reason that that same Psalm concludes with "Arise, O God, judge the earth; for to thee belong all the nations!" (Ps 82:8) Thus, the absence is all the more strange when one notices that the divine rule over the nations is subsumed exclusively under *yahweh* in Genesis 10-11. The conclusion is inevitable: the contrast between *'elohim* and *yahweh* is not one of opposition, as in the case between *yahweh* and Baal, but rather one of subordination. Even as *yahweh* of the Law handed down exclusively to Israel, the scriptural deity is throughout and ultimately under the uncontestable ruling of Elohim, which is precisely what transpires from the above quoted Deuteronomy 7:1-11. Although the passage starts with *yahweh 'elohim* and then even moves to simply *yahweh*, the last three verses are phrased exclusively under the aegis of *yahweh 'elohim as* (the)*'elohim* who is, to boot, more specifically named simply *'el* or rather "the" *'el*, the divine persona par excellence:

> Know therefore that the Lord your God (he) is God, the faithful God (*ha'el hanne'eman*) who keeps covenant and steadfast love with those who love him and keep his commandments, to a thousand generations, and requites to their face those who hate him, by destroying them; he will not be slack with him who hates him, he will requite him to his face. You shall therefore be careful to do the commandment, and the statutes, and the ordinances, which I command you this day. (Deut 7:9-11)

So ultimately, Israel is bound by the statutes and commandments of the *'el* of all nations—if not of the heavens and the earth—and as such he expects *through the wording of his law* that the nations, as strangers and foreigners, that is, as not part of Israel, be treated throughout his "earth" just as God had treated the Israelites in Egypt. How could it be otherwise when the first command—to be obeyed—of *yahweh as* Elohim was uttered to the "human race" (*ha'adam*). It is precisely therein that lies the hurriedness of the Apostle to the nations to bring those nations under the gospel of "obedience" already inscribed in God's (*'elohim's*) scripture (Rom 1:1-6). The universalism of Paul's God extends not only over the Greco-Romans as well as barbarians (vv.14-15) but over the Roman imperial power as well (v.16).[27]

The plural 'elohim

As strange as this may sound to our contemporary ears, the habit of pluralizing the name of a deity was common at the time when scripture was written. The most known example that survived even into our own times is the name of the city Athens where the plural of the original is readily recognizable in the final "s" in English as in the French *Athènes*. The original Greek is *Athēnai*, which is the plural of the goddess *Athēna*. The reason is simple. In order to honor the goddess to whom their city was dedicated many temples were erected in her honor throughout that city. This way a visitor would immediately gather that the city pertained to the goddess Athena. Since, on the other hand, a temple dedicated to a deity had at its center the statue of that deity, to the eye of the visitor as well as citizen, the city of Athena was replete with many statues of Athena. As in the case of a statue of King Louis XIV or an icon of Saint Peter, for instance, one does not say "this is a (the) statue of King Louis" or "this is an icon of Saint Peter" but rather simply "this is King Louis" or "this is Saint Peter," so also would a Greek of ancient times refer to a statue of Athena as simply "Athena." The same habit is detectable in scripture where the plural *ba'alim* (Baals) refers to the many statues and temples of that deity and the plural *'ašerot* (Asheroth) is indicative of the statues and temples of the feminine deity *'ašerah*: "And the people of Israel did what was evil in the sight of the Lord, forgetting the Lord their God, and

---

[27] Power and salvation in v.16 are imperial attributes.

serving the Baals and the Asheroth." (Jdg 3:7) Actually, in the case of the feminine deity, the fact that the reference is to a statue is evident from that the Hebrew feminine plural *'ašerot* (Asheroth) is a unique instance whereas the masculine plural *'ašerim* (Asherim) is found no less than nineteen times in all three parts of the Old Testament. This phenomenon is to be explained in that in all cases save one (1 Kg 14:15) *'ašerim* is used in parallel to the similarly inanimate altars and pillars and the authors opted for a masculine plural corresponding to the plural *selamim* of the noun *selem* (image, statue) found in the following instances:

> then you shall drive out all the inhabitants of the land from before you, and destroy all their figured stones, and destroy all their molten images, and demolish all their high places. (Num 33:52)

> Then all the people of the land went to the house of Baal, and tore it down; his altars and his images they broke in pieces, and they slew Mattan the priest of Baal before the altars. (2Ki 11:18/2Ch 23:17)

> Their beautiful ornament they used for vainglory, and they made their abominable images and their detestable things of it; therefore I will make it an unclean thing to them. (Ezek 7:20)

> You also took your fair jewels of my gold and of my silver, which I had given you, and made for yourself images of men, and with them played the harlot; (16:17)

> But she carried her harlotry further; she saw men portrayed upon the wall, the images of the Chaldeans portrayed in vermilion, (23:14)

> You shall take up Sakkuth your king, and Kaiwan your star-god, your images, which you made for yourselves; (Am 5:26)

This being the reality in those times, it then stands to reason that the scriptural authors' choice for the plural *'elohim* as the most common form reflecting their exclusively *one* supreme god (*'el*) was highly intentional. It served several purposes:

1. The hearers are forced to assume that, wherever they might be and in spite of the many temples they encounter, they stand before—in the presence of (*liphne* [to the face of]; *le'ene* [to the eyes of])—the one who is their sole God. It is interesting in this regard that, for the authors, *yahweh* as nemesis of Baal is never in the plural: "Hear, O Israel: *yahweh* (who is) *our* God, (that) *yahweh* (is) one." (Deut 6:4)

2. The polytheism of the times reflected a practical reality. The multiplicity of the different domains as well as each area of life—sea, earth, mountain, love, war, wisdom—was ruled by a specific deity. By pluralizing *'el* into Elohim instead of *yahweh*, the authors underscored that the scriptural universal deity assumed under its aegis all the possible functions of the pantheon. In order to understand the impact of such literary device on the addressees, my readers are invited to imagine that, in the Yellow Pages telephone book they have at hand, one finds the same "name" for all the possible needs: plumbing; car maintenance; heating and air conditioning; ophthalmology; cardiology; marital services; insurance; etc. It is utterly frustrating and, understandably so, because, if so, then we are not even allowed to seek "a second opinion" regarding a given subject or, for that matter, any subject at all. Just imagine if your "one" plumber were also your "one" physician! There is no possible doubt that the authors knew exactly what they were up to when they prefaced their monumental endeavor with the self-standing statement that functions as a title to the entire scripture: "In the beginning God (*'elohim*) created (*bara'*; made functional) the

heavens and the earth (i.e., our "universe," functionally, that is psychologically as well as literally)." (Gen 1:1) That the scriptural *'elohim* is intentionally pinned down against the totality of the deities and actually dislodges them is evident from that, in that same scripture, the exact same *'elohim* is used to refer to the other (many) gods.[28] Let me here simply refer my readers to the above quoted passage of Deuteronomy: "For they would turn away your sons from following me, to serve other gods (*'elohim*); then the anger of the Lord would be kindled against you, and he would destroy you quickly." (7:4) Furthermore the authors' option to refer to their sole *'elohim* also as *ha'elohim* (*the* gods)—with the definite article *ha(l)*—seals the intentionality of their choice, especially when the two forms appear in the same context: "Now the earth was corrupt in God's (*ha'elohim*) sight, and the earth was filled with violence. And God (*'elohim*) saw the earth, and behold, it was corrupt; for all flesh had corrupted their way upon the earth." (Gen 6:11-12)

3. Still, in order to establish definitely an unbridgeable chasm in the hearers' minds between the scriptural God and the other deities, and thus to keep him as the sole functional *'el*, *ha'el* (*the* El; Deut 7:9), the authors refer to other deities—yet never to the scriptural God, besides

---

[28] See, e.g., Gen 35:2, 4; Ex 12:12; 18:11. The list is endless.

'elohim,[29] also as *'elim* (the plural of *'el*)[30] whose *God* he is: "And the king shall do according to his will; he shall exalt himself and magnify himself above every god, and shall speak astonishing things against *the God of gods* (*'el 'elim*). He shall prosper till the indignation is accomplished; for what is determined shall be done." (Dan 11:36)

I hope that this discussion of *yahweh* and *'elohim* will have convinced my readers that not only the knowledge of scriptural Hebrew but also an intimate knowledge of the scripture in that same Hebrew is a necessity at least on the part of some of the believers in order to clarify unto others what the text is *actually* saying. A caveat is in order here: the interest should be not in what the text is saying about a certain topic, but rather simply in what the text is *plainly* saying. It is from the unbiased hearing of the original text that the listener will gather what the topics are.

---

[29] This is technically the plural of *'eloah*. See especially Ps 18 where both forms are used in the same context and, to boot, followed by *ha'el* (*the* God): "For who is God (*'eloah*), but the Lord? And who is a rock, except our God (*'elohim*)?—the God (*ha'el*) who girded me with strength, and made my way safe." (Ps 18:31-32)

[30] *'el* means deity in general as in Ezek 28: 2 and 9: "you are but a man (*'adam*; human), and no god (*'el*)."

4

The Person and Sex of the Scriptural Deity

The same kind of misconception regarding essence and existence also applies to the "person." In contemporary Western societies the "individual," under the guise of the more sophisticated "person," has been quasi-deified, and is perceived as an "essential" (self-standing) being whose value lies in himself or herself.

The original Greek *prosōpon* and Latin *persona* referred to the mask (face) that an actor wore in order to "impersonate" a character. In scripture the same *prosōpon* refers to the "face" or "forehead" of a human. So the more accurate rendering of those two nouns is our "persona" rather than "person." Clearly, the persona is a functional reality. This is precisely how scripture deals with all its personae or personalities, including God, as characters in the storyline. God is in turn—and not necessarily at the same time—shepherd, king, master, savior, lawgiver, father, and, why not, gardener and mother. When it comes to identifying a father or a mother, the trouble for most of us is that we think in terms of sex, that is, in terms of male and female. Although the human beings and animals are so identified, at no point in scripture is God referred to as either male or female. In the different stories God assumes the function of his character and the sex, if sex is involved. However, one may not extrapolate and deduce that, for instance, God plays the role of a spouse. This statement is definitely incorrect on two counts. First of all, Hebrew does not have a term for our English "spouse"—one is either husband or wife—and God in scripture is never presented as wife; mother, yes, as we shall see, but never wife. Secondly, one has to respect the text. Handling it with liberality is tantamount to re-writing it, and it then becomes our rendition of the text. That God may be a husband[1] and not its counterpart, a wife, is not exceptional. God is always the master, never the slave; always the shepherd, never the sheep; always the senior, never the junior; always the teacher, never the disciple. In scripture, God always has the upper hand in any kind of relationship.

In the patriarchal society of the Ancient Near East a woman was cared for (1) as a daughter by her father and mother of course, however, by the former as the provider; (2) as a wife by her husband; (3) as a widow by either her brother, her father-in-law, her brother-in-law, or her second husband. So it stands to reason that God could never function as a wife or, for that matter, as a woman. However, as I already stated, God does function at times as a mother and sometimes even as a woman in travail. My readers may be quick to interject, "But are these two not women?" Yes, but the inverse is not necessarily true: not every woman is a mother or in travail. And, in each story, it is the function of the character that matters, not the sexuality. In our contemporary world, a single parent must function as mother *and* father, regardless of sexuality. We may speak of a "father figure" or a "mother figure" regarding a person who functions as such and plays that role.[2] We refer to a woman chef as a chef and a woman teacher as a teacher.

In scripture, it is not a woman's potential to bear a child, nor even a pregnancy, but the actual birthing of a living child that defines her motherhood. Her loss of virginity is defined by the birth of her first living child who is referred to as "the opener of the womb."[3] It is that child that confirms that the woman has

---

[1] See Hosea 2:7 (Heb v.9), 16 (Heb v.18); See also Is 54:5-6; Jer 31:32.

[2] The already universal "Be like Mike" is addressed to both boys and girls since one is talking of him in his role as basketball *player*. One could equally come up with "Be like Mia Hamm," which would be addressed equally to boys and girls. How could it not be so when it was she who said to her national team coach: "Coach us like men, treat us like women"?

[3] Genesis 29:31, 30:22. See also Ex 13:2, 12, 15; 34:19; Num 3:12; 18:15.

become a mother in the sense of begetter.[4] In Arabic, a respectful address to a mother (*'um*; Hebrew *'em*) is *'al-walidat* (the begetter) which is the feminine singular active participle of the verb *walada*, corresponding to the Hebrew *hayyoledet* from the verb *yalad*. That same *walidat* is also addressed with the equally respectful title of *'um* followed by the name of her first born, e.g., *'um william* if her first born's name is William. That "title" becomes the name by which she is called as well as known to her community. So the title, "the Mother of William," has a similar functional value as "the President" or, more pertinently for our discussion of scripture, as "the King." It is the noun complement that defines the "being" of the mother rather than vice versa. It is William, the opener of the womb, who makes his mother a begetter. This reality has nothing to do with the sex of the child; it has to do with primogeniture since the "opener of the womb" is obviously the firstborn. This explains why, after the firstborn, we hear only the generic (other) "sons and daughters" in Adam's and Shem's genealogies (Gen 5; 11:10-26).

The most impressive staple of scripture is its consistent belittlement of human power. Given that scripture was written against the background of a patriarchal society, its main nemesis, so to speak, is the macho male human being.[5] This is why from the beginning (Genesis 1), scripture makes sure to point out without any reservation that it is the female, in her function as birth giver, who secures the implementation of the gift of procreation. Man plants the seed but does not give birth. Since ultimately it is God who is the bestower of the seed (Gen 4:25b), man is relegated to a secondary function and thus status. This teaching will be enhanced to its maximum in the story of the barren Sarah conceiving not only without Abraham but also despite her barrenness.[6] What is interesting in this case is that

---

[4] In the Middle East, up to this day, a woman remains a "bride" until the birth of her first child.

[5] The quintessential macho figure was Alexander of Macedon.

[6] This point is picked up by Paul in Romans 4.

Sarah is portrayed as arrogant as her husband in that they both laughed at the thought that God could do the "impossible." The critique of woman as well as man whenever they give themselves value is at its clearest in Ezekiel's unequalled lengthy harangue against prophetesses and prophets, as well as in Amos' criticism of wives and their husbands:

> The word of the Lord came to me: "Son of man, prophesy against the prophets of Israel, prophesy and say to those who prophesy out of their own minds: 'Hear the word of the Lord!' Thus says the Lord God, Woe to the foolish prophets who follow their own spirit, and have seen nothing! Your prophets have been like foxes among ruins, O Israel. You have not gone up into the breaches, or built up a wall for the house of Israel, that it might stand in battle in the day of the Lord. They have spoken falsehood and divined a lie; they say, 'Says the Lord,' when the Lord has not sent them, and yet they expect him to fulfil their word. Have you not seen a delusive vision, and uttered a lying divination, whenever you have said, 'Says the Lord,' although I have not spoken?" Therefore thus says the Lord God: "Because you have uttered delusions and seen lies, therefore behold, I am against you, says the Lord God. My hand will be against the prophets who see delusive visions and who give lying divinations; they shall not be in the council of my people, nor be enrolled in the register of the house of Israel, nor shall they enter the land of Israel; and you shall know that I am the Lord God. Because, yea, because they have misled my people, saying, 'Peace,' when there is no peace; and because, when the people build a wall, these prophets daub it with whitewash; say to those who daub it with whitewash that it shall fall! There will be a deluge of rain, great hailstones will fall, and a stormy wind break out; and when the wall falls, will it not be said to you, 'Where is the daubing with which you daubed it?' Therefore thus says the Lord God: I will make a stormy wind break out in my wrath; and there shall be a deluge of rain in my anger, and great hailstones in wrath to destroy it. And I will break down the wall that you have daubed with whitewash, and bring it down to the ground, so that its foundation will be laid bare; when it falls, you shall perish in the midst of it; and you shall know that I am the Lord. Thus will I

spend my wrath upon the wall, and upon those who have daubed it with whitewash; and I will say to you, The wall is no more, nor those who daubed it, the prophets of Israel who prophesied concerning Jerusalem and saw visions of peace for her, when there was no peace, says the Lord God. And you, son of man, set your face against the daughters of your people, who prophesy out of their own minds; prophesy against them and say, Thus says the Lord God: Woe to the women who sew magic bands upon all wrists, and make veils for the heads of persons of every stature, in the hunt for souls! Will you hunt down souls belonging to my people, and keep other souls alive for your profit? You have profaned me among my people for handfuls of barley and for pieces of bread, putting to death persons who should not die and keeping alive persons who should not live, by your lies to my people, who listen to lies. Wherefore thus says the Lord God: Behold, I am against your magic bands with which you hunt the souls, and I will tear them from your arms; and I will let the souls that you hunt go free like birds. Your veils also I will tear off, and deliver my people out of your hand, and they shall be no more in your hand as prey; and you shall know that I am the Lord. Because you have disheartened the righteous falsely, although I have not disheartened him, and you have encouraged the wicked, that he should not turn from his wicked way to save his life; therefore you shall no more see delusive visions nor practice divination; I will deliver my people out of your hand. Then you will know that I am the Lord." (Ezek 13:1-23)

"Hear this word, you cows of Bashan, who are in the mountain of Samaria, who oppress the poor, who crush the needy, who say to their husbands, 'Bring, that we may drink!' The Lord God has sworn by his holiness that, behold, the days are coming upon you, when they shall take you away with hooks, even the last of you with fishhooks. And you shall go out through the breaches, every one straight before her; and you shall be cast forth into Harmon," says the Lord. (Am 4:1-3)

Motherhood versus Womanhood

Being mostly the heir of a Greco-Roman worldview, our contemporary Western society is fixated on sex. [7] Men and women are viewed sexually rather than as fathers and mothers, that is, as begetters according to the pattern established in Genesis 1. Sex is an individual trait, whereas procreation is an essential societal feature. In the stories throughout Genesis, sexual differentiation is not only systematically subordinate to procreation, but sexual "appetite" is totally absent simply because it does not affect the story line. [8] Consider the following:

- "The man called his wife's name Eve, because she was the mother of all living." (Gen 3:20) Not only is the name of the first woman, Eve (*hawwah*), specifically explained as "the mother of all living (*hay*)," but Eve is grammatically an apposition to "his wife." A contemporary hallmark card or a wedding emcee would have lingered on the word play on *'issah* being the counterpart, the soul mate, of *'is*. The biblical author already pointed that out (2:23), but that aspect spelled out disaster since it reflected man's macho grip over her. Although "Eve" is introduced as the counterpart of Adam, she is also and more importantly the equal of her husband in that she is a progenitor—if not more so than her husband—of the human race since all "living (human)" and thus "life" (*hayyim*) itself comes out of her. This inference is confirmed in the statement concerning the relation between the man and his wife Eve: "Now Adam (*ha'adam*;

---

[7] Compare old movies to modern ones. Even when sexual appetite is assumed, it is never explicit.

[8] The exception to this is the rape of Dinah and Potiphar's wife seducing Joseph. However, both of these stories are not an end in themselves, but rather are functional in that they set the stage for the subsequent events.

the man) knew Eve his wife, and she conceived and bore Cain, saying, 'I have gotten a man with the help of the Lord.'" (Gen 4:1) Notice how she is the main subject of the second part of the verse.[9]

- In the *toledot* of Noah repeatedly we hear of the sons of Noah "and their wives" (6:18; 7:7, 13; 8:16, 18)

- The most striking feature of Sarah's story is that her "person" is relegated to the background when compared to her motherhood, which holds center stage. Not only that, it is within *her* story that we hear of Abram knowing Hagar who conceives Abram's son (16:15-16).

- The story of Lot and his daughters at the end of Genesis 19 would be blacklisted nowadays. Yet, the author is single-mindedly interested in Lot's progeny to the extent that he tells us that it was Lot's daughters who masterminded the scenario to ensure their own progeny.

- Keturah, Abraham's third wife, is exclusively known as a "progenitor" (Gen 25:1-4; 1 Chr 1:32-33). In other words, Keturah is no Jane Eyre, or Cleopatra, Zenobia, Elizabeth I, Queen Victoria, or a Catherine the Great. And yet, there she is "scripturalized" for the ages, even if she is not known to many a scripture aficionado.

- One of the most bizarre stories in scripture is that of Tamar in her relationship with Onan, her brother-in-law (38:2-10), and Judah, her father-in-law (vv.12-30). And yet Tamar is immortalized in the third verse of the first

---

[9] See also my detailed discussion of Genesis 4:25, pp.166-70.

chapter of Matthew, the first and arguably the
most important book of the New Testament.

- Although the rape of Dinah has become not only
  proverbial and a hot topic in contemporary
  theology, in Genesis 34 it functions as a
  backdrop for the story of the betrayal of the
  covenant of circumcision by Simeon and Levi.
  Yet even if Dinah's "person" is not the heroine
  of the story, her name is very much central to the
  story line since it is from the verb *din* (judge).

- In Genesis 39, it is a woman, Potiphar's wife,
  who is the sexual culprit. Yet here again, her
  action is part of the story line. It is the reason
  why Joseph ended in the dungeon whence he
  rose to become Pharaoh's prime minister who
  saved both Egypt and his kin from famine.

Anyone looking to satisfy one's own issues with sexuality
through the scriptural stories of Genesis will be sorely
disappointed. The authors were dealing literally with a much
more serious issue than sex. It was a life and death situation for
all their contemporaries, the good, the bad, and the ugly.

Motherhood and Mercy

Throughout my dealings with scripture I repeatedly
underscored the importance, if not the necessity, of referring to
the original Hebrew in order to understand correctly the
meaning of words and, by extension, the text. I have equally
criticized the understanding of the text based on a Greek term
that does not even exist in Hebrew. This matter is particularly
important in the discussion of motherhood and mercy since
most readers assume that they understand these terms and thus,
even unintentionally, impose their understanding of them on
the scriptural text. The prevailing attitude is that what scripture
says about motherhood and mercy is universally well known.

But is it? Is Hebrew "mercy" the same as English "mercy"? Are Hebrew "motherhood" and "virginity" the same as their assumed English counterparts?

We are used to perceiving mercy as a feeling and associate it with the Hallmark card style "heart," which in our literature is the seat of feelings. The brain is considered to be the seat of "thought" and "will." However, this understanding is the farthest possible from the parallel terms in Hebrew. The Hebrew *leb*, meaning "core," is translated as "heart."[10] However, the Hebrew *leb* is the sole "core" that functions as the seat of "thought" and "will," but not of "feelings" which is reflected in the Hebrew *reḥem* (womb). Indeed, our mercy and compassion are the rendering of the Hebrew *raḥamim*, which is, morphologically, the plural of *reḥem*. So technically *raḥamim* means "wombs." However, one needs to read or to hear scripture "Hebraically." When comparing this plural *raḥamim* with the Hebrew *damim*, we realize that the plural in both cases is functional. Blood is *dam* in Hebrew; however its plural *damim* does not mean bloods; rather it refers to running blood and thus bloodshed. The same applies to *raḥamim*, which refers to the movement of the womb. This being the case, mercy then is a reality that can be felt only by a woman who has given birth, that is, a "mother." So, it is by listening carefully to scripture *in Hebrew* that we eventually comprehend what *raḥamim* is all about. In other words, we should desist injecting our "view" of the matter into scripture. We should stop asking questions such as, "What does scripture say about God?" or "What does scripture say about the virtue of mercy?" or "What does the bible say about "womanhood?" [11] We should simply be asking, "What is scripture saying?"

---

[10] In Latin the heart is *cor* (*cordis* in the genitive), whence our "cordial" and "cordially," while mind (associated with the brain and thought) is *mens* (*mentis* in the genitive) whence our "mental" and "mentally."

[11] Such topics and the meaning of such words are already defined in our minds.

Unlike our contemporary understanding of virginity, in scripture virginity has less to do with intercourse than with birth giving. It is at birth giving that a woman loses her virginity or, more accurately, her womb is "broken out," or "opened" by her first born, the "opener of the womb" (Ex 13:2, 12, 15; 34:19; Num 3:12; 18:15; Ezek 20:26). This in Hebrew is *pheter rehem*.[12] The Hebrew verb *phatar* has the meaning of "breaking out, setting free."[13] The following scriptural usages of the verb *phatar* reveal this connotation of taking some of the inside of an object, such as a blossom or a piece of wood, and breaking or carving it or letting something come "out" of it:

> The cedar within the house was carved in the form of gourds and open (*pheture*) flowers; all was cedar, no stone was seen. (1 Kg 6:18)

> He carved all the walls of the house round about with carved (*phetuhe*; from the verb *phatah* [open]) figures of cherubim and palm trees and open (*pheture*) flowers, in the inner and outer rooms. (6:29)

> He covered the two doors of olivewood with carvings of cherubim, palm trees, and open (*pheture*) flowers; he overlaid them with gold, and spread gold upon the cherubim and upon the palm trees. (6:32)

> On them he carved cherubim and palm trees and open (*pheture*) flowers; and he overlaid them with gold evenly applied upon the carved work. (6:35)

> The beginning of strife is like letting out (*photer*) water; so quit before the quarrel breaks out. (Prov 17:14)

What is of import in the case of giving birth is that it is accompanied with bloodletting (blood shedding), the Hebrew *damim*. This combination of two Hebrew functional plurals, *damim* and *rahamim*, is quite unique: at birth, it is the shedding of

---

[12] In Greek *dianoigon mētran*, in Latin *aperit vulvam*, and in Arabic *phatihu rahmin*.
[13] Arabic uses the same root to speak of "breaking" the fast; hence Arabic *phutur* is breakfast and *'iphtar* is the evening meal of the Muslims at the end of a day of fasting.

a mother's blood, the seat of "breathing," i.e., life,[14] which is the supreme act of "compassion" (*raḥamim*). Thus a woman gives away (her) life in order that someone else receive life, and in so doing she *becomes* a mother.[15] In scripture, what a pregnant woman undergoes in becoming a mother is so serious that her shedding blood is accounted "against" her and thus makes her "unclean" and in need of purification (Lev 12). The reason for this is that God is the sole originator of life and, consequently, only he can "shed blood," that is, take life with impunity:

> then the Lord God formed man of dust from the ground, and breathed into his nostrils the breath of life; and man became a living being. (Gen 2:7)

> Only you shall not eat flesh with its life, that is, its blood. For your lifeblood I will surely require a reckoning; of every beast I will require it and of man; of every man's brother I will require the life of man. (9:4-5)

> And Judah took a wife for Er his first-born, and her name was Tamar. But Er, Judah's first-born, was wicked in the sight of the Lord; and the Lord slew him. Then Judah said to Onan, "Go in to your brother's wife, and perform the duty of a brother-in-law to her, and raise up offspring for your brother." But Onan knew that the offspring would not be his; so when he went in to his brother's wife he spilled the semen on the ground, lest he should give offspring to his brother. And what he did was displeasing in the sight of the Lord, and he slew him also. (38:6-10)

> Vengeance is mine, and recompense, for the time when their foot shall slip; for the day of their calamity is at hand, and their doom comes swiftly. (Deut 32:35)

> Then Nathan went to his house. And the Lord struck the child that Uriah's wife bore to David, and it became sick. David therefore besought God for the child; and David fasted, and went

---

[14] "Only you shall not eat flesh with its life (*nepheš*, breathing) that is, its blood." (Gen 9:4) Notice how in this case RSV translated *nepheš* into "life" rather than "soul".
[15] With all due respect to the sensitivities of my readers, no female teenager, albeit "feminine," and much less a macho young man, undergoes a similar "experience" through her or his "internal, deep" feelings.

in and lay all night upon the ground. And the elders of his house stood beside him, to raise him from the ground; but he would not, nor did he eat food with them. On the seventh day the child died. And the servants of David feared to tell him that the child was dead; for they said, "Behold, while the child was yet alive, we spoke to him, and he did not listen to us; how then can we say to him the child is dead? He may do himself some harm." (2 Sam 12:15-18)

And he said, "Naked I came from my mother's womb, and naked shall I return; the Lord gave, and the Lord has taken away; blessed be the name of the Lord." (Job 1:21)

The scriptural God does not fall under the categories of male and female. He[16] is simply functional.[17] That is why, at the "end," when he will implement his "everlasting covenant, my steadfast, sure love for David" (Is 55:3b), he will act as a mother and he will be more motherly than any mother has ever been:

Hear the word of the Lord, you who tremble at his word: "Your brethren who hate you and cast you out for my name's sake have said, "'Let the Lord be glorified, that we may see your joy'; but it is they who shall be put to shame." Hark, an uproar from the city! A voice from the temple! The voice of the Lord, rendering recompense to his enemies! "Before she was in labor she gave birth; before her pain came upon her she was delivered of a son. Who has heard such a thing? Who has seen such things? Shall a land be born in one day? Shall a nation be brought forth in one moment? For as soon as Zion was in labor she brought forth her sons. Shall I bring to the birth and not cause to bring forth? says the Lord; shall I, who cause to bring forth, shut the womb? says your God. "Rejoice with Jerusalem, and be glad for her, all you who love her; rejoice with her in joy, all you who mourn over her;

---

[16] The Hebrew 'el is a grammatically masculine noun.

[17] This explains how God turns not into a woman, but into a mother (Is 66:13). If protestant female pastors or feminist male pastors in the USA would explain in this manner their posting that God is a "she" at the banners outside their churches, I shall have no qualms. But it is obvious that that is not what they mean; they are hung up on the issue of the equality between man and woman contrary to Paul's scriptural approach whereby he belittles the male instead of equalizing male and female. See my comments on 1 Cor 11:1-16 in C-1Cor 192-200.

that you may suck and be satisfied with her consoling breasts; that you may drink deeply with delight from the abundance of her glory." For thus says the Lord: "Behold, I will extend prosperity to her like a river, and the wealth of the nations like an overflowing stream; and you shall suck, you shall be carried upon her hip, and dandled upon her knees. As one whom his mother comforts, so I will comfort you; you shall be comforted in Jerusalem." (Is 66:5-13)

Lest one, especially a woman, should fall into the self-righteous trap of assuming that God will change sexes or become more "humane," the immediately following verses make sure that he will remain the same judge he has ever been and will implement his essential function of justice:

For behold, the Lord will come in fire, and his chariots like the stormwind, to render his anger in fury, and his rebuke with flames of fire. For by fire will the Lord execute judgment, and by his sword, upon all flesh; and those slain by the Lord shall be many. Those who sanctify and purify themselves to go into the gardens, following one in the midst, eating swine's flesh and the abomination and mice, shall come to an end together, says the Lord. For I know their works and their thoughts, and I am coming to gather all nations and tongues; and they shall come and shall see my glory, and I will set a sign among them. And from them I will send survivors to the nations, to Tarshish, Put, and Lud, who draw the bow, to Tubal and Javan, to the coastlands afar off, that have not heard my fame or seen my glory; and they shall declare my glory among the nations. And they shall bring all your brethren from all the nations as an offering to the Lord, upon horses, and in chariots, and in litters, and upon mules, and upon dromedaries, to my holy mountain Jerusalem, says the Lord, just as the Israelites bring their cereal offering in a clean vessel to the house of the Lord. And some of them also I will take for priests and for Levites, says the Lord. (Is 66:15-21)

Notice how this "divine" function impacts the ending of Isaiah beyond the "new" creation:

For as the new heavens and the new earth which I will make shall remain before me, says the Lord; so shall your descendants and your name remain. From new moon to new moon, and from sabbath to sabbath, all flesh shall come to worship before me, says the Lord. *And they shall go forth and look on the dead bodies of the men that have rebelled against me; for their worm shall not die, their fire shall not be quenched, and they shall be an abhorrence to all flesh.* (Is 66:22-24)

But how does all this take place according to scripture? It does so against the backdrop of shepherd life, as we have seen time and again. In Ezekiel, God is the sole shepherd of his people through his delegate, David, the only shepherd, yet a sheep in God's flock. In Isaiah, we encounter the same approach to the realization of divine mercy. On the one hand:

Behold, the Lord God comes with might, and his arm rules for him; behold, his reward is with him, and his recompense before him. He will feed his flock like a shepherd, he will gather the lambs in his arms, he will carry them in his bosom, and gently lead those that are with young. (Is 40:10-11)

On the other hand, one hears of two emissaries through whom he will accomplish his purpose. The first one is Cyrus who is depicted as a shepherd:

Thus says the Lord, your Redeemer, who formed you from the womb: "I am the Lord, who made all things, who stretched out the heavens alone, who spread out the earth—Who was with me?—who frustrates the omens of liars, and makes fools of diviners; who turns wise men back, and makes their knowledge foolish; who confirms the word of his servant, and performs the counsel of his messengers; who says of Jerusalem, 'She shall be inhabited,' and of the cities of Judah, 'They shall be built, and I will raise up their ruins'; who says to the deep, 'Be dry, I will dry up your rivers'; who says of Cyrus, 'He is my shepherd, and he shall fulfil all my purpose'; saying of Jerusalem, 'She shall be built,' and of the temple, 'Your foundation shall be laid.'" Thus says the Lord to his anointed, to Cyrus, whose right hand I have grasped, to subdue nations before him and ungird the loins of kings, to open doors before him that gates may not be closed: "I will go before you and level the mountains, I will break in pieces the doors of bronze and cut asunder the bars of iron, I will give you the treasures of darkness and the hoards in secret places, that you may know that it is I, the Lord, the God of Israel, who call you by your name. For the sake of my servant Jacob, and Israel my chosen, I call you by your name, I surname you, though you do not know me. I am the Lord, and there is no other, besides me there is no God; I gird you, though you do not know me, that men may know, from the rising of the sun and from the west, that there is none besides me; I am the Lord, and there is no other." (44:24-45:6)

However, beyond this first servant, we hear of another one:

Behold, my servant shall prosper, he shall be exalted and lifted up, and shall be very high. As many were astonished at him—his appearance was so marred, beyond human semblance, and his form beyond that of the sons of men—so shall he startle many nations; kings shall shut their mouths because of him; for that which has not been told them they shall see, and that which they have not heard they shall understand. (52:13-15)

Yet this servant is not depicted as a shepherd, but rather as a lamb that is slaughtered for the sake of the other sheep in the following terms:

All we like sheep (*son*; flock) have gone astray; we have turned every one to his own way; and the Lord has laid on him the iniquity of us all. He was oppressed, and he was afflicted, yet he opened not his mouth; like a lamb (*seh*; lamb, kid) that is led to the slaughter, and like a sheep (*rahel* [Rachel]; ewe) that before its shearers is dumb, so he opened not his mouth. (53:6-7)

Listening more intently to the original, one will readily notice the use of three different nouns to speak of the mission of the servant. The first noun *son* (flock) clearly points to the fact that those who would benefit from that mission are viewed as the domain of a shepherd. The second noun *seh* refers to a lamb, disregarding its sex, since the other scriptural term for lamb is from the root *kbs* and occurs as either *kebes*[18] (lamb), by far the most common, or as *kibsah*[19] (she-lamb), which is found only

---

[18] Greek *amnos*; Latin *agnus*.
[19] Greek *amnas*; Latin *agna*.

eight times in scripture. So by opting for *śeh*, which is also common, over *kebeś*, the author was preparing for the following *rahel* which is specifically "ewe" and occurs only four times in the Old Testament. All the other instances of *rahel* by far more numerous, refer to Rachel, Jacob's wife and mother of Joseph, the father of Ephraim and Manasseh, the two main constitutive tribes of the Kingdom of Israel. So here, the author is playing on two levels, the natural and the scriptural. The final emissary of God, as a member of the flock, still plays the role of the "mother" of the flock.[20] On the one hand, he will emulate the "barren" Rachel who brought about many children. On the other hand, and more importantly, in submitting in total and full obedience to the Lord's will to be bruised (v.10), he will allow God's motherhood to be enacted. The understanding that functionality, rather than sexuality, defines God's emissary, just as it defines the scriptural God himself, is endorsed in the New Testament by the Apostle Paul, who refers to himself endlessly as father, yet portrays himself as a mother: "But we were gentle among you, like a nurse taking care of her children. So, being affectionately desirous of you, we were ready to share with you not only the gospel of God but also our own selves, because you had become very dear to us." (1Thess 2:7-8)[21] Beyond Paul, Jesus himself, clearly a male person scripturally (Mt 1:21, 23, 25; Lk 2:7; 3:23), even compares himself to a hen: "O Jerusalem, Jerusalem, killing the prophets and stoning those who are sent to you! How often would I have gathered your children together as a hen gathers her brood under her wings, and you would not!" (Mt 23:37; Lk 13:34)

---

[20] The Isaianic servant is cast as ewe.
[21] See also 1 Cor 3:2.

Part Two

Genesis 1-11

5

The Creation of Creation (Genesis 1 and 2)

An in depth comparison between the phraseology of chapter 1 and chapter 2 of Genesis will readily reveal that the earth created by God in Genesis 1 corresponds fully to the oasis the Lord God planted in Genesis 2. The creation account in seven days that spans Genesis 1:1-2:4 refers essentially to the "earth" (*'eres*) twenty-three times. At the start of the second account of the creation narrative (2:5-3:24), *'eres* is used three more times in a row (2:5 [twice], 6)[1] only to disappear until 4:12 and 14.[2] In 2:5-6 its obvious function is to transition to the other aspect of it, namely, the "ground" (*'adamah*)— whence the *'adam* was formed (v.7)—which steals the show in chapters 2 and 3 (2:5, 6, 7, 9, 19; 3:17, 19, 23) and the start of chapter 4 (vv.2, 3, 10, 11, 12, 14). This transitioning first appears in chapter 1 with the introduction of the noun *'adamah*, which is functionally parallel to *'eres*:

> And God said, "Let the earth bring forth *living creatures* (*nepheš ḥayyah*; living soul [breath]) according to their kinds: cattle and *creeping things* (*remeš*) and beasts of the earth (*'eres*) according to their kinds." And it was so. And God made the beasts of the earth (*'eres*) according to their kinds and the cattle according to their kinds, and *everything that creeps upon the ground* (*kol remeš ha'adamah*)[3] according to its kind. And God saw that it was good. (Gen 1:24-25)

The total earth that Genesis 1 has in mind is nothing other than the localized earth of the authors themselves. It is only under the impact of philosophical theology based on the

---

[1] In vv.11, 12, and 13, the "earth" connotes a given region, Havilah in vv.11 and 12 and Cush in v.14.

[2] In v.16 it refers to the region of Nod.

[3] Further in the account these same creeping things of the ground are said to be "everything that creeps on the earth (*kol remeš 'al ha'ares*)" (Gen 1:30).

Platonic thinking[4] that the garden of Eden was viewed as a specimen of the reality "earth." This is to say, one starts with Genesis 1 in order to understand Genesis 2-4 instead of realizing that Genesis 1 is only a generalization *by the authors* of their surrounding reality. Genesis 1 is a projection (or retrojection) of Genesis 2. The most compelling argument in favor of this view is to look at how the human being is handled in Genesis 1. The one human being *ha'adam* (*the* man) is in one breath singular and dual and is rendered as such in all translations:

> So God created (the) man in his own image, in the image of God he created *him*; male and female he created *them*. And God blessed *them*, and God said to *them*, "Be fruitful and multiply, and fill the earth and subdue it; and have dominion over the fish of the sea and over the birds of the air and over every living thing that moves upon the earth." (Gen 1:27-28)

The reality of the matter is that sexuality is an incontrovertible given not only in the entire zoological kingdom of which human beings are an integral part, but also in the botanical kingdom:

> And God said, "Let the earth put forth vegetation, plants yielding (*mazria'*; seeding) seed (*zera'*), and *fruit* (*peri*) trees bearing *fruit* (*peri*) in which is their seed (*zera'*), each *according to its kind*, upon the earth." And it was so. The earth brought forth vegetation, plants yielding (*mazria'*; *seeding*) *seed* (*zera'*) according to *their own kinds*, and trees bearing *fruit* (*peri*) in which is their *seed* (*zera'*), each *according to its kind*. And God saw that it was good. (Gen 1:11-12)

> And God said, "Let the waters bring forth swarms of *living creatures* (*nepheš ḥayyah*; living soul [breath]), and let birds fly above the earth across the firmament of the heavens." So God created the great sea monsters and every *living creature* (*nepheš hahayyah*; living soul [breath]) that moves, with which the waters swarm, *according to their kinds*, and every winged bird *according to its kind*." And God saw that it was good. And God *blessed them*, saying, "*Be fruitful* (*peru*)

---

[4] The Platonic premise is that a given reality, like a horse, is only a reflection or a specimen of an eternal reality.

and *multiply* and *fill* the waters in the seas, and let birds *multiply* on the earth." (vv.20-22)

And God said, "Let the earth bring forth *living creatures (nepheš ḥayyah*; living soul [breath]) *according to their kinds*: cattle and *creeping things (remes̱)* and beasts of the earth *('ereṣ) according to their kinds."* And it was so. And God made the beasts of the earth *('ereṣ) according to their kinds* and the cattle *according to their kinds*, and *everything that creeps upon the ground (kol remes̱ ha'adamah) according to its kind*. And God saw that it was good. Then God said, "Let us make man in our image, after our likeness; and let them have dominion over the fish of the sea, and over the birds of the air, and over the cattle, and over all the earth, and over every creeping thing that creeps upon the earth." So God created man in his own image, in the image of God he created him; male and female he created them. And God *blessed them*, and God said to them, *"Be fruitful (peru)* and *multiply*, and *fill* the earth and subdue it; and have dominion over the fish of the sea and over the birds of the air and over every living thing that moves upon the earth." And God said, "Behold, I have given you every plant yielding seed which is upon the face of all the earth, and every tree with seed in its fruit; you shall have them for food. And to every beast of the earth, and to every bird of the air, and to everything that creeps on the earth, everything that has the breath of life, I have given every green plant for food." And it was so. (vv. 24-30)

Even an inveterate disciple of Plato with a modicum of honesty cannot but understand that sexuality controls existence in both the botanical and zoological realms and, in the latter case, *at the express blessing of the scriptural God himself.* It is as though God blessed the DNA itself.[5] There are no immortal, let alone eternal, souls. There is only the blatant reality of our existence: to produce one being there is need for two beings, male and female.[6]

---

[5] Modern science discovered not only the genome but also the discrepancy between the number of chromosomes in the reproductive cells and the number of chromosomes in the rest of the cells in a given body.
[6] Parthenogenesis was obviously unknown to the scriptural writers. I leave it to others to figure out how scripture would have looked like had they been aware of such and,

Still, for a human society to survive, it is not enough to procreate. There needs to be interrelation with other constituents necessary for both its existence and its functionality. Besides other human beings, a society of humans needs at least some animals and some vegetation creating a symbiosis between all three realms. Buildings, although nice and even practical, are not necessary, as proven by shepherd life where the abodes are movable tents.[7] Notice the total absence of buildings until Cain builds a city (Gen 4:17) in contravention of God's express instruction for him to remain a wanderer (v.12). Stone erections, abhorred by the Prophets, are already viewed negatively in Genesis.[8] So it stands to reason that the erudite authors of scripture wielded the reality of shepherdism as a viable alternative to conquests outside one's given area. This applied not only to their peers in Mesopotamia, Indo-Aryan as well as Semite, but also to Alexander's heirs, the Japhethites who came from far away islands.[9] If my thesis is correct, then one should find some indication, albeit indirect, of the authors' favoritism toward shepherdism right at the outset in Genesis 1. I believe there is such indication and very strikingly so.

Scholars, and even a majority of readers, have recognized an oddity in the sequence of creation between the third and the fourth days. The creation of the vegetation preceding that of the animal kingdom in the fifth and six days is to be expected. But it seems quite odd that on the fourth day of the creation, the

---

while at it, to figure out how the teaching of theology at seminaries would have looked had humanity not survived the scriptural flood. As we shall see, the scripture story is simply a parable meant to teach us, humans, how to behave toward one another and not a philosophical treatise about the meaning of life and the value of the human being, let alone a vade-mecum of scientific data.

[7] The Mongolian civilization of Genghis Kahn shows that even a conquering empire that stretched from the steppes of Mongolia to the center of Europe, at least at a time well more recent than the production of scripture, was possible through the use of tents rather than buildings. Even Alexander, although he founded cities and ultimately settled in Babylon, did not carry along stone buildings over the extent of his route of conquest.

[8] Also see further in Genesis 11.

[9] More on this matter later when discussing the Table of Nations in Genesis 10.

lights in the heavenly realm—"the lesser light" and especially "the greater light," the sun—are said to have been made after the creation of vegetation, since it has always been known that the sun is necessary for the growth of vegetation. The reason for this sequence lies in the striking and thus clearly intended omission of the actual names of both the "greater light" and "lesser light," the sun and the moon, whose mention abounds throughout scripture. Since the nouns "sun" and "moon" were also the names of the deities they represented, their mention here would have introduced other deities in the creation story where God has been introduced as the sole and exclusive deity. For the authors, the fate of the Mesopotamian Sun and Moon gods, powerful as they were, was no better than that of Bel and Nebo. Still, since sun and moon gods were universal and found in all cultures, the intent was to include in its purview, not only the Greeks, but also all the neighboring peoples of the area, besides the authors' own populace.[10] For the authors, the scriptural God is the universal deity of "the heavens and the earth" and all their "residents," mineral, botanical and zoological.

I believe that the "switching" between the third and fourth days has a further function that has a direct bearing on corroborating my thesis concerning shepherdism as the backdrop for the entire scriptural story. The phraseology describing the third day of creation reflects that God is the sole factor behind the "emergence" of the earth qua earth, but also does create its vegetation *directly*, that is to say, without the medium of the sun:

> And God said, "Let the waters under the heavens be gathered together into one place, and let the dry land appear." And it was so. God called the dry land Earth, and the waters that were gathered together he called Seas. And God saw that it was good. And God said, "Let the earth *put forth* (*tadśe'*) vegetation (*deśe'*),

---

[10] Later, in my discussion of Genesis 10, we shall see at its clearest the writers' interest in "all" the surrounding nations.

plants yielding seed, and fruit trees bearing fruit in which is their
seed, each according to its kind, upon the earth." And it was so.
The earth *brought forth* (*toṣeh*) vegetation (*deśeʾ*), plants yielding seed
according to their own kinds, and trees bearing fruit in which is
their seed, each according to its kind. And God saw that it was
good. And there was evening and there was morning, a third day.
(Gen 1:9-13)

Not only are both the earth and its vegetation brought about by
God's command, but the terminology used to speak of the
emergence of vegetation looks ahead to that describing the
appearance of the animals (Gen 1:24-25). In the first case his
command to the earth uses a verb *tadśeʾ* from the same root as
vegetation (*deśeʾ*),[11] whereas in the second case the divine
command uses the causative form of the verb "come out" and
thus its meaning is "make something come out," "bring forth."
The action that the earth takes in producing the vegetation at
God's command looks ahead to God's worded command in the
case of the animals. Still, in order that the hearers not be misled,
the authors make sure to describe the emergence of the animals
as the direct action of God himself, "And God made (*wayyaʿaś*)
the beasts of the earth according to their kinds and the cattle
according to their kinds, and everything that creeps upon the
ground according to its kind," using the same verb *ʿasah* that is
found in 1:7, 16, 25, 26,[12] 31 and 2:2 (twice), 3, 4. Such closeness
in "nature" between vegetation and land animals can be beheld
at its clearest in the wilderness setting of shepherdism.[13]

Another feature in Genesis reflective of shepherdism, exactly
as it prevails in the wilderness oases, is that of the sharing

---

[11] Literally rendered, the phrase would sound thus: "Let the earth vegetate
vegetation."

[12] Notice how God "makes" the human being (v.26) in the same manner as he
"makes" the animals (v.25). That "equality" looks ahead to chapter two where both
are "formed" out of the ground.

[13] My hearers are reminded that I am not talking about molecular chemistry. The
scriptural authors were not a CSI (Criminal Scene Investigation) team privy to DNA,
but rather observers of the reality around them as it functionally appears.

between human and animal in the vegetation as food common to both, a situation the humans are summoned to preserve:

> And God said, "Behold, I have given you every plant yielding seed which is upon the face of all the earth, and every tree with seed in its fruit; you shall have them for food. And to every beast of the earth, and to every bird of the air, and to everything that creeps on the earth, everything that has the breath of life, I have given every green plant for food." And it was so. (Gen 1:29-30)

This "way of life" is not only included as a divine summons on the same sixth day on which both land animals and humans were "made" (vv.25 and 26), but it was precisely then that "God saw *everything that he had made*, and behold, *it was very good* " (1:31). The reference to the *totality* of God's establishing the symbiotic life on earth as not only good, but very good, is clearly made with shepherd life in the Syrian wilderness in mind, of which the authors were fully cognizant. Notice that neither killing even of animals, let alone humans—which matter will be dealt with after the flood (9:1-7)—nor erecting buildings, both abominations in the Prophets, are part of the general picture here that is judged as "very good" by God himself. The summons to "the man" (*ha'adam*) in his actuality as "male and female" (1:27)[14] already looks ahead to Micah's chastisement:

> "With what shall I come before the Lord, and bow myself before God on high? Shall I come before him with burnt offerings, with calves a year old? Will the Lord be pleased with thousands of rams, with ten thousands of rivers of oil? Shall I give my first-born for my transgression, the fruit of my body for the sin of my soul?" He has showed you, *O man* (*'adam*), what is *good*; and what does

---

[14] Notice the consistent use of the plural in the divine address to "the man" throughout verses 26-28, no less than nine times. I am talking about the total number of the plural whether in reference to man (twice in vv.26-27; **them ... them**) or in the verbs he uses when describing his address to "man" (twice at the beginning of v.28: and God blessed **them** and God said to **them**) or when addressing "the man" (be fruitful, multiply, fill, subdue, and have dominion are all in the plural in Hebrew, which plural is assumed in English after "said to **them**").

the Lord require of you but to do justice, and to love kindness, and to walk humbly with your God? (Mic 6:6-8)

The scriptural feature of the essential "equality" between human and animal sounds not only strange, but actually unacceptable to our minds that have been shaped by the Platonic notion of the unique value of the human beings in that they partake of the divine *logos*. This thought has stamped theology, starting with Justin the Philosopher, and through it the entire Western world. Consider, however, the following:

1. Whereas the fish (and the sea mammals) and fowl created on the fourth day are honored with the divine blessing for them to procreate and fill the seas and the earth[15] (Gen 1:22), land animals and humans are both made on the same sixth day and are obliquely lumped under the one blessing. It is as though the authors intentionally did not want to separate between the two.

2. Conversely, the "living creatures" (*nepheš hayyah*; living soul [breath]) that open the series of creatures made on the sixth day seem to include the human being, who is, after all, a land mammal. This logical conclusion will soon be confirmed in the next chapter on two levels. First, the "forming" of the same *ha'adam* (the human being) made by God in 1:27 is rendered in these terms: "then the Lord God *formed* (*yaṣar*) man (*ha'adam*) of dust from the ground (*ha'adamah*), and breathed into his nostrils the breath of life; and man (*ha'adam*) became *a living being* (*nepheš hayyah*; living creature, living soul [breath])." (Gen 2:7). Secondly, a few verses

---

[15] Although "birds fly above the earth across the firmament of the heavens" (Gen 1:20) their domain is the earth since they need to alight at some point. That is why, while the flood did not affect the sea animals, birds had to be cared for by Noah and were invited into the ark.

later we hear: "So out of the ground[16] (*ha'adamah*) the Lord God *formed* (*yaṣar*) every beast (*hayyah*; something living) of the field and every bird of the air,[17] and brought them to the man to see what he would call them; and whatever the man called every *living creature* (*nepheš hayyah*), that was its name. The man gave names to all cattle (*behemah*; beast), and to the birds of the air, and to every beast of the field." (vv.19-20)[18]

3. Consequently, the difference between human and animal lies in the responsibility borne by the former. The summons that both are to share the vegetation is expressly addressed to the human being, not the animals (1:29-30). That is why it is the misbehavior of the human beings that brings about both the curse of the ground (3:17), out of which both they and the animals were formed, and God's resolve to blot off the face of that same ground all living beings, man and animal (6:7). Put in terms of shepherdism, besides God himself, only a human can be shepherd.[19]

The handling of the human being in Genesis 1-2 was misread, if not outright mishandled by Alexandrian theology, the "mother" of all theologies,[20] in that it viewed Adam "essentially" rather than "functionally," the latter being the rule for any sound understanding of literature. The same name may

---

[16] The original Hebrew behind "out of" (v.19) is the same *min* that is behind "from" in v.7, thus denoting the same kind of action on God's part in forming man and animal.

[17] Notice how even the birds are said to be "formed" in the same way as man.

[18] That the full "equality" between human and animal is not a passing "exaggeration" but reflects an express authorial intent finds incontrovertible corroboration in Ecclesiastes: "Who knows whether the *spirit* of man (sons of man: *bene' ha'adam*) goes upward and the *spirit* of the beast (*behemah*) goes down to the earth?" (3:21)

[19] 1 Sam 5:2; 7:7; 1 Chr 11:2; 17:6; Ps 78:71; Ezek 34:23; 37:24.

[20] Even Gregory the Theologian admitted that "Origen is the whetstone of us all."

and actually can have two different functions even in the same book, as is evident from the classic cases of Elijah in 1-2 Kings and Peter in Galatians and the Gospels. Each, in turn, is the "good guy" and the "bad guy." Another classic example is the same name Ananias in the Book of Acts. In the first case, the "man named Ananias" (5:1) functions badly, against God's will, while in the second case the "man named Ananias" (9:12) functions positively, according to God's will. The name Ananias, whose Hebrew original means "the Lord's grace or the Lord is graceful," is "betrayed" by its first carrier, whereas it is honored by its second carrier. Another example is found in the case of David, whose Hebrew original means "beloved." While the first David in 1-2 Samuel proves unworthy of his name, the latter David in Isaiah, Jeremiah, and Ezekiel, is shown as worthy of it. The play on the same name does not need to reflect an opposition, but simply a different function according to the context in which it is used. My contention is that Adam has a different function in Genesis 1-4 when compared to that found in Genesis 5:1-6:8. This double functionality was skewed in classical theology that viewed the entire universe anthropocentrically. Hence theology's misunderstanding of the function of Genesis 1:27-28 (So God created [the] man [ha'adam] in his own image, in the image of God he created him; male and female he created them. And God blessed them) in the context of the *toledot* of the heavens and the earth (chapters 1-4) as being the same as its counterpart in Genesis 5:1-2 (This is the book of the generations of Adam ['adam]. When God created man [Adam; 'adam], he made him in the likeness of God. Male and female he created them, and he blessed them and named them [called their name] Man [Adam; 'adam] when they were created) in the context of the *toledot* of Adam (5:1-6:8).

The division of scripture into chapters we are accustomed to appeared much later than the original text of scripture. The only acceptable division is into books. Consequently, in order to correctly hear scripture, one should not only start with Hebrew but also entirely dismiss chapters and verses and try to hear the text of each book in a flow. It is the text itself that forces upon us its intended sections. Luckily for us, in Genesis, one detects readily such division through the series of "these are the *toledot* of" followed by the name of a person: Adam (Gen 5:1), Noah (6:9), sons of Noah (10:1); Shem (11:10); Terah (11:27); Ishmael (25:12); Isaac (25:19); Esau (36:1 and 9), Jacob (37:2).[21] What follows is a list of the descendants of that person, which sometimes includes also some information regarding those descendants.[22] Since the descendants are many, it stands to reason that *toledot* is a plural noun. What is more important, however, is that this noun is from the verbal root *yalad* which means "give birth" as a mammal does, which in turn explains that it is usually followed by a person's name. Thus *toledot* is a reference to the many children and grandchildren and their progeny up to as many as ten generations as in the case of Adam and Shem.[23] Put otherwise it connotes the many that are "procreated" or "produced" by the forebear.

So the question that arises is, "How is it possible that we hear of a *toledot* preceding that of the first human, Adam?" In Genesis 2:4 we are told, "These are the generations (*toledot*) of the heavens and the earth when they were created." Taken in context this means that the *toledot* here cover all the elements that were produced mainly by the heavens and the earth. It is the "story" of the heavens and the earth in their "children," the celestial bodies in the case of the former and the vegetation, animal kingdom, and the humans in the case of the latter. Put otherwise, it is the "family tree" of the heavens and the earth in

---

[21] That this phrase is common is borne out by the fact that it is found also in Num 3:1 of Aaron and Moses, and in Ruth 4:18 of Perez.

[22] This understanding is reflected in RSV that renders "These are the *toledot* of Jacob" into "This is the history of the family of Jacob" (Gen 37:2), the only exception to the rule.

[23] The correctness of my understanding is actually confirmed in Num 3:1-2 where the title "these are the *toledot* of Aaron and Moses" (v.1) is immediately followed by the "explanatory" "these are the sons of Aaron" (v.2).

the same way as the *toledot* of Adam are his "family tree."[24] In a family tree, there is no intrinsic value to the individual. One's value depends on one's "function" in a family tree. If the tree is my *toledot*, then I am the forebear, the "progenitor," the "producer," whereas the others are the children, the "produced," and thus I am *not* part of the family represented in that tree. I produce the tree and there would not have been a tree were it not for me. On the other hand, if I am a member of a family tree, then I am one of many, and thus part of the totality, the "family," even when I am the first-born. The tree would have still been there had I not been. Put otherwise, I am still the same person, but I function differently, and thus I have a different value. So one may *not* speak of me in one breath by combining the two "personalities" or "personae" into one. I am not the same persona in a setting where I am *a* student compared to a setting where I am *the* professor. I, the priest Paul, am not the same persona when I am officiating the liturgy compared to when I am sitting in a pew as one of the parishioners.

Similarly, the same Adam functions differently, and thus is a different persona, in Genesis 1-4 compared to Genesis 5:1-6:8.[25] In the former he is "produced" among many other "productions" in the *toledot*, the "story," of the heavens and the earth, whereas in chapter 5, in *his toledot*, in *his* story, he is the producer. In chapter 1 the subject matter Adam is viewed in a generic way—the human being (*ha'adam*)—just like the vegetation and the animal kingdom.

---

[24] The intentionality on the author's part in this matter is borne out by the fact that, in either case, the *toledot* are described, *with the same wording*, as being the product of God's will: "These are the *generations* (*toledot*) of the heavens and the earth *when they were created* (*behibbare'am*) *on the day* (*beyom*) that the Lord God made the earth and the heavens" (Gen 2:4); "This is the book of the *generations* (*toledot*) of Adam. When God created man, he made him in the likeness of God. Male and female he created them, and he blessed them and named them Man *when they were created* (*beyom hibbare'am*; on the day they were created)." (Gen 5:1-2)
[25] At which point begins the following section "the *toledot* of Noah" in v.9.

> Then God said, "Let us make man (*'adam*) in our image, after our likeness; and let them have dominion over the fish of the sea, and over the birds of the air, and over the cattle, and over all the earth, and over every creeping thing that creeps upon the earth." So God created (the) man (*ha'adam*) in his own image, in the image of God he created him; male and female he created *them*. And God blessed *them*, and God said to *them*, "*Be fruitful and multiply*, and fill the earth and subdue it; and have dominion over the fish of the sea and over the birds of the air and over every living thing that moves upon the earth." (Gen 1:26-28)

This approach carries over into the other version of the creation story. The unique mention of *'adam* in 2:5 is followed by twenty-four instances of *ha'adam* in chapters 2-3 up to and inclusively of 4:1. In chapter 5, however, we have repeatedly six times only *'adam* in vv.1-5 *even* in the statement in v.1b-2 that takes up 1:27 where one hears of *ha'adam*: [26]

> This is the book of the generations of Adam (*'adam*). When God created man (*'adam*), he made him in the likeness of God. Male and female he created them, and he blessed them and named them Man (*'adam*) when they were created. (Gen 5:1-2)[27]

Thus Adam here is taken not as a species, but rather *as an individual* just like the rest of the individuals in his *toledot*. Still, the author's reprisal of the phraseology found at the end of chapter 1 is clearly intentional: the human realm of chapter 5 is not a different world than that of chapter 1-3. The intentionality in stressing the oneness of the world, be it human or animal, will be revisited in Noah's *toledot* where both his descendants and the animal kingdom are preserved in the one ark in order that the creation of the scriptural story may carry on as God intended it. This divine intention concerning the oneness of

---

[26] This in turn corroborates my thesis that chapters 1-4 are a unit entitled "the *toledot* of the heavens and the earth" followed by a second literary unit entitled "the *toledot* of Adam" covering chapter 5.

[27] RSV is misleading in translating the same original *'adam* in three different ways: Adam, man, and Man.

humanity as well as creation will be revisited time and again
throughout Genesis.

6

The Sound of God Walking
(Genesis 3)

After we hear of the story of the serpent luring Adam and Eve, we encounter the odd phrase regarding the sound of God walking in the garden:

> And they heard the sound (*qol*) of the Lord God walking (*mithallek*) in the garden in the cool of the day, and the man and his wife hid themselves from the presence of the Lord God among the trees of the garden. But the Lord God called (*wayyiqra'* from *qara'*) to the man, and said to him, "Where are you?" And he said, "I heard the sound (*qol*) of thee in the garden, and I was afraid, because I was naked; and I hid myself." (vv. 8-10)

"The sound of Lord God walking" is usually dismissed as being metaphoric without further examination or discussion of the original Hebrew. Moreover, the sound (*qol*) is usually taken as being that of God's footsteps. Notice how the RSV blatantly reflects this understanding in translating the original *qoleka*, usually rendered as "your voice," as "the sound of thee." KJV has in both cases (vv.8 and 10) simply "your voice," which is much more natural and fitting the context.[1] Listening to the original at face value, verses 9-10 are an expansion of verse 8: Adam and Eve heard the voice of the Lord God asking Adam where he was. Their guilt made them hide from "the presence of the Lord God," which is legal court terminology. In other words, they feared the punishment he, as judge cognizant of "the good and the evil," would issue against them. However, the original implies more than meets the ear at first hearing, due to the author's use of *mithallek*, the participle of the verb *hithallek*, the seventh verbal form (reflexive) of the verb *halak* (walk), whose meaning is "walk to and fro, walk around" *with a certain aim*[2]—

---

[1] LXX and Vulgate also use "voice" in both cases.
[2] In this particular case, the aim is to locate the culprit.

and not wandering aimlessly—when compared to the first verbal form *halak* that has the connotation of walking from one point to another. A good example where "walking to and fro" is clearly expressed is found in Job:

> The Lord said to Satan, "Whence have you come?" Satan answered the Lord, "From going to and fro on the earth, and from *walking up and down (hithallek)* on it." And the Lord said to Satan, "Have you considered my servant Job, that there is none like him on the earth, a blameless and upright man, who fears God and turns away from evil?" ... And the Lord said to Satan, "Whence have you come?" Satan answered the Lord, "From going to and fro on the earth, and from *walking up and down (hithallek)* on it." And the Lord said to Satan, "Have you considered my servant Job, that there is none like him on the earth, a blameless and upright man, who fears God and turns away from evil? He still holds fast his integrity, although you moved me against him, to destroy him without cause." (Job 1:7-8; 2:2-3)

The verb *hithallek* reflects the habitual continuous movement of a shepherd and his flock in the wilderness whether it is over the area of grazing where they settle for a time or the relocation from one grazing spot to another within the boundaries of that same wilderness. A pertinent instance of such is encountered in the Book of Genesis itself. I am asking my readers' indulgence for my quoting chapter 13 in its entirety. Apart from shedding a light on the meaning and function of *hithallek*, it presents us with two extra features: (1) it has a bearing on our entire discussion and (2) it betrays an intimate link with chapter 3, terminology wise.

> [1] So Abram went up from Egypt, he and his wife, and all that he had, and Lot with him, into the Negeb. [2] Now Abram was very rich in cattle, in silver, and in gold. [3] And he journeyed on from the Negeb as far as Bethel, to the place where his tent had been at the beginning, between Bethel and Ai, [4] to the place where he had made an altar at the first; and there Abram called on the name of the Lord. [5] And Lot, who went with Abram, also had flocks (*son*) and herds and tents, [6] so that the land could not support

both of them dwelling together; for their possessions were so great that they could not dwell together, ⁷and there was strife between the herdsmen (*ro'im*; shepherds) of Abram's cattle and the herdsmen (*ro'im*; shepherds) of Lot's cattle. At that time the Canaanites and the Perizzites dwelt in the land. ⁸Then Abram said to Lot, "Let there be no strife between you and me, and between your herdsmen (*ro'im*; shepherds) and my herdsmen (*ro'im*; shepherds); for we are kinsmen. ⁹Is not the whole land before you? Separate yourself from me. If you take the left hand, then I will go to the right; or if you take the right hand, then I will go to the left." ¹⁰And Lot lifted up his eyes, and saw that the Jordan valley was well watered everywhere like the garden of the Lord, like the land (*'eres*; earth) of Egypt, in the direction of Zoar; this was before the Lord destroyed Sodom and Gomorrah. ¹¹So Lot chose for himself all the Jordan valley, and Lot journeyed east; thus they separated from each other. ¹²Abram dwelt in the land of Canaan, while Lot dwelt among the cities of the valley and moved his tent as far as Sodom. ¹³Now the men of Sodom were wicked, great sinners against the Lord. ¹⁴The Lord said to Abram, after Lot had separated from him, "Lift up your eyes, and look from the place where you are, northward and southward and eastward and westward; ¹⁵for all the land (*'eres*; earth) which you see I will give to you and to your descendants for ever. ¹⁶I will make your descendants as the dust of the earth (*'eres*); so that if one can count the dust of the earth, your descendants also can be counted. ¹⁷Arise, walk (*hithallek*) through the length and the breadth of the land (*'eres*; earth), for I will give it to you." ¹⁸So Abram moved his tent, and came and dwelt by the oaks of Mamre, which are at Hebron; and there he built an altar to the Lord. (Gen. 13)

The setting of the passage is unmistakably shepherd life. It is against this background that Abram is asked to *hithallek* "through the length and breadth of the earth" (v.17) that extends "northward and southward and eastward and westward" as far as Abram's "eyes can see" (vv.14-15). This is clearly shepherd terminology that is to be taken metaphorically—actually hyperbolically—rather than literally. Indeed, it is impossible to "see" Hebron (v.18) from Bethel (v.3).

Rather, the phrase's intent is twofold. On the one hand, it applies to wherever Abram is at any given moment; on the other hand, and more importantly for my overall thesis, it applies to the fact that the "earth" granted to Abram extends over the vast expanse of the Syrian Wilderness, inclusive of the "ten" nations that abide there:[3]

> On that day the Lord made a covenant with Abram, saying, "To your descendants I give this land, from the river of Egypt to the great river, the river Euphrates, the land of the Kenites, the Kenizzites, the Kadmonites, the Hittites, the Perizzites, the Rephaim, the Amorites, the Canaanites, the Girgashites and the Jebusites." (15:18-21)

The link between these two passages is further underscored in the unexpected additional aside in 13:7b, "At that time the Canaanites and the Perizzites dwelt in the land."[4]

Besides pointing ahead to chapter 15, chapter 13 harks back to the story of the garden where we encountered *hithallek* for the first time. The case for this can readily be made due to the following features that seem to be unnecessary additions. In literature, unnecessary is usually to be equated with intentional. Let me begin with the most striking feature. In order to justify Lot's choice of the "Jordan valley" (v.11) it would have been sufficient to say that it "was well watered everywhere" without the unnecessary addition "like the garden of the Lord, like the land of Egypt, in the direction of Zoar" (v.10). At most, one would have expected the mention of the locality Zoar to indicate how far south Lot's portion extended. It is the likening of that portion not only to "the garden of the Lord" but also to "the land of Egypt" which is exceptional, unless the author intended to draw the hearer's attention to chapter 2 where one

---

[3] The numeral ten reflects universal totality. See *NTI₄* 22-25.
[4] See later on why and how these two nations are the shortest rendition of the totality of nations.

finds both the verb "water"[5] and "the land of Cush" that lies south of Egypt:

> And the Lord God planted a garden in Eden, in the east; and there he put the man whom he had formed ... A river flowed out of Eden to water the garden, and there it divided and became four rivers. The name of the first is Pishon; it is the one which flows around the whole land of Havilah, where there is gold; and the gold of that land is good; bdellium and onyx stone are there. The name of the second river is Gihon; it is the one which flows around the whole land of Cush. And the name of the third river is Tigris, which flows east of Assyria. And the fourth river is the Euphrates. (vv.8, 10-14)

The author is intentionally bringing into the picture the land of Cush (and Egypt) irrigated by the Gihon. Later in chapter 15, he will include in Abram's portion the Euphrates and the Tigris, the two rivers encompassing the "garden of the Lord." As for the land of Havilah irrigated by the Pishon, it is brought obliquely into the same picture through the mention of "gold" (13:2) alongside *miqneh* (translated as cattle, but technically means movable possession comprising both animals in general as well as personal items) whose main intent is the flocks as is clear from both Genesis 13:5 (And Lot, who went with Abram, also had flocks [*son*] and herds and tents) and the reference specifically to *ro'im* (shepherds) repeatedly in verses 7 and 8. Since "gold" is non-functional in the story of chapter 13, its obvious intent is to bring to mind the earlier two occurrences of gold in conjunction with the land of Havilah (2:11-12). In other words, the story of the shepherds Abram and his nephew Lot takes place within the confines of the Syrian Wilderness, the locale of the scriptural "earth (land) of Canaan:"[6] "At that time

---

[5] The occurrence of the root *šaqah* in 13:10 is the first after its occurrence in 2:6 (but a mist went up from the earth and watered the whole face of the ground) and 10 and later does not appear again until 19:21-38 in conjunction with both Lot and Zoar. If that is not intentionality, then what is?

[6] I shall discuss this matter in detail later.

the Canaanites and the Perizzites dwelt in the land" (13:7b);
"Abram dwelt in the land of Canaan" (v.12a).

Given all the preceding, it stands to reason to take the Lord
God's "walking" in the garden as the behavior of a shepherd
looking for his "lost sheep" around the oasis.[7] This view of God
is not farfetched since in Genesis we hear that, in spite of being
mighty, God acts as the shepherd of Israel. We find this in
Jacob's blessing to Joseph:

> Joseph is a fruitful bough, a fruitful bough by a spring; his
> branches run over the wall. The archers fiercely attacked him,
> shot at him, and harassed him sorely; yet his bow remained
> unmoved, his arms were made agile by the hands of the Mighty
> One of Jacob (by the name of the Shepherd [ro'eh], the Rock of
> Israel), by the God of your father who will help you, by God
> Almighty who will bless you with blessings of heaven above,
> blessings of the deep that couches beneath, blessings of the breasts
> and of the womb. (49:22-25)

Later in the Pentateuch we hear the following passage at the
end of which God walks (hithallek) among his people as a
shepherd among his flock:

> You shall make for yourselves no *idols* and erect no *graven image or
> pillar*, and you shall not set up *a figured stone* in your *land*, to bow
> down to them; for I am the Lord your God. You shall *keep my
> sabbaths* and reverence my sanctuary (*miqdas*): I am the Lord. If
> you *walk in my statutes* and *observe my commandments* and *do them* ...
> And I will give *peace* in the land, and you shall lie down, and none
> shall make you afraid; and I will remove *evil beasts* from the land,
> and the sword shall not go through your land ... And I will make
> my abode (*miskan*) among you (*betokekem*; in the midst of you), and
> my soul shall not abhor you. And I will walk (*[we]hithallakti*)
> among you (*betokekem*; in the midst of you), and *will be your God*,
> and *you shall be my people*. (Lev 26:1-3, 6, 11-12)

---

[7] It is not just "ambulating" or "taking a stroll" during which he decides to play hide
and seek with the man who is hiding among the trees!

The same thought, cast in the same terms, is found again in Ezekiel, where it appears in conjunction with God being depicted as shepherd of his flock:

> Therefore say, "Thus says the Lord God: I will gather you from the peoples, and assemble you out of the countries where you have been scattered, and I will give you the *land* of Israel." (Ezek 11:17)

> And when they come there, they will remove from it *all its detestable things and all its abominations*. And I will give them one heart, and put a new spirit within them; I will take the stony heart out of their flesh and give them a heart of flesh, that they may *walk in my statutes* and *keep my ordinances* and *obey them*; and *they shall be my people, and I will be their God*. (11:18-20)

> And they shall bear their punishment—the punishment of the prophet and the punishment of the inquirer shall be alike—that the house of Israel may go no more astray from me, nor defile themselves any more with all their transgressions, but that *they may be my people and I may be their God*, says the Lord God. (14:10-11)

> So they were scattered, because there was no shepherd; and they became food for all the *wild beasts*. My sheep (My flock) were scattered, they wandered over all the mountains and on every high hill; my sheep (My flock) were scattered over all the face of the earth, with none to search or seek for them. Therefore, you shepherds, hear the word of the Lord: As I live, says the Lord God, because my sheep (my flock) have become a prey, and my sheep (my flock) have become food for all the *wild beasts*, since there was no shepherd; and because my shepherds have not searched for my sheep, but the shepherds have fed themselves, and have not fed my sheep; therefore, you shepherds, hear the word of the Lord: Thus says the Lord God, Behold, I am against the shepherds; and I will require my sheep (my flock) at their hand, and put a stop to their feeding the sheep; no longer shall the shepherds feed themselves. I will rescue my sheep from their mouths, that they may not be food for them. For thus says the Lord God: Behold, I, I myself will search for my sheep, and will seek them out. *As a shepherd seeks out his flock when some of his sheep*

have been scattered abroad, so will I seek out my sheep; and I will rescue
them from all places where they have been scattered on a day of
clouds and thick darkness. And I will bring them out from the
peoples, and gather them from the countries, and will bring them
into their own land; and I will feed them on the mountains of
Israel, by the fountains, and in all the inhabited places of the
country. I will feed them with good pasture, and upon the
mountain heights of Israel shall be their pasture; there they shall
lie down in good grazing land, and on fat pasture they shall feed
on the mountains of Israel. *I myself will be the shepherd of my sheep*,
and I will make them lie down, says the Lord God. (34:5-15)

I will make with them a covenant of *peace* and banish *wild beasts*
from the land, so that they may dwell securely in the wilderness
and sleep in the woods. And I will make them and the places
round about my hill a blessing; and I will send down the showers
in their season; they shall be showers of blessing. (34:25-26)

They shall no more be a prey to the nations, nor shall *the beasts of
the land* devour them; they shall dwell securely, and none shall
make them afraid. And I will provide for them prosperous
plantations so that they shall no more be consumed with hunger
in the land, and no longer suffer the reproach of the nations. And
they shall know that I, the Lord their God, am with them, and
that *they, the house of Israel, are my people*, says the Lord God. *And you
are my sheep, the sheep of my pasture, and I am your God, says the Lord God.*
(34:28-31)

I will make a covenant of *peace* with them; it shall be an everlasting
covenant with them; and I will bless them and multiply them, and
will set my sanctuary (*miqdaš*) in the midst of them (*betokam*) for
evermore. My dwelling place (*miškan*) shall be with them; and *I
will be their God, and they shall be my people*. Then the nations will
know that I the Lord sanctify Israel, when my sanctuary (*miqdaš*)
is in the midst of them (*betokam*) for evermore." (37:26-28)

7

Cain and Seth
(Genesis 4)

Since Cain and Abel are not part of the *toledot* of Adam, arguably the author could have skipped Genesis 4 by proceeding directly to the genealogy of Adam outside the garden in chapter 5. So one is to inquire as to the value of chapter 4 and its function in the author's purview. First and most importantly, the story of Cain and Abel is the first scriptural story that pins down in the clearest of terms two ways of life, shepherdism and city life, one against the other. At the same time it is a clear invitation to opt for the former. So already in the first tackling of human social life outside the garden of Eden, the authors betray their bias as well as their interest. This matter will be revisited at the end of Isaiah where Zion, the heavenly city, will be likened to a wilderness and desert where Eden-like life will blossom: "For the Lord will comfort Zion; he will comfort all her waste places, and will make her wilderness like Eden, her desert like the garden of the Lord; joy and gladness will be found in her, thanksgiving and the voice of song." (51:3) This view reappears at the close of the entire scripture, New as well as Old Testament, where we hear of "the holy city, new Jerusalem, coming down out of heaven from God" (Rev 21:2) described in terms that recollect the garden of Eden:

> Then he showed me *the river of the water of life*, bright as crystal, flowing from the throne of God and of the Lamb through the middle of the street of the city; also, on either side of the river, *the tree of life with its twelve kinds of fruit, yielding its fruit each month*; and the leaves of the tree were for the healing of the nations. There shall no more be anything accursed, but the throne of God and of the Lamb shall be in it, and his servants shall worship him; they shall see his face, and his name shall be on their foreheads. And night shall be no more; they need no light of lamp or sun, for the

Lord God will be their light, and they shall reign for ever and ever. (22:1-5)

Cain, as tiller of the ground (Gen 4:2b) like his father (2:15), is obviously sedentary while Abel is introduced as "shepherd of flock" (ro'eh son)[1] and, as such, is unequivocally the preferred of the Lord: "And the Lord had regard for Abel and his offering, but for Cain and his offering he had no regard." (Gen 4:4b-5a) The lack of a given reason for the homicide is obviously intended: it is what it is. God in scripture is biased toward shepherdism, without which bias there would not have been scripture.[2] This bias is at its clearest in the subsequent story of Cain. His punishment by God should have been death (The voice of your brother's blood is crying to me from the ground; 4:10b), however, rather than death, he is given an alternative, that is, to lead a life similar to that of Abel: wandering in the earth of wandering.[3] Notice also how the earth of Nod is in a location right outside Eden where Adam and Eve, and their descendants, were exiled for good. Thus the proposition is for Cain to live "Eden-ly" in the wilderness after the manner of his brother Abel:

> He drove out the man; and at the east of (miqqedem) the garden of Eden he placed the cherubim, and a flaming sword which turned every way, to guard the way to the tree of life. (3:24)

> Then Cain went away from the presence of the Lord, and dwelt in the land of Nod, east of (qidmat) Eden. (4:16)

However, Cain's proclivity toward sedentary life lured him to contravene the divine command—just as his father did—and he became the first to commit the ultimate mistake of building a city. Not content with this misconceived feat, he even named the city after his son Enoch (4:17), thus turning God's gift of

---

[1] A rare phrase instead of the simpler "shepherd." I shall point out later how it is used specifically in conjunction with key personalities in scripture.

[2] The later explanations by the Christian intelligentsia smacks of Greek philosophy: there *must* have been a reason. My readers are reminded that reason in Greek is *logos*.

[3] The name Nod in Hebrew is from the same root as the verb *nad* (wander).

flesh into one of stone. This situation will be redressed at the end when the human beings will be restored to their original "natural" status of beings of flesh:

> And when they come there, they will remove from it all its detestable things and all its abominations. And I will give them one heart, and put a new spirit within them; I will take the stony heart out of their flesh and give them a heart of flesh, that they may walk in my statutes and keep my ordinances and obey them; and they shall be my people, and I will be their God. But as for those whose heart goes after their detestable things and their abominations, I will requite their deeds upon their own heads, says the Lord God. (Ezek 11:18-21)

> I will sprinkle clean water upon you, and you shall be clean from all your uncleannesses, and from all your idols I will cleanse you. A new heart I will give you, and a new spirit I will put within you; and I will take out of your flesh the heart of stone and give you a heart of flesh. And I will put my spirit within you, and cause you to walk in my statutes and be careful to observe my ordinances. (36:25-27)

> "And I will lay sinews upon you, and will cause flesh to come upon you, and cover you with skin, and put breath in you, and you shall live; and you shall know that I am the Lord." So I prophesied as I was commanded; and as I prophesied, there was a noise, and behold, a rattling; and the bones came together, bone to its bone. And as I looked, there were sinews on them, and flesh had come upon them, and skin had covered them; but there was no breath in them. (37:6-8)

Scripture's Anti-Kingly Emphasis

Before proceeding to the *toledot* of Adam I should like to examine scripture's anti-kingly bias that I stressed time and again as being one of the most important crimson threads throughout scripture, if not its actual trigger. The fact that the authors did not entitle the genealogy of Cain (Gen 4:17-24) as *toledot* indicates that, in spite of his great accomplishments and those of his progeny, he ended up not leaving a mark on human history. I shall go into more detail as to how the content of that passage reflects the anti-kingly and anti-city bias at each turn.

Genesis 4:17-24 has a double function. On the one hand, it shows that indeed God's blessing is still working in spite of man's misbehavior: "Cain knew his wife, and she conceived and bore Enoch" (v.17) just as "Adam knew Eve his wife, and she conceived and bore Cain" (v.1). On the other hand, however, the path chosen by man takes him farther away from the original setting of the garden where everything needed was provided by God, and the little work man did was for his benefit and enjoyment. This path led to civilization, the most grandiose expression of which is the (imperial) city[4] that will ultimately stand arrogantly against God (11:1-9).

Eve's reaction to her having conceived and given birth to Cain is to acknowledge that the child is the gift of God rather than her own making: "I have gotten a man with the help of the Lord." (4:1).[5] Instead of Eve's attitude of thanksgiving, Cain's reaction to his wife's bearing his son was that he "built a city, and called the name of the city after the name of his son, Enoch" (v.17). The intended extreme irony can be seen in the name Enoch, from the root *ḥnk*, which has the connotation of "dedication."[6] Instead of taking his son's name seriously and dedicating him back to God, Cain makes his son, who is as much God's gift *as he himself is*, into a city. Cain, the man of (living) flesh, begets a man of (dead) stone! In other words, Cain circumvented God's decision to have him "dwell" in a "land of wandering" and decided to "dwell" in a city of his own making. Cain's legacy becomes, by choice, one of stone. Ultimately, God will correct this human propensity within the scriptural odyssey in a terminology reminiscent of the first chapters of Genesis:

---

[4] Civilization and city (*civitas*) are from the same root in the original Latin.

[5] See however later my comments on this statement in comparison with that about Adam's wife in 4:25.

[6] *ḥanukkah* (Hanukkah), which is the Feast of the (Re)dedication of the Temple under the Maccabees, comes from the same root.

And I will give them one heart, and put a new spirit within them; I will take the stony heart out of their flesh and give them a heart of flesh, that they may walk in my statutes and keep my ordinances and obey them; and they shall be my people, and I will be their God. But as for those whose heart goes after their detestable things and their abominations, I will requite their deeds upon their own heads, says the Lord God. (Ezek 11:19-21)

Therefore I will judge you, O house of Israel, every one according to his ways, says the Lord God. Repent and turn from all your transgressions, lest iniquity be your ruin. Cast away from you all the transgressions which you have committed against me, and get yourselves a new heart and a new spirit! Why will you die, O house of Israel? For I have no pleasure in the death of any one, says the Lord God; so turn, and live. (18:30-32)

I will sprinkle clean water upon you, and you shall be clean from all your uncleannesses, and from all your idols I will cleanse you. A new heart I will give you, and a new spirit I will put within you; and I will take out of your flesh the heart of stone and give you a heart of flesh. And I will put my spirit within you, and cause you to walk in my statutes and be careful to observe my ordinances. (36:25-27)

This sad state of affairs is carried through the seventh generation of Cain's progeny, that is, to its fullest extent with God's approval and under his control.[7] As in Genesis 2 with the building of woman and in 1 Samuel 8 with the rise of kingship, God allows Cain's decision to take its course in order to show the hearers the calamitous end of such. The series of names in Cain's progeny reflect the fact that they are furthering his ways, that is, following man's own will while ignoring God's initial plan. The name of Enoch's son, Irad (*'irad*), is a combination of the noun *'ir* (city) and the verb *radah* (rule [over], have dominion [over]); thus the son of Enoch was to rule over the city named

---

[7] For the value of the numerical 7, see the Excursus on Number Symbolism in *NTI₃* 22-28.

after his father.[8] The following in line is Mehujael (*meḥuya'el*) meaning "what he undertakes will be erased (they will erase)," and his son's name Methushael (*metuša'el*) means "what he asks for will die," reflecting the biblical end of the city founded by Cain. Next is Lemech (*lemek*),[9] which is a play on the Hebrew noun *melek* (king) through metathesis.[10] Two extra features that are related to him confirm this. On the one hand, he had more than one wife, which was a kingly prerogative, as one can see from the examples of Saul (2 Sam 12:7-8), David (2 Sam 5:13; 12:11; 19:5), Solomon (1 Kg 10:8; 11:1-4), Rehoboam (2 Chr 11:21), Ahab (1 Kg 20:3-7), and Jehoiachin (2 Kg 24:15). On the other hand, in his statement to his wives he acts as a judge, the way a king—and thus a god—would: he emits a verdict of death: "I have slain a man for wounding me, a young man for striking me. If Cain is avenged sevenfold, truly Lemech seventy-sevenfold." [11] (Gen 4:23-24) Notice that in the case of Cain, it is God who is the avenger (v.15), while Lemech, de facto, usurps the place of God. In doing so, Lemech commits the ultimate blasphemy of which the kings of Judah and Israel were culprits[12] (Ezek 34). So Cain's wish to build a city to protect himself ends with the rise of kingship that will destroy it. This is the biblical story in a nutshell.

---

[8] *'irad* from *'ir-rad* without the repetition of the letter *r*. Keeping the final *h* of *radah* would have resulted in a feminine proper noun.

[9] Unfortunately the traditional English Lamech, starting with the King James Version, is incorrect. Lamech (*lamek*) is found only in Gen 4:18. In the following four instances of the same name (vv.19, 23 [twice], 25) we have the Hebrew *lemek* (Lemech). This is repeated in Gen 5:25-31 where the first instance in v.25 is *lamek*, whereas, the following four (vv.26, 28, 30, 31) are *lemek*. The first instance in each passage is due to the fact that the personal noun is the last word of the verse. In this case, in Hebrew, we have what is called the pausal form where the vowel of the accented syllable in the word is lengthened, in this case from the short *e* to a long *ā*.

[10] Metathesis is the switch in place between two consonants in the same word.

[11] Notice the use of "seven" and "seventy seven," reflective of the divine.

[12] The two most striking examples are David taking the life of Uriah (2 Sam 11:14-15) and Ahab taking that of Naboth (1 Kg 21:1-16).

Chapter 7

God's Choice of Seth over Cain

The assumption that Cain would be well established throughout the ages is reflected in the seven generations issued from him culminating in Lemech, the king. Although a fully developed civilization is encompassed within Cain's legacy,[13] God dismisses his progeny as illustrative of human destiny. Instead it is Seth, the replacement of Abel, the "shepherd of flock," and his son Enosh who are shown to be the divinely willed *'adamic* progeny:

> And Adam knew his wife again, and she bore a son and called his name Seth, for she said, "*God has appointed for me another child instead of Abel*, for Cain slew him." To Seth also a son was born, and he called his name Enosh. *At that time men began to call upon the name of the Lord.* This is the book of the generations of Adam. When God created man, he made him in the likeness of God. Male and female he created them, and he blessed them and named them Man when they were created. When Adam had lived a hundred and thirty years, he became the father of a son in his own likeness, after his image, and named him Seth. The days of Adam after he became the father of Seth were eight hundred years; and he had other sons and daughters. Thus all the days that Adam lived were nine hundred and thirty years; and he died. When Seth had lived a hundred and five years, he became the father of Enosh. Seth lived after the birth of Enosh eight hundred and seven years, and had other sons and daughters. Thus all the days of Seth were nine hundred and twelve years; and he died. (Gen 4:25-5:8)

The story of Cain and Abel outside the garden conveys the author's double thesis of the garden being an oasis and the directive to handle God's creation as its shepherd, and not as its king. By the same token, the story reveals that the human being committed the same error twice, once in the garden and the

---

[13] And Lamech took two wives; the name of the one was Adah, and the name of the other Zillah. Adah bore Jabal; he was the father of those who dwell in tents and have cattle. His brother's name was Jubal; he was the father of all those who play the lyre and pipe. Zillah bore Tubalcain; he was the forger of all instruments of bronze and iron. (Gen 4:19-22)

other time outside it, underscoring man's preference for urban civilization, which is "created through human hands," over life in the wilderness, which is fully God's handicraft. This repeated error will set the stage for presenting human wickedness in Genesis 6:1-8 as the third and final straw that broke the camel's back and brought about the seemingly inconceivable[14]—God regretted his original plan conceived in chapters 1 and 2: "And the Lord was sorry that he had made man on the earth, and it grieved him to his heart. So the Lord said, 'I will blot out man whom I have created from the face of the ground, man and beast and creeping things and birds of the air, for I am sorry that I have made them.'" (Gen 6:6-7)

---

[14] See *NTI₃* 22-23 on the function of the third time.

8
Revisiting Genesis 1-4

Considering that the books constituting the Latter Prophets and the Ketubim are conceived as a ministory of the stubbornly repeated disobedience on the part of the scriptural Israel,[1] which story is expanded upon in the Prior Prophets where God intervenes to restore the original order of things according to his will, one would expect to find the same "story" in Genesis 1-4. This is precisely what one finds when hearing the original Hebrew. The kingly terminology of Genesis 1:28 (subdue; have dominion) does not entail a free rein for human beings to do as they please. Such dominion is to be exercised with the view of maintaining the order willed by God, so that they and the land animals may enjoy life granted to them both through consumption of the vegetation provided for them by God himself on the third day (vv.29-30). This matter is of central importance for the authors since it is revisited again at the beginning of the second creation narrative: "In the day that the Lord God made the earth and the heavens, when no plant of the field was yet in the earth and no herb of the field had yet sprung up—for the Lord God had not caused it to *rain upon the earth*, and there was no man to till *('abad*; serve) the ground." (Gen 2:4b-5) Two features are of import in this statement: (1) there is no vegetation to sustain animal life *unless* the Lord God sends his rain upon the ground and (2) man is to "serve" that ground, which will be iterated in 2:15. The rendering of *'abad* into "till" in the sense of "work" the ground, as it is usually understood, is not only incorrect, but goes against the intent of the text. The Hebrew *'abad* is from the same root as *'ebed* (slave). Put otherwise, *'adam* is to act as a slave who would facilitate the "work" of his master who provides the rain necessary for the growth of every plant and herb *of the field*, and not of the

_____

[1] See, e.g., my comments on Isaiah in *OTI₁* 39 and *C-Is* 19, 29-33, and my handling of Psalms in *OTI₃* 97-104.

vineyard, for instance, that is the product of man's work.[2] The shepherd maintains the status quo and in no way "improves" on it.[3] Accordingly, 'adam was positioned as the caretaker of the 'adamah, not as its proprietor. The authors' intention is reflected in their cunning choice of terminology: ṣelem (image) and demut (likeness) carry a double-edged, rather than an outright positive, connotation. ṣelem—from ṣel (shadow)—means "shadowy" reflection[4] and demut denotes a speechless (lifeless) resemblance.[5] Together they are an unambiguous invitation for human beings to realize that they are "representations" and, by extension, mere "representatives" that can be easily "blotted out, wiped out, deleted, erased" (from the verb maḥah) as with an eraser,[6] as in Genesis 6:7. That is definitely a far cry from how the human beings came to be perceived in Alexandrian theology.

After having established human frailty, especially as expressed by those in positions of governance, whether monarchs or any sort of socio-political leaders, Genesis 2-4 proceeds to show the hearers that such frailty was revealed soon enough and was proven to be the rule rather than the exception until God's corrective intervention. The costly "error" of Adam and Eve in wanting to play the "role" of God brought about their exile out of the garden and their children being born in that exile.[7] Cain like Adam was put in the position of "servant" of the ground (Gen 4:2b). In spite of God's corrective punishment, he rebelliously established a city and a kingly dynasty. He surpassed his father in believing that he was indeed *a* if not *the*

---

[2] This matter will be revisited in the story of Noah, where the fruit of the vineyard will set the stage for the divine curse, which in turn brings to mind the scenario of Genesis 3.

[3] This scenario has already in mind Ezekiel 34 where the kings of Israel are addressed as its shepherds, and not its kings. My readers are reminded that the Hebrew *melek* (king) means owner, proprietor, which appellative in scripture is due solely to God.

[4] See *C-Gen* 42 fn 18.

[5] See *C-Gen* 42 fn 19.

[6] In Arabic the word "eraser" is from the same root *mḥḥ*.

[7] Already this story looks forward to Ezekiel who addressed *in the land of exile* the children of the exiles.

king, as reflected in both his attitude and in the naming of his heir Lemech.[8] However, God dismisses Cain's lineage and establishes a new one through Seth, who took the place of the shepherd Abel (4:25-26). This new genealogy, Adam-Seth-Enosh, forms a trilogy whose meaning in the original Hebrew is "a human being posits (begets) another human being."[9] By limiting the genealogy to three generations, the author is inviting the hearers to fill in the blanks and realize that procreation is a revolving reality through natural begetting sanctioned by God himself for humans as well as animals (1:20-28). According to scripture the human being is a "living creature," and as chief among this realm is responsible and accountable for the future of every other "living creature" (*nepheš ḥayyah*) *in the eyes of the scriptural God.*

It is through this new genealogy that "men began to call upon the name of the Lord" (Gen 4:26b). So the beginning of true worship coincided with God's reestablishment of his original plan in "the *toledot* of the heavens and the earth." The genealogy via Seth, which is clearly presented as an alternative to Cain's, offers humanity another path. Notice the parallelism in terminology reflecting a new start:

> Now Adam (*ha'adam*; the man)[10] knew Eve his wife, and she conceived and bore Cain, saying, "I have gotten a man with the help of the Lord." (Gen 4:1)

---

[8] One can see how Cain prefigures David who, from shepherd, became a king and made out the conquered city of Jebus "the city of David" (2 Sam 5:9), his personal property.

[9] The Hebrew *'enoš* is from the same root as *iš* (the male human being) whose counterpart is *iššah* (the female human being): "Then the man said, 'This at last is bone of my bones and flesh of my flesh; she shall be called Woman (*iššah*), because she was taken out of Man (*iš*).'" (Gen 2:23)

[10] I shall deal momentarily with the difference between *ha'adam* in v.1 and *'adam* in v.25.

And Adam (*'adam*)[11] knew his wife again, and she bore a son and called his name Seth (*šet*), for she said, "God has appointed (*šat*)[12] for me another child instead of Abel, for Cain slew him." (4:25)

In contradistinction to both Cain and Seth, Abel is introduced summarily without the mention of Adam knowing Eve: "And again, she bore his brother Abel." (4:2) However, Seth is presented as taking the place of Abel (*hebel*), an indication to the hearer that the will of God was "set"[13] in the way he originally intended: the human being is a mere *hebel* (vanishing breath) and should never endeavor to become a king "like God." This is the teaching of Genesis 2-3, and is corroborated in that Seth produces Enosh (*'enoš*), which is the other Hebrew word for human being.[14] The complete cycle[15] is thus "man (*'adam*) sets (Seth) man (Enosh)" and so on and so forth. It is this true man Enosh, the son of Seth, son of Adam, who is *the* man said to have initiated the true worship of the Lord (Gen. 4:26b). In other words, the genealogy of Seth and that of Cain offer two very different ways of life: (1) relying on God's earth, of which humanity is an integral part, and thus relying on God Himself, or (2) in contradistinction, relying on oneself and one's accomplishments built in stone. In these two alternative genealogies of Genesis 4 looms the specter of Ezekiel, the son of man, and his teaching against the city and its king, the son of God. Genesis will opt for Seth over Cain, as will become clear in the genealogy of Adam (Gen 5:3).

The incontrovertible feature that seals my thesis that "the *toledot* of the heavens and earth" (Gen 1-4) function as a mini-

---

[11] See previous note.

[12] Both *šet* and *šat* are from the same Hebrew root *šit* meaning "place, set, appoint."

[13] See previous note.

[14] From the same root as the Hebrew *'iš* (man, male human being) whose plural *'anašim* has the additional letter *n* found in *'enoš*. Similarly, *'iššah*, the singular feminine of *'iš*, has the plural form *našim*.

[15] Three is the numeral expressing fullness and "indeed-ness." It is the lowest plural numeral beyond the numeral two (the dual in Semitic languages) reflecting an either-or situation. Semitic languages, just as ancient Greek, have the singular, the dual, and the plural in their verbal conjugations.

scripture lies in the wording of Genesis 4:25-26, the concluding passage to that *toledot*:

And Adam (*'adam*) knew his wife (*'iššah*) again, and she bore a son and called his name (*šem*) Seth (*šet*), for she said, "God (*'elohim*) has appointed (*šat*; the verb from the same root as the noun *šet*) for me another child (*zera'*; seed) instead of Abel, for Cain slew him." To Seth also a son was born (*yullad*), and he called his name (*šem*) Enosh (*'enoš*; from the same root as *'iššah*). At that time *men began to call* (*huḥal liqro'*; it was allowed/permitted that it be called) upon the name of the Lord.

In chapters 1-4 reference is consistently made to *ha'adam* (the man), except for the first instance in 1:26 where we have *'adam* (Adam). This is intentional since even, outside the garden, we hear: "Now *ha'adam* (the man)[16] knew Eve his wife (*'iššah*), and she conceived and bore Cain, saying, 'I have gotten a man with the help of the Lord.'" (4:1) Genesis 4:25 clearly harks back to 4:1 since it uses the adverb "again" to refer to the man having known his wife "who bore a son" whose name she defines in an explanatory statement. However, in the latter case, the story is about *'adam* (Adam) instead of *ha'adam* (the man). The author does this to prepare the hearer for the immediately subsequent *toledot* of *'adam* (Adam), the individual who is thus referred to no less than six times in a row (5:1 [twice], 2, 3, 4, 5) and whose son and grandson are none other than Seth (vv.3, 4, 6, 7, 8) and Enosh (vv.6, 7, 9, 10, 11) who were already introduced in 4:25-26. Consequently, these two verses (4:25-26) serve as straddle between the *toledot* of "the heavens and the earth," of which *ha'adam*, both male and female, is one product among many others, and the *toledot* of Adam the individual from whom came all individual human beings who, in turn, are never Adam—as construed later in theological thought—since Adam is

---

[16] RSV has "Adam."

THE RISE OF SCRIPTURE

unrepeatable.[17] The rest of humanity are merely *bene 'adam* (children of Adam).

However, and very strikingly for that matter, besides looking forward to 5:1 *'adam* (Adam) in 4:25 recalls *'adam* (Adam) of 1:26. No other instance of such is found between these two occurrences. One cannot escape this intentional choice since it is *ha'adam* (the man) that is found no less than nineteen times in chapters 1-2 in between these two occurrences of *'adam*. Literarily speaking, the two instances of *'adam* (Adam) bracket the author's dealing with *ha'adam* (the man) in the *toledot* of "the heavens and the earth."

The plausible explanation for such a literary device is to invite the hearer to realize that *'adam* is the subject matter of the book of his *toledot* (5:1), and that his great grandson Noah is nothing other than the prototypical specimen of the species *ha'adam* (the human being) that is an integral part of the *toledot* of the heavens and earth, God's creation. The hearers are not surprised when the subsequent lengthy narrative of the *toledot* of Noah (6:9-9:29) will have in its purview not only the human species, but all the different species of the animal world, birds as well as land animals, that are an integral part of "the heavens and the earth" God created (ch.1) and all are included in the divine blessing:

> Then God said to Noah and to his sons with him, "Behold, I establish my covenant with you and your descendants after you,

---

[17] To make the point to my male students, I always remind them—to their chagrin, of course—that Adam *according to the scriptural text* had no navel, since he was formed of *ha'adamah* (the ground; Gen 2:7); whereas all the rest of us have one! And, in order that the women in my class would not gloat, I remind these too that they all have a navel whereas Eve, "the mother of all living" (Gen 3:20b), did not have one either since she was built out of the rib of *ha'adam* (2:22). The Arabic language refers to the men as "sons of Adam" and to the women as "daughters of Eve." It is so precise concerning this matter that it uses the Semitic generic *'adamiy* (*'adam*-ic, *'adam* like) to refer to a "humane" person. Arabic uses the generic ending -*iy* (-*i* in the spoken language) that corresponds to the Hebrew generic ending –*i*. To give an example, the Hebrew *yehudi* (Judahite, Jew, pertaining to Judah) would be *yahudiy* in Arabic (*yahudi* in the spoken Arabic). In other words, *yehudah* (Judah) the patriarch is unrepeatable whereas his progeny are the *yehudim* (plural of *yehudi*).

and with every living creature that is with you, the birds, the cattle, and every beast of the earth with you, as many as came out of the ark. I establish my covenant with you, that never again shall all flesh be cut off by the waters of a flood, and never again shall there be a flood to destroy the earth." And God said, "This is the sign of the covenant which I make between me and you and every living creature that is with you, for all future generations: I set my bow in the cloud, and it shall be a sign of the covenant between me and the earth. When I bring clouds over the earth and the bow is seen in the clouds, I will remember my covenant which is between me and you and every living creature of all flesh; and the waters shall never again become a flood to destroy all flesh. When the bow is in the clouds, I will look upon it and remember the everlasting covenant between God and every living creature of all flesh that is upon the earth." God said to Noah, "This is the sign of the covenant which I have established between me and all flesh that is upon the earth." (9:8-17)

Thus, Genesis 1-4 functions as a unique preamble to the scriptural "book" of "the toledot of *'adam* (Adam)." It is an ever reminder that whatever Adam's stature as the unique and unrepeatable forefather in his own "tree," he remains but one of the constituents in the "tree" of "the heavens and the earth," and was lumped together with the other "living beings" on the sixth day. His uniqueness as a functional representative of God in the management of God's creation does not take effect until chapter 5 where the statement of 1:26-27 is picked up with Seth, and *not with Cain* whose "presence" is confined to chapter 4:

Then God said, "Let us make man (*'adam*) in our image, after our likeness; and let them have dominion over the fish of the sea, and over the birds of the air, and over the cattle, and over all the earth, and over every creeping thing that creeps upon the earth." So God created man (*ha'adam*) in his own image, in the image of God he created him; male and female he created them. (1:26-27)

This is the book of the generations of Adam (*'adam*). When God created man (*'adam*), *he made him in the likeness of God*. Male and female he created them, and he blessed them and named them Man (*'adam*) when they were created. When Adam (*'adam*) had lived a hundred and thirty years, he became *the father of a son in his own likeness, after his image*, and named him Seth. (5:1-3)[18]

The uniqueness and thus unrepeatability of Genesis 1-4 is corroborated in the last scriptural "book" of 1 and 2 Chronicles in that its opening reflects Genesis 5, sealing the intent that it contains not the "chronicles" of "the heavens and the earth" that are confined to Genesis 1-4, but rather the "chronicles" of the human beings, the "children of Adam" of Genesis 5: Adam, Seth, Enosh; Kenan, Mahalalel, Jared; Enoch, Methuselah, Lamech; Noah, Shem, Ham, and Japheth (1 Chr 1:1-4). Notice again that Cain is nowhere to be found.[19]

Seth, God's Seed

A series of features in Genesis 4:25-26 will support my thesis that Genesis 1-4 functions as a mini-scripture.[20] Let me begin

---

[18] It is this Adam that is the main topic of interest of the authors in the rest of scripture. Only at the final restoration, as reflected in the Latter Prophets and the Psalms, are the heavens and the earth, the subject of the first scriptural *toledot*, reincorporated in God's purview with the human beings in whose care they had been entrusted (Gen 1:26-30). Once again the Apostle captured that scriptural teaching fully as well as masterfully: "For the creation waits (*apekdekhetai*) with eager longing for the revealing of the sons of God; for the creation was subjected to futility, not of its own will but by the will of him who subjected it in hope; because the creation itself will be set free from its bondage to decay and obtain the glorious liberty of the children of God. We know that the whole creation has been groaning (*systenazei*) in travail together until now; and not only the creation, but we ourselves, who have the first fruits of the Spirit, groan (*systenazomen*) inwardly as we wait (*apekdekhomenoi*) for adoption as sons, the redemption of our bodies." (Rom 8:19-23)

[19] It is imperative for my readers—who are used to the LXX canon where 1 and 2 Chronicles, Ezra, and Nehemiah, follow 1 and 2 Kings—to realize that Ezra, Nehemiah, 1 and 2 Chronicles (in this *unexpected order*—since the latter two cover a period that is prior to the one covered by Ezra and Nehemiah), are entered as the last books of the Writings (*ketubim*) that are the third part of the Hebrew Old Testament. In other words, 1 and Chronicles *conclude* the Old Testament by harking back to Genesis before moving to the stories of Israel and Judah covered in 1 and 2 Samuel and 1 and 2 Kings.

[20] I must immediately caution my readers that I have repeatedly shown RSV to be wanting, if not outright biased, in my commentaries, and is at the highest level of distortion of the original, especially in its handling of the birth of Seth. In defense of my choice of it throughout the years, it was the most "common" translation upon my

with the authors' handling of God, which parallels their handling of *'adam*. Throughout the first narrative of the creation (1:1-2:3) one hears consistently of the deity as *'elohim* (God). Starting with 2:4, again consistently, one hears *yahweh 'elohim* (the Lord God) until 4:25 where we have *'elohim* (God) followed, in verse 26 with *yahweh* (the Lord) on its own. Just as *'adam* brackets the *toledot* of "the heavens and the earth" and opens up the *toledot* of Adam, so does *'elohim* that occurs, beyond 4:26, in 5:1 (twice), 22, and 24 (twice), that is, throughout these *toledot*.[21] It is as though God, the originator of the *toledot* of "the heavens and the earth," decided suddenly to intervene *directly* in the origin of Seth. That such is the author's intention is evident from a comparison between this origination and that of Cain, the slayer of Abel, whom Seth is supposed to replace:

> Now Adam (*ha'adam*; the man) knew Eve his wife (*'iššah*; woman),[22] and she conceived and bore Cain (*qayn*), saying, "I have gotten (*qaniti*) a man (*'iš*) with (the help of) the Lord." (4:1)

> And Adam (*'adam*) knew his wife (*'iššah*; woman) again, and she bore a son and called his name (*šem*) Seth (*šet*), for she said, "God (*'elohim*) has appointed (*šat*; the verb from the same root as the noun *šet*) for me another child (*zera'*; seed) instead of Abel, for Cain slew him." (4:25)

And since God's interventions in chapter 1 produced something totally new, the like of which was never before, here also Seth, whose name reflects a direct "appointment, positing, placing,"[23] is brought about as *zera'* (seed) *'aḥer* (other, different), and not as

---

arrival to the USA and was printed in an ecumenical edition that comprised all the additional books found in the LXX. Thus it was a "practical" tool in my classes.

[21] The Lord occurs in verse 29 in a reference to the curse pronounced by the Lord God against the ground in 3:17: "and called his name Noah, saying, 'Out of the ground which the Lord has cursed this one shall bring us relief from our work and from the toil of our hands.'"

[22] The Hebrew *'iššah*—just as the Greek *gynē*, the French *femme* and the German *Frau*—means basically "woman" and secondarily "wife," which allows a word play in all those languages.

[23] Which is the meaning of the Hebrew verb *šit*.

"another child" per RSV.[24] The importance of the original was fully captured by the Vulgate, which has *semen,* as well as the LXX that has *sperma.* The linkage to the divine activity in chapter 1 is evident in that there we find the earliest instances of the root *zrʿ* in reference to vegetation and where *zeraʿ* is used in its original connotation of a seed that is planted:

> And God said, "Let the earth put forth vegetation, plants *yielding seed* (*mazriaʿ zeraʿ*), and fruit trees bearing fruit in which is their *seed,* each according to its kind, upon the earth." And it was so. The earth brought forth vegetation, plants *yielding seed* (*mazriaʿ zeraʿ*) according to their own kinds, and trees bearing fruit in which is their *seed,* each according to its kind. And God saw that it was good ... And God said, "Behold, I have given you every plant *yielding seed* (*zoriaʿ zeraʿ*) which is upon the face of all the earth, and every tree *with seed* (*zoriaʿ zeraʿ*; yielding seed [KJV]) in its fruit; you shall have them for food." (1:11-12, 29)

The only exception is found in 3:15, which refers to human progeny as in 4:25:

> The Lord God said to the serpent, "Because you have done this, cursed are you above all cattle, and above all wild animals; upon your belly you shall go, and dust you shall eat all the days of your life. I will put enmity between you and the woman, and between your *seed* and her *seed*; he shall bruise your head, and you shall bruise his heel." (3:14-15)

One cannot miss that 4:25 is the realization of the divine promise of 3:15.[25] First and foremost, the "kingly" genealogy of Cain, which wanted to enact the initial wish of Adam and Eve to be "like God (gods),"[26] was sidelined by God in favor of a "human" genealogy whereby a human being (Adam) posits

---

[24] That the RSV read the original in an individualizing and historicizing manner is outright unforgivable since not only the LXX and the Vulgate, but also its parent, the KJV, has "another seed." Even the JB has *postérité* and the Arabic has *nasl-an,* both meaning "posterity, progeny."

[25] Unless one subscribes to the Alexandrian Christology that controls theology and sees virtually any verse of the Old Testament as not only pointing to but also actually speaking directly of Jesus Christ.

[26] My readers are reminded that the Hebrew *ʾelohim* is a plural noun.

(Seth) another human being (Enosh). In the book of the *toledot* of Adam, Cain is nowhere to be found. So, God starts afresh, with a new and different (*'aḥer*) seed.

The author's interest in underscoring that it is the same God who is the originator in both cases becomes of the essence when one carefully lends one's ear to the original Hebrew: at the close of the *toledot* of "the heavens and the earth" God is fully discarding *ha'adam* and his progeny through Cain and is starting a totally new humankind—kind of humans—with *'adam* and his progeny Enosh through Seth. This new beginning was "prophesied" by the Lord himself in 3:15. Consider the phraseology of 4:1 and 4:25. In 4:1 we encounter the last mention of *ha'adam* in chapters 1-4 and the second and last mention of Eve in the Old Testament. The two subjects are the same protagonists introduced in 2:23 (Then the man [*ha'adam*] said, "This at last is bone of my bones and flesh of my flesh; she shall be called Woman [*'iššah*], because she was taken out of Man [*'iš*]") and in 3:20 (The man [*ha'adam*] called his wife's [*'iššah*] name Eve, because she was the mother of all living"). On the other hand, in 4:25 we have, literarily speaking, two different protagonists Adam (*'adam*) and his woman (*'iššah*) that is not named. Thus, the new "seed" (*zeraʻ*), harbinger of a new beginning initiated by the God who created the heavens and the earth, is the product of a human male whose name is Adam and "his" woman, that is, any "male and female" as announced in 1:26, and not *ha'adam* who, together with his Eve, bone of his bones, have compromised God's original plan that God had found to be "very good" (v.31). Not only did *ha'adam* force the Lord's hand to have his *'iššah* "built" out of himself as *'iš* (2:23b) rather than formed out of the ground as he and all the animals were formed (vv.8 and 19), but that same *'iššah* who was graced with the most beautiful name Eve, "mother of all living" or, alternatively,[27] "mother of all life," viewed her son as "a thing to be grasped, held unto as a personal possession" (Phil 2:6b) by

---

[27] When the original is heard, as it should be, consonantally.

declaring the child she has acquired "with the Lord" as an *'iš* (male human being) (Gen 4:1). Just as *ha'adam* viewed the *'iššah* as a reflection of his being an *'iš* instead of as a gift from the Lord, Eve also viewed her son as an *'iš*, reflection of her being an *'iššah*, instead of as a gift from the Lord. Contrary to this, the *'iššah* of Adam fully acknowledged her son as the gift of God: "God (*'elohim*) has appointed (*šat*; the verb from the same root as the noun *šet*) for me another child (*zera'*; seed) instead of Abel, for Cain slew him." (v.25) Notice how the idea of gift is underscored in the latter statement where the subject of the action is God (God has appointed), whereas in the former case it is Eve herself who is the subject (I acquired). The difference is also evident in the names of the two children: Cain (*qayn*) is from the same root as the verb "acquire" (*qanah*), whereas Seth (*šet*) is from the same root as the verb "appoint" (*šit*).

The result is that Cain, Eve's progeny, disappears, together with his mother Eve, from the horizon of humankind; whereas Seth, Adam's wife's progeny, survives and produces a being, Enosh (*'enoš*), as much human as his grandfather Adam (*'adam*).[28] The epitome of the irony is that *'enoš* is from the same root as *'iš*, but with a more encompassing connotation. Put otherwise, Adam's wife, in her humility, ultimately got the *'iš* that Eve, in her arrogance, only thought she had. Notice how the divine gift is further recognized: instead of hearing that Seth begat (the active voice *yalad*) Enosh, as was in the case of Adam's wife (and she bore [*watteled*] a son and called his name Seth), the authors intentionally used the passive voice: "To Seth also a son was born (*yullad*), and he called his name Enosh." (v.26a) The hearer cannot escape the distinct impression that both Seth and Enosh were "produced" by God himself.

---

[28] See my comments earlier.

yalad *and Its Cognates*

The authors ingeniously used the different verbal forms of *yalad* whose meaning, in the basic form *qal*, is "give birth (as a mammal would)" and thus, technically speaking, only a woman could be its subject. One will find that whenever the author uses *yalad* with a man as its subject, it has a negative connotation. Consequently, the same author uses a different verbal form in conjunction with the *toledot* of Adam in chapter 5.

In Genesis 3:16; 4:1, 2, 17, 20, 22, 25; and 6:4, it is women that "give birth." What is striking is that, just between 4:17, where it is Cain's wife that gives birth to Enoch, and verses 20 and 22, where it is Lamech's wives who give birth, we hear: "To Enoch was born (*wayyiwwaled*; the passive form *niphal*) Irad; and Irad was the father of (*yalad*; gave birth to) Mehujael, and Mehujael the father of (*yalad*; gave birth to) Methushael, and Methushael the father of (*yalad*; gave birth to) Lamech." (4:18) The intention behind this is unmissable. All three men who "gave birth" disappear completely and are not taken up in the *toledot* of Adam. On the other hand, Cain, Enoch, and Lamech, who are not said to "give birth," will be taken up there. In the case of Cain and Lamech, it is their wives who give birth, whereas Irad "was born" as a gift to Enoch, just as later Enosh was to Seth. All this was done to posit into the *toledot* of Adam the "revised" Enoch who comes from Seth. This Enoch will be the "perfect" human being (5:21-24).[29] The special value of Enosh is underscored through the use of another passive form, the fourth verbal form *pual*, which has the connotation of either an iterative action—stressing intentionality or causality—thus underscoring that the action was indeed willed by God: "To Seth also a son was born (*yullad*), and he called his name Enosh." (4:26a) The passive *pual* is found again in conjunction with the birth of "the daughters of man" (daughters were born [*yulladu*] to them; 6:1) who are viewed positively in opposition to the

---

[29] See my comments later.

"sons of God" who are presented as imposing themselves on the women or taking advantage of them (v.2).[30] The passive *niphal* will be used to speak of the *toledot* of the sons of Noah, with whom the new chapter initiated by God will be implemented: "These are the generations (*toledot*) of the sons of Noah, Shem, Ham, and Japheth; sons were born (*wayyiwaledu*) to them after the flood." (10:1) As for the *toledot* of Adam, the author systematically uses the active fifth verbal form *hiphil*, which is essentially causative, to speak of the begetting, no less than twenty eight times[31] after the following pattern: "When Adam had lived a hundred and thirty years, he became the father of (*wayyoled*; caused to be borne/begotten) a son in his own likeness, after his image, and named him Seth. The days of Adam after he became the father of (*holido*; his having caused to be borne/begotten) Seth were eight hundred years; and he had (*wayyoled*; caused to be borne/begotten) other sons and daughters." (5:3-4)

'adam *versus* ha'adam

One can hear the ingenuity of the authors in their conceiving Genesis 1-4 as a mini-scripture impacting not only the "spirit" of all subsequent stories, but also their terminology and phraseology. God *literally* as well as *literarily* discarded the progeny of Cain and replaced it with that of Seth through Enosh to the extent that *ha'adam* of 1:27 was sidelined in 4:25 in favor of *'adam* of 1:26. The mechanism through which Enosh was produced—the causative passive *yillud* (verbal form *pual*, passive of *piel*)—was picked up as the basic and systematic mechanism of the production—the causative active *yoled* (verbal form *hiphil*)—of all humankind in chapter 5. The option for two different verbal forms to render the idea of causality is intended to differentiate between the divine and the human modes of origination. The author's bias toward *'adam* over *ha'adam* is

---

[30] See further below my comments on that passage.
[31] Twenty-nine if one counts 6:10 which is a repetition of 5:32.

transparent in the way he subsumes the phraseology of 1:26-27 into that of 5:1-3:

> Then God said, "Let us make man (*'adam*) in our *image*, after our *likeness*; and let them have dominion over the fish of the sea, and over the birds of the air, and over the cattle, and over all the earth, and over every creeping thing that creeps upon the earth." So God created man (*ha'adam*) in his own *image*, in the *image* of God he created him; male and female he created them. (1:26-27)

> This is the book of the generations of Adam (*'adam*). When God created man (*'adam*), he made him in the *likeness* of God. Male and female he created them, and he blessed them and named them Man (*'adam*) when they were created. When Adam (*'adam*) had lived a hundred and thirty years, he became the father of a son in his own *likeness*, after his *image*, and named him Seth. (5:1-3)

In both texts, the combination of "image" and "likeness" to describe the reflection of God in the human being is restricted to *'adam*, whereas *ha'adam* is merely in the "image" of God. The author had the opportunity to add "likeness" in 1:27, however, he opted for repeating "image," purposely avoiding "likeness." In chapter 5, the author again betrays his preference in that the first time he mentions exclusively "likeness" (v.1), relegating "likeness" and "image" to v.2. It is *'adam*—and not *ha'adam* as in 1:27—who communicates the fullness of God's reflection. This confirms what I pointed out earlier, namely, that it is *'adam*—and not *ha'adam*—who carries *through animal-like begetting* (*wayyoled*; caused to be borne/begotten) the bridging of the *toledot* of the heavens and earth with the *toledot* of the human beings. Put otherwise, man is not a Platonic eternal "idea"—of the same "essence" as God—that is reflected in the individual being. Rather *ha'adam*, who was lured to fathom that he could be like God, is just a mere "living breathing" (*nepheš ḥayyah*) individual whose name is Adam (*'adam*), and who perpetrates himself through animal-like begetting. Thus, just as Abel, he is bound to disappear as a "passing breath" (*hebel*). The author's insistence on this matter is evident in his tedious drilling of "begetting" into the hearer's ear twenty eight times over thirty-two verses.

Further confirmation of the intended differentiation between *'adam* and *ha'adam* can be found in another feature of 1:26-28. Whereas *'adam* is granted to "have dominion over" (*radah*) the rest of creation (v.26), in the case of *ha'adam* one hears two verbs: "subdue" (*kabaš*) and "have dominion over" (*radah*) (v.28). However, the first is not simply an addition since it is given precedence. More importantly, an "additional" verb would have had the same complement, however, "subdue" is part of an additional *phrase* that includes its own complement:

> And God blessed them, and God said to them, "Be fruitful and multiply, and *fill the earth and subdue it*; and have dominion over the fish of the sea and over the birds of the air and over every living thing that moves upon the earth." (v. 28)

The passage is an intentional set up since *ha'adam* will be asked to "serve" (*'abad*) the earth and "keep/protect" (*šamar*) it (2:15),[32] and not "subdue" it. This is borne out by the difference in connotation between *radah* and *kabaš*. The latter is from a Semitic root (*kbš*) connoting pressure in order to compact something and thus oppression by bringing something or someone "under the boot" so to speak. A few examples would suffice:

> But afterward they turned around and took back the male and female slaves they had set free, and *brought them into subjection* (*wayyikbešum*) as slaves. (Jer 34:11)

> but then you turned around and profaned my name when each of you took back his male and female slaves, whom you had set free according to their desire, and *you brought them into subjection* (*wattikbešu*) to be your slaves. (34:16)

---

[32] See earlier my comments on that verse where I point out then RSV's "till," to render *'abad*, is incorrect. Moreover, *šamar* is the same verb that is used to speak of "keeping" the (commandments of the) Law. That is to say that *ha'adam* is to serve the earth and keep it "with his own life" in view of the following statement (vv.16-17) whereby breaking the divine commandment is punishable by death.

And now you intend *to subjugate* (*likboš*) the people of Judah and Jerusalem, male and female, as your slaves. Have you not sins of your own against the Lord your God? (2 Chr 28:10)

He will again have compassion upon us, *he will tread* (*yikboš*) our iniquities under foot. Thou wilt cast all our sins into the depths of the sea. (Mic 7:19)

And Moses said to them, "If the sons of Gad and the sons of Reuben, every man who is armed to battle before the Lord, will pass with you over the Jordan and the land *shall be subdued* (*nikbešah*) before you, then you shall give them the land of Gilead for a possession." (Num 32:29)

Then the whole congregation of the people of Israel assembled at Shiloh, and set up the tent of meeting there; the land *lay subdued* (*nikbešah*) before them. (Josh 18:1)

"Is not the Lord your God with you? And has he not given you peace on every side? For he has delivered the inhabitants of the land into my hand; and the land *is subdued* (*nikbešah*) before the Lord and his people." (1 Chr 22:18)

On the other hand, *radah* means "rule," the way a senior or someone in charge would:

For *he had dominion over* (*rodeh*) all the region west of the Euphrates from Tiphsah to Gaza, over all the kings west of the Euphrates; and he had peace on all sides round about him (1 Kg 4:24)

Solomon also had seventy thousand burden-bearers and eighty thousand hewers of stone in the hill country, besides Solomon's three thousand three hundred chief officers who were over the work, *who had charge of* (*rodim*) the people who carried on the work. (5:15-16)

These were the chief officers who were over Solomon's work: five hundred and fifty, *who had charge of* (*rodim*) the people who carried on the work. (9:23)

It shall be the most lowly of the kingdoms, and never again exalt itself above the nations; and I will make them so small that they will never again *rule over* (*redot*) the nations. (Ezek 29:15)

This, in turn, explains why *radah* needs to be qualified when used in a negative connotation, the like of subjection:

You shall not rule over him *with harshness*, but shall fear your God. (Lev 25:43)

You may bequeath them to your sons after you, to inherit as a possession for ever; you may make slaves of them, but over your brethren the people of Israel you shall not rule, one over another, *with harshness.* (25:46)

As a servant hired year by year shall he be with him; he shall not rule *with harshness* over him in your sight. (25:53)

Most importantly for my overall thesis is what we hear in Ezekiel concerning the behavior of the shepherds of Israel:

The weak you have not strengthened, the sick you have not healed, the crippled you have not bound up, the strayed you have not brought back, the lost you have not sought, and *with force and harshness* you have ruled them. (Ezek 34:4)

Still the real icing on the cake is to be heard in the concluding statement of the story of the *toledot* of the heavens and the earth: "At that time men began to call upon the name of the Lord." (Gen 4:26) RSV follows KJV in supplying "men" as the subject of the verb "began." The Vulgate and JB supply "he," in referring to Enosh as the subject, following the LXX. The discrepancy is due to the fact that the original verb is in the passive voice *huhal* (it was begun) without either a subject or an indirect complement indicating the agent that performed the calling. All the other instances of that verb in Genesis that are rendered as "began," starting with the LXX, are in the active voice *hehel*:

When men began (*hehel*) to multiply on the face of the ground, and daughters were born to them. (6:1)

Noah was the first (*yahel*) tiller of the soil. He planted a vineyard. (9:20)

Cush became the father of Nimrod; he was the first (*hehel*) on earth to be a mighty man (10:8)

And the Lord said, "Behold, they are one people, and they have all one language; and this is only the beginning (*ḥillam*; their beginning, their starting) of what they will do; an nothing that they propose to do will now be impossible for them." (11:6)

And the seven years of famine began (*teḥillenah*) to come, as Joseph had said. There was famine in all lands; but in all the land of Egypt there was bread. (41:54)

And he searched, beginning (*heḥel*) with the eldest and ending with the youngest; and the cup was found in Benjamin's sack. (44:12)

In all these instances the LXX, followed by all other translations, uses the verb *arkhomai* (begin, start). However, in 4:26, it reads: "This one [he; viz Enosh] *ēlpisen* (hoped, looked forward) that the name of the Lord be called upon." The full "awareness" of the original on the LXX's part militates for my thesis that both texts have the same authors. But, more importantly, the LXX captured the fact that the original presented the first statement regarding true worship as a gift from God—and not something initiated by Enosh (a human being)—which Enosh could only hope that his progeny would follow, which hope will be soon shattered, as reflected in all the four following instances of "began" (6:1; 9:20; 10:8; 11:6).

Calling upon the Name

Let us delve more into the meaning of the phrase "to call upon the name of the Lord" (4:26) and its far reaching connotation, and thus function, in this context. Even a first time hearer of scripture will at one point gather that it is the most succinct expression of worship: doing something and anything after first invoking the name of the deity. Given the sudden switch from "God" (v.25) to "the Lord" (v.26) who issued a "command" for the man to abide by (2:16), attention is drawn to the fact that the true worship required of Enosh and his descendants boils down to unquestioning obedience to God's will, which alone secures the continuance of the life granted by God. Breaking of the command will bring about the punishment of death (v.17b).

This is precisely what will be heard time and again in the law issued at Sinai. That the author had obedience to that law as true worship in mind in 4:26b is borne out by the fact that the law is expressly linked to "the Lord"—the deity of the "command"—rather than to "God": "I am the Lord. I appeared to Abraham, to Isaac, and to Jacob, as God Almighty, but by *my name the Lord* I did not make myself known to them." (Ex 6:2-3)[33] By the same token, up to the end of Genesis 4, there is no reference to any temple and its service. The only "sacrifice" is that of a slaughtered lamb (4:4) by a "shepherd of flock"[34] (v.2). One can sense even in 4:26b the background of the Syrian Desert which I believe to be underlying the stories of the first four chapters of scripture. This can be corroborated in the obvious interplay on "calling the name of" in the episode covering God's new start through a new "seed" in a mere two verses:

> And Adam knew his wife again, and she bore a son and called (*qara'*) his name (*šem*) Seth (*šet*), for she said, "God has appointed for me another seed (RSV has "child") instead of Abel, for Cain slew him." To Seth also a son was born, and he called (*qara'*) his name (*šem*) Enosh. At that time men began to call (*qara'*) upon the name (*šem*) of the Lord. (4:25-26)

This use of the noun *šem* (name) cannot be overlooked especially when it appears in all three cases with the verb "call." It is the "name" when "called" that establishes a being as a valid entity:

> So out of the ground the Lord God formed every beast of the field and every bird of the air, and brought them to the man to see what he would call (*qara'*) them; and whatever the man called (*qara'*) every living creature, that was its name (*šem*). The man gave (*qara'*) names (*šem*) to all cattle, and to the birds of the air, and to every beast of the field but for the man there was not found a helper fit for him. (2:19-20)

---

[33] I discussed earlier in detail the scriptural functional differentiation between *'elohim* (God) and *yahweh* (the Lord), which differentiation is usually eliminated in classical theological thought.

[34] Rendered as "keeper of sheep" by RSV.

Later the man will name that helper fit for him: "The man called (*qara*) his wife's name (*šem*) Eve, because she was the mother of all living." (3:20) This naming is so important that one can argue that Cain and Abel disappeared from the map of humankind *because* they were not "named" as Seth and Enosh were: "Now Adam knew Eve his wife, and she conceived and bore Cain, saying, 'I have gotten a man with the help of the Lord.' And again, she bore his brother Abel." (4:1-2) It is the "naming" of Seth and Enosh that explains their survival in Adam's family tree. The centrality of the "naming" is evident in that, although his wife had already named her son Seth, it is repeated again to establish that Adam is indeed the "begetter" of Seth: "When Adam had lived a hundred and thirty years, he became the father of (*wayyoled*) a son in his own likeness, after his image, and named him Seth." (5:3) Thus, scripturally speaking, the divine image and likeness granted to *'adam* (1:26) is, in turn, transmitted to his son by begetting him through a woman (the *hiphil wayyoled*). Subsequently, the naming of the firstborn son is included in the following "begettings."

Since the calling of the name of a given reality brings that reality to the fore and thus makes it functional for the speaker, the "name" is the audibly tangible "form" of that reality. This is so much so that the name of a reality is, to all purpose and intent, fully equivalent to that reality as is evident from the following statement: "If you are not careful to do all the words of this law which are written in this book, that you may fear *this glorious and awful name*, the Lord your God, then the Lord will bring on you and your offspring extraordinary afflictions, afflictions severe and lasting, and sicknesses grievous and lasting." (Deut 28:58-59) Even more, in another instance the Lord God himself is referred to simply as "the name" (*haššem*): "Now an Israelite woman's son, whose father was an Egyptian, went out among the people of Israel; and the Israelite woman's son and a man of Israel quarreled in the camp, and the Israelite woman's son blasphemed *the Name*, and cursed." (Lev 24:10-11a) That is why the "first commandment" of the covenant comprises the following prohibition: "You shall not take the name of the Lord your God in vain; for the Lord will not hold him guiltless who takes his name in vain." (Ex 20:7) The meaning is incontrovertible: the "name" of the Lord God is not vain, that is not empty, but carries his "functional presence" and thus effectiveness. There is no need to further philosophize or theologize as though this rule applies only to the divine name. The same applies to the utterance of the noun "elephant"; its mere utterance "calls" that animal into a functional presence between the speaker and the hearer. It is a practical matter that allows us to immediately make real an otherwise absent animal without the necessity of bringing a specimen from the zoo! Let me iterate: it is the name in and of itself that carries that reality. However, the same name does not exist in and of itself, but rather is bestowed through its "calling" in a loud utterance— and thus officially stated before witnesses—which is the literal meaning of the Hebrew *qara'*. This is precisely what the man did with his wife (3:20) as well as with the animals (2:19-20a). The difference between these and God is that God is the judge. Calling his name is tantamount to calling or appealing to a judge, and such appeal is as irreversible as an appeal to Caesar; it has to be acted on:

> "If then I am a wrongdoer, and have committed anything for which I deserve to die, I do not seek to escape death; but if there is nothing in their charges against me, no one can give me up to them. I appeal (*epikaloumai*) to Caesar." Then Festus, when he had conferred with his council, answered, "You have appealed (*epikeklēsai*) to Caesar; to Caesar you shall go." ... "But when Paul had appealed (*epikalesamenou*) to be kept in custody for the decision of the emperor, I commanded him to be held until I could send him to Caesar." ... And Agrippa said to Festus, "This man could have been set free if he had not appealed (*epikeklēto*) to Caesar." (Act 25:11-12, 21; 26:32)

The verb rendered into "appeal" is none other than the Greek *epikal(e)ō* found in LXX Genesis 4:26b: "At that time men began to call (*epikaleisthai*) upon the name of the Lord."

So true worship to any deity is tantamount to acknowledging that that deity is a judge, and it is the judge that defines the court of law and the seat of judgment, and not vice versa. Any seat a deity sits on functions as a throne.[35] That is why a true deity is the one that acts factually as a judge, as is evident from Psalm 82:

> A Psalm of Asaph. God has taken his place in the divine council; in the midst of the gods he holds judgment: "How long will you judge unjustly and show partiality to the wicked? *Selah* Give justice to the weak and the fatherless; maintain the right of the afflicted and the destitute. Rescue the weak and the needy; deliver them from the hand of the wicked." They have neither knowledge nor understanding, they walk about in darkness; all the foundations of the earth are shaken. I say, "You are gods, sons of the Most High, all of you; nevertheless, you shall die like men, and fall like any prince." Arise, O God, judge the earth; for to thee belong all the nations!

This is precisely how God shows to the man that he—and not the man—is the sole deity that can differentiate between the good and the evil. However, he did so *as a shepherd* in the garden of Eden where there are no stone buildings. This is precisely how true worship originated with God in Genesis 4:26b. It did not come from the human being who, as we saw with Cain and we shall see later in chapters 10 and 11, is prone to erect cities, towers and temples. These will be completely discarded by God in Isaiah 1 and 66 in favor of true behavior:

> "Hear the word of the Lord, you rulers of Sodom! Give ear to the teaching of our God, you people of Gomorrah! What to me is the multitude of your sacrifices? says the Lord; I have had enough of

---

[35] The Christian Orthodox should have no qualms regarding this reality. Any seat provided for their bishop to sit on during services is referred to as "throne." A pertinent factual anecdote is in the statement of the Late Patriarch of Antioch Ignatius IV. When he was seated in one of the chairs along the length of the dining table, someone suggested to him that he should move to the "head" of the table where there was only one chair. "My friend," he said, "where I am sitting *is* the head of the table."

burnt offerings of rams and the fat of fed beasts; I do not delight
in the blood of bulls, or of lambs, or of he-goats. When you come
to appear before me, who requires of you this trampling of my
courts? Bring no more vain offerings; incense is an abomination
to me. New moon and sabbath and the calling of assemblies -- I
cannot endure iniquity and solemn assembly. Your new moons
and your appointed feasts my soul hates; they have become a
burden to me, I am weary of bearing them. When you spread
forth your hands, I will hide my eyes from you; even though you
make many prayers, I will not listen; your hands are full of blood.
Wash yourselves; make yourselves clean; remove the evil of your
doings from before my eyes; cease to do evil, learn to do good;
seek justice, correct oppression; defend the fatherless, plead for
the widow. Come now, let us reason together, says the Lord:
though your sins are like scarlet, they shall be as white as snow;
though they are red like crimson, they shall become like wool. If
you are willing and obedient, you shall eat the good of the land;
But if you refuse and rebel, you shall be devoured by the sword;
for the mouth of the Lord has spoken." How the faithful city has
become a harlot, she that was full of justice! Righteousness lodged
in her, but now murderers. Your silver has become dross, your
wine mixed with water. Your princes are rebels and companions
of thieves. Every one loves a bribe and runs after gifts. They do
not defend the fatherless, and the widow's cause does not come
to them. (1:10-23)

Thus says the Lord: "Heaven is my throne and the earth is my
footstool; what is the house which you would build for me, and
what is the place of my rest? All these things my hand has made,
and so all these things are mine, says the Lord. But this is the man
to whom I will look, he that is humble and contrite in spirit, and
trembles at my word. He who slaughters an ox is like him who
kills a man; he who sacrifices a lamb, like him who breaks a dog's
neck; he who presents a cereal offering, like him who offers
swine's blood; he who makes a memorial offering of frankincense,
like him who blesses an idol. These have chosen their own ways,
and their soul delights in their abominations; I also will choose
affliction for them, and bring their fears upon them; because,
when I called, no one answered, when I spoke they did not listen;

but they did what was evil in my eyes, and chose that in which I did not delight." (66:1-4)

What is compelling in this regard is that this attack on ritual worship brackets the first book of the Latter Prophets. This bracketing does not leave room for the hearer to think that God might change his mind concerning this matter.

ḥalal

I should like to revisit here the verb *huḥal* (the *hophal* [passive voice] of the verb *ḥalal*) found in Genesis 4:26 in order to underscore that any other form of worship, especially temple services of any sort, are not only an abhorrence, but outright blasphemy according to scripture. This is to say that the concluding verse of the *toledot* of the heavens and the earth, God's total creation, is setting up the hearer to perceive immediately the blasphemy in the action of the human beings in 11:1-9, which is described through the *hiphil* (active voice) of the same verb *ḥalal* (v.8). First and foremost, it is imperative to realize that the intentionality behind *huḥal* is evidenced in that the *hophal* form of that verb occurs once, and only once, in the entire Old Testament, in Genesis 4:26b.

The original connotation of the Semitic *ḥalal* is to undo, untie, and thus solve, resolve. In Arabic it is used to speak about solving a mathematical problem or resolving an issue, as well as untying a knot. It is used in churchly vocabulary to speak of absolution whether of sins or of something binding as an oath or a church rule, such as fasting. Hence, its connotation of something "allowed." Most of my readers living in the Western hemisphere are familiar with the stores that sell meat *ḥalal*, that is, meat that may be consumed without contravening the rule that forbids a Muslim from consuming meat of animal whose blood has not been fully drained. The opposite of *ḥalal* is *ḥaram*, which is from the same root as *ḥerem* that connotes excommunication, anathema, blacklisting, marking as taboo.[36] When used as an adjective in Arabic, *halal* means "allowed" whereas *haram* means "prohibited."   True worship was "allowed," "initiated" (passive voice *hophal*; 4:26b) by God. All the other "initiations" (active voice *hiphil* [*hehel*]), whose agents are human beings, are expressions of arrogance. The seriousness of this matter is evidenced in that both the causative form *hiphil* and its cognate *piel* (*hillel*),[37] which is also causative, appear profusely in scripture, especially in Leviticus and Ezekiel,[38] to reflect the sense of profanation, sacrilege, blasphemy. Note the following instances where the noun complement is precisely the "name" of God:

> You shall not give any of your children to devote them by fire to Molech, and so profane (*piel*) the name of your God: I am the Lord. (Lev 18:21)

> And you shall not swear by my name falsely, and so profane (*piel*) the name of your God: I am the Lord. (19:12)

> I myself will set my face against that man, and will cut him off from among his people, because he has given one of his children to Molech, defiling my sanctuary and profaning (*piel*) my holy name. (20:3)

> They shall be holy to their God, and not profane (*piel*) the name of their God; for they offer the offerings by fire to the Lord, the bread of their God; therefore they shall be holy. (21:6)

> And you shall not profane (*piel*) my holy name, but I will be hallowed among the people of Israel; I am the Lord who sanctify you, (22:32)

> As for you, O house of Israel, thus says the Lord God: Go serve every one of you his idols, now and hereafter, if you will not listen

---

[36] See my discussion of *herem* in *C-Josh* 127-30.

[37] The corresponding Arabic *hallala* is used in churchly vocabulary to speak of allowing food on certain days of Lent, which is otherwise not allowed, that is to say, to "render something admissible [*halal*]."

[38] I have shown in my commentary on Ezekiel *C-Ezek* how these two books are closely interrelated.

to me; but my holy name you shall no more profane (*piel*) with
your gifts and your idols. (Ezek 20:39)

But when they came to the nations, wherever they came, they
profaned (*piel*) my holy name, in that men said of them, but I had
concern for my holy name, which the house of Israel caused to
be profaned (*piel*) among the nations to which they came.
Therefore say to the house of Israel, Thus says the Lord God: It
is not for your sake, O house of Israel, that I am about to act, but
for the sake of my holy name, which you have profaned (*piel*)
among the nations to which you came. And I will vindicate the
holiness of my great name, which has been profaned (passive *pual*)
among the nations, and which you have profaned (*piel*) among
them; and the nations will know that I am the Lord, says the Lord
God, when through you I vindicate my holiness before their eyes.
(36:20-23)

The last instance sheds light on our discussion. In it the *piel*
parallels its passive voice *pual* (passive voice) that corresponds to
the passive voice *hophal* found also in Genesis 4:26b instead of a
hiphil (active voice). Still, unlike Genesis where the unnamed
agent is obviously God, in Ezekiel the agent of the action are
the disobedient people as is evident from the parallel statement
where they function as the grammatical subject of the *piel* form.
Consequently, it is only when God himself allows an action
relating to his name, that the result is positive: his name is
sanctified (hallowed) or glorified. When we are the initiators,
then we are committing perjury, sacrilege, and blasphemy.
Moreover, the centrality as well as the seriousness of the matter
concerning the "calling" of the "name" will be apparent in the
toledot of Noah, that of his sons, and that of Shem (chapters 6-
11).

laqaḥ *(take)*

It would be well worth our while to delve into the phraseology
of Genesis 2-3 in order to perceive how the authors set the stage
for that scriptural thesis in those two chapters. I should like to
concentrate on the interplay between the two nouns, ground

and dust, and the verb "take" that are found together in 3:19 as part of the divine curse addressed to *ha'adam*.[39] In order to make our task simpler, let me post the different pertinent passages where the nouns and the verb occur:

> then the Lord God formed man *of dust from the ground,* and breathed into his nostrils the breath of life; and man became a living being (Gen 2:7)

> The Lord God took *(qal)* the man and put him in the garden of Eden to till it and keep it (2:15)

> So the Lord God caused a deep sleep to fall upon the man, and while he slept took *(qal)* one of his ribs and closed up its place with flesh; and the rib which the Lord God had taken *(qal)* from the man he made into a woman and brought her to the man. Then the man said, "This at last is bone of my bones and flesh of my flesh; she shall be called Woman, because she was taken out *(pual)* of Man." (2:21-23)

> So when the woman saw that the tree was good for food, and that it was a delight to the eyes, and that the tree was to be desired to make one wise, she took *(qal)* of its fruit and ate; and she also gave some to her husband, and he ate. (3:6)

> In the sweat of your face you shall eat bread till you return to the ground, for out of it you were taken *(pual)*; you are dust, and to dust you shall return. The man called his wife's name Eve, because she was the mother of all living. And the Lord God made for Adam and for his wife garments of skins, and clothed them. Then the Lord God said, "Behold, the man has become like one of us, knowing good and evil; and now, lest he put forth his hand and take *(qal)* also of the tree of life, and eat, and live for ever"— therefore the Lord God sent him forth from the garden of Eden, to till the ground from which he was taken *(pual)*. (3:19-23)

---

[39] I said "addressed to" and not "against" because the target of the curse is *ha'adamah* (the ground) rather than *ha'adam* (vv.17-19): "And to Adam he said, 'Because you have listened to the voice of your wife, and have eaten of the tree of which I commanded you, 'You shall not eat of it,' cursed is the ground because of you; in toil you shall eat of it all the days of your life.'"

It is evident that in all these instances of "take" (*laqah*) whenever the agent is God himself, the connotation is constructive. However, whenever the agent is the human being, male or female, the connotation is negative in the sense that the action taken is forbidden. The same approach is found in the following chapters through the *toledot* of both Adam and Noah that run until the end of chapter 9. Whenever God is the agent, or whenever a human being—or even the earth—"takes" or "receives"[40] someone or something at the command of God, or at least according to the will of God, the connotation is positive:

> And now you are cursed from the ground, which has opened its mouth to receive your brother's blood from your hand. (4:11)[41]

> Enoch walked with God; and he was not, for God took him. (5:24)

> Also take with you every sort of food that is eaten, and store it up; and it shall serve as food for you and for them. (6:21)

> Take with you seven pairs of all clean animals, the male and his mate; and a pair of the animals that are not clean, the male and his mate. (7:2)

> But the dove found no place to set her foot, and she returned to him to the ark, for the waters were still on the face of the whole earth. So he put forth his hand and took her and brought her into the ark with him. (8:9)

> Then Noah built an altar to the Lord and took of every clean animal and of every clean bird, and offered burnt offerings on the altar. (8:20)

> Then Shem and Japheth took a garment, laid it upon both their shoulders, and walked backward and covered the nakedness of their father; their faces were turned away, and they did not see their father's nakedness. (9:23)

---

[40] *laqah* can mean either as in our English when one takes something that is given to one. A classic cultic example is the full equation in meaning between "taking communion" and "receiving communion."

[41] The verb "receive" renders the original *laqah* that is translated as "take" in the following instances.

To the contrary, whenever action is taken by a human being of his own will and choosing, then the connotation is negative:

> And Lamech took two wives; the name of the one was Adah, and the name of the other Zillah. (4:19)

> The sons of God saw that the daughters of men were fair; and they took to wife such of them as they chose. (6:2)

The last quotation fully justifies my having brought into the picture 3:19 and 2:17 while commenting on the intention behind the action of the "sons of God" in "taking" for themselves whomever they pleased among the "daughters of men" (6:2) in order to produce a progeny of assumedly "mighty men." Whatever and whomever they may "grab" in order to ensure their presumed trait of immortality has been preemptively foiled by God himself in chapters 2 and 3.

In all three instances where reference is made to a divine action in the passive voice, the fourth verbal form *pual* (passive of the third verbal form, the active *piel*) is used instead of the logically expected second verbal form *niphal* (passive of the basic form *qal*). This may not seem a big deal in and of itself until one recalls that the authors handled the verb *yalad* (give birth) in the same way by using the form *pual* instead of the expected form *niphal*.[42] Since the *niphal* of both verbs is extant in scripture, the use of the causative form *pual* must be taken as deliberate with the view of underscoring God's objectives in the biblical narrative. In other words, God intended to accomplish the action of taking and that of giving birth in the way each is described as having taken place.

banah

In the scriptural stories, God alone controls his plan: he pursues and realizes it despite the human beings' consistently disobedient behavior. It is through the use of an ingenious play

---

[42] See above.

on another important verb, *banah* (build), that the authors disclose this plan. Since the basic connotation of *banah* is erecting a building, it is by definition a negative term in scripture. Suffice it to point out here that four of the seven instances of that verb in Genesis 1-11 occur in the last two chapters in conjunction with the erection of kingly buildings in Babel:

> From that land he (Nimrod) went into Assyria and built Nineveh. (10:11)

> Then they said, "come, let us build ourselves a city, and a tower with its top in the heavens, and let us make a name for ourselves, lest we be scattered abroad upon the face of the whole earth. And the Lord came down to see the city and the tower, which the sons of men had built. And the Lord said, "Behold, they are one people, and have all one language; and this is only the beginning of what they will do; and nothing that they propose to do will now be impossible for them" ... So the Lord scattered them abroad from there over the face of all the earth, and they left off building the city. (11:4-6, 8)

If you add the reference to Cain's building a city (4:17), the ratio is five out of seven instances that refer to urban civilization. The remaining two instances of the author's handling of the verb *banah* (2:22; 8:20) are worthy of our attention. The latter occurrence only *seems* to reflect a positive connotation because it speaks of building an altar to the Lord: "Then Noah built an altar to the Lord, and took of every clean animal and of every clean bird, and offered burnt offerings (*wayya'al 'olah*) on the altar." (8:20) On the one hand, the sacrificial act entailed killing animals, which was not officially allowed until 9:3-4. On the other hand, an altar is an erection of stones that is reflective of a sedentary life. In fact 8:20 is phrased in such a way to presage Noah's opting for a sedentary life around the vineyard whose planting he initiated (9:20). This intention of the authors can be seen in that earlier, when describing the offering of Abel the "shepherd of flock," they avoided the technical sacrificial phrase "offered burnt offerings" and used instead the generic "brought": "and Abel brought (*hebi'*) of the firstlings of his flock and of their fat portions." (4:4a)

The earlier occurrence of *banah* deals with the "building" of woman in conjunction with her being "taken from" the man:

> Then the Lord God said, "It is not good that the man should be alone; I will make him a helper *fit for him*" (*kenegdo*, from the preposition *neged*). So out of the ground the Lord God formed every beast of the field and every bird of the air, and brought them to the man to see what he would call them; and whatever the man called every living creature, that was its name. The man gave names to all cattle, and to the birds of the air, and to every beast of the field; but for the man there was not found a helper *fit for him* (*kenegdo*). So the Lord God caused a deep sleep to fall upon the man, and while he slept took (*laqah*) one of his ribs and closed up its place with flesh; and the rib which the Lord God had taken (*laqah*) from the man he made (*banah*; built) into a woman and brought her to the man. Then the man said, "This at last is bone of my bones and flesh of my flesh; she shall be called Woman, because she was taken (*luqqah*) out of Man." (2:18-23)

The Togetherness of Human and Animal

The versatility of this passage is astounding in that it foresees as well as prepares for the following chapters that concern procreation as a blessing from God and the respective roles of the man and the woman in begetting children for the perpetuity of humankind. What is remarkable is how the tension between those roles, which will be resolved in 6:1-8, is set up in chapters 1-3. Any hearer of scripture cannot possibly miss that procreation is of paramount interest for the authors. Anthropology, that is to say, the concern for the "human person," let alone any comment on the psychology of human male or female, is totally absent in chapters 1-11. Men and women are presented solely from the perspective of sexuality, which is *the* means of procreation. This is borne out in how the authors handle the pair "male and female" (*zakar uneqebah*). Not only does this phrase qualify *'adam* (5:2) as well as *ha'adam* (1:27), but it is used repeatedly in conjunction with all the other animals:

> So God created man *ha'adam* in his own image, in the image of God he created him; male and female (*zakar uneqebah*) he created them. (1:27)

> When God created man *'adam*, he made him in the likeness of God. Male and female (*zakar uneqebah*) he created them, and he blessed them and named them Man *'adam* when they were created. (5:1-2)

> And of every *living* (*hay*) thing of *all flesh*, you shall bring two of every sort into the ark, to *keep them alive* (*hayot*) with you; they shall be male and female (*zakar uneqebah*) (6:19)

> Take with you seven pairs of all clean animals, *the male and his mate* (*'iš we'išto*); and a pair of the animals that are not clean, *the male and his mate* (*'iš we'išto*); and seven pairs of the birds of the air also, male and female (*zakar uneqebah*), to keep their kind alive upon the face of all the earth. (7:2-3)

> Of clean animals, and of animals that are not clean, and of birds, and of everything that creeps on the ground, two and two (*šenayim šenayim*), male and female (*zakar uneqebah*), went into the ark with Noah, as God had commanded Noah. (7:8-9)

> And they that entered, male and female (*zakar uneqebah*) of *all flesh*, went in as God had commanded him; and the Lord shut him in (7:16)

Four points are relevant to our discussion. First and foremost, in the Old Testament the phrase "male and female" is confined to the just quoted passages that are found in Genesis 1-7 where the topic is not only procreation, but also survival of the *toledot* of the heavens and the earth.[43] Secondly, the stress that the pair are to be taken together can be seen in the parallel phrase "two (and) two" (*šenayim šenayim*; 7:9). Thirdly, the same phrase applies equally to the entire animal realm so that animal life

---

[43] Thereafter, the phrase "male *or* female" occurs a few times starting, much later, with Leviticus 3:1.

would be maintained along with human life: "And of every living (*ḥay*) thing of all flesh, you shall bring two of every sort into the ark, to keep them alive (*ḥayot*) *with you*." (6:19) Last, and in no way least, the oneness between human and animal realms, or rather realm, resonates in the parallel phrase *'iš we'išto*, literally "a man and his woman/wife," to refer to animals (7:2). And as though all this underscoring were not enough, at the end of the flood story one hears the totally unexpected, "So Noah went forth, and his sons and his wife and his sons' wives with him. And every beast, every creeping thing, and every bird, everything that moves upon the earth, went forth *by families* (*lemišpeḥotehem*; *according to their families*) out of the ark." (Gen 8:18-19) This is the sole instance in scripture where the noun *mišpaḥah* occurs in reference to animals.[44] Not only that, but this is the first occurrence of that noun in scripture. When a few verses later, one encounters, no fewer than five times, the same *mišpeḥot* used in conjunction with the descendants of Noah's three sons (10:5, 18, 20, 31, 32), the hearer is already programmed to understand it in function of its first occurrence. That is to say, it is the animal "setting of communal life" that defines the human setting. This is reflective of shepherd-like life where the shepherd and his family are "at one" with their flock.

The togetherness, if not oneness, between humans and especially land animals is found only in Genesis 1, where the creation of both takes place on the sixth day and both are included under one blessing for their procreation. In chapter 2, the mention on God's lips of "a helper fit for" the man refers to the animals (v.18) and, only thereafter, to the woman (v.20). Moreover the animals were formed out of the ground (v.19) just as the man was (v.7). The woman was not even formed, but rather "built" (*banah*; v.22). One can see how this is disconcerting for "scholars" and "theologians" who opt for "political correctness" at the expense of the authorial integrity.

---

[44] Normally *mišpaḥah* (plural *mišpeḥot*) refers to a human clan and by extension a village.

The Semitic Arabic (*bana'*) as well as the LXX *ō[i]kodomēsen* and the Vulgate *aedificavit* kept in tune with the original Hebrew. However, the more recent European translations shy away from using built: KJV and RSV use "made," whereas JB has "fashioned" that corresponds to "modelled" (vv.7 and 19), and the Spanish has "formed" in all three instances (vv. 7, 19, 22).

It was the arrogance of *ha'adam* that forced God to resort to the "artificiality" of building the woman out of building blocks provided by *ha'adam* instead of forming her out of the ground. Indeed, *ha'adam* asserted boastfully that the woman was not only "bone of his bones" but "flesh of his flesh" (v.23) to the extent that they became "one flesh," that is to say, the flesh of *ha'adam*. In other words, *ha'adam* wanted the woman to be defined not only through him, but actually by him, as is clear from his statement concerning the origin of the "name" he bestowed on the woman: the *'iššah* is *'iššah* because she is from *'iš* linguistically and literally. In scripture, naming is functional. So in the mind and attitude of *ha'adam*, the connotation is that woman is subordinate to him. This prepares for the later divine statement describing that relationship: "To the woman he [the Lord God] said, 'I will greatly multiply your pain in childbearing; in pain you shall bring forth children, yet *your desire shall be for your husband, and he shall rule over you.*'" (3:16). Notice how this subjection is framed within the context of begetting. This state of affairs will culminate in 6:1-2 where it will be addressed and corrected by God himself. As in the case of the institution of kingship in 1 Samuel 8, and as I have repeatedly pointed out, because God allows something is not to be taken as reflecting his will regarding that matter. The solution to the dilemma, brought about by the propensity of *ha'adam* to implement his own will, will be resolved by *ha'elohim* in 6:1-8 within the context of begetting. This solution will be revisited time and again with a series of "barren" women who will give birth "with the Lord" rather than with their husbands. The first and most striking story is that of Sarah.[45] She is followed by a series of others, such as Manoah's wife and Samson's mother (Judg 13), and Hannah, Samuel's mother (1 Sam 1), down to Mary, mother of Jesus. Theology continues to tax the common believers' wits and is still losing energy as well because it historicizes the scriptural stories and individualizes the scriptural personalities. In doing so, classical theology, which was originally devised and written by Greco-Romans, perceived scripture à la Iliad and Odyssey and then seasoned it with Plato's eternal *logos* terminology. This resulted in the inexplicable "mysteries" of "the trinity" and "the incarnation." Theology should have followed Paul's authoritative teaching in Galatians 4 where he points out what was already clear in the Old Testament namely, the Sarah of Genesis and the new Jerusalem of Isaiah are *one and the same* scriptural "entity":

> For it is written that Abraham had two sons, one by a slave and one by a free woman. But the son of the slave was born according to the flesh, the son of the free woman through promise. Now this is an allegory: these women are two covenants. One is from Mount Sinai, bearing children for slavery; she is Hagar. Now Hagar is Mount Sinai in Arabia; she corresponds to the present Jerusalem, for she is in slavery with her children. But the Jerusalem above is free, and she is our mother. For it is written, "Rejoice, O barren one who does not bear; break forth and shout, you who are not in travail; for the children of the desolate one are many more than the children of her that is married." Now we, brethren, like Isaac, are children of promise. (Gal 4:22-28)

Even a first time hearer of scripture cannot be but struck by the fact that the mention of Sarah is confined to Genesis and Isaiah 51:2 in the entire Old Testament. This can hardly be taken as coincidental, especially since the new divine city is depicted in

---

[45] See later my comments on the circumstances surrounding Sarah's begetting her son Isaac.

Isaiah—and specifically referenced in Galatians—in terms of shepherd life:

> Sing, O barren one, who did not bear; break forth into singing and cry aloud, you who have not been in travail! For the children of the desolate one will be more than the children of her that is married, says the Lord. Enlarge the place of your tent, and let the curtains of your habitations be stretched out; hold not back, lengthen your cords and strengthen your stakes. (Is 54:1-2)

What I tried to show up to this point is that this same "entity"—or rather proposed scriptural "story"—of a woman begetting without the interference of a man, yet through God himself, is intimated in Genesis 6:1-8 and even earlier in 4:25-26. Put otherwise, any "seed" (*zeraʿ*) that is deemed to live is the making of God (Genesis 1); its survival depends on the promise of the Lord God in 3:15 that is realized in 4:25-26. A realized promise functions as a judgment on any future lack of trust in a divine promise. Both Abraham and Sarah who laughed at God's promise were stuck with the gift of Isaac. Gift it is, and yet it will function as a constant reminder that it is God who will forever remain "laughing" at them and, through them, at their progeny, the *toledot* of Isaac whose name in Hebrew literally means "he [God] laughs." Moreover, the same God who "laughs" at Israel, the *toledot* of Jacob, Isaac's son, will also "laugh" at all nations who, through sheer force and presumed superiority, assume that they can prevail against the Lord and his city Zion:

> Why do the nations conspire, and the peoples plot in vain? The kings of the earth set themselves, and the rulers take counsel together, against the Lord and his anointed, saying, "Let us burst their bonds asunder, and cast their cords from us." He who sits in the heavens laughs; the Lord has them in derision. Then he will speak to them in his wrath, and terrify them in his fury, saying, "I have set my king on Zion, my holy hill." (Ps 2:1-6)

> Thou, Lord God of hosts, art God of Israel. Awake to punish all the nations; spare none of those who treacherously plot evil. *Selah* Each evening they come back, howling like dogs and prowling

about the city. There they are, bellowing with their mouths, and
snarling with their lips—for "Who," they think, "will hear us?"
But thou, O Lord, dost laugh at them; thou dost hold all the
nations in derision. (Ps 59:5-8)

We see how the circle started in Genesis 1-4 reaches its fullness
not only in Isaiah, the first book of the Latter Prophets, but also
in Psalms, the first book (the Hebrew canon) of the Ketubim. As
we shall see later, the New Testament does not bring anything
new content wise—if it were so, then it would be a heresy—
rather its novelty is one of approach: whereas the addressee of
the Old Testament is the scriptural Israel, thus bringing it under
direct divine judgment, the New Testament, containing the
exact same teaching as the Old Testament, is addressed directly
to the scriptural nations thus putting them also under divine
judgment:

> For I want you to know, brethren, that our fathers were all under
> the cloud, and all passed through the sea, and all were baptized
> into Moses in the cloud and in the sea, and all ate the same
> supernatural food and all drank the same supernatural drink. For
> they drank from the supernatural Rock which followed them, and
> the Rock was Christ. Nevertheless with most of them God was
> not pleased; for they were overthrown in the wilderness. Now
> these things are warnings for us, not to desire evil as they did. Do
> not be idolaters as some of them were; as it is written, "The
> people sat down to eat and drink and rose up to dance." We must
> not indulge in immorality as some of them did, and twenty-three
> thousand fell in a single day. We must not put the Lord to the
> test, as some of them did and were destroyed by serpents; nor
> grumble, as some of them did and were destroyed by the
> Destroyer. Now these things happened to them as a warning, but
> they were written down for our instruction, upon whom the end
> of the age has come. (1 Cor 10:1-11)

With the scriptural message already etched in stone in the first
two *toledot* (Genesis 1-5), the authors are ready to move their
hearers on to the next scenario of their overarching scriptural
story by implementing their thesis that shepherd-like life is the
answer to all the ills of urban civilization anchored around

kingship. In the following *toledot*, those of Noah, the authors include *during his lifespan* the lengthy parenthesis of the flood where Noah will "remain" not only through begetting, but also through the fully harmonious symbiosis between him, his children *and their wives*, on the one hand, and the vegetation and the animal kingdom on the other hand. As we shall see, primacy is given to the vegetation, brought forth on the third day of creation (1:11-13) that would insure the survival of both animals and humans throughout the generations:

> And God said, "Behold, I have given you every plant yielding seed which is upon the face of all the earth and every tree with seed in its fruit; you shall have them for food. And to every beast of the earth, and to every bird of the air, and to everything that has breath of life, I have given every green plant for food." And it was so. (vv.29-30)

It is the *'adamah*/ground, lacking *nephesh*/breathing yet full of life, that sustains *nephesh*-ic life on earth and under the heavens. Such is the reality of shepherd life in the Syrian Desert.

The flood story contained within the span of the *toledot* of Noah is not alarming news to the hearers simply because they are alive and well, listening to scripture. This is proof enough that the Lord did not carry through his decision to blot out *all* life upon the ground. The overwhelming stretching of the flood story over almost three full chapters is meant to convey instruction. What is definitely striking, however, is that the instruction straddles both the *toledot* of Adam and of Noah. At the end of the former, we hear that "Noah found favor in the eyes of the Lord" (6:8) who had just decided "to blot out all life he had created from the face of the ground" (v.7). The original Hebrew does not have the adversative "but" (v.8) before Noah, rather it has simply the conjunction "and." This in itself piques the hearer's attention to look forward to the reason behind that. Yet, the reason is not given within the confines of the *toledot* of Adam, but rather in a parenthetical phrase in the opening statement of the *toledot* of Noah: "These are the generations of

Noah. Noah was a righteous man, blameless in his generation;
Noah walked with God. And Noah had (*wayyoled*; gave birth
indirectly to) three sons, Shem, Ham, and Japheth." (Gen 6:9-
10) The addition of 9b (Noah was a righteous man, blameless in
his generation; Noah walked with God) interrupts the natural
flow between verse 9a (These are the generations of Noah) and
verse 10 (Noah had three sons, Shem, Ham, and Japheth). Not
only that, 9b starts with the repetition of the name Noah instead
of being attached through the relative pronoun *'ašer* (who). The
straddling of this information concerning Noah is the reason for
the Lord's rescinding his initial decision. It is an additional
literary device that tightens the link between the *toledot* of Adam
and that of Noah and, in its own way, seals the scriptural
premise that humankind is one and uninterrupted and will
remain forever anchored in Genesis 1. In other words, the one
God has only one world. This will be corroborated in the flood
story where "all living beings" will be joined with the human
beings in Noah's ark just as they were lumped together in the
divine verdict of 6:7.

   The reason behind Noah's finding favor in the Lord's eyes is
a matter of "behavior," which behavior is living according to
God's will. So the lengthy testing story of the flood both looks
ahead and prepares for the even lengthier story of the issuance
of the Law and the ominous and testing trek through the
wilderness   covered   in   four   books,   Exodus   through
Deuteronomy. Beyond that, the re-reading of the Law of
Deuteronomy to both the scriptural Israel and the scriptural
nations (Josh 8:32-35) will preface the still lengthier story of
these two scriptural entities throughout the Prophets, the second
part of the Old Testament. In the Pentateuch and in the
Prophets, both Israel and the nations will prove to be "*neither
righteous nor blameless*," and thus *not* having "walked with
God." However, at the end time, there will not be mercy as in
the times of Noah. Given that one hears in Psalms of the
repeated failure of all ("there is none that does good, no, not
one"; Ps 14:3; 53:3), the voice of the Lord God will resound

through Ezekiel's lips or rather in his scroll written on both sides (Ezek 1:9-10):

> Son of man, when a land sins against me by acting faithlessly, and I stretch out my hand against it, and break its staff of bread and send famine upon it, and cut off from it man and beast, even if these three men, Noah, Daniel, and Job, were in it, they would deliver but their own lives by their righteousness, says the Lord God. If I cause wild beasts to pass through the land, and they ravage it, and it be made desolate, so that no man may pass through because of the beasts; even if these three men were in it, as I live, says the Lord God, they would deliver neither sons nor daughters; they alone would be delivered, but the land would be desolate. Or if I bring a sword upon that land, and say, Let a sword go through the land; and I cut off from it man and beast; though these three men were in it, as I live, says the Lord God, they would deliver neither sons nor daughters, but they alone would be delivered. Or if I send a pestilence into that land, and pour out my wrath upon it with blood, to cut off from it man and beast; even if Noah, Daniel, and Job were in it, as I live, says the Lord God, they would deliver neither son nor daughter; they would deliver but their own lives by their righteousness. For thus says the Lord God: "How much more when I send upon Jerusalem my four sore acts of judgment, sword, famine, evil beasts, and pestilence, to cut off from it man and beast! Yet, if there should be left in it any survivors to lead out sons and daughters, when they come forth to you, and you see their ways and their doings, you will be consoled for the evil that I have brought upon Jerusalem, for all that I have brought upon it. They will console you, when you see their ways and their doings; and you shall know that I have not done without cause all that I have done in it, says the Lord God." (14:13-23)

9

The Toledot of Adam (Genesis 5)

The most compelling indication that the author intended a different angle in dealing with *ha'adam* of Genesis 1-4 and *'adam* in Genesis 5:1-6:8 is found at the start of chapter 5. The *toledot* of Adam are introduced with the unique instance of "this is (*zeh*; singular corresponding to book) the *book of* the *toledot* of," which sounds like a "title" of an independent and self-contained literary work. All the other *toledot* in the biblical narrative are introduced with the phrase "these are (*'elleh*; plural corresponding to *toledot*) the *toledot* of." In doing this, the authors wanted to draw attention to the "independence" of Genesis 5:1-6:8 in order that it be heard on its own ground as a book. By the same token, it ensured that the topic "the *toledot* of the heavens and the earth" was closed, thus locking Genesis 1-4 into a self-standing section that encompasses the *complete story* of the heavens and the earth from the scriptural perspective. This intention is confirmed by the fact that the authors did not entitle the genealogy of Cain (Gen 4:17-24) as *toledot*, which they could have easily as well as justifiably done.

But, one would inquire, if the entire scriptural message is subsumed in Genesis 1-4, what is the function of the *toledot* of Adam in the scheme of Genesis 1-11, which does not yet deal with Abraham and his descendants who are the main proponents of the scriptural story?

Its function is pivotal on many levels. Besides its most striking feature, which is repeated again and again, that man begets his children indirectly through woman, the *toledot* of Adam presents us with a series of important characteristics. The first one underscores the centrality of the main feature of the scriptural premise, that is, the repeated and stubborn disobedience and the equally repeated divine "repentance" offering a second

202 THE RISE OF SCRIPTURE

chance to the human beings. In the first instance, Adam contravenes God's command not to eat of the tree of the knowledge of the good and the evil, however, instead of the promised capital punishment, Adam is "exiled" and allowed to live. In the second instance, Cain kills his brother Abel and is punished to wander "in exile" instead of the expected capital punishment. Rather than wandering and living a life as a shepherd, Cain establishes a city and a dynasty. God puts an end to this dynasty and opts in its stead for that of Seth and Enosh. The third time, at their apex, in their tenth generation, the human beings, subsumed as *ha'adam* (6:1), commit, at its fullest scale, the aberration of considering themselves divine beings, which is strictly forbidden early on in Genesis 2; they start acting as "sons of *the* divinity (what is divine by definition)" (*bene ha'elohim*).[1]

Just as he salvaged Abel's memory through Seth (4:25), God salvages Cain's memory, however, in a more subdued way through the *toledot* of Adam. Cain (*qayn*), being the epitome of disobedience in not having repented of his homicide, is preserved in an indirect manner through Kenan (*qe[y]nan*), the son of Enosh—the second Adam[2] (5:10). He is belittled, however, in that he appears as the son of *'adam* via Seth and Enosh, whereas in chapter 4 he is the immediate son of *ha'adam*. In other words, the *toledot* of Adam "salvages" the Cain of the *toledot* of the heavens and the earth by "humanizing" him. This complete turnabout is reflected in the change of the name from Cain to Kenan. The Hebrew consonantal original of Kenan *qynn* is the same as *qyn* (Cain) with the addition of the consonant *n*. Later we shall encounter the descendants of this Kenan (*qynn*) as Kenites (Num 24:21; Judg 1:16; 4:11, 17 [twice]; 5:24); the consonantal Hebrew for Kenite is *qyni*, someone pertaining to *qyn* (Cain).

---

[1] Notice the definite article *ha(l)* before *'elohim*.
[2] See above.

This genuine interest in Cain is evident in that not only Enoch but also Lemech is subsumed in the *toledot* of Adam.[3] These three men, who are said to have begotten indirectly in chapter 4, are "salvaged" in that they are part of Adam's progeny, whereas the other three men of Cain's family—Irad, Mehujael, and Methushael (4:18)—are "eliminated." However, this inclusion offers more than meets the eye at first glance. A closer look will reveal that the newly introduced Noah as well as Enoch and Lemech, the two names taken from Cain's "family tree," play a special role in giving a few twists to that otherwise iterative genealogy. These twists are interrelated as well as essential from the purview of the biblical story.

Enoch

I showed earlier that, in Cain's genealogy, Enoch (*hanok*) had been hijacked by his father Cain to function against his original destiny: instead of acknowledging him as a gift from God and dedicating him to this same God, Cain opted to dedicate to him the city he built. In Adam's genealogy, Enoch recovers his true destiny. He is reestablished to reflect the meaning of his name, "renewal." In chapter 4, his father Cain wanted to change him from a being of flesh, that is, a "human being" according to God's will by the standard of Genesis 1, into a being of stone, a city (4:17). God intervenes to "renew" that Enoch into a being of flesh who is obedient to God's will. This teaching echoes that of Ezekiel, "the father of scripture":

> And I will give them one heart, and put a new spirit within them; I will take the *stony heart* out of their flesh and give them a *heart of flesh*, that they may *walk* (*halak*) in my statutes and keep my ordinances and obey them; and they shall be my people, and I will be their God. (11:19-20)

---

[3] As we shall see later this divine concern in *all* human beings, even those who look as though they are pushed aside, in the detailed *toledot* of Esau (Gen 36:9-43) and Ishmael (25:12-16).

A new heart I will give you, and a new spirit I will put within you; and I will take out of your flesh the *heart of stone* and give you a *heart of flesh*. And I will put my spirit within you, and cause you to *walk* (*halak*) in my statutes and be careful to observe my ordinances. (36:26-27)

The new Enoch's obedience is expressed in his "walking with God." Twice he is said to have walked (*hithallek*) with God: "Enoch walked with God after the birth of Methuselah three hundred years ... Enoch walked with God." (5:22, 24) Put otherwise, Enoch actualizes the full image and likeness of God himself. Furthermore, instead of the phrase "and he died," used with the other patriarchs before as well as after him, we are told that "and he was not, for God took him" (v.24). Thus, this Enoch is presented as "the man" who lived according to God's will and consequently "did not die," but he went to abide with God, thus realizing the destiny originally assigned to "the man" (Gen 2-3). He was granted the life promised in the tree of life, a life that Adam could not attain due to his disobedience.

However, what is most important for my thesis is that Enoch's "walking" is rendered both times through *hithallek*, the *hiphil* (fifth verbal form of the verb *halak*) that we encountered in the description of God's "walking" (*mithallek*; 3:8): *wayyithallek ḥanok 'et-ha'elohim* (vv.22a and 24a). This again brings to mind Ezekiel in his depiction of God as shepherd and the invitation to God's locum tenens to follow in his Lord's footsteps: "I myself will be the shepherd of my sheep, and I will make them lie down, says the Lord God ... And I will set up over them one shepherd, my servant David, and he shall feed them: he shall feed them and be their shepherd." (Ezek 34:15, 23) In the latter passage, the prophet is referring to the "renewed" David. Here in Genesis the author is speaking of the "renewed" Enoch[4] *as shepherd* and thus, taking the place of Abel through his grandfather Seth who

---

[4] My readers are reminded that the name *ḥanok* (Enoch) is from the verb *ḥanak* whose meaning is "dedicate, initiate, renew" whence we have *ḥanukkah* (Hanukkah) the feast of the rededication of the temple under the Maccabees.

Chapter 9   205

was begotten to "replace" Abel (4:25). Later the hearer will
realize that Enoch functions as the prototype for Noah and
Abraham and even Isaac:

> Noah was a righteous man, blameless (*tamim*) in his generation;
> Noah walked (*hithallek*) with God. (6:9)

> When Abram was ninety-nine years old the Lord appeared to
> Abram, and said to him, "I am God Almighty; walk (*hithallek*)
> before me, and be blameless (*tamim*)." (17:1)

> But he said to me, "The Lord, before whom I (viz. Abraham)
> walk (*hithallakti*), will send his angel with you and prosper your
> way; and you shall take a wife for my son from my kindred and
> from my father's house." (24:40)

> And he blessed Joseph, and said, "The God before whom my
> fathers Abraham and Isaac walked (*hithalleku*), the God who has
> led (*ro'eh*;[5] shepherded) me all my life long to this day." (48:15)

Although his lifespan is much shorter than that of the others in
his family tree, Enoch nevertheless lives the fullness of life
expressed in the number 365, a "full" year (Gen 5:23). The
absolute uniqueness of Enoch is not to be equaled by anyone
else thus making of him a challenge to all *'adamic* generations.

Enoch's uniqueness in walking with God will receive another
kind of seal. Noah also "walked (*hithallek*) with God," and for
that reason God promises an everlasting covenant beyond the
punishment of the flood. Although his lifespan was almost triple
that of Enoch's (v.29), Noah falters at the end of his life (Gen
9:20-28) and ends up dying. In the case of Enoch, it is his son
and grandson, not he, who will "die." Whereas Enoch followed
in the "footsteps" of God, Noah's downfall lies in that he
followed in the "footsteps" of Cain: "In the course of time Cain
brought to the Lord an offering of the fruit of the ground

---

[5] This active participle of the verb *ro'eh* functions as a noun as well. My readers are
reminded that this is a basic rule in Semitic languages.

[*ha'adamah*]" (Gen 4:3); "Noah was a man of the ground (*'iš ha'adamah*). He planted a vineyard." (Gen 9:20)[6]

Enoch's uniqueness is further reflected in that he occupies position number seven in the genealogy, which is the full divine number, in contradistinction with the number ten, which is the full human number. In other words, the fullness of any human story is at hand when and whenever God's will is implemented. Man, however, is allowed to proceed on his own way, if God so chooses. Later we hear of Israel reaching the land promised by God the King of Israel. Rather than being satisfied, Israel will decide to proceed on its own way by requesting a human king (1 Sam 8). Just as later, the post-Samuel period or "route" will end with annihilation through exile, from a nationhood perspective, the post-Enoch period or "route" will end with Noah, in whose time God threatens the man and the earth with annihilation (Gen 6:1-8). This "route" is initiated with Methuselah (*metušelaḥ*; Gen 5:22, 25-27) whose name means "(someone) sends his death" or "(someone) sends (him) to his death." This will happen via Lemech who keeps the penultimate position in Adam's genealogy, which was his in Cain's. He also keeps the same function, that of the "king (son of God)" who acts willfully, and not according to God's will.

Lemech

Contrary to Enoch who was "salvaged" through authorial "renewal," Lemech was "salvaged" unchanged for a very simple reason: once more, according to Ezekiel and all the Prophets, Prior as well as Latter, a king is a king is a king. A king is essentially bad news in scripture that upholds God as the sole King. Actually, Lemech looks worse in Adam's *toledot*. Notice how the arrogance of Lemech in Genesis 5 is compounded when compared to that in Genesis 4. Lemech's lifespan covers

---

[6] I shall discuss Noah more in detail later.

777 years, which seemingly reflects divine perfection, the test and eventual pitfall for all kings.

In Cain's genealogy it is Enoch who ended up not being what he was supposed to be; here in Adam's genealogy it is Lemech who assumes that role. Although his life(span) looks perfect, still it is bogus perfection. Enoch, who lived as a "son of man" for 365 years, is the one who attained real perfection. The play on "son of man" versus "son of God" will be picked up in Genesis 6:1-8 and, as we shall see, will remain throughout the Bible as the choice that Noah and his descendants will have to deal with time and again.

Another dig at the kingly institution and its "length of years" can be detected in Lemech's age of 182 when he begets Noah. Since this number is the half of the lifespan of Enoch, the author may well have been intending to say that Lemech's real value was in his progeny Noah,[7] and that he actually accomplished his mission in life at age 182, well short of the "perfect" Enoch.

The reason behind "salvaging" Lemech as well as Enoch will soon be revealed in the story of Lemech's son Noah and Noah's three sons. The scriptural God never discards his original plan and replaces it with a "new" one, but vies, in spite of and against all odds, to change the human beings' hearts of stone into hearts of flesh. This intention is evident in the last verse of chapter 5: "After (When) Noah was five hundred years old, Noah became the father of Shem, Ham, and Japheth." (v.32) Notice the sudden change from mentioning just the first born, as was the case with all the preceding "fathers," to mentioning all three sons together. The intentionality of the matter finds corroboration in that the matter is taken up again at the beginning of the *toledot* of Noah: "These are the generations (*toledot*) of Noah. Noah was a righteous man, blameless in his generation; Noah walked with God. And Noah had (*wayyoled*; became the father of) three sons, Shem, Ham, and Japheth."

---

[7] See below on Noah.

(6:9-10) On the other hand, Noah's forebears are said to have begotten many other sons and daughters, whereas Noah's progeny is restricted to his three sons. Here again one can see the centrality of the naming for "existence": while Noah's three sons are named, the many "other" children of his predecessors are not and thus are functionally relegated to oblivion. Still, what is more important for the scriptural thesis of the oneness of humankind is that the *toledot* of the three sons will be presented in the following words: "These are the generations (*toledot*) of the sons of Noah, Shem, Ham, and Japheth; sons were born to them after the flood." (10:1) Their posterities are lumped into one progeny instead of three progenies, one for each, which is the rule elsewhere. Even Ham, who dishonored his father unleashing a curse against his own son, Canaan (9:21-25), is included. It could not have been otherwise since the everlasting covenant promised to Noah (6:18) includes his *three* sons and all the constituents of God's one creation:

> And God said *to Noah* ... "But I will establish my covenant *with you*; and you shall come into the ark, you, your sons, your wife, and your sons' wives with you." (6:13a, 18)

> Then God said *to Noah and to his sons with him*, "Behold, I establish my covenant *with you and your descendants after you*, and with every living creature that is with you, the birds, the cattle, and every beast of the earth with you, as many as came out of the ark. I establish my covenant with you, that never again shall all flesh be cut off by the waters of a flood, and never again shall there be a flood to destroy the earth." And God said, "This is the sign of the covenant which I make between me and you and every living creature that is with you, for all future generations..." (9:8-12)

It is important to note that the flood story is an integral part of the *toledot* of Noah, whereas the *toledot* of his three sons—and thus of humankind as we as well as the author know it—will be initiated *after* the flood (10:1). And as we shall see in chapter 10, the oneness of the totality of humankind does not preclude differentiation between the diverse nations. The descendants of each of Shem, Ham, and Japheth reflect three different "kinds" of societies that function differently throughout the scriptural story.[8]

The way the *toledot* of Adam is handled gives the clue as to why "the Lord saw that the wickedness of man was great in the earth, and that every imagination of the thoughts of his heart was only evil continually" (Gen 6:5) to the extent that "the Lord was sorry that he had made man on the earth, and it grieved him to his heart. So the Lord said, 'I will blot out man whom I have created from the face of the ground, man and beast and creeping things and birds of the air, for I am sorry that I have made them'" (Gen 6:6-7).

The most striking feature of the *toledot* is undoubtedly the extravagant lifespans of those forebears. Trying to use Genesis 6:3 (Then the Lord said, "My spirit shall not abide in man for ever, for he is flesh, but his days shall be a hundred and twenty years") to "explain" the oddity does not hold water on two levels. On the one hand, keeping the lifespans within the range of three hundred or even four hundred years would have sufficed. On the other hand, the restriction to one hundred twenty years as the intended punishment does not make sense since thereafter human beings lived much longer than that.[9] I believe one should take verse 3 together with the following four verses and understand it as a first thought, but after assessing the gravity of the situation, this limit of lifespan was upped to total annihilation. Hence, verse 3 should be understood as a literary device to impress upon the readers that, *indeed*, the wickedness of man "grieved" the Lord "to his heart" (Gen 6:6b).[10]

So what is the reason for these long lifespans? A plausible explanation is the *toledot* of Adam was meant as a parody of the Sumerian Kings List, which was very well known to the original addressees and which left its impact on the Akkadian and

---

[8] I shall go in detail over this matter in my discussion of that chapter.

[9] Gen 11:10-26.

[10] See my comments on the original Hebrew in *C-Gen* 88.

Babylonian King Lists. It is a well-attested phenomenon that established civilizations, especially when they become powerful and extend over a wide expanse, did not want to be viewed as newcomers on the historical scene, but wanted to appear "ancient," which would give them an aura and, more importantly, legitimize them in the eyes of the peoples conquered by them. The reason is that a "newcomer" is tantamount to "usurper" and thus illegitimate. Put otherwise, the leaders of the new power use the device of retrojection: they project their actual situation into the very distant past. A classic example is the way the city of Rome came to perceive itself. Not only do we hear of the mythic twins Romulus and Remus who were raised by a she-wolf, but also that the Romans were the descendants of Aeneas of Troy.[11] Thus Rome presents itself as the heir of the ancient Greek civilization. Moreover, it is the city of Rome that gives its name to the Roman empire and civilization, in the same way as Sumer, Assur (Assyria), and Babylon did in the East. The city was viewed as a deity's domain: the deity founded its city and assigned a monarch to rule over it in that deity's name. See, for instance, the classic depiction of this state of affairs in scripture itself:

> Why do the nations conspire, and the peoples plot in vain? The kings of the earth set themselves, and the rulers take counsel together, against *the Lord and his anointed*, saying, "Let us burst their bonds asunder, and cast their cords from us." He who sits in the heavens laughs; the Lord has them in derision. Then he will speak to them in his wrath, and terrify them in his fury, saying, "*I have set my king on Zion, my holy hill.*" I will tell of the decree of the Lord: He said to me, "*You are my son, today*[12] *I have begotten you. Ask of me, and I will make the nations your heritage, and the ends of the earth your possession.*" (Ps 2:1-8)

---

[11] Hence, the name of Virgil's epic poem, the Aeneid.
[12] Which is the day of the monarch's coronation.

Since the deity cannot be a deity except over a domain, i.e., its city,[13] and since that same deity, the "heavenly" monarch, assigns an "earthly" monarch to rule over its domain, it ensues that the "earthly" kingship had to stretch back in the past as far as possible in order to "eternalize" the city and, by the same token, legitimize the actual monarch. This is precisely why the lengthy catalogues of kings that were produced extend back into mythical times when monarchs lived tens of thousands of years. The nearer the monarchs are to the time of the writing, their lifespans dwindle to the hundreds of years. With this in mind, one can understand what the scriptural authors were doing. They were replacing the kingly line with a "human" line. The reality on earth is not the result of the rule of a monarch as representative of a deity; rather it is the result of the human progeny through procreation that was blessed by God himself in Genesis 1; hence, the intentional repetition of Genesis 1:26 at the beginning of the *toledot* of Adam (5:1b-2). In order to impress the hearers, the authors presented the forebears in a "kingly" manner just as they did in Genesis 1:27. Notice also how it is only the first-born that is of import since it is through him that the "dynasty" proceeds: "When Seth had lived a hundred and five years, he became the father of Enosh. Seth lived after the birth of Enosh eight hundred and seven years, and had other sons and daughters. Thus all the days of Seth were nine hundred and twelve years; and he died." (Gen 5:6-8, see also all the following generations.) However—and therein lies the low blow—the human "dynasty" has one up over the kingly "dynasty." In the case of the latter, the primogeniture does not automatically secure the heirship since the one in line still has to be endorsed and declared by the deity as monarch in a ceremony of investiture. We are all familiar with the repeated battles for succession that can turn bloody. Scripture itself dedicates two full chapters to such within the household of

---

[13] See the Ugaritic story of Baal who begged his sister/consort Anat to accompany him in order to secure from their father El a mountain where Baal could build his temple (abode).

God's elect, David (1 Kg 1-2). In the case of the human "dynasty," God does not need to intervene at each turn since he himself has already implanted his choice in the process of procreation. The authors unequivocally insist on this matter right from the start: "When God created man, *he made him in the likeness of God*. Male and female he created them, and he blessed them and named them Man when they were created. When Adam had lived a hundred and thirty years, *he became the father of a son in his (Adam's) own likeness, after his (Adam's) image*, and named him Seth." (Gen 5:1b-3) The message is clear: the only King is God and the human beings, all of them, are accountable in that they are responsible for his entire creation since, with Adam's death, Seth is put, ipso facto, in a similar position as his father in Genesis 1:28-30. What a literary tour de force!

Still, as I pointed out early on, the authors are anti-heroes. They are not interested in glorifying their own culture over that of Ancient Greece and Macedonia. That is why, they conceived the *toledot* of Adam in a way that would not allow the hearer to deduce that the "human" dynasty they presented is in and of itself superior to the "kingly" dynasty. Their thesis is precisely that the kings are as "human" as the other humans. The human "dynasty" itself is challenged by Enoch, not the son of Cain (Gen 4:17), but by Enoch as revisited in the *toledot* of Adam through Seth. This Enoch was the one who truly enacted the meaning of his name, "dedicated" (5:21-24). Yet, even he could not save humankind from the divine ire in Genesis 6. Just as Adam and his progeny faltered in Genesis 2-3 and 4, humankind falters again even more miserably here. In spite of the fact that God carried the human race through ten generations amounting to 8125 years, he is forced to regret having created what he did and decided to obliterate it (6:1-7).

So, the author plants in the hearer's mind the seed of thought that the last word will be God's and not that of man. He does so by ending Adam's genealogy, beyond Methuselah and Lemech, with Noah in the tenth position, ten being the numeral of the full human story. Momentarily, we shall hear of the virtual annihilation of all life on earth. Still, Noah stands out, already at birth, as the sign of assuredness that God will ultimately intervene to salvage life on earth. Noah is, in Adam's genealogy, the only descendant whose name is introduced the way Cain's and Seth's were in the previous genealogies (4:1, 25). However, the difference lies in that the naming of Cain and Seth is linked to their birth, whereas the text concerning the naming of Noah not only "looks ahead" but also goes beyond the catastrophe:

> When Lemech had lived a hundred and eighty-two years, he became the father of a son, and called his name Noah, saying, "Out of the ground (*min ha'adamah*)[14] which the Lord has *cursed* [15] this one shall bring us relief (*yenaḥamenu*) from our work and from the toil (*'iṣṣabon*)[16] of our hands." (5:28-29)

Since the terminology is clearly reminiscent of Genesis 2-3, the hope is the reversal of the curse that befell Adam. However, the play on words is very astute and helps build the bridge between the curse of the earth in Adam's time and the impending annihilation of the earth with the promise of a fresh start beyond both disasters. Instead of playing on the root of the Hebrew personal name, as was the case with Cain and Seth, the author changes the root of the name Noah by adding a letter, thus introducing a new root *nḥm* (consolation; relief) instead of the expected *nḥ* (rest; enjoyment).[17] The root of the name itself harks back to when God put Adam in the garden "to enjoy himself" (Gen 2:15);[18] yet it also looks ahead beyond the flood to when Noah will have enough respite on earth to plant a

---

[14] Gen 2:7, 9, 19

[15] See Gen 3:17.

[16] See Gen 3:17.

[17] My readers are reminded that in Hebrew the alphabet is made only of consonants (our vowels are just vocalic sounds in Hebrew and do not count especially when it comes to the root of a word). Consequently, adding or subtracting a letter is of momentous value.

[18] See my comments on that verse in *C-Gen* 53-55.

vineyard (9:20), which will be the trigger for the curse issued by
Noah against Canaan his grandson (v.25). The introduced root
nḥm also encourages the hearer not to lose hope when God
announces his intention to annihilate the earth, since the verb
used to describe God's repentance (feeling sorry) for having
made man (6:6) is also *nḥm*.[19]

This back and forth literary play seems to reflect
indecisiveness on God's part. However, it is a scriptural trait
through which the authors are promoting their sui generis
message: matters go sour due to human proclivity toward self-
assertion and thus disobedience. Yet, *in spite of* their attitude,
God remains in control and pushes further his original plan to
preserve his creation. Thus he alone is the "beneficent
shepherd." This scenario will be repeated time and again
throughout scripture.[20] The most compelling paradigm passage
in this regard is found in Ezekiel where the Lord will accomplish
the mission of saving "all Israel, all of them" is spite of their
rebellion and through a purge that decimates part of them:

> What is in your mind shall never happen—the thought, "Let us
> be like the nations, like the tribes of the countries, and worship
> wood and stone." As I live, says the Lord God, surely with a
> mighty hand and an outstretched arm, and with wrath poured
> out, I will be king over you. I will bring you out from the peoples
> and gather you out of the countries where you are scattered, with
> a mighty hand and an outstretched arm, and with wrath poured
> out; and I will bring you into the wilderness of the peoples, and
> there I will enter into judgment with you face to face. As I entered
> into judgment with your fathers in the wilderness of the land of
> Egypt, so I will enter into judgment with you, says the Lord God.
> I will make you pass under the rod, and I will let you go in by
> number. I will purge out the rebels from among you, and those

---

[19] More on this below when I shall discuss Gen 6:1-8.
[20] My readers are reminded that, if and when God allows something to take place
according to the will of humans, it does not mean that he agrees with it, a matter I
referred to earlier in my discussion of God's allowing Cain to go his way in building
a city instead of accepting the divine punishment for him to wander.

who transgress against me; I will bring them out of the land where they sojourn, but they shall not enter the land of Israel. Then you will know that I am the Lord. As for you, O house of Israel, thus says the Lord God: Go serve every one of you his idols, now and hereafter, if you will not listen to me; but my holy name you shall no more profane with your gifts and your idols. For on my holy mountain, the mountain height of Israel, says the Lord God, there all the house of Israel, all of them, shall serve me in the land; there I will accept them, and there I will require your contributions and the choicest of your gifts, with all your sacred offerings. (20:32-40)

This way of looking at the surviving remainder as representing the totality of a given entity that has lost part of its constituency is a classic literary device and has survived in the human way of speaking up to our days. The most telling example is how one refers to the victorious army in spite of its many—sometimes innumerable—losses in individuals: In the Second World War the Allies went to war, lost many of the soldiers and came back victorious. Notice how one uses the same grammatical subject "the Allies" without any apprehension that the hearers would misunderstand. In this case one is viewing the entire army as one "flock."

10

Before Noah and the Flood

One would have expected that the "story" of Noah begin immediately after his mention and that of his three sons in 5:32, however, such is not the case. His *toledot* starts at 6:9, again with the repeated mention of his sons (v.10). Consequently, the passage 6:1-8 is still part of Adam's *toledot*.

It opens with reference to the "multiplying" of *ha'adam* (v.1) according to the divine plan for him to "multiply" (1:28):

When men (*ha'adam*) began (*hehel*) to multiply (*rab* from the root *rab*) on *the face of the ground*, and daughters were born to them, the sons of God saw that the daughters of men were fair; and they took to wife such of them as they chose. Then the Lord said, "My spirit shall not abide in man for ever, for he is flesh, but his days shall be a hundred and twenty years." The Nephilim were on the earth in those days, and also afterward, when the sons of God came in to the daughters of men, and they bore children to them. These were the mighty men that were of old, *the men of renown* (*'anše* [plural of *'iš*] *haššem*). The Lord saw that the wickedness (*ra'ah* [feminine of *ra'*]; evil) of man was great (*rabbah* from the root *rab*) in the earth, and that every imagination of the thoughts of his heart was only evil (*ra'*) continually. And the Lord was sorry that he had made man on the earth, and it grieved him to his heart. So the Lord said, "I will blot out man whom I have created from *the face of the ground*, man and beast and creeping things and birds of the air, for I am sorry that I have made them." But Noah found favor in the eyes of the Lord. (6:1-8)

So God created man (*ha'adam*) in his own image, in the image of God he created him; male and female he created them. And God blessed them, and God said to them, "Be fruitful and multiply (*rebu* from the root *rab*), and fill the earth and subdue it; and have dominion over the fish of the sea and over the birds of the air and over every living thing that moves upon the earth." (1:27-28)

The short passage 4:25-26 linking the *toledot* of the heavens and the earth with that of Adam played an axial role in the development of the origins of the scriptural story. A close look at 6:1-8, a passage linking the *toledot* of Adam and that of Noah, will prove to be of a similar value. Those verses hark back to chapters 1-4 as well as look ahead to the flood story. Only a careful hearing of the original Hebrew will unlock the insinuations in its far-reaching layers.

From the outset one hears a clear reference to God's command in 1:28 for *ha'adam* to "multiply." The centrality of the root *rab* (6:1) in the author's mind is evident from its reemergence in verse 5 and, no less, in conjunction with the root *ra'* (evil) that is central to the story of that same *ha'adam* in the garden (chapters 2-3). In the garden story the mistake lay in that *ha'adam* contravened God's express command (2:17); here the misbehavior is more cunning in that it plays on a different connotation of the same verb *rab* used in an earlier divine command for *ha'adam* to "multiply." The same verb also means "become greater, more powerful." By combining *rab* and *ra'* in the same verse (6:5), the author is emphasizing that the same *ha'adam* has reached a yet unheard of level of wickedness. This prepares the hearer for the divine decision to blot off the face of the ground all living beings that had populated that same ground. The exception, of course, is the sea animals that will not be affected by the flood (v.7). The divine "crisis" was so extreme that it is expressed through the phrase "it grieved him to his heart (v.6).[1]

Once more, an attentive ear can hear in the first two verses the relentless bias against kingship and the seemingly unbridled power inherent to it. The author gives an explanation as to how the human beings distorted the divine intention behind the verb *rab*. The fact that they "began *(hehel)*" the process of multiplying has a negative connotation.[2] Instead of letting God initiate the

---

[1] See my comments on the Hebrew verb *hit'asseb* in *C-Gen* 88.
[2] See my comments on 4:26b.

process that would have made it indeed an expression of his "blessing" (1:28), they took over the lead and implemented it according to "every imagination of the thoughts of his [their] heart." Therein lay the evil which is stressed through the repetition of *ra'* in the same verse (6:5).

Moreover, the perpetrators of that "evil (wickedness)" are said to be *bene ha'elohim* (the sons of *the* deity; v.2).[3] Without resorting to a lengthy aside concerning the distinction between *'elohim* (God) and *ha'elohim* (with the definite article, *the* god), suffice it to point out here that up until 17:18, *ha'elohim* occurs only six times, all of which are found in close proximity (5:22, 24; 6:2, 4, 6, 11). The last instance occurs in the tightly knit passage justifying God's decision to launch his annihilating flood:

> Now the earth *was corrupt* (*tiššahet*; *niphal* of the verb *šahat*) in God's (*ha'elohim*) sight, and the earth was filled with violence. And God (*'elohim*) saw the earth, and behold, it *was corrupt* (*nišhatah*; *niphal*); for all flesh *had corrupted* (*hišhit*; *hiphil*) their way upon the earth. And God (*'elohim*) said to Noah, "I have determined to make an end of all flesh; for the earth is filled with violence through them; behold, I *will destroy* (*mašhit*; *hiphil*) them with the earth … For behold, I will bring a flood of waters upon the earth, to *destroy* (*šahet*; *piel*) all flesh in which is the breath of life from under heaven; everything that is on the earth shall die." (6:11-13, 17)

The quintessentially scriptural approach to divine punishment found time and again is to let the culprits taste the outcome of their own sin, i.e., let them proceed on their path of self-destruction.[4] The play on the different verbal forms of the same root *šahat* supports this. The earliest instances of *šahat*— five times within verses 11-17—are followed by two instances more in 9:11 and 15 that hark back to 6:13 and 17:

---

[3] "The sons of God" in RSV.

[4] Earlier, I have referred in detail to 1 Samuel 8 where the Lord punishes Israel with their own wish to be "like the other nations"—which he had destroyed time and again before their eyes—by granting them their request for an earthly king.

I establish my covenant with you, that never again shall all flesh
be cut off by the waters of a flood, and never again shall there be
a flood to *destroy* (*šaḥet; piel*) the earth ... I will remember my
covenant which is between me and you and every living creature
of all flesh; and the waters shall never again become a flood to
destroy (*šaḥet; piel*) all flesh. (Gen 9:11, 15)

The next occurrence concerns the destruction of Sodom: "And
Lot lifted up his eyes, and saw that the Jordan valley was well
watered everywhere like the garden of the Lord, like the land of
Egypt, in the direction of Zoar; this was before the Lord *destroyed*
(*šaḥet; piel*) Sodom and Gomorrah." (13:10).

There is no actual need for *ha'elohim* (6:11) just before the
repeated reference *in the same context* to *'elohim* (vv.12 and 13).
Because of this the hearer is forced to link it to the preceding
instance of its use (6:9), especially since it will not be heard again
until 17:18. This instance of *ha'elohim* gives the rationale behind
God's rescinding his original decision to destroy everything on
earth: "Noah was a righteous man, blameless in his generation;
Noah walked (*hithallek*) with God (*'et-ha'elohim*)" (6:9). This is an
exact mimicking of 5:22 and 24:

> Enoch walked (*hithallek*) with God (*'et-ha'elohim*) after the birth of
> Methuselah three hundred years, and had others sons and
> daughters. (5:22)

> Enoch walked (*hithallek*) with God (*'et-ha'elohim*); and he was not,
> for God took him. (v. 24)

Noah's behavior, which made him both blameless and
righteous, thus "walking" according to God's will, was that of a
shepherd.[5] The irony of the flood story lies in that, logistically
speaking, it would be almost impossible for the Syrian-Arabian
Desert to be flooded due to its expanse, while the area of the

---

[5] As I explained in dealing with God's "walking" (*mithallek*) in Gen 3:8. Later, of
course, Noah will renege on such behavior by tilling the ground and planting a
vineyard (9:20), thus treading in the footsteps of Cain, the tiller of the ground, instead
of proceeding in the footsteps of Abel, the "shepherd of the flock."

Two Rivers, where many prosperous cities as well as the mighty Babylon lay, could well be.

It is against that background that one is to look for the meaning and function of *bene ha'elohim* (the sons of the god[s]; 6:2 and 4) that occurs twice in a row and in the same context as the last two instances of *ha'elohim* (vv.6 and 11). The passage 6:1-4 is constructed very cunningly. It gives the impression that *bene ha'elohim* are all-powerful vis-à-vis "the daughters of men," but the reality of the matter is that it makes fun of that apparent power. Unlike *ha'elohim*—whether one takes it as meaning "the God" or "the gods"—*bene ha'elohim* are in need of procreation in order to secure their dynasty, that is to say, their "existence" into the future. The classic text that illustrates this is found in Psalm 45 that unequivocally calls the king *'elohim* (v.5, following KJV that renders the Hebrew more literally). It is dedicated to his wedding, yet with the view of procreation in mind:

> ... daughters of kings are among your ladies of honor; at your right hand stands the queen in gold of Ophir. Hear, O daughter, consider, and incline your ear; forget your people and your father's house; and the king will desire your beauty. Since he is your lord, bow to him; the people of Tyre will sue your favor with gifts, the richest of the people with all kinds of wealth. The princess is decked in her chamber with gold-woven robes; in many-colored robes she is led to the king, with her virgin companions, her escort, in her train. With joy and gladness they are led along as they enter the palace of the king. Instead of your fathers shall be your sons; you will make them princes in all the earth. I will cause your name to be celebrated in all generations; therefore the peoples will praise you for ever and ever. (Ps 45:9-17)

Although the queen bows in submission to the king as her "lord" (*'adon*), his "name" will not persist forever unless she bears sons for him just as his own mother bore him for his father before him.

In Genesis 6:1-4 one notices that the progeny is "men of renown" (*'anše haššem*; the men of "the name") as well as "mighty men (*gibborim*) of old," who are introduced with their proper name of Nephilim, an appellation meant to impress the hearer. The only other passage where we hear of the Nephilim describes them as men of great strength and stature:

> At the end of forty days they [the men who were sent to scout the land of Canaan] returned from spying out the land. And they came to Moses and Aaron and to all the congregation of the people of Israel in the wilderness of Paran, at Kadesh; they brought back word to them and to all the congregation, and showed them the fruit of the land. And they told him, "We came to the land to which you sent us; it flows with milk and honey, and this is its fruit. Yet the people who dwell in the land are strong, and the cities are fortified and very large; and besides, we saw the descendants of Anak there. The Amalekites dwell in the land of the Negeb; the Hittites, the Jebusites, and the Amorites dwell in the hill country; and the Canaanites dwell by the sea, and along the Jordan." But Caleb quieted the people before Moses, and said, "Let us go up at once, and occupy it; for we are well able to overcome it." Then the men who had gone up with him said, "We are not able to go up against the people; for they are stronger than we." So they brought to the people of Israel an evil report of the land which they had spied out, saying, "The land, through which we have gone, to spy it out, is a land that devours its inhabitants; and all the people that we saw in it are men of great stature. And there we saw the Nephilim (the sons of Anak, who come from the Nephilim); and we seemed to ourselves like grasshoppers, and so we seemed to them." (Num 13:25-33)

The hearer will soon learn that the Nephilim are only paper tigers—"men of great stature" (*'anše middot*) and not so much *'anše haššem* (the men of *the* name)—since God, who is the only true *haššem* (the name), will invalidate their dread as Anakim (sons of Anak; Num 13:33) in the Book of Joshua (11:21-22). Still an attentive hearer does not need to wait until Numbers and Joshua to hear this since the name itself means "the falling ones, those about to fall" and thus "the fallen." The preceding instance of the verb *fell* (*naphal*) occurs in conjunction with the "fall" of Cain: "So Cain was very angry, and his countenance

fell (naphal). The Lord said to Cain, 'Why are you angry, and
why *has* your countenance *fallen (naphal)*?'" (Gen 4:5b-6) What is
striking is that the agent behind the "fall" of Cain's countenance
is none other than the Lord who appeared earlier as the subject
of the causative form *(hiphil)* of that same verb: "So the Lord
God *caused* a deep sleep *to fall (wayyap[h]p[h]el)* upon the man."
(Gen 2:21a) Such is a work of ingenuity, not just happenstance.
The result is that "the sons of God" in 6:1-4 are not only fake,
but their "power" lies in God's original blessing of procreation.
That is why the subject matter of the entire passage is "the man"
(ha'adam; v.1) whose last mention was in 3:24. However, *ha'adam*
in 6:1-4 is used in contradistinction to *ha'elohim*. More
importantly, it is "the daughters of *ha'adam*" that are presented
as the positively viewed counterpart to the negatively viewed
"the sons of *ha'elohim*." Let us review the original:

> When men *(ha'adam)* began *(hehel)* to multiply *(larob)* on the face of
> the ground, and daughters were born *(yulledu)* to them, the sons
> of God *(ha'elohim)* saw that the daughters of men *(ha'adam)* were
> fair; and they took to wives[6] *(našim*; plural of *'iššah)* such of them
> as they chose. Then the Lord said, "My spirit shall not abide in
> man *(ha'adam)* for ever, for he is flesh, but his days shall be a
> hundred and twenty years." The Nephilim were on the earth in
> those days, and also afterward, when the sons of God *(ha'elohim)*
> came in to the daughters of men *(ha'adam)*, and they bore
> *(weyaledu)* [children][7] to them. These were the mighty men that
> were of old, the men of renown. (6:1-4)

First and foremost it is awkward, to say the least, that one hears
solely of daughters having been born to *ha'adam*. The
awkwardness lies in that no less than nine times before we are
told that each of the "fathers," except for Noah,[8] brought forth
through birth *(hiphil* of the verb *yalad)* "sons and daughters" after
he brought forth through birth *(hiphil* of the verb *yalad)* his
primogeniture: "When Adam had lived a hundred and thirty

---

[6] As per KJV; RSV has the singular "wife."

[7] Not in the original that has only "gave birth."

[8] See earlier my comments concerning this matter.

years, he became the father *(wayyoled)* of a son in his own likeness, after his image, and named him Seth. The days of Adam after he became the father of *(holido)* Seth were eight hundred years; and he had *(wayyoled)* other sons and daughters." (5:3-4)[9] So the authors clearly intended to include human beings of both sexes in Adam's progeny thus preparing the readers to perceive that *ha'adam* in 6:1-8 encompasses the entire humankind which "started" to misconstrue the divine blessing of multiplication into a license for arrogance (v.1a), which attitude in turn provoked God's anger and punishment. However, unexpectedly, we are told that the result of that "multiplication" was that "daughters were born *(yulledu;* passive causative *piel)* to them" (v.1b). As for the "sons," they are introduced as "sons of *ha'elohim*" (v.2). Not only that, but, in verses 2 and 4, twice we are presented with these "sons of *ha'elohim*" as imposing themselves willfully on the "daughters of *ha'adam*." In other words, it is the males that usurped the females by usurping the status of deity reserved only to God. The latter usurpation was done through the medium of kingship as will become clear in chapter 10.

All this is borne out by the fact that the noun *gibbor* (mighty man) is restricted to only five occurrences in the Pentateuch, four of which are found in Genesis (6:4; 10:8, 9 [twice]) and one in Deuteronomy (10:17). The prime prototype of the "mighty men" *(gibborim)* issued from the intercourse between "the sons of *ha'elohim*" and "the daughters of *ha'adam*" (Gen 6:4) is Nimrod, the king of Babel, whose status is underscored through its mention thrice in two verses: "Cush became the father of Nimrod; he was the first on earth to be a mighty *(gibbor)* man. He was a mighty *(gibbor)* hunter before the Lord; therefore it is said, 'Like Nimrod a mighty *(gibbor)* hunter before the Lord.'"

---

[9] Notice how RSV disrupts the original by translating the same verb into "had" in the third instance, when its parent the KJV has "begat" in all three cases. One begins to wonder whether RSV is intent to adulterate the original. It chews and digests the original for the hearers/readers instead of presenting them with the original as KJV has systematically honestly tried.

(10:8-9) Later one hears that it is in Babel, Nimrod's city, where the "tower with its top in the heavens" is erected, in order that men might "make a name (*šem*) for ourselves" (11:4), thus proclaiming themselves as *anše haššem*, literally rendered, "the male human beings of the name" (6:4). This is done in express defiance to God's will. However, God was not about to be outmaneuvered by those who are, in spite of what they think of themselves, merely "sons of *ha'adam*" (11:5), the same *ha'adam* to whom the Lord God (3:14) said "you are dust, and to dust you shall return" (3:19). The same Lord God will state, in no uncertain terms, what is required of humankind, in the last Book of the Pentateuch, as an ever reminder to those who are about to enter the Syrian wilderness:

> And now, Israel, what does the Lord your God require of you, but to fear the Lord your God, to *walk* in all his ways, to love him, to serve the Lord your God with all your heart and with all your soul, and to keep the commandments and statutes of the Lord, which I command you this day for your good? Behold, to the Lord your God belong heaven and the heaven of heavens, the earth with all that is in it; yet the Lord set his heart in love upon your fathers and chose their descendants (*zera'*; seed)[10] after them, you above all peoples, as at this day. Circumcise therefore the foreskin of your heart, and be no longer stubborn. *For the Lord your God is God of gods and Lord of lords, the great, the mighty (*gibbor*), and the terrible God, who is not partial and takes no bribe.* He executes justice for the fatherless and the widow, and loves the sojourner, giving him food and clothing. Love the sojourner therefore; for you were sojourners in the land of Egypt. You shall fear the Lord your God; you shall serve him and cleave to him, and by *his name* you shall swear. He is your praise; he is your God, who has done for you these great and terrible things which your eyes have seen. Your fathers went down to Egypt seventy persons; and now the Lord your God has made (*śim*; put, set, posit)[11] you as the stars of heaven *for multitude* (*larob*; to mulitply).[12] (Deut 10:12-22)

---

[10] As in 4:25.

[11] The verb *śim* has the same connotation as the verb *šit* found in 4:25.

[12] The same expression as in 6:1.

Notice further how the same male human beings who were introduced earlier as "sons of *ha'elohim*" (Gen 6:2) are belittled into "sons of *ha'adam*" at the exact time they were asserting their arrogance against God in order to make a "name" for themselves, a name that they were intending to pass on to their progeny:

> Then they said, "Come, let us build ourselves a city, and a tower with its top in the heavens, and let us make a name (*šem*) for ourselves, lest we be scattered abroad upon the face of the whole earth." And the Lord came down to see the city and the tower, which the sons of men (*bene ha'adam*) had built. (11:4-5)

In actuality, they are of the same exact stock as their counterparts, the daughters of men (*benot ha'adam*) as has been asserted time and again. "Fathers" give birth through the medium of their wives (*našim*; plural of *'iššah*) to "sons *and* daughters" (chapter 5). The height of irony is that even "sons of *ha'elohim*" are in need of "daughters," who are said to have been born (*yulledu*), to ensure their own progeny. The *bene ha'adam* are presented as the same "kind" of human beings as Enosh: "To Seth also a son was born (*yullad*),[13] and he called his name Enosh." (4:26a) What the author is stressing, in his own way,[14] is that while the "sons" *as monarchs*, the like of Nimrod, are busy asserting themselves as almost Platonic beings having their value in and of themselves, the value of the "daughters" lies in that they "are born" as much a gift from God as Enosh whose name is from the same root as *našim* that means "wives" as well as "women." Put otherwise, in spite of the fact that the *'iššah* of

---

[13] *yulledu* (plural) and *yullad* (singular) reflect the same verbal form *pual*, the passive of *piel* on which I commented earlier showing its parallelism in its causative connotation with the *hiphil* used extensively in chapter 5.

[14] When *hearing* the text rather than trying to comprehend it with our mind that is bound to its own axioms, one realizes what the author is describing. It is in this same vein that the author of a parable imposes his own rules to the parabolic story he is expounding. The most striking example is found in the parable of the lost son where we are told that a father divides his own *inheritance* between his two sons *before his death!* Yet, without this impossible premise, there would not have been that Lukan parable with the "lesson" it is conveying.

ha'adam was told that "your desire shall be for your husband, and he shall rule over you" (3:16), four verses later she is "called" by none other than *ha'adam* himself "the mother of all living (life)" (v.20), including those who proclaim themselves as "divine beings." These "divine beings" are castigated in Ezekiel in the harshest possible terms:

> The word of the Lord came to me: "Son of man, say to the prince of Tyre, Thus says the Lord God: Because your heart is proud, and you have said, 'I am a god, I sit in the seat of the gods, in the heart of the seas,' *yet you are but a man, and no god, though you consider yourself as wise as a god*—you are indeed wiser than Daniel; no secret is hidden from you; by your wisdom and your understanding you have gotten wealth for yourself, and have gathered gold and silver into your treasuries; by your great wisdom in trade you have increased your wealth, and your heart has become proud in your wealth—therefore thus says the Lord God: Because you consider yourself as wise as a god, therefore, behold, I will bring strangers upon you, the most terrible of the nations; and they shall draw their swords against the beauty of your wisdom and defile your splendor. They shall thrust you down into the Pit, and you shall die the death of the slain in the heart of the seas. Will you still say, 'I am a god,' in the presence of those who slay you, though you are but a man, and no god, in the hands of those who wound you? You shall die the death of the uncircumcised by the hand of foreigners; for I have spoken, says the Lord God." (28:1-10)

It is hardly a coincidence that Sidon, the sister city of Tyre, is introduced in Genesis 10:15 as the "first-born" of Canaan who was cursed in no uncertain terms a few verses earlier (9:25-27).

The repeated belittling of man by depriving him of being the source of life, and placing the perpetration of the "seed" (*zera'*) in the act of "begetting (giving birth)" (*yalad*), which is factually a woman's trait, is a literary set-up that will find its resolution in the story of Abram/Abraham and Sarai/Sarah and the birth of Isaac. It is worth noting that that story of Abram/Abraham is not titled *toledot*, but is part of the *toledot* of Terah that starts in Genesis 11:27, and is followed by the *toledot* of Ishmael (25:12)

and Isaac (v.19). If Abraham is robbed of *toledot*, it is because his
scriptural heir, Isaac, was not born, even indirectly, of him.
Sarah gives birth to Isaac as a result of the divine promise to
her, and not due to Abram's having known her as he did Hagar:
"And he [Abram] went in to Hagar, and she conceived ... And
Hagar bore Abram a son; and Abram called the name of his
son, whom Hagar bore, Ishmael" (Gen 16:4, 15). Nowhere is it
mentioned that Abraham knew Sarah. Actually, they both
"laughed" at God's "promise" of the "birth" of Isaac:

> And God said to Abraham, "As for Sarai your wife, you shall not
> call her name Sarai, but Sarah shall be her name. I will bless her,
> and moreover I will give you a son by her; I will bless her, and
> she shall be a mother of nations; kings of peoples shall come from
> her." Then Abraham fell on his face and laughed, and said to
> himself, "Shall a child be born to a man who is a hundred years
> old? Shall Sarah, who is ninety years old, bear a child?" (17:15-
> 17)

> The Lord said, "I will surely return to you in the spring, and
> Sarah your wife shall have a son." And Sarah was listening at the
> tent door behind him. Now Abraham and Sarah were old,
> advanced in age; it had ceased to be with Sarah after the manner
> of women. So Sarah laughed to herself, saying, "After I have
> grown old, and my husband is old, shall I have pleasure?" The
> Lord said to Abraham, "Why did Sarah laugh, and say, 'Shall I
> indeed bear a child, now that I am old?' Is anything too hard for
> the Lord? At the appointed time I will return to you, in the spring,
> and Sarah shall have a son." But Sarah denied, saying, "I did not
> laugh"; for she was afraid. He said, "No, but you did laugh."
> (18:10-15)

Without mentioning that Abraham knew Sarah, we hear that
she conceived and bore a son in the following way:

> The Lord visited Sarah as he had said, and the Lord did to Sarah
> as he had promised. And Sarah conceived, and bore Abraham a
> son in his old age at the time of which God had spoken to him.
> Abraham called the name of his son who was born to him, whom
> Sarah bore him, Isaac (21:1-3)

This scriptural scenario was picked purposely by Paul in both Galatians and Romans:

> For *it is written* that Abraham had two sons, one by a slave and one by a free woman. But the son of the slave was born according to the flesh, the son of the free woman *through promise*. (Gal 4:22-23)[15]

> That is why it depends on faith, in order that the promise may rest on grace and be guaranteed to all his descendants—not only to the adherents of the law but also to those who share the faith of Abraham, for he is the father of us all, *as it is written*, "I have made you the father of many nations"—in the presence of the God in whom he believed, who gives life to the dead and calls into existence the things that do not exist. In hope he believed against hope, that he should become the father of many nations; as he had been told, "So shall your descendants be." He did not weaken in faith when he considered his own body, which was as good as dead because he was about a hundred years old, or when he considered the barrenness of Sarah's womb. No distrust made him waver concerning the promise of God, but he grew strong in his faith as he gave glory to God, fully convinced that God was able to do what he had promised (Rom 4:16-21)

The ultimate message of scripture, stated in its opening chapters and repeated throughout, is that the male human being, whether as *ha'adam*—an element of the heavens and the earth, God's total and one creation, or as simply *'adam*—the progenitor of the human family tree, shall forever remain what he is, and shall "return to the ground" (*ha'adamah*) out of which he was taken (*luqqaḥta*) (Gen 3:19b). Not only that, but he is mere dust (of that ground): "then the Lord God formed man of dust from the ground, and breathed into his nostrils the breath of life; and man became a living being" (2:7) and "to that dust he shall return" (19c). This extreme belittling is unmissable: while a ground is a recognizable entity, its dust can be scattered and

---

[15] Notice the omission of "was born" before "through promise," which is only understandable since "was born," technically speaking, cannot be except "according to the flesh."

as such is an unrecognizable entity. According to the premise in the scriptural story, the only way for the male human being to "remain" is through procreation, which was blessed by God himself. That is to say, *the* human being, *ha'adam*, cannot "remain" except as *'adam*, an individual human being through begetting (*yalad*).[16] *However*, this begetting is the function of a woman, who alone can "give birth" (*yalad*); man can only *holid*: beget *indirectly* through the woman.[17] Since the mechanism of begetting was launched through God's blessing, ultimately every human being is as Enosh (*'enoš* from the same root as *'iššah* [female human being] or *'iš* [male human being])—daughters and sons (chapter 5)—a gift from God (4:26a), that is, a living being "posited" (*šet*; Seth) by him (4:25), as will be unequivocally demonstrated in *the scriptural story* of Sarah and Isaac.[18]

yelud 'iššah

That the defining characteristic of the human being, female as well as male, is being born of a woman (his or her mother) finds full confirmation in the *Ketubim*, where we find the phrase *yelud 'iššah* (born of a woman):

> Man (*'adam*) that is born of a woman (*yelud 'iššah*) is of few days, and full of trouble. (Job 14:1)

> What is man (*'enoš*), that he can be clean? Or he that is born of a woman (*yelud 'iššah*), that he can be righteous? (15:14)

> How then can man (*'enoš*) be righteous before God? How can he who is born of woman (*yelud 'iššah*) be clean? (25:4)

---

[16] The openly anti-Platonic stand is unmistakable.

[17] The scriptural authors would never subscribe to the contemporary statement of a man "*we* are pregnant." I hope the day will not come when men would say "*we* gave birth"!

[18] This way of perceiving one's progeny as a gift from God is still ingrained in the Semitic mind. Up to this day, whenever an Arab is asked as to how many children one has, the answer is either "that many—according to the number of children—who are God's" or "God has not (yet) granted us any."

These three instances offer more than meets the ear when one *hears* them in the original. In Job 14:1 the original *'adam yelud 'iššah* is literally "man, born of a woman" where the phrase "born of a woman" is in apposition to "man," the end result being "man (or, put otherwise), born of a woman."[19] That is to say, the noun "man" and the phrase "born of a woman" are fully equivalent meaning wise and thus interchangeable: man is by definition "born of a woman." Furthermore, *yelud* is the construct form[20] of *yalud* that is the passive participle of the verbal form *qal yalad* (give birth) and thus, functionally, is the direct result—the outcome—of birth giving which I discussed in detail in conjunction with Genesis 4:25 and 6:1-6 and showed that giving birth is an action that technically applies exclusively to a woman in travail, and not to the male human being.[21] When one considers that the Book of Job pertains to Wisdom Literature and thus the discussion takes place between "elders" discussing matters of life in general terms, that is, their statements are intended to apply to the human beings of all walks of life,[22] then one can see the closeness with Genesis 1-11 that is essentially concerned with all the "nations." The closeness between Job and Genesis 1-11 is evident in the other two instances of *yelud 'iššah* in Job. On the one hand, we hear, not of *'adam*, but of his "counterpart" *'enoš* that occurs for the first time in Genesis 4:26 and then several times in 5:6-11, only to disappear completely until Isaiah 8:1. On the other hand, *'enoš* himself is in turn viewed as totally equivalent to *yelud 'iššah* in that the statements concerning each of these two entities are

---

[19] RSV would have been correct had it put "that is" between commas, giving to that phrase an explanatory function: "Man, that is (to say), someone (anyone) born of a woman, is of a few days."

[20] The form a noun take when followed by another noun (complement).

[21] See earlier my discussion, in conjunction with the *toledot* of Adam, of the different verbal forms of the verb *yalad* that are used whenever a woman is the progenitor (the basic form *qal* whose meaning is "give birth") or a man (the fifth verbal form *hiphil* whose meaning is "give birth through someone else").

[22] My readers are reminded that Job himself, though a keeper of the Law, lived and died in the land of Uz, outside the confines of the scriptural Kingdoms of Israel and Judah,

reversed in Job 15:14 and 25:4: what is said of the one in the first instance is said of the other in the second instance and vice versa.

11

The Toledot of Noah
(Genesis 6-10)

As in the case of the *toledot* of the heavens and the earth and of that of Adam, the *toledot* of Noah (6:9-9:29) functions as a mini-scriptural story: in spite of the human behavior, matters end up on the right track solely due to God's mercy. However, the content of Noah's *toledot* is much more impressive and encompassing than that of Adam, not only due to its length but also and more importantly—precisely due to its length—it incorporates the terminology of the expanded scriptural story of Israel and Judah, their ancestors and the "patriarchs," that starts in Genesis and ends in 2 Chronicles. A detailed discussion of the matter will prove worthwhile in that it will corroborate my thesis as well as clarify the authors' intention.

At the beginning, we hear that God rescinded his decision to wipe out his creation because "Noah found favor in the eyes of the Lord" (6:8), which functions as an introduction to his *toledot*. Still, the *toledot* proper opens up with the reason behind that favor: "Noah was a righteous (*saddiq*) man, blameless (*tamim*) in his generation; Noah walked (*hithallek*) with God." (6:9) The pivotal importance of that statement is evident in that it interrupts the flow between "These are the generations of Noah" (6:9a) and its natural follow-up "And Noah had three sons, Shem, Ham, and Japheth" (6:10). Righteous (*saddiq*) is a legal term and is used throughout scripture to qualify someone who lives according to God's law and thus is declared innocent of any wrongdoing in the court of the righteous judge. Blameless (*tamim*) is a cultic term used to speak of the sacrifices and the priests who offer them: both are to be in a state of "sane completeness" without any missing or blemished limb in the presence of God.[1] Thus, Noah is presented as perfect on two levels, the legal and the cultic, meaning that God had nothing whatsoever against him. Still, what is even more important is that the statement about Noah's "perfection" ends with "Noah walked (*hithallek*) with God," which is word for word the repeated description of Enoch in Genesis 5:22 and 24. However, Noah emulated not only Enoch but God himself who also "walked" (*hithallek*), that is, in the same way a shepherd does.[2]

Unlike his predecessor Adam, Noah proved to be both righteous and blameless in obedience to God's command. His obedience is repeatedly pointed out in the flood story through an interesting literary device. His actions following God's directives to build the ark and to enter into it together with all the other beings living on earth (6:13-21) are not described; we are simply told that "Noah did this; he did all that God commanded him" (v.22). The author underscores this by repeating it: at the end of a similar directive by the Lord regarding the pure animals (7:1-4), we hear that "Noah did all that the Lord had commanded him" (v.5). It sounds as though Noah did not "do" anything save be obedient to God; his activity is subsumed in God's words of command to the effect that his obedience *was* his action. Even the actual entrance into the ark is described twice as an action on the part of Noah and his company (7:7-9 and 13-16); twice we are told at the end "as God had commanded Noah (him)" (vv.9 and 16). In the last instance we hear that it is God himself who consummated and sealed the "actions" of Noah and his companions: "and the Lord closed (the entrance door of the ark) after him." (v.16)

As later in the scriptural story of Israel and Judah, all seems to be well until the hour of the test. Instead of Noah's persisting in his shepherd-like attitude and understanding that it is God's

---

[1] See, e.g., Lev 1:3, 10; 3:1, 6 for the offered animals, and Lev 21:17-21 for the priests.
[2] See my comments earlier in conjunction with God's and Enoch's "walking" (*hithallek*).

consolation (*nhm*) that ultimately ensures the human beings' enjoyment (*nuaḥ*)[3] on the ground granted them by God, Noah opts for sedentary life by planting a vineyard. The vineyard, like the olive orchard, is the ultimate sign of sedentary life since it takes a long time for it to grow and requires continual attention and care:

> Say to the people of Israel, When you come into the land which I give you, the land shall keep a sabbath to the Lord. Six years you shall sow your field, and six years you shall prune your vineyard, and gather in its fruits; but in the seventh year there shall be a sabbath of solemn rest for the land, a sabbath to the Lord; you shall not sow your field or prune your vineyard. (Lev 25:2-4)

> Moreover you have not brought us into a land flowing with milk and honey, nor given us inheritance of fields and vineyards. (Num 16:14)

> I gave you a land on which you had not labored, and cities which you had not built, and you dwell therein; you eat the fruit of vineyards and oliveyards which you did not plant. (Josh 24:13)

> Let me sing for my beloved a love song concerning his vineyard: My beloved had a vineyard on a very fertile hill. He digged it and cleared it of stones, and planted it with choice vines; he built a watchtower in the midst of it, and hewed out a wine vat in it; and he looked for it to yield grapes, but it yielded wild grapes. (Is 5:1-2)

> Again I will build you, and you shall be built, O virgin Israel! Again you shall adorn yourself with timbrels, and shall go forth in the dance of the merrymakers. Again you shall plant vineyards upon the mountains of Samaria; the planters shall plant, and shall enjoy the fruit. (Jer 31:4-5)

> For thus says the Lord of hosts, the God of Israel: Houses and fields and vineyards shall again be bought in this land. (Jer 32:15)

> Thus says the Lord God: When I gather the house of Israel from the peoples among whom they are scattered, and manifest my

---

[3] See earlier on the word play between these two roots.

holiness in them in the sight of the nations, then they shall dwell in their own land which I gave to my servant Jacob. And they shall dwell securely in it, and they shall build houses and plant vineyards. (Ezek 28:25-26)

Therefore, behold, I will allure her, and bring her into the wilderness, and speak tenderly to her. And there I will give her vineyards, and make the Valley of Achor a door of hope. (Hos 2:14-15)

"I will restore the fortunes of my people Israel, and they shall rebuild the ruined cities and inhabit them; they shall plant vineyards and drink their wine, and they shall make gardens and eat their fruit. I will plant them upon their land, and they shall never again be plucked up out of the land which I have given them," says the Lord your God. (Am 9:14-15)

Their goods shall be plundered, and their houses laid waste. Though they build houses, they shall not inhabit them; though they plant vineyards, they shall not drink wine from them. (Zeph 1:13)

The Flood

Now the earth was corrupt in God's sight, and the earth was filled with violence...And God said to Noah, "I have determined to make an end of all flesh; for the earth is filled with violence through them; behold, I will destroy them with the earth." (Gen 6:11, 13)

Just as was the case with the *toledot* of Adam as well as that of the heavens and the earth, the flood story is woven with the phraseology evocative of the sin of arrogance of the kings of Jerusalem and Samaria. Both the violence (*hamas*; 6:11, 13) and its punishment, the end (*qeṣ*; v.13), are standard prophetic terminology.[4] As for the means of salvation from the threatening waters it is the same as that of Moses since the term *tebah* translated as "ark" in Genesis 6:14 is found only twice

---

[4] See especially Ezek 7. Also, e.g., Am 8:2; Hab 2:3.

again, in Exodus 2:3 and 5. RSV is misleading in that it translates into "ark" the *tebah* of Noah and the *'aron* of testimony (Ex 25:16-22), whereas it uses "basket" to speak of the *tebah* that carried the child Moses (2:3, 5). In fact, the "basket" that saved Moses is similar to the "ark" that saved Noah and his progeny. The close correspondence can be detected in two more features:

1. The word *qinnim* (consonantal *qnym*) in Genesis 6:14 is translated into "rooms" (nests), whereas the same consonantal *qnym* can be vocalized as *qanim*, the plural of *qaneh* meaning "reed." The closeness between the two explains why the Jerusalem Bible translates Genesis 6:14 into "Make yourself an ark out of resinous wood. *Make it of reeds* and caulk it with pitch inside and out" instead of "Make yourself an ark of gopher wood; *make rooms in the ark*, and cover it inside and out with pitch" (RSV). Another term for "reeds" is *suph*, a word encountered in Exodus 2:3 and 5 to indicate the reeds among which the basket (*tebah*) was laid. [5]

2. Note the similarity with which each *tebah* is prepared against the eventually inimical waters: "Make yourself an ark of gopher wood; make rooms in the ark (make it of reeds), and *cover it inside and out with pitch*" (Gen 6:14); "And when she could hide him no longer she took for him a basket made of bulrushes, and *daubed it with bitumen and pitch*." (Ex 2:3)[6]

The flood episode reflects all the essential features of the scriptural angles as well as its total perspective. One notices very

---

[5] It is also the word used to qualify the "sea of reeds" that the Israelites traversed upon their leaving Egypt. Hence, the connection is not only between Noah and Moses, but also indirectly between Noah and Israel.

[6] This protection against the waters, in turn, looks ahead to Israel's exodus from Egypt.

clearly that God pushes his plan forward *in spite of* the humans' stubborn recalcitrance. In this particular case, God foregoes any upcoming behavior on the part of Noah and his sons by announcing the irrevocable covenant he will be making with them and their descendants at the end of the flood: "But I will establish my covenant with you" (Gen 6:18a); "Behold, I establish my covenant with you and your descendants after you." (9:9) The hearer is at once cognizant of God's resolve as well as his incontrovertible control over the events involving humans, animals, and vegetation. As we shall hear time and again, God is the sole valid "agent" or "actor" in the scriptural story.[7]

The land animals and the birds are included as an integral part of the one world God created on earth. Vegetation is an essential element in the sustenance of that one creation, and it is the resurgence of that vegetation—just as it was on the third day of creation—that becomes the sure sign (8:6-12) of the possibility for humans and animals to thrive again: "Then God said to Noah, 'Go forth from the ark, you and your wife, and your sons and your sons' wives with you. Bring forth with you every living thing that is with you of all flesh—birds and animals and every creeping thing that creeps on the earth—that they may breed abundantly on the earth, and be fruitful and multiply upon the earth.'" (8:15-17) Notice also, since the land animals were as locked as the humans were in the ark, it was birds, which "fly above the earth across the firmament of the heavens" (1:20b), that brought the sign of new life to them. This all-encompassing symbiosis between life in "the heavens and the

---

[7] We hear this very clearly in Isaiah, immediately after his totally unexpected choice of Cyrus to implement his plan (44:24-45:6): "I form (*yaṣar*, as from clay) light and create (*bara'*) darkness, I make (*'aśah*) weal and create (*bara'*) woe, I am the Lord, who do all these things. Shower, O heavens, from above, and let the skies rain down righteousness; let the earth open, that salvation may sprout forth (*para'*; bear fruit, be fruitful), and let it cause righteousness to spring up (*ṣamah*; sprout, spring up) also; I the Lord have created (*bara'*) it." (Is 45:7-8) All the verbs are found in Genesis 1-2: *yaṣar* (2:7, 8, 19); *bara'* (1:1, 21, 27 [thrice], 2:3); *'aśah* (1:7, 11, 12, 16, 25, 26, 31; 2:2 [twice], 3, 4, 18); *ṣamah* (2:5).

earth" without any artificiality is immediately visible, if not tangible, and is reminiscent of shepherd life set in the wilderness.

The wilderness in the author's purview is none other than the Syrian Wilderness as reflected in the mention—otherwise totally unwarranted—of "the mountains of Ararat" (8:4), a unique instance of that phrase in the Hebrew Old Testament. To be sure, Ararat is referred to only three more times[8], all three much later in the canon (2 Kg 19:37; Is 37:38; Jer 51:27), however, never as "the mountains of Ararat." Since the scriptural flood is presented as universal, why would the authors mention Ararat specifically unless they were interested in that region and specifically refer to the plural "mountains" instead of the singular "mountain"? Even if one supposes that the plural is intended to refer to Little Ararat as well as to Mount Ararat proper, the result is the same: one has in mind a region rather a given spot. Furthermore, how could an ark whose length is 450 feet land at once on two peaks over seven miles apart? My reading that it is an intended region is corroborated in that one hears "the land (*'ereṣ*; earth) of Ararat" in the parallel instances of 2 Kings 19:37 and Isaiah 37:38. The LXX has *gēn Ararat* (earth [land] of Ararat) in the former case while *Armenian* (Armenia) in the latter case.[9] If the region of Ararat is intended, then the reason is that there lie the sources of both the Euphrates and the Tigris, the rivers that encompass the locale of the scriptural story, a locale established early on in Genesis 2:14. The incontrovertibility of the immediate "clarity" as to the meaning of the phrase "the mountains of Ararat" lies ultimately in that an original hearer was not expected to wait until 2 Kings—let alone the erudite commentaries of centuries later— to figure out the authors' intention! For such hearer, "mountains of Ararat" was as "clear" as *babel* (Babel, Babylon)

---

[8] Actually only twice, since the texts of 2 Kings and Isaiah are copies of one another.
[9] This evidence is sealed in that the Vulgate has the converse: *terram Armeniorum* (land [earth] of the Armenians; 2 Kg 19:37) and *terram Ararat* (Is 37:38).

in Genesis 10:10 and 11:9, which is also situated between the two rivers and also does not occur again until 2 Kings 17:24.

God's intent of a severe fatherly punishment unto instruction rather than a judge's verdict unto obliteration is sealed in the mention of a covenant immediately after the announcement of the devastating flood: "For behold, I will bring a flood of waters upon the earth, to destroy all flesh in which is the breath of life from under heaven; everything that is on the earth shall die. But I will establish my covenant with you." (Gen 6:18-19) Later, in chapter 9, we shall learn that this covenant is binding on God alone, which confirms that God assumes full responsibility for having created the earth and all that lives on it (6:6-7). An essential aspect of the divine instruction is that it was not easy for God to redress the calamity in which man's sin jeopardized the entire earth. The hearer cannot escape both the lengthiness of the flood story line and the tentativeness of its resolution. Forty days of flooding that gradually submerges the entire earth (7:17-23) are followed by 150 days of full submersion (v.24), at the end of which God happens to remember Noah and the animals (8:1). The reversal of the flood takes another 150 days, during which the waters abated and the ark came to rest on Mount Ararat (vv.3-4). After that, two and half months are needed before the tops of other mountains could scarcely be seen (vv.4-5). Even then, it is only forty days later that Noah dares to "open the window of the ark" (v.6). The released crow kept "going to and fro" an indefinite number of times "until the waters were dried up from the earth" (v.7). Then came the turn of the dove, sign of God's peace, which peace ensures that the earth become a "*manoah*[10] (resting place) for the sole of the foot," but no such rest was to be found (v.9). It took seven days and then another seven days for the earth to become again habitable (vv.10-12) as God originally intended it to be (1:9-13). It took God one full year (7:6; 8:13) to commit his instructional

---

[10] From the same root as *noah* and *nuh*.

punishment and turn the page to initiate a fresh start on the first day of the first month of a new year (8:13).

Here again, under the influence of Platonic philosophy, the classic theological approach to scripture followed the path of individualistic anthropology and misread the flood narrative along the same lines as it did the creation narrative. Classical theology viewed the creation narrative as being the story of the "individual" Adam, and also read the flood narrative as dealing with the salvation of the "individual" Noah. However, a closer look at the latter narrative will show that the author's concern is still the same "earth" with which he was concerned in Genesis 1-4. The lesson of Genesis 6-8 is the following: due to the wickedness of Adam, "the man," the earth was threatened with obliteration, and it is only through the righteousness of Noah, "the son of man (Adam)," that God will condescend to salvage the earth he created with its vegetation and its inhabitants— animals as well as humans.

12

The Toledot of Noah's Sons

As the *toledot* of Noah are thus closely linked to those of Adam, they are also closely knit with the *toledot* of Noah's sons (Gen 10:1). This is evident in that the mention of Noah's progeny brackets the passage 6:1-8:

> And Noah was five hundred years old: and Noah begat Shem, Ham, and Japheth. (Gen 5:32)

> These *are* the generations of Noah: ... and Noah begat three sons, Shem, Ham, and Japheth. (6:9-10 KJV)[1]

The repetition of Noah's giving birth indirectly to three sons is clearly a departure from how his forefathers were handled:

> When Seth had lived a hundred and five years, he became the father of Enosh. Seth lived after the birth of Enosh eight hundred and seven years, and had other sons and daughters. Thus all the days of Seth were nine hundred and twelve years; and he died. (5:6-8)

These give birth to their son and then, after the birth of that son, to many other "sons and daughters." Noah, on the other hand, fathers *three sons*; we are not told that he had other sons and daughters. Furthermore, the births of the three sons are lumped together as though they were triplets, although later we hear of Ham being the "younger (or youngest)" (9:24). The reason is that in Noah's case the marker between "before" and "after" is not the birth of a son, but rather the flood: "*After the flood* Noah lived three hundred and fifty years. All the days of Noah were nine hundred and fifty years; and he died." (9:28-29) It only makes sense since, had God's decision not been

---

[1] I opted for KJV over RSV because here again the latter, in total disregard to both the original and its parent KJV, does not actually translate since it renders the same original *wayyoled* into "became the father of" in 5:32 and into "had" in 6:10. It sounds like a term paper where the student tries not to use twice the same expression back to back!

rescinded, both Noah and his sons would have died at the same time. However, according to the scriptural scenario, Noah's sons continue living and procreating. Still, what is important in the flood being the marker between "before" and "after" lies in that it is not so much Noah and his wife, but rather the three sons *and their wives* who straddled that marker, which in turn secured the continuation of the human race: "These three were the sons of Noah; and from these *the whole earth was peopled.*" (9:19) The centrality of that point for the story is not only logical and thus assumed, but is also underscored:

> But I will establish my covenant with you; and you shall come into the ark, you, your sons, your wife, and your sons' wives with you. (6:18)

> And Noah and his sons and his wife and his sons' wives with him went into the ark, to escape the waters of the flood. (7:7)

> On the very same day Noah and his sons, Shem and Ham and Japheth, and Noah's wife and the three wives of his sons with them entered the ark, (7:13)

> Go forth from the ark, you and your wife, and your sons and your sons' wives with you. (8:16)

> So Noah went forth, and his sons and his wife and his sons' wives with him. (8:18)

In its own way this underscoring enhances the vital importance already given "the daughters of men" in the prelude to the flood (6:1-8) as well as in the *toledot* of Noah and his sons.

The covenant of God in the flood story is unique on two levels. On the one hand, one hears of it *before* the flood, thus giving assuredness to the hearer that all will end well: "For behold, I will bring a flood of waters upon the earth, to destroy all flesh in which is the breath of life from under heaven; everything that is on the earth shall die. But I will establish my covenant with you; and you shall come into the ark, you, your sons, your wife, and your sons' wives with you." (6:17-18) The covenant "contains" the flood, which threatened total annihilation of the entire creation living on the (dry) "ground," within the lifespan of Noah. More importantly, the covenant was *one-sided*, that is, binding on God alone, who would allow his creation to "remain" and "continue" on the basis of God's blessing of procreation:

> And when the Lord smelled the pleasing odor, the Lord said in his heart, "I will never again curse the ground because of man, for the imagination of man's heart is evil from his youth; neither will I ever again destroy every living creature as I have done. While the earth remains, seedtime and harvest, cold and heat, summer and winter, day and night, shall not cease." (8:21-22)

When compared with the subsequent covenants with Abraham and Moses, the one-sidedness of that first covenant is evident in that the "sign" of the rainbow linked to it lies solely in God's hands and does not depend on the human being in any way. On the other hand, and because it is "one-sided," this covenant has a perennial value. It functions as a harbinger of the final covenant of peace that will be concluded with the "new" David at the end of the scriptural odyssey where God commits himself unilaterally: "For this is like the days of Noah to me: as I swore that the waters of Noah should no more go over the earth, so I have sworn that I will not be angry with you and will not rebuke you. For the mountains may depart and the hills be removed, but my steadfast love shall not depart from you, and my covenant of peace shall not be removed, says the Lord, who has compassion on you." (Is 54:9-10) It is interesting to note that that covenant of peace will be concluded with *all peoples* just as the one with Noah was with *all the descendants of Noah's sons*: "Incline your ear, and come to me; hear, that your soul may live; and I will make with you an everlasting covenant, my steadfast, sure love for David. Behold, I made him a witness to the peoples, a leader and commander for the peoples." (55:3-4) The concern for all peoples in Genesis is evident in the detailed list of nations in the ensuing lengthy chapter 10.

The Curse of Canaan

Both the *toledot* of the heavens and the earth and those of Adam
end with closing remarks (Gen 4:25-26 and 6:1-8) that not only
prepare for the following *toledot*, but also encapsulate the entire
message of scripture. This particular interest of the authors is
found again, and for the third time,[2] at the conclusion of the
toledot of Noah (9:18-29). This passage seems an unnecessary
aside at first hearing; however, it is as overarching in its value
and function for the entire scripture as its predecessors, if not
more so, since it introduces Canaan which is, to say the least,
one of the most central scriptural "entities":

> [18] The sons of Noah who went forth from the ark were Shem,
> Ham, and Japheth. Ham was the father of Canaan.[19] These three
> were the sons of Noah; and from these the whole earth was
> peopled. [20] Noah was the first tiller of the soil. He planted a
> vineyard; [21] and he drank of the wine, and became drunk, and lay
> uncovered in his tent. [22] And Ham, the father of Canaan, saw the
> nakedness of his father, and told his two brothers outside. [23] Then
> Shem and Japheth took a garment, laid it upon both their
> shoulders, and walked backward and covered the nakedness of
> their father; their faces were turned away, and they did not see
> their father's nakedness. [24] When Noah awoke from his wine and
> knew what his youngest son had done to him, [25] he said, "Cursed
> be Canaan; a slave of slaves shall he be to his brothers." [26] He also
> said, "Blessed by the Lord my God be Shem; and let Canaan be
> his slave." [27] God enlarge Japheth, and let him dwell in the tents
> of Shem; and let Canaan be his slave." [28] After the flood Noah
> lived three hundred and fifty years. [29] All the days of Noah were
> nine hundred and fifty years; and he died. (9:18-29)

This passage is ingeniously constructed in that it introduces
both the *toledot* of the sons of Noah (10:1) and the aside
concerning the blessing of Shem and the curse of Canaan. Both
subjects are preceded by the statement concerning "the sons of
Noah" (9:18-19). Notice how the two topics are introduced in
the order in which they will be dealt with: first one hears that

---

[2] The numeral three reflects fulfilment and assurance in the sense of "it is indeed so."

Ham was the father of Canaan (v.18b), whose cursing is the subject of the story that follows (vv.20-27), then one hears of the populating of the earth (v.19b), which is the subject matter of chapter 10. However, as we shall see, this passage is more than a simple aside. Canaan will be highly profiled in the list of nations where he is dealt with over five verses (10:15-19). The prominent feature of repopulating the earth will use the verb *naphesah* (was peopled) under the form *phus* in 11:4, 8, 9 as well as 10:18. Hence, it will behoove us to give closer attention to Genesis 9:18-29 to unlock its versatile functionality.

The peopling of the earth after the flood is through Noah's sons:

These are the sons of Japheth in their lands, each with his own language, by their families, in their nations. (10:5)

These are the sons of Ham, by their families, their languages, their lands, and their nations (10:20)

These are the sons of Shem, by their families, their languages, their lands, and their nations. (10:31)

The people and the areas where they live often coalesce in scripture. A "personal" name is often used to identify a locality. This applies not only to Japheth, Ham and Shem in the list of nations, but also to other well-known areas or cities:

The sons of Ham: Cush, Egypt, Put, and Canaan (10:6)

The sons of Cush: Seba, Havilah, Sabtah, Raamah, and Sabteca. The sons of Raamah: Sheba and Dedan. (10:7)

Canaan became the father of Sidon his first-born (10:15)

The sons of Shem: Elam, Asshur, Arpachshad, Lud, and Aram (10:22)

Joktan became the father of Almodad, Sheleph, Hazarmaveth, Jerah, Hadoram, Uzal, Diklah, Obal, Abimael, Sheba, Ophir, Havilah, and Jobab; all these were the sons of Joktan (10:26-29)

As I showed earlier the lapse or imperfection of Noah lay in that he planted a vineyard (9:20b). This action was that of a

sedentary and thus urban person. I should like to linger on
Genesis 9:20b in order to point out the necessity of the original
to perceive the author's intention and thus the actual meaning
of the text. Except for the LXX, which kept the syntax of the
original at the price of sounding awkward,[3] most of the other
translations either supply the verb "to be" (KJV) or avoid the
original "began" (RSV) in order to make sense of the original.
One of the translations that capture the original is the Jerusalem
Bible: "Noé, le cultivateur, commença de planter la vigne.
(Noah, the farmer [husbandman], began to plant the vine.)"
This is precisely how the Hebrew sounds: *'iš ha'adamah* (the man
of the ground) is an apposition describing Noah. However,
given the play we witnessed in the original on these two nouns
and their interconnection, it is hard to imagine that the author
not only intended this apposition but also expressed it in this
phrase, unique in scripture. Both literally and technically
speaking, this phrase is untranslatable; it must be *heard* in the
original in order to be understood. We have seen that *(ha)'adam*
understood himself as *'iš*. Although equivalent, they are
functionally different: *(ha)'adam* is the counterpart of *ha'adamah*
(the ground), whereas *'iš* is the counterpart of *'iššah* (woman). In
either case, the "man" is in a relation of either "son" or
"husband" to the ground whence he was taken. Since *'adam* is
also the personal name of the first human being, the author
opted for *'iš* to speak of Noah in relation to the ground.[4] So
Noah, as Adam before him in the garden God had planted, was
supposed to remain dependent on the ground as its "son",
feeding with his flock on the herb and trees of the earth—that
is to say as a shepherd. He decided instead to take the role of
God as planter. However, the vine made him a sedentary and
thus on his way to becoming as Cain before him, that is to settle
and build a city. Noah's propensity for building had already
been hinted at earlier: "Then Noah built an altar to the Lord,
and took of every clean animal and of every clean bird, and

---

[3] "And began Noah farmer of the earth and planted a vineyard."
[4] Besides, *'adam ha'adamah* instead of *'iš ha'adamah* would have sounded awkward.

offered burnt offerings on the altar" (8:20). To be sure, he built an altar to offer sacrifices as did Abel before him, and he used "lawfully" pure animals; moreover, one can safely assume, since he had just gone forth out of the ark, that he didn't take his time to erect a stone building but used any rudimentary material available for a one time altar. Still, by using the verb "build," the author was preparing the hearer for Noah's intention to "settle." Instead of remaining the man (male person) of the ground (thus husband or son), that is Adamic, living out of whatever the ground produces automatically, he decided to plant a garden with vegetation (herbs) and trees, the way only God can do. In other words, he decided to take care of the ground instead of letting it take care of him; instead of *'iš* (*'adam* from *ha'adamah*) he became the *'adon* (master) and *ba'al* (ruler), while scripture unequivocally declares that God is not only the sole universal King but also, and by the same token, the only *'adon* (master):

> Behold, the ark of the covenant of *the Lord* ('adon) *of all the earth* is to pass over before you into the Jordan. Now therefore take twelve men from the tribes of Israel, from each tribe a man. And when the soles of the feet of the priests who bear the ark of the Lord (*yahweh*), *the Lord* ('adon) *of all the earth*, shall rest in the waters of the Jordan, the waters of the Jordan shall be stopped from flowing, and the waters coming down from above shall stand in one heap. (Josh 3:11-13)

What is interesting concerning this last passage is that it comes at the crossing of the waters of the Jordan that were contained by God, which is reminiscent of Genesis 9 where Noah and his companions were allowed to enjoy the dry land after the same God had contained the waters of the flood. However, unlike human lordship, God, as in the case of the crossing of the Jordan, uses his being *'adon* for the good of his subjects. That is why, at the end, toward his repentant subjects he will show his true face, that of being their *'iš* (husband) instead of appearing as their *ba'al* (suppressive ruler):

> And in that day, says the Lord, you will call me, 'My husband,'
> (*'išši*) and no longer will you call me, 'My Baal' (*ba'ali*). (Hos 2:16
> RSV)

> And it shall be at that day, saith the Lord, *that* thou shalt call me
> Ishi; and shalt call me no more Baali. (Hos 2:16 KJV)

Another feature of drinking wine is that it is linked to festivities
that only the rich and powerful can afford: "Hear this word, ye
kine of Bashan, that *are* in the mountain of Samaria, which
oppress the poor, which crush the needy, which say to their
masters (*'adonim*), Bring, and let us drink." (Am 4:1 KJV) And
those husbands-masters are accused of committing violence
while enjoying their festivities:

> O you who put far away the evil day, and bring near the seat of
> violence? Woe to those who lie upon beds of ivory, and stretch
> themselves upon their couches, and eat lambs from the flock, and
> calves from the midst of the stall; who sing idle songs to the sound
> of the harp, and like David invent for themselves instruments of
> music; who drink wine in bowls, and anoint themselves with the
> finest oils, but are not grieved over the ruin of Joseph! (6:3-6)

The same violence, together with robbery, is linked earlier to
human power:

> Proclaim to the strongholds in Assyria, and to the strongholds in
> the land of Egypt, and say, "Assemble yourselves upon the
> mountains of Samaria, and see the great tumults within her, and
> the oppressions in her midst." "They do not know how to do
> right," says the Lord, "those who store up violence and robbery
> in their strongholds." (3:9-10)

Still, what is more important for our case is that it was violence
upon the earth which triggered God's wrath and unleashed the
flood:

> Now the earth was corrupt in God's sight, and the earth was filled
> with violence. And God saw the earth, and behold, it was corrupt;
> for all flesh had corrupted their way upon the earth. And God
> said to Noah, "I have determined to make an end of all flesh; for

the earth is filled with violence through them; behold, I will destroy them with the earth." (Gen 6:11-13)

So, by excessively indulging in wine, Noah was paving the way toward the reverting of the earth and its population (9:1-2, 9-12, 15-17) to their pre-flood state. Later, we shall see how Jeremiah will offer to the "urban" Jerusalem a way out of its impasse using the Rechabites, dwellers of tents as well as abstinent from wine, as an example to follow:

The word which came to Jeremiah from the Lord in the days of Jehoiakim the son of Josiah, king of Judah: "Go to the house of the Rechabites, and speak with them, and bring them to the house of the Lord, into one of the chambers; then offer them wine to drink." So I took Jaazaniah the son of Jeremiah, son of Habazziniah, and his brothers, and all his sons, and the whole house of the Rechabites. I brought them to the house of the Lord into the chamber of the sons of Hanan the son of Igdaliah, the man of God, which was near the chamber of the princes, above the chamber of Maaseiah the son of Shallum, keeper of the threshold. Then I set before the Rechabites pitchers full of wine, and cups; and I said to them, "Drink wine." But they answered, "We will drink no wine, for Jonadab the son of Rechab, our father, commanded us, 'You shall not drink wine, neither you nor your sons for ever; you shall not build a house; you shall not sow seed; you shall not plant or have a vineyard; but you shall live in tents all your days, that you may live many days in the land where you sojourn.' We have obeyed the voice of Jonadab the son of Rechab, our father, in all that he commanded us, to drink no wine all our days, ourselves, our wives, our sons, or our daughters, and not to build houses to dwell in. We have no vineyard or field or seed; but we have lived in tents, and have obeyed and done all that Jonadab our father commanded us. But when Nebuchadrezzar king of Babylon came up against the land, we said, 'Come, and let us go to Jerusalem for fear of the army of the Chaldeans and the army of the Syrians.' So we are living in Jerusalem." Then the word of the Lord came to Jeremiah: "Thus says the Lord of hosts, the God of Israel: Go and say to the men of Judah and the inhabitants of Jerusalem, Will you not receive instruction and listen to my words? says the Lord. The command which Jonadab the son of Rechab gave to his sons, to drink no wine, has been kept; and they drink none to this day, for they have obeyed their father's command. I have spoken to you persistently, but you have not listened to me. I have sent to you all my servants the prophets, sending them persistently, saying, 'Turn now every one of you from his evil way, and amend your doings, and do not go after other gods to serve them, and then you shall dwell in the land which I gave to you and your fathers.' But you did not incline your ear or listen to me. The sons of Jonadab the son of Rechab have kept the command which their father gave them, but this people has not obeyed me. Therefore, thus says the Lord, the God of hosts, the God of Israel: Behold, I am bringing on Judah and all the inhabitants of Jerusalem all the evil that I have pronounced against them; because I have spoken to them and they have not listened, I have called to them and they have not answered." But to the house of the Rechabites Jeremiah said, "Thus says the Lord of hosts, the God of Israel: Because you have obeyed the command of Jonadab your father, and kept all his precepts, and done all that he commanded you, therefore thus says the Lord of hosts, the God of Israel: Jonadab the son of Rechab shall never lack a man to stand before me." (Jer 35:1-19)

The kingly undertone concerning Noah's planting a vineyard is detectable in the use of "began" (*heḥel*) which looks ahead to the following two occurrences of that verb in Genesis 10:8 and 11:6 that are interconnected in that they both refer to Babel. In the first instance we hear:

Cush became the father of Nimrod; he *was the first* (*heḥel*) on earth to be a *mighty* man. He was a *mighty* hunter before the Lord; therefore it is said, "Like Nimrod a *mighty* hunter before the Lord." The beginning of his *kingdom* was *Babel*, Erech, and Accad, all of them in the land of Shinar. (10:8-10)

In the second instance we hear:

And they said to one another, "Come, let us make bricks, and burn them thoroughly." And they had brick for stone, and bitumen for mortar. Then they said, "Come, let us build ourselves a city, and a tower with its top in the heavens, and let us make a name for ourselves, lest we be scattered abroad upon the face of the whole earth." And the Lord came down to see the city and the tower, which the sons of men had built. And the Lord said, "Behold, they are one people, and they have all one language; and this is only the *beginning of what they* (*hillam*) will do; and nothing that they propose to do will now be impossible for them..." (11:3-6)

Therefore is the name of it called *Babel*; because the Lord did there confound the language of all the earth: and from thence did the Lord scatter them abroad upon the face of all the earth. (11:9)

So having started his story in the footsteps of Enoch, "walking (*hithallek*) with *ha'elohim*" (6:9; compare with 5:22 and 24) as a shepherd would, Noah reneges on that way of life in favor of urbanism, which introduces a curse on his progeny. Consequently, the scriptural story dismisses him in order to prepare the scene for the true "heir" of Enoch, Shem whose progeny, as I shall show, is essentially one of shepherds. Moreover, Shem and his descendants beget "sons and daughters," as did Adam and his progeny before Noah; neither Noah nor his sons are said to have begotten "daughters."[5] In other words, although it appears that Noah and his sons, together with their wives, harbinger *a* new beginning, it is only the *toledot* of Shem *the shepherd* that instate *the* new beginning. Shem tops Adam in that Adam's *toledot* (5:1-6:8) end up with those multiplying self-aggrandizement (6:1-2, 4) and with Noah (v.8), ultimately a renegade (9:20-27). The *toledot* of Shem (11:10-26) culminate with Terah "the father of Abram" (v.26). Abram's wife Sarai was *barren* (vv.29-30) and, apparently, without progeny. All this, in turn, looks forward to the prophetic promise concerning the fruitfulness of the "barren" wilderness of the shepherds where God will be the sole true *iš* of his followers, those who *hithallek* on the path of his commandments:

"For their mother has played the harlot; she that conceived them has acted shamefully. For she said, 'I will go after my lovers, who

---

[5] See earlier my comments concerning this matter.

give me my bread and my water, my wool and my flax, my oil
and my drink.' Therefore I will hedge up her way with thorns;
and I will build a wall against her, so that she cannot find her
paths. She shall pursue her lovers, but not overtake them; and she
shall seek them, but shall not find them. Then she shall say, 'I will
go and return to my first husband, for it was better with me then
than now.' And she did not know that it was I who gave her the
grain, the wine, and the oil, and who lavished upon her silver and
gold which they used for Baal. Therefore I will take back my
grain in its time, and my wine in its season; and I will take away
my wool and my flax, which were to cover her nakedness. Now I
will uncover her lewdness in the sight of her lovers, and no one
shall rescue her out of my hand. And I will put an end to all her
mirth, her feasts, her new moons, her sabbaths, and all her
appointed feasts. And I will lay waste her vines and her fig trees,
of which she said, 'These are my hire, which my lovers have given
me.' I will make them a forest, and the beasts of the field shall
devour them. And I will punish her for the feast days of the Baals
when she burned incense to them and decked herself with her
ring and jewelry, and went after her lovers, and forgot me, says
the Lord. "Therefore, behold, I will allure her, and bring her into
the wilderness, and speak tenderly to her. And there I will give
her her vineyards, and make the Valley of Achor a door of hope.
And there she shall answer as in the days of her youth, as at the
time when she came out of the land of Egypt. "And in that day,
says the Lord, you will call me, 'My husband,' and no longer will
you call me, 'My Baal.' For I will remove the names of the Baals
from her mouth, and they shall be mentioned by name no more.
*And I will make for you a covenant on that day with the beasts of the field,
the birds of the air, and the creeping things of the ground;* and I will abolish
the bow, the sword, and war from the land; and I will make you
lie down in safety. And I will betroth you to me for ever; I will
betroth you to me in righteousness and in justice, in steadfast love,
and in mercy. I will betroth you to me in faithfulness; and you
shall know the Lord. "And in that day, says the Lord, I will
answer the heavens and they shall answer the earth; and the earth
shall answer the grain, the wine, and the oil, and they shall answer
Jezreel; and I will sow him for myself in the land. And I will have
pity on Not pitied, and I will say to Not my people, 'You are my
people'; and he shall say 'Thou art my God.'" (Hos 2:5-23)

Notice how the author intentionally brings into the picture the covenant of Genesis where "the beasts of the field, the birds of the air, and the creeping things of the ground" are included (Hos 2:18a; Gen 9:10).

Unfortunately, we were all trained in the "good guy/bad guy" approach to reality. What is even worse is that we tend to associate ourselves with the "good guys," which explains why we cannot fathom that *in scripture* not even Jesus is good; only God is good (Mk 10:17-18/Lk 18:18-19): "None is righteous, no, not one; no one understands, no one seeks for God. All have turned aside, together they have gone wrong; no one does good, not even one." (Rom 3:10-12) Hence, except for Enoch, not even Noah can sustain his "perfection." After having begun by "walking with God" as Enoch did and being "righteous" and "blameless in his generation" (Gen 6:9), Noah falters as Adam did before him. Not only did he follow in Cain's footsteps by planting a vineyard and opting for a sedentary life, but he also indulged in overdrinking its produce, instead of just "enjoying" (*nuaḥ*) it.[6] The result was that he became inebriated, which in turn led to Ham's temptation. Scripture is not ambivalent regarding this matter (Mt 18:6/Mk 9:42/Lk 17:2). Still, it is striking that the one who is cursed is Canaan rather than his father Ham. This is done in view of the function the *scriptural* Canaan will have in the *scriptural* story. Canaan, the "earth of the divine promise," is tantamount to the Syrian Desert where the scriptural story is played out. That earth will be the area where the divine blessing or the divine curse will be implemented, depending on the people's obedience or disobedience to the divine commandments. We see consequences of this in the first few chapters of Genesis, and it will resurface time and again throughout scripture, especially when it concerns the "earth" granted to the people to live on. The curse or blessing in the Law (Lev 26) is the "sword of

---

[6] See earlier my discussion concerning the similar root behind the name *noaḥ* (Noah) and the verbal root *nuaḥ* (enjoy).

Damocles" hanging over the heads of the people. This message is so central to scripture that the words of the Law are repeated in Deuteronomy (28) just before the scriptural Israel steps into Canaan, and repeated again upon stepping into Canaan (Josh 8:30-35). It is also found unexpectedly at the close of the Latter Prophets and, to boot, repeated over the heads of the *righteous* as the *last words* of the God who spoke in the Prophets, represented by Elijah, and the Law, represented by Moses. This scenario will be revisited in the pericopes of the Transfiguration (Mt/Mk/Lk):

> For behold, the day comes, burning like an oven, when all the arrogant and all evildoers will be stubble; the day that comes shall burn them up, says the Lord of hosts, so that it will leave them neither root nor branch. But for you who fear my name the sun of righteousness shall rise, with healing in its wings. You shall go forth leaping like calves from the stall. And you shall tread down the wicked, for they will be ashes under the soles of your feet, on the day when I act, says the Lord of hosts. Remember the law of my servant Moses, the statutes and ordinances that I commanded him at Horeb for all Israel. Behold, I will send you Elijah the prophet before the great and terrible day of the Lord comes. And he will turn the hearts of fathers to their children and the hearts of children to their fathers, lest I come and smite the land with a curse. (Mal 4:1-6)

The significance of this thought in scripture, New as well as Old Testament, will find resonance in its last words where blessing and curse are cast against the scenario of its first words in Genesis 2:

> I warn every one who hears the words of the prophecy of this book: if any one adds to them, God will add to him the plagues described in this book, and if any one takes away from the words of the book of this prophecy, God will take away his share in *the tree of life* and in the holy city, which are described in this book. (Rev 22:18-19)

Noah's Last Days

The description of Noah's last days (Gen 9:18-29) not only
prepares for the curse of Canaan (vv.20-27) through the
mention of Ham as "father of Canaan" (v.18b), but also for the
subsequent chapter that deals with populating the earth: "These
three were the sons of Noah; and from these the whole earth
was peopled (*naphesah*)." (v.19) The verb *naphas* that is translated
as "was peopled," is rare in scripture and is found only in this
instance in the Pentateuch. The safest way to figure out its
meaning and function here is to appeal to Jeremiah where it
occurs nine times in a row:

> You are my hammer and weapon of war: with you I *break* nations
> *in pieces*;[7] with you I destroy kingdoms; with you I *break in pieces*[8]
> the horse and his rider; with you I *break in pieces*[9] the chariot and
> the charioteer; with you I *break in pieces* man and woman; with you
> I *break in pieces*[10] the old man and the youth; with you I *break in
> pieces*[11] the young man and the maiden; with you I *break in pieces*[12]
> the shepherd and his flock; with you I *break in pieces*[13] the farmer
> and his team; with you I *break in pieces*[14] governors and
> commanders. (51:20-23)

In all instances the LXX renders *naphas* through the verb
diaskorpizō whose meaning is "scatter, disperse." It is clear from
the context this is accomplished through shattering, which is
captured in the Vulgate's *conlido/collido* (collide, make collide)
and can be heard in the paraphrase "break into pieces" in both
KJV and RSV. Still, what is peculiar to Genesis 9:19 when
compared to the passage in Jeremiah is that in Genesis the verb
is used intransitively, that is, without a direct object; hence the
RSV's use of the passive "was peopled." KJV retains the spirit

---

[7] Heb *niphasti*, LXX *diaskorpizeis*, VUL *conlidis*.
[8] Heb *niphasti*, LXX *diaskorpiō*, VUL *conlidam*.
[9] Heb *niphasti*, LXX *diaskorpiō*, VUL *conlidam*.
[10] Heb *niphasti*, LXX *diaskorpiō*, VUL *conlidam*.
[11] Heb *niphasti*, LXX *diaskorpiō*, VUL *conlidam*.
[12] Heb *niphasti*, LXX *diaskorpiō*, VUL *conlidam*.
[13] Heb *niphasti*, LXX *diaskorpiō*, VUL *conlidam*.
[14] Heb *niphasti*, LXX *diaskorpiō*, VUL *conlidam*.

of the original with its active voice "overspread." However, both
KJV and RSV miss the negative connotation of the original,
which is preserved in the LXX and Vulgate. The awkwardness
of the original is that the subject of the verb connoting
"shattering, division, scattering, dispersion" is the "earth,"
which is a technical impossibility. So the LXX and Vulgate
resorted to paraphrasing, thus changing the grammatical
function of the "earth" from subject to recipient of the action of
the "dispersion" of the human beings, which makes much more
sense:

τρεῖς οὗτοί εἰσιν οἱ υἱοὶ Νωε ἀπὸ τούτων διεσπάρησαν ἐπὶ πᾶσαν
τὴν γῆν (Gen 9:19 LXX)

tres isti sunt filii Noe et ab his disseminatum est omne hominum
genus super universam terram (Gen 9:19 VUL)

Still the awkwardness of this verse in the original Hebrew
needs to be addressed. The author opted for the verb *naphaṣ* in
preparation for the use of the related verb *phuṣ*[15] which occurs
no less than four times in the subsequent story of the *toledot* of
Noah's three sons: Genesis 10:18; 11:4, 8, 9. The intentional use
of *naphaṣ* in 9:9 is confirmed in the immediately following
instance of *phuṣ*, which is consonantally composed of the same
three Hebrew letters to the extent that both sound identical. It
is as though they are from the same verb with different
conjugational endings. In the first case the subject is the singular
feminine *'ereṣ* (earth), whereas in the second case the subject is
the plural *mišpaḥot* (families):

These three were the sons of Noah; and from these the whole
earth was peopled (*naphesah*). (9:19)

Afterward the families of the Canaanites spread abroad (*naphoṣu*).
(10:18b)

---

15 In scripture, the verb *phuṣ* is used much more frequently than *naphaṣ*.

Those of my readers who know Hebrew will realize that these two verbs coalesce meaning wise, which is reflected in all translations.[16]

Since all three instances of *phuṣ* in chapter 11 clearly have a negative connotation, one can safely surmise that the same connotation should be applied to *phuṣ* in 10:18b: "Afterward the families of the Canaanites spread abroad (*naphoṣu*)." Notice how here RSV follows KJV that has used the same translation of "spread" in 9:18. Undoubtedly, the author used *naphaṣ* in 9:19b with an eye on 10:19b precisely because he "unwarrantedly" introduced Canaan at the end of 9:18: "The sons of Noah who went forth from the ark were Shem, Ham, and Japheth. Ham was the father of Canaan." This is corroborated in the use of a different verb *pharad*, which has a clearly positive connotation, to speak of the "spreading" of all the "nations" descending from all three sons as well as to speak specifically of the Japhethites, the "nations" par excellence as I shall show momentarily:

> From these the coastland peoples spread (*niphredu*). These are the sons of Japheth in their lands, each with his own language, by their families, in their nations. (10:5)

> These are the families of the sons of Noah, according to their genealogies, in their nations; and from these the nations spread abroad (*niphredu*) on the earth after the flood. (10:32)

That verb's positive connotation is borne out by its use in 2:10. There it describes the "division" of the river that watered the garden of the Lord God into the four major rivers that water the scriptural universe:

> A river flowed out of Eden to water the garden, and there it divided (*yiphphared*) and became four rivers (2:10)

As we shall see, instead of "spreading" all over the earth in order to multiply and fill the earth, the nations opted to

---

[16] The most plausible explanation is that the two verbs *naphaṣ* and *phuṣ* are "weak" verbs in that the consonant *nun* at the beginning of the first and the consonant *waw* (sounding as *u*) of the second either change or even drop out during conjugation.

congregate. That is why God will "break" them "apart" as a corrective punishment to further his original plan. The only exception are the descendants of Canaan because of the curse linked to him, that is to say, linked to the earth of Canaan, the earth of promise, which proved to be, due to the people's disobedience, cursed instead of blessed. In other words, the author played ingeniously on two verbs, *pharad* and *phus*; the effect of both appears to be the same, scattering and dispersion, yet the first is an expression of blessed multiplication and the second a punishment. Only God, in his own time, will turn the scattering of Israel residing in Canaan to exile among the nations into a blessing for all those nations (Isaiah, Jeremiah, Ezekiel). This is precisely what is implied in Genesis 9-11, at the conclusion of which we shall hear:

> Now the Lord said to Abram, "Go from your country and your kindred and your father's house to the land that I will show you. And I will make of you a great nation, and I will bless you, and make your name great, so that you will be a blessing. I will bless those who bless you, and him who curses you I will curse; and by you all the *families* (*mishpahot*) of the earth shall bless themselves." (12:1-3)

Notice how *mishpahot* here harks back to *mishpahot* in Genesis 10, which encompass all nations inclusive of the renegade Canaan, and beyond this to 8:19:

> From these the coastland peoples spread. These are the sons of Japheth in their lands, each with his own language, by their *families*, in their nations ... Afterward the *families* of the Canaanites spread abroad ... These are the sons of Shem, by their *families*, their languages, their lands, and their nations. These are the *families* of the sons of Noah, according to their genealogies, in their nations; and from these the nations spread abroad on the earth after the flood. (10:5, 10, 31-32)

> And every beast, every creeping thing, and every bird, everything that moves upon the earth, went forth by *families* out of the ark. (8:19)

As I indicated previously, in literature, it is the first instance of a term that defines it. Thus one is to perceive the human *mishpaḥah* as an animal *mishpaḥah* and not vice versa. The families of the earth, understood in the context of Genesis 12:1-3, are to be viewed as the "family" of Abram who, a few verses later, is presented as shepherd[17] and, by the same token, his *mishpaḥah* is to be viewed as a *mishpaḥah* of sheep. Accordingly, the blessing includes—and I would even venture to say, primarily—the *mishpaḥot* of the animal realm, that is, it is a repeat of Genesis 1 where the animals are blessed before the human being. Now one can understand why the authors of Genesis subsumed the blessing of the land animals into that of the human beings, which was preceded by the blessing of the fowl with whom they share the earth. That is why, in the so-called "messianic" era of universal peace, the land animals are incorporated in that purview:

> The wolf shall dwell with the lamb, and the leopard shall lie down with the kid, and the calf and the lion and the fatling together, and a little child shall lead them. The cow and the bear shall feed; their young shall lie down together; and the lion shall eat straw like the ox. The sucking child shall play over the hole of the asp, and the weaned child shall put his hand on the adder's den. (Is 11:6-8)

So one can see that the families of the nations issued from Noah's three sons include the animals that went forth with them out of the ark where they all were preserved in order to populate the earth. As stressed through repetition, the covenant instated is between God and "all living beings" (Gen 6:18-21; 9:1-3, 9-17). This is an invitation for the hearers to include mentally at the mention of "families" also the families of the animals, which is reflective of shepherdism. My conclusion finds support in that, after the lumping of all three brothers in one *toledot* (10:1) whose story runs until 11:9, comes the *toledot* of specifically one of them,

---

[17] That aspect of Abram was prepared for in the genealogy of his forebear Shem where the majority of the descendants' names reflect shepherdism (see later my comments on that genealogy).

Shem (v.10), whose progeny, as I shall show, is made up mainly of names that reflect shepherd life. Moreover, the following *toledot* that propels ahead the scriptural story is that of the last descendant of Shem, Terah (vv.26-27), whose first-born is none else than Abram *the shepherd* (13:5-9) through whom God's blessing will be secured for all the nations issued from the sons of Noah (12:2-3). Such cannot possibly be a coincidence. How the authors prepare for this culmination can be seen in the way they handle the *toledot* of the three sons of Noah and, more specifically, the function of each of those sons.

The Overlapping of Shem and Ham

We saw earlier how the closing of Adam's *toledot* (Gen 6:1-8) underlined the negative behavior of Adam's progeny and thus set up the scenario of the punishment through the flood that takes the lion's share in Noah's *toledot*. The closing of Noah's *toledot* (9:18-29) performs a similar function: it ends up with a negative aspect of Noah, the one who "found favor in the eyes of the Lord" because he "was a righteous man, blameless in his generation; and walked with God" (6:8-9). He not only ended up living a sedentary life à la Cain (9:20) instead of living as a shepherd à la Abel, but was the main culprit in introducing a "curse" in God's renewed creation (v.25) just as his forerunner Adam did in the garden of the original creation. Yet, in the same breath one hears of the blessing of Shem and that of Japheth through Shem (vv.26-27), which blessing will be secured through the promise made to the shepherd Abram.

A striking feature of the *toledot* of the three sons of Noah is the overlapping of the geographical "areas" of Shem and Ham to the extent that their supposedly two ethnicities are intermingled, much to the chagrin of the "historicizing" scholars:

- Canaan the "Semite" is said to be the son of Ham in 10:6.

- Nimrod, the king of the "Semitic" "Babel, Erech, and Accad, all of them in the land of Shinar" (v.10) is presented as the grandson of Ham through Cush (vv.6-9).

- Havilah is ascribed to both Shem (v.7) and Ham (v.29) and so is Sheba (vv.7, 28).

On the other hand, although Japheth originates in the faraway coastlands of Greece, in order for his descendants to share in Shem's blessing he is to "dwell in Shem's tents" (9:25-26), that is to say, accept the shepherd way of life and enjoy, as Shem does, God's gift of the earth with the animals, and receive God's blessing of procreation without curse when everything God has made was "very good" (1:29-31a). However, Japheth, through Alexander of Macedon, opts for the legacy of Nimrod, a descendant of Ham, by making Babel, Nimrod's city, his capital. Put otherwise, Japheth opted, through Alexander and his heirs, for the sedentary life and its buildings. That attitude, which will be visited in Genesis 10:1-9, will bring about on all the descendants of Noah God's "curse" in a similar manner as the flood. In both cases, the rain that is supposed to give life to the earth (2:5) will either submerge that earth through flooding or dismantle the human lofty stone buildings by "moistening" them into complete erosion.[18] Still, immediately after the episode of the tower of Babel (10:1-9) humankind is given a glimpse of a sure hope in the *toledot* of Shem the "shepherd" (vv.10-26). The *toledot* of Noah's three sons (10:1) carries on in the *toledot* of only one of them, Shem (*šem*; name) by whom God's chosen, from both Gentiles and Israel (Is 66:17-21), will be known at the end: "For as the new heavens and the new earth which I will make shall remain before me, says the Lord; so shall your descendants (Hebrew *zera*; Greek *sperma*; seed) and your name (Hebrew *šem*; Greek *onoma*) remain." (v.22)

---

[18] See later my comments on the destruction of the tower of Babel, Alexander's capital, through "moisture" (Gen 11:9).

13

The Nations and
the Peoples of the Earth

Just as Noah's name is functional so are the names of his children. The first Shem, *šem*, means "name," and thus "fame" as in "to make a name for oneself."[1] It fits perfectly the patriarch whose progeny will include Abraham "by whom all the families of the earth shall bless themselves" (Gen 12:3). The second, *ham*, is from the same root as "heat" and thus "ire." He, or at least his descendant Canaan, incurs the divine wrath and curse. As for Jepheth (Japheth), Noah's statement concerning him—"God enlarge (open up) Jepheth" (Gen 9:27)—sounds thus in Hebrew: *yapht 'elohim leyephet*. The correspondence between the verb "open" and the personal name is audible. Whereas Shem is blessed and Ham is cursed, Jepheth is neither blessed nor cursed; he simply shares in his brother's blessing:

> When Noah awoke from his wine and knew what his youngest son had done to him, he said, "Cursed be Canaan; a slave of slaves shall he be to his brothers." He also said, "Blessed by the Lord my God be Shem; and let Canaan be his slave. God enlarge Jepheth, and let him dwell in the tents of Shem; and let Canaan be his slave." (9:24-27)

Scripture is adamant about the oneness of the human race. Just as the pre-diluvial humanity is Adamic, the post-diluvial human race stems from Noah. The oneness of humanity is underscored in the way the *toledot* of the three children are presented together:[2] "These are the *toledot* of *the sons of Noah*, Shem, Ham, and Japheth." (Gen 10:1a) The addition of "sons were born to them after the flood" after these just mentioned

---

[1] See, e.g., Gen 11:14; 12:2; Ps 72:17-19.
[2] The numeral 3 reflects assured totality (see the Excursus on Number Symbolism in *NTI₃* 22-28). The *toledot* of Shem will be the subject of Gen 11:10-26.

sons is to anchor this reality in the hearer's mind. To further anchor the oneness of mankind, the author closes with the mention of Noah after the three family trees: "These are the families of *the sons of Noah*, according to their genealogies, in their nations; and from these the nations spread abroad on the earth after the flood." (v.32)

There is a preferential tilt for Jepheth over Ham that is detected in the phraseology used to speak of the spreading of their descendants. Whereas the progeny of Jepheth is said to have spread out (from the root *pharad*; v.5) just as the totality of the peoples did (v.32), it uses the verb *phuṣ* (v.18) concerning the descendants of Ham, which has the negative connotation of separate (from one another; scatter). This intended connotation is evident since this same verb *phuṣ* occurs later in the story of the tower of Babel (Gen 11). There the peoples planned to unite "lest we be scattered abroad (*naphuṣ*) upon the face of the whole earth" (v.4), and yet end up by being scattered by God himself as a punishment: "Therefore its name was called Babel, because there the Lord confused the language of all the earth; and from there the Lord scattered them abroad (*hephiṣam*, from *phuṣ*) over the face of all the earth." (v.9) The close link between the progeny of Ham and the story of the tower of Babel is evident in the names used in both (Shinar and Babel) and in the reference to building a majestic city:

> The sons of Ham: Cush, Egypt, Put, and Canaan. The sons of Cush: Seba, Havilah, Sabtah, Raamah, and Sabteca. The sons of Raamah: Sheba and Dedan. Cush became the father of Nimrod; he was the first on earth to be a mighty man. He was a mighty hunter before the Lord; therefore it is said, "Like Nimrod a mighty hunter before the Lord." The beginning of his kingdom was Babel, Erech, and Accad, all of them in the land of Shinar. From that land he went into Assyria, and built Nineveh, Rehoboth-Ir, Calah, and Resen between Nineveh and Calah; that is the great city. (10:6-12)

Now the whole earth had one language and few words. And as
men migrated from the east, they found a plain in the land of
Shinar and settled there. And they said to one another, "Come,
let us make bricks, and burn them thoroughly." And they had
brick for stone, and bitumen for mortar. Then they said, "Come,
let us build ourselves a city, and a tower with its top in the
heavens, and let us make a name for ourselves, lest we be
scattered abroad upon the face of the whole earth." And the Lord
came down to see the city and the tower, which the sons of men
had built. And the Lord said, "Behold, they are one people, and
they have all one language; and this is only the beginning of what
they will do; and nothing that they propose to do will now be
impossible for them. Come, let us go down, and there confuse
their language, that they may not understand one another's
speech." So the Lord scattered them abroad from there over the
face of all the earth, and they left off building the city. Therefore
its name was called Babel, because there the Lord confused the
language of all the earth; and from there the Lord scattered them
abroad over the face of all the earth. (11:1-11)

Moreover, Nimrod, whose name is from the root *marad* (rebel),
fits the attitude of the kings of Nineveh and Babylon, as well as
that of the protagonists in the story of Genesis 11:1-9.

The artificiality of the names of Noah's sons is at its clearest
in the way the author handles Ham's progeny. On the one
hand, he includes under Ham names that should have been
under Jepheth, such as the Philistines (10:14) whom he links to
Egypt (v.13), or under Shem, such as Canaan and all those
mentioned under him (vv.15-19) as well as Babel (v.10) and
Nineveh (v.11) whom he links to Cush (v.8), which is Upper
Egypt. On the other hand, he includes Elam (Persia) under
Shem (v.22) instead of under Jepheth as he did Media (Madai;
v.2)[3], and he names Havilah and Sheba under both Ham (v.7)
and Shem (vv.27-28). Thus, when orchestrating his list of

---

[3] Media was a kingdom adjacent to Elam/Persia. Cyrus I who conquered Babylon
in the 6th century B.C. was the king of both kingdoms. These two kingdoms are
mentioned as a pair *paras umaday* (Persia and Media) in Esther 1:3, 14, 16, 19. In the
last instance the pair is rendered as "the Persians and the Medes."

nations, the biblical author had two working references in mind. Firstly, the nations are lumped not only geographically, but also in spheres of influence. Secondly, the "enemies" of later Israel and Judah, which enemies will earn the divine "ire" in the prophetic books, are entered under Ham (*ham*; heat, ire). The corollary is that the areas of Ham and Shem overlap within the biblical scene of the Ancient Near East. The difference between them is not racial, but rather behavioral. Ham represents all the "wicked" who will be under divine ire and curse, whereas Shem is a stand-in for all the "blessed" who abide by God's will and to whom God will give a "name" (*šem*; fame), as he will promise Abram the Shemite (12:1-3). However, as Jeremiah will make clear, it is not fleshly circumcision that will differentiate between Israel and the others, but rather circumcision of the heart: "Behold, the days are coming, says the Lord, when I will punish all those who are circumcised but yet uncircumcised—Egypt, Judah, Edom, the sons of Ammon, Moab, and all who dwell in the desert that cut the corners of their hair; for all these nations are uncircumcised, and all the house of Israel is uncircumcised in heart." (Jer 9:25-26)

How about Jepheth? He functions as representative of the "nations," that is, all the outsiders who are ultimately invited to join in Shem's blessing: "God enlarge Jepheth, and let him dwell in the tents of Shem." (Gen 9:27) There are plenty of textual indications that militate for this. Jepheth, as a totality, is said to have spread just as did the totality of Noah's progeny: "*From these* (Jepheth's sons) *the coastland nations spread* [4] in their lands, each with his own language, by their families, in their nations" (10:5); "These are the families of the sons of Noah, according to their genealogies, in their nations; and *from these the nations spread* on the earth after the flood." (v.32) On the other hand, the term *'iyyim* (coastlands; isles), encountered only here in v. 5

---

[4] I am following the original Hebrew and even the Greek Septuagint in omitting the addition found in translations (such as RSV) that read: "From these the coastland peoples spread. *These are the sons of Japheth* in their lands, each with his own language, by their families, in their nations."

throughout the entire Pentateuch (*'iyye haggoyim*, the coastlands [isles] of the nations), will appear frequently in Isaiah and Ezekiel in reference to the (far) nations in contradistinction to Israel. Those *'iyyim* will one day be preached, together with Israel, the good news of salvation:

> Behold my servant, whom I uphold, my chosen, in whom my soul delights; I have put my Spirit upon him, he will bring forth justice to the nations. He will not cry or lift up his voice, or make it heard in the street; a bruised reed he will not break, and a dimly burning wick he will not quench; he will faithfully bring forth justice. He will not fail or be discouraged till he has established justice in the earth; and *the coastlands* wait for his law. Thus says God, the Lord, who created the heavens and stretched them out, who spread forth the earth and what comes from it, who gives breath to the people upon it and spirit to those who walk in it: "I am the Lord, I have called you in righteousness, I have taken you by the hand and kept you; I have given you as a covenant to the people, a light to the nations, to open the eyes that are blind, to bring out the prisoners from the dungeon, from the prison those who sit in darkness. I am the Lord, that is my name; my glory I give to no other, nor my praise to graven images. Behold, the former things have come to pass, and new things I now declare; before they spring forth I tell you of them." Sing to the Lord a new song, his praise from the end of the earth! Let the sea roar and all that fills it, *the coastlands* and their inhabitants. (Is 42:1-10)

Later, in Isaiah, we are told that the inhabitants of those far off coastland nations, the foreigners, will be granted a "name" (*šem*):

> Let not *the foreigner* who has joined himself to the Lord say, "The Lord will surely separate me from his people"; and let not the eunuch say, "Behold, I am a dry tree." For thus says the Lord: "To the eunuchs who keep my sabbaths, who choose the things that please me and hold fast my covenant, I will give in my house and within my walls a monument and *a name* better than sons and daughters; I will give them an everlasting *name* which shall not be cut off. "And *the foreigners* who join themselves to the Lord, to minister to him, to love the name of the Lord, and to be his servants, every one who keeps the sabbath, and does not profane

it, and holds fast my covenant—these I will bring to my holy mountain, and make them joyful in my house of prayer; their burnt offerings and their sacrifices will be accepted on my altar; for my house shall be called a house of prayer for all peoples. (Is 56:1-7)

And at the end of Isaiah we are told of the gathering of many nations in the new Jerusalem without differentiation between insider and foreigner. What is impressive, however, is that we hear, in conjunction with coastlands, the names of some Jephethite nations of Genesis. Notice the closeness in terminology:

> The sons of Japheth: Gomer, Magog, Madai, *Javan*, *Tubal*, Meshech, and Tiras. The sons of Gomer: Ashkenaz, Riphath, and Togarmah. The sons of *Javan*: Elishah, *Tarshish*, Kittim, and Dodanim. From these *the coastland nations* spread in their lands, each with his own language (tongue; *lašon*), by their families, in their nations. (Gen 10:2-5)

> For I know their works and their thoughts, and I am coming to gather *all nations* and tongues (*lešonot*); and they shall come and shall see my glory, and I will set a sign among them. And from them I will send survivors to *the nations*, to *Tarshish*, Put, and Lud,[5] who draw the bow, to *Tubal* and *Javan*, to *the coastlands* afar off, that have not heard my fame or seen my glory; and they shall declare my glory among *the nations*. And they shall bring all your brethren from *all the nations* as an offering to the Lord, upon horses, and in chariots, and in litters, and upon mules, and upon dromedaries, to my holy mountain Jerusalem, says the Lord, just as the Israelites bring their cereal offering in a clean vessel to the house of the Lord. And some of them also I will take for priests and for Levites, says the Lord. (Is 66:18-21)

The Tower of Babel

Between the *toledot* of Noah's sons (Gen 10) and the *toledot* of Shem (11:10-26) we have the episode of the tower of Babel,

---

[5] Notice the inclusion of the Hamite Put (Gen 10:6) and the Shemite Lud (v.22) as if the biblical author intended to include *all* nations in his purview.

which is linked to the previous passage through the term "language" (10:31 and 11:2). In the table of nations the languages or tongues are many (10:5 and 31), but the tower story starts with the one language: "Now the whole earth had one language and the same words."[6] (11:1) Since the end of this episode is the confusion of speech (11:7), the story functions as an appendix to the *toledot* of Noah's sons intending to explain the factual multiplicity of languages among the progeny of the originally one family.

Still, the explanation is scriptural, that is to say, from the scriptural perspective whose core is the critique of human arrogance. Taking over the position of majesty and authority that befits God alone[7] is tantamount to rebellion. Accordingly, the story is woven around Babel (11:8), one of the cities of Nimrod's kingdom or empire (10:10). Scripturally, as we hear time and again, the epitome of human arrogance lies in mishandled kingship, whether it is Pharaoh, or Solomon, or Sennacherib, or Nebuchadnezzar. Each is a Nimrod in his own way. In scripture solely "The Lord is (the good and righteous) King." He alone is the fatherly shepherd who tends his (scattered) sheep as "one" flock, whereas the arrogant kings scatter them unto oblivion and death (Ezek 34; 37:15-28). My referring to Ezekiel is due to the similarity in terminology. The noun *biq'ah* translated as "plain" (Gen 11:2) is the same word that occurs in Ezekiel and there is translated as plain or valley. Its original meaning is "a (watery) spot in the open," and thus is the opposite of a high and mighty summit. Ezekiel maintains that God in all his glory chose to appear to his prophet, not on the Mount of Jerusalem, but rather in a *biq'ah* (Ezek 3:22-23;

---

[6] RSV translates *debarim 'aḥadim* into "few words," which does not make sense. The idea behind Gen 11:1 is to stress the oneness and the mutual understanding between the peoples of the entire earth, as a premise for God's "confusing their speech, that they may not understand one another's speech" (v.7).

[7] See, e.g., Is 2.

8:4), and it is in that same *biq'ah* that he chose to bring his people
from the death of exile back into life (37:1-2).[8]

Instead of just dwelling on the plain, the people decided to
build a city, just as Cain did. [9] But they even surpassed Cain and
planned to "build a tower with its top in the heavens" and
"make a name (*šem*) for themselves." They disregarded the fact
that the only valid city and tower are the ones that God erects
as his vineyard (Is 5:1-2).[10] When the people "chip in" they mess
it up (vv.3-4) as the Psalmist—ironically Solomon—asserts:
"Unless the Lord builds the house, those who build it labor in
vain. Unless the Lord watches over the city, the watchman stays
awake in vain." (Ps 127:1)

God's intervention was not to allow the human beings to
realize *their* project. They wanted to build a city in order not to
be scattered (Gen 11:4). God turns the table against them: "So
the Lord scattered them abroad from there over the face of all the
earth, and *they left off building the city*. Therefore its name was
called Babel, because there the Lord confused the language of
all the earth; and from there *the Lord scattered them* abroad over
the face of all the earth." (vv.8-9) The repetition of the reference
to the city as well as of the action of scattering intends to
underscore that God *indeed* undid their doing, which "doing"
had just been mentioned doubly in God's description of man's
endeavor: "… and this is only the beginning of what *they will do*;
and nothing that they propose *to do* will now be impossible for
them." (v.6) I would be remiss if I didn't point out the functional
value of the verb *balal* which is usually translated as "confound."
However, its most common meaning is "moisten." As such, it
counteracts the action of building with bricks that have to be
burned (with fire) thoroughly (v.3) to dry. It is as though the aim
of *balal* is to extinguish the fire necessary to prepare the bricks

---

[8] These are the only instances of *biq'ah* in Ezekiel.

[9] This, in essence, is the same theme of disobedience that was seen earlier—Adam
was to simply settle in the garden of Eden; Cain was to dwell in the land of wandering.
See also my comments on "land of Nod."

[10] In both Genesis and Isaiah we have the same noun *migdal* to speak of the tower.

or alternatively to keep the bricks moist and not allow them to dry. The irony is exquisite. Instead of burning the (already erected) cities with fire, as he usually does in the prophetic books, God here intervenes during the construction by not allowing man to fulfill his project of construction. This understanding is supported by the fact that up to this point it is water rather than fire that has been the medium of divine chastisement. However, since God committed himself not to use water as a destructive flood that would have engulfed men, he used it to stop the construction of their city and mighty tower. By the same token, by "scattering" them (vv.8-9), God graciously preserved them in their initial calling, willed by God, of "spreading over the earth" (10:5, 32) in order to "fill it" (1:28; 9:1).

The Continuation of the Scriptural Story

The scriptural story line proceeds through Shem and does so without being affected by the flood which is presented as a period within the lifespan of Noah and his sons who were born before the flood (5:32) and survived it (8:15). The author's intention to point out the continuity in the Adamic humanity created by God is evident in that the *toledot* of Shem (11:10-26) is patterned after that of Adam. In each *toledot* a person begets his firstborn at a certain age, then lives so many years during which he begets other sons and daughters;[11] and each genealogy ends with the last person engendering three children (5:32; 11:26). The difference lies in the point of reference: the creation of man in the case of Adam (5:1-2); the flood in the case of Shem. However—and herein lies the contrast—in Adam's *toledot* we hear of Kenan, a stand-in for Cain who was the first builder of a city and of Lemech, the kingly ruler, whereas, the

---

[11] Mention of the death and the total number of years is not necessary with Shem as it was with Adam (see my comments above).

names of Shem's descendants reflect shepherdism. The choice of these names could not have been but intentional.

> These are the descendants of Shem. When Shem was a hundred years old, he became the father of Arpachshad two years after the flood; and Shem lived after the birth of Arpachshad five hundred years, and had other sons and daughters. When Arpachshad had lived thirty-five years, he became the father of Shelah; and Arpachshad lived after the birth of Shelah four hundred and three years, and had other sons and daughters. When Shelah had lived thirty years, he became the father of Eber; and Shelah lived after the birth of Eber four hundred and three years, and had other sons and daughters. When Eber had lived thirty-four years, he became the father of Peleg; and Eber lived after the birth of Peleg four hundred and thirty years, and had other sons and daughters. When Peleg had lived thirty years, he became the father of Reu; and Peleg lived after the birth of Reu two hundred and nine years, and had other sons and daughters. When Reu had lived thirty-two years, he became the father of Serug; and Reu lived after the birth of Serug two hundred and seven years, and had other sons and daughters. When Serug had lived thirty years, he became the father of Nahor; and Serug lived after the birth of Nahor two hundred years, and had other sons and daughters. When Nahor had lived twenty-nine years, he became the father of Terah; and Nahor lived after the birth of Terah a hundred and nineteen years, and had other sons and daughters. When Terah had lived seventy years, he became the father of Abram, Nahor, and Haran. Now these are the descendants of Terah. Terah was the father of Abram, Nahor, and Haran; and Haran was the father of Lot. Haran died before his father Terah in the land of his birth, in Ur of the Chaldeans. And Abram and Nahor took wives; the name of Abram's wife was Sarai, and the name of Nahor's wife, Milcah, the daughter of Haran the father of Milcah and Iscah. (11:10-28)

The name Arpachshad (11:10) is clearly of non-Semitic origin.[12] In the previous chapter we heard that he was the

---

[12] There is no need to get bogged down into figuring out its origin. What is of import is its functionality.

middle of five brothers, the other four being Elam, Asshur, Lud, and Aram (Gen 10:22). The authorial predilection if not outright bias for Arpachshad is evident on two counts. First of all, he is not the eldest. Secondly, his two grandsons, Peleg and Joktan, are mentioned (v.25), and Joktan's progeny is detailed in the next four verses (vv.26-29). The intention is obviously to foil the expectations of the hearers.[13] After hearing that Arpachshad and not one of his two older brothers is chosen as heir (11:10-12), and given the author's expansion of his progeny, the hearers will expect the same for the younger Joktan.[14] Still, the author's remarkable ingenuity lies in how he prepared in "Shem's progeny" in chapter 10 for the actual *toledot* of Shem in chapter 11 by introducing Arpachshad's grandsons (10:25). The verb *palag* means divide (mainly in two). Peleg and Joktan "divide" the scriptural world of the Syro-Arabian Desert. Joktan's progeny populate the southern part of the Arabian Desert. His three sons—Sheba, Ophir, and Havilah—are clearly representative of areas in its southernmost part; Hazermaveth is undoubtedly the area of contemporary Hadramawt east of Yemen. Peleg's progeny populate the Syrian Wilderness located in the northern part of the Arabian Desert.[15] The progeny of Peleg living in the Syrian Wilderness prepare for the "shepherd" style *toledot* of Shem.

In addition to Arpachshad, who was shown to be de facto the father of the residents of the Syro-Arabian Wilderness, all the other names in Shem's *toledot* betray shepherdism. The first *'eber* (Eber) is clearly the forefather of the *'abarim* (Hebrews) who are insistently as well as consistently presented a shepherds in

---

[13] A similar literary twist will be heard in Terah's *toledot*. Hearing that Abram's wife, Sarai, is barren and that his brother, Haran, had a son, the hearers cannot but assume that the legacy will be carried on through Haran's son Lot.

[14] The Hebrew *yoqtan* is from the root *qaton* (young), which is so obvious that the author did not need to explain it as he did Peleg: "To Eber were born two sons: the name of the one was Peleg, for in his days the earth was divided, and his brother's name was Joktan." (10:25)

[15] It is this area (the Syrian Wilderness) that the scriptural authors are most interested in.

Genesis. Early on Abram is introduced out of the blue sky as
"*the* Hebrew" (*haʿibri*; 14:13) which, in Hebrew, is literally
"pertaining to Eber." Reu (*reʿu*) is the most eloquent of all names
since it literally means "ye shepherd (graze)" (imperative plural
of the verb *raʿah* [shepherd; graze]), so it applies to both the
shepherds and their sheep. Serug (*serug*), the passive participle of
a very rare verb *sarag* meaning "intertwine," could well
reference the tight knit relation between members of the same
family (*mishpaḥah*) of either shepherds or sheep who have only
one another in the wilderness. Nahor (*naḥor*) is from a rarely
used root that connotes the sound emitted by an animal, more
specifically the snorting of horses, but it could apply to any herd
of animals.

Terah is meant to function at the end of the *toledot* of Shem as
Noah did at the end of the *toledot* of Adam. However, in the case
of Noah, there was hope that was only shattered much later,
after four chapters. By now, the hearers should have learned
that it is only by "walking with God" unflinchingly, as in the
case of Enoch, that there is assurance of life (5:22, 24), a life that
had been promised to and missed by Adam (Gen 2-3). The
powerful lesson of Enoch is that he appears as part of the
"ungodly" progeny of Adam. Appearances, however, can be
deceptive, and this is so with Terah. The name *terah* is already
a harbinger of bad news since its Semitic root *trḥ* connotes
sadness. One of Terah's sons, Haran, died before him while still
in Ur of the Chaldeans (Gen 11:28), that is, the earth of the later
exile. In other words, Haran was not part of the company that
was headed to Canaan, the earth of the promise (v.31).
Listening carefully to the original, an attentive ear will detect
word play that brings to mind the sad episode recounted in the
beginning of the chapter where the high building intended to be
raised in the plain of Shinar was razed and thus flattened to the
level of the plain. The original *haran* (personal name) is from the
noun *har* (mountain) with the ending *n*, typically a suffix of
profession or attribution; thus *haran* would be "mountaineer."
The original *ḥaran* (name of locality) is from the root *ḥr(r)*

connoting heat, again with the ending *n*; thus *ḥaran* would be a hot expanse corresponding to the Syrian Desert, which is precisely where the scriptural *ḥaran* is located.[16] So, in a manner of speaking, the "lofty" *haran* was not allowed to reach *ḥaran*, the "garden" planted in the Syrian Wilderness by the Lord God himself around the oasis Tadmor, but instead was left to die in the plain of rivers and buildings.

What is exceptional in the scriptural story of Abraham is that he does not have a *toledot*. The story line between chapters 12 and 24 is subsumed under Terah's *toledot*.[17] These chapters are replete with unfortunate stories and behaviors that are a letdown for the hopeful hearers of scripture. Suffice it to mention a few:

- Abram resorting to Egypt for food and forced to lie about Sarai.

- Abraham's feud with Lot, his nephew.

- The mistreatment of Hagar and her son, by her mistress Sarai who had used her for her own benefit. Add to this, that Ishmael was not only Abram's actual son but also circumcised on the same day as Abraham himself.

- Even after the covenant, when the Lord asked Abram to "walk before me and be blameless," both Abraham and Sarah "laughed" at God's promise.

- Abraham's shameless bargaining with God concerning God's justice in the episode with Sodom.

---

[16] Unfortunately, KJV and RSV render both *ḥaran* and *haran* as "Haran," which is confusing, whereas the LXX and the Vulgate differentiate between the two.

[17] The following *toledot*, those of Ishmael and of Isaac, occur in Genesis 25.

- The death punishment of the disobedient wife of Lot, which ended with Lot lying with his daughters to secure a progeny.

- A repeat of the experience with Pharaoh when Abraham again resorted to subterfuge to save his skin.

- Again the casting out of Hagar and her son by Sarah.

Even after God's covenant and their renaming, Abraham and Sarah did not improve their behavior. Thus, for the hearers of scripture, the only hope is in God who keeps *his* promise to keep *his* flock as a functional and living unit, in spite of the tendency of his sheep to wander away.

The *toledot* of Shem ends the story of the "beginnings of the heavens and (especially) the earth" which, in spite of man's misbehavior, God manages to salvage and keep. The *toledot* of Terah (11:27) starts the story of the "beginnings of the biblical Israel" who, when granted an earth to live on, end up abusing it and thus forcing God to intervene with another punishment unto instruction.[18] At the end of that lengthy and detailed sad story, God will commit himself to yet another one-sided and unconditional covenant, the covenant of peace (Is 55), through which he will establish "the new heavens and the new earth" (66:22-24).

---

[18] Given that scripture is filled with stories of man's bad behavior and chronic disobedience to God's laws, it is puzzlingly arrogant for both Jews and Christians to praise their own sociological "histories" as a continuation of the scriptural parabolic and thus non-historical story, and to defend the deception that they are the actual biological descendants of the scriptural Israel.

14

Three Threads Woven Throughout Scripture

In the following I should like to go over the three parts of scripture in order to show that the three concomitant concerns for shepherdism, Syrian Wilderness, and all the surrounding nations constitute the three crimson threads around which was woven the entire scriptural epic. The scriptural authors' main object was to equalize the Hellenes with other residents of the Two Rivers area. To do so they belittled any civilization that developed around major urban centers —their own as well as that championed by Alexander of Macedon—in both its material[1] and intellectual[2] aspects. They offered shepherdism as *the* way of life and behavior that would ensure the continuity of natural life, that is to say, a way *of* and *for* life simultaneously.

Shepherdism

Sheperdism cannot be created, made up, built, or constructed by the human mind and hands, but rather "it is what it is," that is, a "natural" way of life where humans, animals, and vegetation co-exist in a necessary and complete symbiosis. One does not need to prove the reality of shepherdism as though it were a construct, one simply needs to point to it since it is "out there" to behold. The authors actually had it in their front yard, so to speak, and thus they simply had to "depict" it, in the language of their time, as having been "set" or "made" by God (Gen 1):

> And God said, "Behold, I have given you every plant yielding seed which is upon the face of all the earth, and every tree with

---

[1] Buildings, especially palaces and temples.
[2] Human knowledge misconstrued as guiding wisdom for correct behavior.

seed in its fruit; you shall have them for food. And to every beast
of the earth, and to every bird of the air, and to everything that
creeps on the earth, everything that has the breath of life, I have
given every green plant for food." And it was so. And God saw
everything that he had made, and behold, it was very good.
(Gen 1:29-31).

Their front yard was the Syrian Wilderness—extending into
the Arabian Desert—whose "capital" or center was the oasis
Tadmor.[3] What was impressive about that Wilderness was the
fact that it was practically "inhabited" by the many nations
whose territories of origin surrounded it. The result was that all
those nations "shared" in its blessings, which point is made early
on in scripture in an unmatchable succinct and precise passage:

And the Lord God planted a garden in Eden, in the east; and
there he put the man whom he had formed. And out of the
ground the Lord God made to grow every tree that is pleasant to
the sight and good for food, the tree of life also in the midst of the
garden, and the tree of the knowledge of good and evil. A river
flowed out of Eden to water the garden, and there it divided and
became four rivers. The name of the first is Pishon; it is the one
which flows around the whole land of Havilah, where there is
gold; and the gold of that land is good; bdellium and onyx stone
are there. The name of the second river is Gihon; it is the one
which flows around the whole land of Cush. And the name of the
third river is Tigris, which flows east of Assyria. And the fourth
river is the Euphrates. The Lord God took the man and put him
in the garden of Eden to till (*'abad*; serve) it and keep it. (Gen 2:8-
15)

As early as the story of Cain and Abel one encounters God's
obvious bias (Gen 4:4b-5a) toward Abel (v.2), the "shepherd of
flock" (*ro'eh ṣo'n*; keeper of sheep), over Cain, the "tiller of the
ground" (v.2) and "builder" of cities (v.17). The genealogy of
Shem, the chosen among Noah's three sons, is replete with

---

[3] The capital of Saudi Arabia that extends over the Arabian Desert is Ar-Riyadh
whose translation is "the gardens," that is, "the oases."

"shepherds" residing in open stretches of wilderness.[4] The blessing of Jepheth consists in his dwelling in the "tents" of Shem (10:27). Repeatedly Abraham, Isaac, Jacob and Jacob's sons are presented as shepherds whether they reside in Canaan[5] or between the Two Rivers in Haran[6] or even during their sojourn in Egypt, the land of majestic constructions.[7]

In the Book of Exodus the verse that introduces the lengthy story[8] of the trek through the wilderness between Egypt and Canaan sounds like the blue print reflecting the authors' mindset: "Now Moses was keeping the flock (*ro'eh 'et-ṣo'n;*[9] keeper of the sheep) of his father-in-law, Jethro, the priest of Midian; and he led his flock to the west side of the wilderness, and came to Horeb, the mountain of God." (3:1) Moses the lawgiver is said to be a "shepherd of flock" (3:1) just as Abel was. This basic trait is evident in that, in spite of his upbringing in the house of Pharaoh (2:9-11), he marries into the family of Jethro, a shepherd whose flock grazed the "wilderness" of Midian where lay Horeb, the divine mountain (*har ha'elohim*; the mountain of *the* deity) (3:1). The relation between Moses and Jethro was triggered by the fact that both were shepherds (2:16-19). It is as though Moses' "profession" of "shepherd of flock" prepared him to lead the people as God's "flock" in the wilderness:

> Thou didst lead thy people like a flock by the hand of Moses and Aaron. (Ps 77:20)

> He smote all the first-born in Egypt, the first issue of their strength in the tents of Ham. Then he led forth his people like sheep, and guided them in the wilderness like a flock. (Ps 78:51-52)

---

[4] See my comments earlier on Gen 11:10-26.
[5] See Gen 29.
[6] See Gen 37.
[7] See Gen 46-47.
[8] Four volumes: Exodus, Leviticus, Numbers, Deuteronomy.
[9] The additional particle *'et* does not affect the meaning since it is simply an indicator that the following noun is grammatically a direct complement.

It is precisely Jethro's profession that allowed him to counsel
Moses in the matter of caring for God's people sojourning in the
wilderness (Ex 18:17-26) where presumably they were abiding
in tents as Jethro himself was: "Moses went out to meet his
father-in-law, and did obeisance and kissed him; and they asked
each other of their welfare, and went into the tent." (v.7) Even
God himself acted as the shepherd of his people, his flock:

> A Psalm of David. The Lord is my shepherd, I shall not want; he
> makes me lie down in green pastures. He leads me beside still
> waters; he restores my soul. He leads me in paths of righteousness
> for his name's sake. (Ps 23:1-3)

> O save thy people, and bless thy heritage; be thou their shepherd,
> and carry them for ever. (28:9)

> To the choirmaster: according to Lilies. A Testimony of Asaph.
> A Psalm. Give ear, O Shepherd of Israel, thou who leadest Joseph
> like a flock! Thou who art enthroned upon the cherubim, shine
> forth (80:1)

What is impressive in the last instance is that it is the same God
"enthroned upon the cherubim" who is *shepherd* and, more
specifically, à la Moses and Jethro, that is to say, as a Midianite
Bedouin sheik. Scripture itself supports my conclusion. Just as
Moses meets Jethro in his tent as we heard earlier (Ex 18:7) so
also does God meet Moses in his—God's—tent which is
specifically called "the tent of meeting" (27:1).[10] Granted the
divine tent is much more elaborate, yet nonetheless a tent that
can be folded and transported through the wilderness to be
pitched again in a new place:

> Now Moses used to take the tent and pitch it outside the camp,
> far off from the camp; and he called it the tent of meeting. And
> every one who sought the Lord would go out to the tent of
> meeting, which was outside the camp. (Ex 33:7)

> The whole number of the camp of Reuben, by their companies,
> is a hundred and fifty-one thousand four hundred and fifty. They

---

[10] See also chapters 28-30 throughout.

shall set out second. Then the tent of meeting shall set out, with the camp of the Levites in the midst of the camps; as they encamp, so shall they set out, each in position, standard by standard. (Num 2:16-17)

In this regard I should like to suggest that Sunday school curricula discard Platonism and Alexandrian theology when speaking of God to children. It would be more beneficial to speak of him in terms of Genghis Khan and his famous elaborate movable tents. On the one hand, this approach is more understandable, credible, and exciting for them, and, on the other hand, it corresponds to God in both the wilderness and Canaan as "the Lord of hosts (armies; *ṣeba'ot*)" who threatens with his power not only the nations but also his own people:[11]

> "Behold, I will press you down in your place, as a cart full of sheaves presses down. Flight shall perish from the swift, and the strong shall not retain his strength, nor shall the mighty save his life; he who handles the bow shall not stand, and he who is swift of foot shall not save himself, nor shall he who rides the horse save his life; and he who is stout of heart among the mighty shall flee away naked in that day," says the Lord. (Am 2:13-16)[12]

---

[11] One can even add the fact that the tomb of Genghis Khan was purposely concealed in order that his body—and thus he—*not* "be found," which corresponds perfectly with the non-iconic (non-statuesque) scriptural God who, unlike the other deities, does not need temples and mausoleums to remind his followers of his "presence" in spite of the fact that he seems "absent" to their sight. Nonetheless the unbridgeable chasm between the two lies in that Genghis Khan has a—even made—"history," whereas the scriptural God has—is cast as a character in—merely a literary "story." The first could still be "seen" during his lifetime, whereas the second can only be "heard" while being "read aloud" from a canonized (sealed off) writ. It is the "theologians" and "preachers" who distort this scriptural reality by giving the impression they can "re-write" the scriptural "data" for their own times in the same way as historians and scholars try to "re-write" the history of Genghis Khan for their own times.

[12] In this instance it is noteworthy that a few verses later we hear of a shepherd salvaging the rest of one of his sheep: "Thus says the Lord: 'As the shepherd rescues from the mouth of the lion two legs, or a piece of an ear, so shall the people of Israel who dwell in Samaria be rescued, with the corner of a couch and part of a bed.'" (Am 3:12)

The lion has roared; who will not fear? The Lord God has
spoken; who can but prophesy? (3:8)

For he said, "Surely they are my people, sons who will not deal
falsely; and he became their Savior. In all their affliction he was
afflicted, and the angel of his presence saved them; in his love and
in his pity he redeemed them; he lifted them up and carried them
all the days of old. But they rebelled and grieved his holy Spirit;
therefore he turned to be their enemy, and himself fought against
them." (Is 63:8-10)

The scriptural wilderness scenario carries on in the Prophets
where kingship—by definition divine since, on the one hand,
God is the King of Israel and, on the other hand, the king is the
"son of God"—is pinned down against, and even belittled in
favor of, shepherdism. The most compelling figure that
overarches this literature is David who is first depicted as a
shepherd (1 Sam 16:11, 19) who with a sling won a decisive
victory for his people against the Philistine champion Goliath (1
Sam 17). This same David ended up bringing catastrophe for
his people when he imagined he would be "king" instead of
recognizing that the sole king is God himself. In spite of the fact
that he himself was shepherd and the people still abided in
tents[13] David looked down at the tent that housed the ark of the
Lord, whence God shepherded his people under the judges until
the times of Eli.[14] He planned to erect a building to house the
ark of the Lord, however, he was harshly reprimanded for this
decision. He was reminded that even in Canaan with its giant
cities (Num 13:28), God still abides in his tent of meeting and,
even within the gates of his temple, the worshipping people
remain the sheep of God's pasture (Ps 100:3-4):

---

[13] Saul chose three thousand men of Israel; two thousand were with Saul in
Michmash and the hill country of Bethel, and a thousand were with Jonathan in
Gibeah of Benjamin; the rest of the people he sent home, every man to his tent. (1
Sam 13:2)

[14] Now Eli was very old, and he heard all that his sons were doing to all Israel, and
how they lay with the women who served at the entrance to the tent of meeting.
(1Sam 2:22)

As the ark of the Lord came into the city of David, Michal the daughter of Saul looked out of the window, and saw King David leaping and dancing before the Lord; and she despised him in her heart. And they brought in the ark of the Lord, and set it in its place, inside the tent which David had pitched for it;[15] and David offered burnt offerings and peace offerings before the Lord. (2 Sam 6:16-17)

Now when the king dwelt in his house, and the Lord had given him rest from all his enemies round about, the king said to Nathan the prophet, "See now, I dwell in a house of cedar, but the ark of God dwells in a tent." And Nathan said to the king, "Go, do all that is in your heart; for the Lord is with you." But that same night the word of the Lord came to Nathan, "Go and tell my servant David, 'Thus says the Lord: Would you build me a house to dwell in? I have not dwelt in a house since the day I brought up the people of Israel from Egypt to this day, but I have been moving about in a tent for my dwelling. In all places where I have moved with all the people of Israel, did I speak a word with any of the judges of Israel, whom I commanded to shepherd my people Israel, saying, "Why have you not built me a house of cedar?"' (7:1-7)

The situation will be redressed when God will promise through his prophets Isaiah, Jeremiah, and Ezekiel, a new David who would act as a shepherd for God's flock on and in behalf of God the sole shepherd.[16]

The interest in shepherdism remains within the authors' purview throughout the story of scriptural kingship. This is evident from the following three instances:

1. In his criticism of King David assuming absolute power to do as he pleases—killing Uriah and taking his wife Bathsheba—the prophet Nathan resorts to a parable cast in a setting reflecting

---

[15] Notice how here David follows the example of Moses in Ex 33:7.
[16] See Ezek 34 and especially 37:24-28 where the stone sanctuary (*miqdaš*) of God will be turned anew into a dwelling place (*miškan*; tent abode). See my comments earlier on this passage as well as on David's scriptural "epic."

shepherd life: "There were two men in a certain city, the one rich and the other poor. The rich man had very many flocks and herds; but the poor man had nothing but one little ewe lamb, which he had bought. And he brought it up, and it grew up with him and with his children; it used to eat of his morsel, and drink from his cup, and lie in his bosom, and it was like a daughter to him." (2 Sam 12:1-3)

2. When Rehoboam wanted to push ahead his father Solomon's policies of imposing a kingly societal structure over all the tribes of Israel (1 Kg 12:1-15), the people reacted in the following manner: "And when all Israel saw that the king did not hearken to them, the people answered the king, 'What portion have we in David? We have no inheritance in the son of Jesse. To your tents, O Israel! Look now to your own house, David.' So Israel departed to their tents." (v.16)

3. Finally, and most compellingly per scriptural chronology, over three hundred years later when "the word which came to Jeremiah from the Lord in the days of Jehoiakim the son of Josiah, king of Judah" (Jer 35:1), it offered the Rechabites who "live in tents all their days" (v.7) as the example to be followed by the Judahite subjects of Jehoiakim.

The Syrian Wilderness

The Platonic *logos* that controlled Christian theological constructs is merely a figment of the imagination of philosophers and theologians alike. It is utopic or utopian, that is pertaining to utopia (from the Greek *ou* and *topos* [no place or not a place]). It is thus important that we not imagine that the scriptural authors' shepherdism is simply a mental projection similar to an Eden-like Narnia. Scriptural shepherdism had an actual locale, the Syrian Wilderness at whose center was the actual Tadmor and filled with actual oases.[17] The Syrian Wilderness motif pervades the scriptural epic throughout the writings of the Prophets that deal with the two scriptural Kingdoms of Israel and Judah on their "ground."

The thorniest of issues is the location and borders of Canaan, the earth of the promise where the scriptural epic unfolded from the times of Joshua to the Babylonian exile. Its location is virtually always handled as an assumption that everybody roughly agrees upon: we assume it spread over southern Lebanon and Palestine. But, is that so? Is the scriptural Canaan co-extensive with the geographic historical Canaan? The question is legitimate since many Jewish and Christian Zionists use scripture to validate that the extant of the biblical land of Israel stretches all the way to the Euphrates. Instead of superimposing "our" assumption of the location of the scriptural Canaan, the question that needs to be dealt with is, "What is the expanse of *scriptural* Canaan?"

After the repeated promise that God is about to grant the Israelites he saved from Egypt "the earth of Canaan, the earth of their sojournings, where they sojourned"[18] (Ex 6:4)[19] we suddenly hear the following detailed descriptions of that "earth (land RSV) of Canaan":

> Moses sent them to spy out *the land of Canaan*, and said to them, "Go up into the Negeb yonder, and go up into the hill country, and see what the land is, and whether the people who dwell in it are strong or weak, whether they are few or many, and whether the land that they dwell in is good or bad, and whether the cities that they dwell in are camps or strongholds, and whether the land

---

[17] See earlier fn.3 concerning Ar-Riyadh, the major city of the Arabian Wilderness that is the extension of the Syrian Wilderness.

[18] Literal rendering of the original. RSV has "the land of Canaan, the land in which they dwelt as sojourners."

[19] See also Lev 25:38; Num 32:30, 32.

is rich or poor, and whether there is wood in it or not. Be of good
courage, and bring some of the fruit of the land." Now the time
was the season of the first ripe grapes. So they went up and spied
out the land from the wilderness of Zin to *Rehob (reḥob), near the
entrance of Hamath.* (Num 13:17-21)

The Lord said to Moses, "Command the people of Israel, and say
to them, When you enter the land of Canaan (this is the land that
shall fall to you for an inheritance, the land of Canaan *in its full
extent* [*ligbulotehah*]), your south side shall be from the wilderness of
Zin along the side of Edom, and your southern boundary shall be
from the end of the Salt Sea on the east; and your boundary shall
turn south of the ascent of Akrabbim, and cross to Zin, and its
end shall be south of Kadeshbarnea; then it shall go on to
Hazaraddar, and pass along to Azmon; and the boundary shall
turn from Azmon to the Brook of Egypt, and its termination shall
be at the sea. For the western boundary, you shall have the Great
Sea and its coast; this shall be your western boundary. This shall
be your northern boundary: from the Great Sea you shall mark
out your line to Mount Hor; from Mount Hor you shall mark it
out *to the entrance of Hamath,* and the end of the boundary shall be
at Zeded; then the boundary shall extend to Ziphron, and its end
shall be at Hazarenan; this shall be your northern boundary. You
shall mark out your eastern boundary from Hazarenan to
Shepham; and the boundary shall go down from Shepham to
Riblah on the east side of Ain; and the boundary shall go down,
and reach to the shoulder of the sea of Chinnereth on the east;
and the boundary shall go down to the Jordan, and its end shall
be at the Salt Sea. This shall be your land with its boundaries all
round." (34:1-12)

The Lord our God said to us in Horeb, "You have stayed long
enough at this mountain; turn and take your journey, and go to
the hill country of the Amorites, and to all their neighbors in the
Arabah, in the hill country and in the lowland, and in the Negeb,
and by the seacoast, *the land of the Canaanites,* and *Lebanon, as far as
the great river, the river Euphrates.*" (Deut 1:6-7)

After the death of Moses the servant of the Lord, the Lord said to
Joshua the son of Nun, Moses' minister, "Moses my servant is
dead; now therefore arise, go over this Jordan, you and all this

people, into the land which I am giving to them, to the people of Israel. Every place that the sole of your foot will tread upon I have given to you, as I promised to Moses. *From the wilderness and this Lebanon as far as the great river, the river Euphrates, all the land of the Hittites to the Great Sea* toward the going down of the sun shall be your territory." (Josh 1:1-4)

Then Joshua gathered all the tribes of Israel to Shechem, and summoned the elders, the heads, the judges, and the officers of Israel; and they presented themselves before God. And Joshua said to all the people, "Thus says the Lord, the God of Israel, 'Your fathers lived of old *beyond* (*'eber*)[20] *the Euphrates*, Terah, the father of Abraham and of Nahor; and they served other gods. Then I took your father Abraham from beyond (*'eber*) the River and led him through **all** the land of Canaan, and made his offspring many. I gave him Isaac.'" (24:1-3)

This view of Canaan is so engrained in the scriptural story that it even supersedes the no less scriptural borders of the Kingdoms of Israel and Judah that extended over the territory of the twelve tribes which cover the area of modern-day Palestine/Israel. Compare, on the one hand, the allotment in the Book of Joshua (chs. 13-19) and even the post-exilic allotment in Ezekiel 48 with, on the other hand, the descriptions of the Davidic kingdom that are reminiscent of those pertaining to Canaan as the earth of the promise:

After this David defeated the Philistines and subdued them, and David took Methegammah out of the hand of the Philistines. And he defeated Moab, and measured them with a line, making them lie down on the ground; two lines he measured to be put to death, and one full line to be spared. And the Moabites became servants to David and brought tribute. David also defeated Hadadezer the son of *Rehob*, king of Zobah, *as he went to restore his power at the river Euphrates*. And David took from him a thousand and seven hundred horsemen, and twenty thousand foot soldiers; and David hamstrung all the chariot horses, but left enough for a hundred chariots. And when the Syrians (*'aram*) of *Damascus* came

---

[20] Whence *'ibri* (Hebrew). See my comments earlier on the origin of the connotation of that noun.

to help Hadadezer king of *Zobah*, David slew twenty-two
thousand men of the Syrians (*'aram*). Then David put garrisons in
Aram of Damascus; and the Syrians (*'aram*) became servants to
David and brought tribute. And the Lord gave victory to David
wherever he went. And David took the shields of gold which were
carried by the servants of Hadadezer, and brought them to
Jerusalem. And from Betah and from Berothai, cities of
Hadadezer, King David took very much bronze. When Toi king
of *Hamath* heard that David had defeated the whole army of
Hadadezer, Toi sent his son Joram to King David, to greet him,
and to congratulate him because he had fought against
Hadadezer and defeated him; for Hadadezer had often been at
war with Toi. And Joram brought with him articles of silver, of
gold, and of bronze; these also King David dedicated to the Lord,
together with the silver and gold which he dedicated from all the
nations he subdued, from Edom, Moab, the Ammonites, the
Philistines, Amalek, *and from the spoil of Hadadezer the son of Rehob,
king of Zobah.* (2 Sam 8:4-12)[21]

After this David defeated the Philistines and subdued them, and
he took Gath and its villages out of the hand of the Philistines.
And he defeated Moab, and the Moabites became servants to
David and brought tribute. David also defeated *Hadadezer king of
Zobah, toward Hamath, as he went to set up his monument (*yado*; hand
[power])* at the river Euphrates.[22] And David took from him a
thousand chariots, seven thousand horsemen, and twenty
thousand foot soldiers; and David hamstrung all the chariot
horses, but left enough for a hundred chariots. And when the
Syrians of *Damascus* came to help Hadadezer king of *Zobah*, David
slew twenty-two thousand men of the Syrians. Then David put
garrisons in Syria of *Damascus*; and the Syrians became servants
to David, and brought tribute. And the Lord gave victory to
David wherever he went. (1 Chr 18:1-6)

---

[21] See also 2 Sam 10:6-19.
[22] eo tempore percussit David etiam Adadezer regem Suba regionis Emath quando
perrexit ut *dilataret imperium suum* (expand his command [absolute power; empire])
usque ad flumen Eufraten (VUL); And David smote Hadarezer king of Zobah unto
Hamath, as he went *to stablish his dominion by the river Euphrates.* (KJV).

The result is unmissable. The scriptural Canaan, "earth of the promise," is co-extensive with Aram that is co-extensive with the Syrian Wilderness; it starts at the wilderness of the Negev (Southern Palestine) and ends at the Euphrates passing through Damascus and Hamath. The most compelling sign that seals this conclusion is the unique, yet strange, mention of Tadmor/Palmyra as having been built by Solomon and, to boot, in a similar context as David's taking over Aram/the Syrian Desert:

> At the end of twenty years, in which Solomon had built the house of the Lord and his own house, Solomon rebuilt the cities which Huram had given to him, and settled the people of Israel in them. And Solomon went to *Hamathzobah*, and took it. He *built* Tadmor **in the wilderness** and all the store-cities which he *built* in *Hamath*. He also *built* Upper Bethhoron and Lower Bethhoron, fortified cities with walls, gates, and bars, and Baalath, and all the store-cities that Solomon had, and all the cities for his chariots, and the cities for his horsemen, and whatever Solomon desired to build in Jerusalem, in Lebanon, and *in all the land of his dominion* (realm; *mimšelah*). All the people who were left of the Hittites, the Amorites, the Perizzites, the Hivites, and the Jebusites, who were not of Israel, from their descendants who were left after them in the land, whom the people of Israel had not destroyed – these Solomon made a forced levy and so they are to this day. (2 Chr 8:1-8)

The last two verses of the above quoted passage leave no doubt that the authors' ultimate interest lies in the nations (*ha'adam*; the human beings) residing in and around the Syrian Wilderness (Aram). That wilderness and the shepherd life that it sustains form the setting of scripture's instructional parable (*mashal*) addressed to *one and all alike* with no exception. Interestingly, this finds evidence in a peculiar passage from Zechariah:

> The burden of the word of the Lord in the land of Hadrach, and Damascus *shall be* the rest thereof: when *the eyes of man* (*'eyn 'adam*), as of all the tribes of Israel, *shall be* toward the Lord. And Hamath

also shall border thereby; Tyrus, and Zidon, though it be very
wise. (Zech 9:1-2 KJV)

I chose KJV over RSV precisely because RSV translates "the
eyes of man" into "the cities of Aram":

An Oracle The word of the Lord is against the land of Hadrach
and will rest upon Damascus. For to the Lord belong the cities of
Aram, even as all the tribes of Israel; Hamath also, which borders
thereon, Tyre and Sidon, though they are very wise. (Zech 9:1-
2 RSV)

RSV's translation is understandable in view of the difficulty of
the original and that the middle consonant of *'adam* (אדם) and
'aram (ארם) look alike and can be easily confused by the copyists.
Add to this that Aram fits perfectly the context that includes
Damascus, Hamath, Tyre, and Sidon. The more serious French
translation of the Jerusalem Bible opts for Aram, though it keeps
the original *'eyn* which means also "source (fountain) of water"
besides "eye"[23] : "… Car à Yahvé appartient la source d'Aram
et toutes les tribus d'Israël." (Zech 9:1 FBJ)

dabar *versus* logos

Before dealing with the third scriptural "thread," the interest in
the nations rather than Israel proper, I should like to discuss a
matter of axial importance that goes hand in hand with
shepherdism and the Syrian Wilderness, namely, the choice of
midbar to speak of that wilderness. A cursory look at a
concordance will readily show that, out of the many terms
referring to arid or deserted areas—such as *ḥorbah*, *yešimon*, and
'arabah—*midbar* is by far the most common. The most
compelling explanation is that this noun is from the same root
as the noun *dabar* (word), which is translated as *logos* in the LXX,
and the verbal root *dabar* (speak). This intended connection is
virtually sealed in the one instance in the Book of Song of Songs

---

[23] A source of water looks like, or at least reminds the onlooker of, an eye. That is
why the same Semitic word *'eyn* can mean either.

where the plural *midbarim* (deserts, wildernesses) is used in reference to the ("words, utterances" of the) "mouth" as is evidenced in the parallelism with "lips": "Your lips are like a scarlet thread, and *your mouth* (*midbarek*) is lovely. Your cheeks are like halves of a pomegranate behind your veil." (Song 4:3) The original Hebrew is very precisely reflected in the LXX's *hē lalia* (speech, speaking) *sou* and the Vulgate's *eloquium* (eloquence) *tuum*, both nouns in the singular form.[24] However, what is still more impressive is that within the same context of the description of the beloved one hears a list of terms pertaining to life around an oasis:

> Behold, you are beautiful, my love, behold, you are beautiful! Your eyes are *doves* behind your veil. Your hair is like a *flock of goats*, moving down the slopes of Gilead. Your teeth are like a *flock of shorn ewes* that have come up from the washing, all of which bear twins, and not one among them is bereaved. Your lips are like a scarlet thread, and your mouth is lovely. Your cheeks are like halves of a *pomegranate* behind your veil. Your neck is like the tower of David, built for an arsenal, whereon hang a thousand bucklers, all of them shields of warriors. Your two breasts are like two *fawns*, twins of a *gazelle*, that feed among the lilies... A *garden* locked is my sister, my bride, a garden locked, a *fountain*[25] sealed... a *garden fountain*, a *well of living water*, and *flowing streams* from Lebanon. Awake, O north wind, and come, O south wind! Blow upon my *garden*, let its fragrance be wafted abroad. Let my beloved come to his *garden*, and eat its choicest *fruits*. (Song 4:1-5, 12, 15-16)

On the other hand we have two instances where the trilateral *dbr* is vocalized as *dober* and undoubtedly connotes pastureland:

> Then shall the lambs graze (*ra'u* from the verb *ra'ah*) as in their pasture (*kedobram*), fatlings and kids shall feed among the ruins (*horbot*, plural of *horbah*). (Is 5:17)

> I will surely gather all of you, O Jacob, I will gather the remnant of Israel; I will set them together like sheep in a fold, like a flock

---

[24] JB preserved the plural in translating *deborek* as *tes discours* (your discourses).
[25] As in "spring" (*'eyn*).

in (the midst of; *betok*) its pasture (*haddobro*), a noisy multitude of men. (Mic 2:12)

Still translating *haddobro* as "its pasture" goes against the rule in Hebrew where a noun cannot be defined simultaneously by the definite article and a pronoun. Literally *haddobro* would be "the its pasture." The logical solution would be to parse the consonantal *hdbro* as *hodbero*, which would be the infinitive of the *hophal* (the passive form of *hiphil*) *hodbar* followed by the pronoun *o* (its): its being pastured, that is, (the area) where it (the flock) is being pastured. Although my surmise seems farfetched, still it is plausible due to the fact that the *hiphil hidbir* is encountered twice in Psalms 18:47 (Heb v.48) and 47:3 (Heb v.4) where it has the meaning of "drive back, move away, bring under control, subdue":

> the God who gave me vengeance and subdued peoples under me (*yadber 'ammim tahtay*) (Ps 18:47 RSV; Heb v.48)

> He subdued peoples under us (*yadber 'ammim tahtenu*), and nations under our feet. (Ps 47:3 RSV; Heb v.4)

The same connotation is further found at the end of 2 Chronicles where we encounter the *piel* form *dibber*, which otherwise usually refers to "speaking":

> Now when Athaliah the mother of Ahaziah saw that her son was dead, she arose and destroyed (*wattedabber*) all the royal family of the house of Judah. (2 Chr 22:10)

This being the understanding of both KJV and RSV, it is totally bewildering, to say the least, that both versions stick to the traditional translation of "speak" even against the general "flow" of the verse that reflects the movement of turning one's back, spurning:

> I opened to my beloved; but my beloved had withdrawn himself, *and* was gone: my soul failed when he spake (*bedabbero*; at his speaking): I sought him, but I could not find him; I called him, but he gave me no answer. (Song 5:6 KJV)

> I opened to my beloved, but my beloved had turned and gone. My soul failed me when he spoke (*bedabbero*; at his speaking). I sought him, but found him not; I called him, but he gave no answer. (Song 5:6 RSV)

What is even more stunning is that the same criticism must be leveled against both the LXX and Vulgate, which in spite of their translating *wattedabber* in 2 Chronicles as "destroyed,"[26] understood *bedabbero* as speaking.[27]

The only logically plausible way to solve this apparent conundrum is to dismiss the influence of Platonism that plagued our "theological" purview while listening to scripture. The *dabar* of scripture is a far cry from Plato's *logos*. The latter, as is evident from Plato's "Dialogues," is through and through dialogical in that more than one person entertain the "discourse." Notice how both patristic theology and all other theologies thrive on "quotations" from different authors and sources. Actually, unless one does so, one is dubbed as non-scholarly. Not so the scriptural *dabar* that is exclusively one-directional: God speaks not to give his "opinion," but to issue orders while the recipients of his *dabar* have no say whatsoever in the matter and are utterly silenced whenever they open their mouths.

> And the word of the Lord came to me: "Son of man, what is this proverb that you have about the land of Israel, saying, 'The days grow long, and every vision comes to nought'? Tell them therefore, 'Thus says the Lord God: I will put an end to this proverb, and they shall no more use it as a proverb in Israel.' But say to them, The days are at hand, and the fulfilment of every vision. For there shall be no more any false vision or flattering divination within the house of Israel. But I the Lord will speak the word which I will speak, and it will be performed. It will no longer be delayed, but in your days, O rebellious house, I will speak the word and perform it, says the Lord God." Again the word of the

---

[26] *apōlesen* (LXX) and *interfecit* (VUL).

[27] I hope by now my readers will indulge my general caveat against all translations. At least the LXX has *exēlthen en logō avtou* (went out/away in his word [while speaking]).

Lord came to me: "Son of man, behold, they of the house of Israel
say, 'The vision that he sees is for many days hence, and he
prophesies of times far off.' Therefore say to them, Thus says the
Lord God: None of my words will be delayed any longer, but the
word which I speak will be performed, says the Lord God."
(Ezek 12:21-28)

The word of the Lord came to me again: "What do you mean by
repeating this proverb concerning the land of Israel, 'The fathers
have eaten sour grapes, and the children's teeth are set on edge'?
As I live, says the Lord God, this proverb shall no more be used
by you in Israel." (18:1-3)

His *dabar* is administered in the wilderness and proceeds from
his shepherd's mouth while the sheep's dilemma lies in that the
utterly non-Platonic, non-Shakespearian "to obey or not to
obey" is not even the question. It does not matter whether a
"baa" is emitted or not. Obeying maintains the life that the
sheep is already enjoying, while disobedience posits the same
sheep as *'obed* (unto destruction) as an Aramean by himself in
the wilderness.

In other words, the words of God have always to be heard
from the perspective of their place of origin, in the wilderness of
Egypt or that of the nations. This is precisely what the
unmatchable Paul did in 1 Corinthians 10:1-11 until his
teaching was perverted within the Alexandrian "school" of
theology, that is, within the walls of Plato's academy in
Alexandria and since within the walls of all "schools." It is
within such schools *of stone* that the non-scriptural *logos* prospers
unto the great glory of the misled *'adam* while the scriptural *dabar*
is uttered out during the "readings"—rather than the
sermons[28]—heard in the house churches by the human ears *of
flesh*. And, as always, whether the recipients obey or not shall be
revealed on judgment day, and not before, when all *'adam* of all
generations shall stand before the King of all. It is no wonder

---

[28] Unless they consist of explanatory footnotes to the literal meaning and function of
the original scriptural words.

then that, in view of that judgment, scripture's primary interest is the totality of the nations rather than the scriptural Israel.

Scripture's Interest in the Nations

The prime interest in the nations throughout scripture is sealed early on in the story of *'adam*—the primary stand-in for *ha'adam*—(Gen 5) and his progeny who are all the nations (Gen 10) as descendants of his great-grandchild Noah's three sons. This in turn explains the mention of the long series of nations in conjunction with the promise to the progeny of Abraham concerning the "earth of Canaan":

> On that day the Lord made a covenant with Abram, saying, "To your descendants I give this land, from the river of Egypt to the great river, the river Euphrates, the land of the Kenites, the Kenizzites, the Kadmonites, the Hittites, the Perizzites, the Rephaim, the Amorites, the Canaanites, the Girgashites and the Jebusites." (Gen 15:18-21)

This in a shorter form is repeated in the introduction to the book of Joshua describing the implementation of that promise:

> After the death of Moses the servant of the Lord, the Lord said to Joshua the son of Nun, Moses' minister, "Moses my servant is dead; now therefore arise, go over this Jordan, you and all this people, into the land which I am giving to them, to the people of Israel. Every place that the sole of your foot will tread upon I have given to you, as I promised to Moses. From the wilderness and this Lebanon as far as the great river, the river Euphrates, all the land of the Hittites to the Great Sea toward the going down of the sun shall be your territory." (Josh 1:1-4)

The singling out of the Hittites in Joshua as representatives of all ten nations in Genesis is to be explained by the fact that their place of residence was at the west of the sources of the Euphrates and Tigris rivers in actual Turkey. It is a literary case of "all the more so": if I am mentioning the Hittites, one should the more so include all the other nations from the Euphrates all the way south to (the river of) Egypt and the Great (Mediterranean) Sea.

By the same token, since the scriptural "list of nations" does not
always contain the same names, one is to conclude that the
numeral ten is a literary device reflecting the totality of all
nations residing in the area.[29] This understanding is
corroborated in that, except for Genesis 13:7b, Genesis 15:18-
21 contains the first scriptural "list" of nations residing in the
earth of the promise and is the only "list" that contains ten of
them. Consequently, all the subsequent "lists" are intentionally
partial in order to impress upon the hearers that they are
dealing with the same reality without taxing them time and
again with an endless series of names. The seeming exception
of Genesis 13:7b (At that time the Canaanites and the Perizzites
dwelt in the land [earth]) actually confirms this conclusion since
the two names are as all-encompassing as those of the following
"list" of ten. Canaanites are by definition the inhabitants
pertaining to Canaan, which explains why the earlier rendition
of 13:7b was phrased thus: "At that time the Canaanites were
in the land." (Gen 12:6b) For a Semite hearer the root *p(h)araz*,
whence Perizzite, connotes "putting aside in the open" and thus
"separating (with the intention of allotting)"[30] as is the case in
the following examples:

- In Judges 5:7 and 8 *perazon* is translated as
  "inhabitants of villages" in KJV and "peasantry"
  in RSV, both indicating an "open" area as in
  "countryside."

- The same applies to *perazot* in Ezekiel 38:11
  (villages in both KJV and RSV) and Zechariah
  2:8 (towns in KJV and villages in RSV).

- Similarly *peruzi*—which is the passive participle
  of *paraz*—is rendered as "unwalled" and thus "in
  the open" (villages) in Deut 3:5 and 1 Sam 6:18

---

[29] See Numerological Symbolism in *NTI₃* 22-28.
[30] In Arabic the verb *pharaza* has precisely this meaning and is used specifically in
reference to land allotment. An earth that is *maphruzat* means an earth that has been
surveyed and separated in lots.

(both KJV and RSV). The plural *peruzim* occurs in Esther 9:19 as an adjective describing the Jews "of the villages" "who live in open towns": "¹⁸ But the Jews who were in Susa gathered on the thirteenth day and on the fourteenth, and rested on the fifteenth day, making that a day of feasting and gladness. ¹⁹ Therefore the Jews *of the villages*, who *live in the open towns*, hold the fourteenth day of the month of Adar as a day for gladness and feasting and holiday-making, and a day on which they send choice portions to one another." (Esth 9:18-19)

Put otherwise, in Genesis 13:7b, Perizzites is a generic term used in conjunction with the Canaanites, mentioned in 12:6b, to underscore the fact that the authors are referring to the entirety of the inhabitants of that area, which will be confirmed in the encompassing list of ten nations in 15:18-21.

At the same time Perizzites may be a cryptic allusion to Alexander and his Macedonian cohort who spread all over the Syrian Wilderness, the scriptural earth of Canaan. If so, then the authors are intentionally expanding the horizon of their scriptural setting, i.e., the Syrian Wilderness, as representative—a microcosm—of the entire "earth" that God created together with the heavens in Genesis 1. That is to say, whatever applies to the Syrian Wilderness should apply to the rest of the earth even if the authors themselves are not aware of its expanse. In other words, they devised their scripture as authoritatively prescriptive over the entire realm of *ha'adam*, the human beings wherever they may be found on the "dry land" (Gen 1:9) of the world. This concern for inclusiveness is further reflected in that some of the names of the nations refer to actual peoples while others, like the Perizzites, are symbolic. The Hittites, the Amorites, the Canaanites, and the Jebusites in the list of ten (Gen 15:18-21) refer to actual societies, the rest are generic names:

- The Kenites (*qeyni* son[s] of *qayn*), as I explained earlier, are the Cain-like people. The intention is to impress on the hearers that God does not forget those who appear to be on the side track.

- The same concern of including the "outsiders" and even "cast out" applies to the Kenizzites. They are the descendants of Kenaz who is both of the progeny of Esau (Gen 36:11, 15, 42) and "uncle" of Caleb—the outsider "dog" (Josh 15:17).[31] It is striking that the generic Kenizzite appears long before one hears of Kenaz. So the hearers have to *wait* before they figure out the author's intention as they had to *wait* to figure out what the author intended with the strange, at first hearing, plural *'elohim* of Genesis 1:1.

- The Kadmonites (*qadmoni* son[s] of *qadmon*) have a similar function as Kenites. They refer to those who live in the East (*qedem*) and thus outside the garden (Gen 3:24) and represented those who planned to revolt against God: "And as men migrated from the east, they found a plain in the land of Shinar and settled there." (Gen 11:2)

- Although mention of the Rephaim occurs in Genesis 14:5 (In the fourteenth year Chedorlaomer and the kings who were with him came and subdued the Rephaim in Ashterothkarnaim, the Zuzim in Ham, the Emim in Shavehkiriathaim, and the Horites in their Mount Seir as far as Elparan on the border of the wilderness; vv.5-6) the hearers again have to *wait* until Numbers and Deuternomy to figure out that Rephaim are "men of great stature— physically as well as socially" similar to the

---

[31] See also Judg 1:13; 3:9, 11.

Nephilim of 4:4[32]: "And there we saw the Nephilim (the sons of Anak, who come from the Nephilim); and we seemed to ourselves like grasshoppers, and so we seemed to them" (Num 13:33); "The Emim formerly lived there, a people great and many, and tall as the Anakim; like the Anakim they are also known as Rephaim, but the Moabites call them Emim." (Deut 2:10-11)

- The strange tetra-consonantal name Girgashites can be explained as a made-up name from the verb *garash* (*garaš*) whose meaning is "drive out, cast out" and whose aim is to include the "outcast," the "outsiders," of any kind. It comes from the doubling of the first letter before the last, just as the name Gilgal is formed from the verb *galal* (roll and thus surround) by doubling the first letter before the last. The result is that Gilgal refers to a town that is surrounded by walls or a camp of tents delineated by a circumference. The general meaning of Gilgal explains the different cities with such name in scripture.

- The names of these nations as being symbolic is corroborated by other names found elsewhere in the list of nations. The most prominent is Hivites (*ḥiwwi*) from the verb *ḥawah* (contain, encompass) and thus refers to tent or camp dwellers. Although such people live outside the cities, they are still part of the authors' purview. The most famous of such tent dwellers are the Rechabites of Jeremiah 35.

---

[32] See my comments earlier.

Once the author has used the comprehensive list of ten nations at the start, he could afford, without any misunderstanding, to shorten it into a list of two, three, four, six, or seven nations. The final impression on the hearer's ear remains the same: all surrounding nations will be integrated together with Israel on a totally equal footing in Zion, God's city of the end times (Is 66:19-21). However, one does not need to wait until the Latter Prophets and the end of Isaiah to detect the divine beneficence toward the nations. It is already and glaringly so in the Prior Prophets. There Aram is not only a prize for David and his kingly heirs to conquer and subdue, but it is also the "realm" of prophetic activity on the part of Elijah and Elisha whose stories overarch nineteen chapters (1 Kg 17 through 2 Kg 13) out of the total forty seven chapters of those two books assumedly purporting the story of the kingdoms of Israel ad Judah.[33] What is strikingly impressive in the case of those two prophetic giants is the amount of attention the author gives to their activity among outsiders and even among presumed enemies. The hearer cannot evade utter astonishment at the repeated story of the care for a stranger widow by raising her son from the dead (Elijah in 1 Kg 17:17-24) or providing her with a son (Elisha in 2 Kg 4:8-17) and then raising him from the dead (vv.18-37). Again, twice we are told that those prophets provided bread where it was needed to strangers (the same widow in the case of Elijah in 1 Kg 17:7-16) and compatriots (Elisha in 2 Kg 4:38-44) alike.[34] Still, and more importantly, we have the lengthy and detailed story of Elisha's healing of Naaman, the top commander of the enemy army of Aram, which cannot but startle the Judahite hearer of scripture especially that it ends with the punishment of Elisha's helper

---

[33] The LXX names them the (third and fourth) Books of the Kingdoms together with 1 and 2 Samuel (first and second Books of the Kingdoms).

[34] The New Testament authors were so impressed by this repetition that they emulated it in the two accounts of the multiplication of the bread in Matthew, Mark, and Luke!

with the same leprosy that had plagued Naaman the "enemy." It is worth quoting the passage in its entirety:[35]

> Naaman, commander of the army of the king of Syria, was a great man with his master and in high favor, *because by him the Lord had given victory to Syria.* He was a mighty man of valor, but he was a leper. Now the Syrians on one of their raids had carried off a little maid from the land of Israel, and she waited on Naaman's wife. She said to her mistress, "Would that my lord were with the prophet who is in Samaria! He would cure him of his leprosy." So Naaman went in and told his lord, "Thus and so spoke the maiden from the land of Israel." And the king of Syria said, "Go now, and I will send a letter to the king of Israel." So he went, taking with him ten talents of silver, six thousand shekels of gold, and ten festal garments. And he brought the letter to the king of Israel, which read, "When this letter reaches you, know that I have sent to you Naaman my servant, that you may cure him of his leprosy." And when the king of Israel read the letter, he rent his clothes and said, "Am I God, to kill and to make alive, that this man sends word to me to cure a man of his leprosy? Only consider, and see how he is seeking a quarrel with me." But when Elisha the man of God heard that the king of Israel had rent his clothes, he sent to the king, saying, "Why have you rent your clothes? Let him come now to me, that he may know that there is a prophet in Israel." So Naaman came with his horses and chariots, and halted at the door of Elisha's house. And Elisha sent a messenger to him, saying, "Go and wash in the Jordan seven times, and your flesh shall be restored, and you shall be clean." But Naaman was angry, and went away, saying, "Behold, I thought that he would surely come out to me, and stand, and call on the name of the Lord his God, and wave his hand over the place, and cure the leper. Are not Abana and Pharpar, the rivers of Damascus, better than all the waters of Israel? Could I not wash in them, and be clean?" So he turned and went away in a rage. But his servants came near and said to him, "My father, if the prophet had commanded you to do some great thing, would you not have done it? How much rather, then, when he says to

---

[35] It is imperative for my readers to supply mentally "Aram" every time they hear/read "Syria" or "Syrians."

you, 'Wash, and be clean'?" So he went down and dipped himself seven times in the Jordan, according to the word of the man of God; and his flesh was restored like the flesh of a little child, and he was clean. Then he returned to the man of God, he and all his company, and he came and stood before him; and he said, "Behold, I know that there is no God in all the earth but in Israel; so accept now a present from your servant." But he said, "As the Lord lives, whom I serve, I will receive none." And he urged him to take it, but he refused. Then Naaman said, "If not, I pray you, let there be given to your servant two mules' burden of earth; for henceforth your servant will not offer burnt offering or sacrifice to any god but the Lord. In this matter may the Lord pardon your servant: when my master goes into the house of Rimmon to worship there, leaning on my arm, and I bow myself in the house of Rimmon, when I bow myself in the house of Rimmon, the Lord pardon your servant in this matter." He said to him, "Go in peace." But when Naaman had gone from him a short distance, Gehazi, the servant of Elisha the man of God, said, "See, my master has spared this Naaman the Syrian (*the Aramean*), in not accepting from his hand what he brought. As the Lord lives, I will run after him, and get something from him." So Gehazi followed Naaman. And when Naaman saw some one running after him, he alighted from the chariot to meet him, and said, "Is all well?" And he said, "All is well. My master has sent me to say, 'There have just now come to me from the hill country of Ephraim two young men of the sons of the prophets; pray, give them a talent of silver and two festal garments.'" And Naaman said, "Be pleased to accept two talents." And he urged him, and tied up two talents of silver in two bags, with two festal garments, and laid them upon two of his servants; and they carried them before Gehazi. And when he came to the hill, he took them from their hand, and put them in the house; and he sent the men away, and they departed. He went in, and stood before his master, and Elisha said to him, "Where have you been, Gehazi?" And he said, "Your servant went nowhere." But he said to him, "Did I not go with you in spirit when the man turned from his chariot to meet you? Was it a time to accept money and garments, olive orchards and vineyards, sheep and oxen, menservants and maidservants? Therefore the leprosy of Naaman shall cleave to you, and to your descendants for ever." So he went out from his presence a leper, as white as snow. (2 Kg 5:1-27)

Let me point out a few features of this account that have a bearing on our discussion:

1. It is the Lord of Israel who granted victory to Aram over Israel. This is the behavior of a universal deity that is God of Judahites, Israelites, and Gentiles (Am 1-2), of "both Jews and Gentiles" (Rom 3:29).

2. The Lord's gracefulness toward an enemy of his people is detectable in the name *na'aman* whose verbal root means "be pleasant, graceful (toward someone else)": "I am distressed for you, my brother Jonathan; *very pleasant have you been* (*na'amta*) to me." (2 Sam 1:26)

3. Naaman is purposely surnamed "the Aramean" (2 Kg 5:20) in view of the confession required by no less than the Law: "And you shall make response before the Lord your God, 'A wandering Aramean was my father; and he went down into Egypt and sojourned there, few in number; and there he became a nation, great, mighty, and populous. And the Egyptians treated us harshly, and afflicted us, and laid upon us hard bondage.'" (Deut 26:5-6) The original *'obed* rendered as "wandering" literally means "unto extinction." The correspondence between the two predicaments of Naaman and the Israelites is unmissable.

4. Still, just as important, is the fact that, in scripture, Aram and the Syrian Wilderness refer to the same geographical reality, which explains

why the LXX[36] renders the Hebrew *'aram* into
Syria and *'arammi* into *Syros* (Syrian).

This primary interest in the nations takes full precedence
understandably in the *ketubim* that are addressed to the members
of the synagogue listening to the Law and the Prophets to be
fully open to and inviting of the nations. A bird's eye view of
that literature will show the following:

- The Book of Psalms underscores God's full
  control of the nations at the beginning,[37] toward
  the center,[38] and at the closure[39] of the Book.

- The Book of Job is about a faithful follower of
  the Law who lived his entire life far away from
  the land of the two Kingdoms of Israel and
  Judah, and managed to fare well "in the fear of
  the Lord."

- The Book of Proverbs offers the teaching of the
  Law in the garb of "wisdom" that was so
  cherished by the Greeks of the times.

- The Book of Ruth presents us with a Moabite
  woman, Naomi (*no'omi*)—corresponding to
  Naaman (*na'aman*) the Aramean—who ends by

---

[36] Followed by the Vulgate, KJV, and RSV.
[37] Why do the nations conspire, and the peoples plot in vain? The kings of the earth
set themselves, and the rulers take counsel together, against the Lord and his
anointed, saying, "Let us burst their bonds asunder, and cast their cords from us."
(Ps 2:1-3) "Ask of me, and I will make the nations your heritage, and the ends of the
earth your possession. You shall break them with a rod of iron, and dash them in
pieces like a potter's vessel." Now therefore, O kings, be wise; be warned, O rulers of
the earth. Serve the Lord with fear, with trembling kiss his feet, lest he be angry, and
you perish in the way; for his wrath is quickly kindled. (Ps 2:8-12)
[38] Arise, O God, judge the earth; for to thee belong all the nations! (Ps 82:8)
[39] Let the faithful exult in glory; let them sing for joy on their couches. Let the high
praises of God be in their throats and two-edged swords in their hands, to wreak
vengeance on the nations and chastisement on the peoples, to bind their kings with
chains and their nobles with fetters of iron, to execute on them the judgment written!
This is glory for all his faithful ones. (Ps 149:5-9)

being likened to "Rachel and Leah, who together built up the house of Israel" (4:11) and even surpasses them by becoming the great-grandmother of David (v.17). She was honored together with only two other women at the "head" of the New Testament canon (Mt 1:5).

- The Song of Songs describes the new Jerusalem where the king weds a dark skinned outsider.

- In the Book of Esther the unnamed and thus "inexistent"[40] God rules over the power of the times, Persia.

- In Daniel the same God rules throughout the centuries over all the kingdoms around the Syrian Wilderness, including the most recent, that of the Seleucids.

Co-inheritance with the Nations

There is a curious feature in the Book of Joshua, the book that describes Israel's settlement in Canaan, the earth of the promise. We have been programmed by the presupposition that all the nations that were abiding there before the entrance of the Israelites were annihilated in order to give way to the newcomers who then populated that entire earth. Yet scripture itself flatly belies such a presupposition:

> So the anger of the Lord was kindled against Israel; and he said, "Because this people have transgressed my covenant which I commanded their fathers, and have not obeyed my voice, I will not henceforth drive out before them *any of the nations that Joshua left when he died*, that by them I may test Israel, whether they will take care to walk in the way of the Lord as their fathers did, or not." So the Lord left those nations, not driving them out at once, and *he did not give them into the power of Joshua*. (Judg 2:20-23)

---

[40] In the sense of "non-egregious."

What is still more impressive, however, is the way in which those nations co-existed with the Israelites. Here again, we have been programmed to assume that the Israelites became the actual "owners" of the earth while the nations were just allowed to reside among them. Nothing is farther from the scriptural truth. Looking back at the itinerary of the entrance into Canaan that culminates with its inheritance (Josh 14), one detects a sub-theme of the book, which is the corollary of its main theme that the Lord is the lord (master) of all the earth (3:11, 13). The sub-theme is that this same Lord's plan as well as his initial decision is the co-inheritance of his earth by Israel and the nations. The story encompassing both the preparation for and the actual crossing into Canaan is bracketed with the case of Rahab, the Canaanite harlot (2:1 and 6:25). At the heart of this lengthy episode we have the passage about the "covenant" of circumcision, which in turn brings to mind Genesis 17 where Abraham is specifically introduced as "the father of a multitude of nations" (v.4) and, on such basis, circumcision is intended as encompassing "both he that is born in your house and he that is bought with your money from any foreigner who is not of your offspring" (vv.12-13). That is why "she [Rahab] dwelt in (the midst of; *beqereb*) Israel *to this day*" (Josh 6:25b).

Since the "crossing" into Canaan was marred by the people's disobedience in spite of their being circumcised, the second part of Joshua, which deals with the beginning of the "settlement" in Canaan (chs.7-12), revolves around the proclamation of the Law (8:30-35). In this regard, Israel's obedience to the "covenant" of the Law had to be tested as to whether they would keep a "covenant" of peace with the inhabitants of Gibeon (ch.9) who were Hivites (11:19). The centrality of this test for the story is evident in that the "need" of the Gibeonites triggered the first period in the "settlement" (10:1-9) that ended with chapter 12. This "covenant" with the Gentile Hivites will haunt Israel and its kings throughout the centuries (2 Sam 21:1-14).

The last indication of the sub-theme of co-inheritance with the nations is found after the interlude of chapter 13 covering the heritage of the Trans-Jordan tribes. The author prefaces the final stage of the settlement in Canaan by the nine and half tribes with a special section on the "Gentile" Caleb. Thus, when listening to the settlement of the Israelite tribes, the hearer will realize that these are co-inheriting that earth with the nations. A series of passages corroborate that God's will for Canaan is that it be a prototype for all parts of God's earth—an earth intended for co-habitation for all children of Adam:

> Yet the people of Israel did not drive out the Geshurites or the Maacathites; but Geshur and Maacath dwell in the midst of Israel *to this day*. (Josh 13:13)

> But the Jebusites, the inhabitants of Jerusalem, the people of Judah could not drive out; so the Jebusites dwell with the people of Judah at Jerusalem *to this day*. (15:63)

> However they (the Ephraimites) did not drive out the Canaanites that dwelt in Gezer: so the Canaanites have dwelt in the midst of Ephraim *to this day*. (16:10)

> But the people of Benjamin did not drive out the Jebusites who dwelt in Jerusalem; so the Jebusites have dwelt with the people of Benjamin in Jerusalem *to this day*. (Judg 1:21)[41]

> Manasseh did not drive out the inhabitants of Bethshean and its villages, or Taanach and its villages, or the inhabitants of Dor and its villages, or the inhabitants of Ibleam and its villages, or the inhabitants of Megiddo and its villages; but the Canaanites persisted in dwelling in that earth. When Israel grew strong, they put the Canaanites to forced labor, but did not utterly drive them out. And Ephraim did not drive out the Canaanites who dwelt in Gezer; but the Canaanites dwelt in Gezer among them. Zebulun did not drive out the inhabitants of Kitron, or the inhabitants of

---

[41] An indication that Caleb was originally an outsider can be seen in the phraseology concerning his inheritance: "According to the commandment of the Lord to Joshua, he gave to Caleb the son of Jephunneh a portion (*ḥeleq*; lot) *among the people (children) of Judah*, Kiriatharba, that is, Hebron (Arba was the father of Anak)." (Josh 15:13)

Nahalol; but the Canaanites dwelt among them, and became
subject to forced labor. (Judg 1:27-30)

Furthermore, just as other populations dwell in the midst of or
with the children of Israel, so the converse is true:

Asher did not drive out the inhabitants of Acco, or the inhabitants
of Sidon, or of Ahlab, or of Achzib, or of Helbah, or of Aphik, or
of Rehob; but *the Asherites dwelt among the Canaanites, the inhabitants
of the earth*; for they did not drive them out. *Naphtali* did not drive
out the inhabitants of Bethshemesh, or the inhabitants of Beth-
anath, but *dwelt among the Canaanites, the inhabitants of the earth*;
nevertheless the inhabitants of Bethshemesh and of Beth-anath
became subject to forced labor for them. (Judg 1:27-33)

The conclusion is inescapable. No one is the proprietor of the
earth of Canaan and, by extension, of the entire earth except
God the King himself since the Hebrew *melek* (king) literally
means "proprietor." He is not only the proprietor of the earth
but also of all "those who dwell therein" (Ps 24:1). In this regard
David only imagined he was the "king" (proprietor) of Uriah *the
Hittite* and his wife Bathsheba. He ends learning that lesson the
hard way, a way that would never be condoned by either
classical theology or modern ethics; God himself strikes David's
newborn to death:

David said to Nathan, "I have sinned against the Lord." And
Nathan said to David, "The Lord also has put away your sin; you
shall not die. Nevertheless, because by this deed you have utterly
scorned the Lord, the child that is born to you shall die." Then
Nathan went to his house. And *the Lord struck*[42] *the child* that Uriah's
wife bore to David, and it became sick. David therefore besought
God for the child; and David fasted, and went in and lay all night
upon the ground. And the elders of his house stood beside him,
to raise him from the ground; but he would not, nor did he eat
food with them. On the seventh day *the child died*. (2 Sam 12:13-
18)

---

[42] It is the same verb *nagaph* that is used to describe God's actions against Egypt,
including the slaying of their firstborn (Ex 12:23, 27).

Part Three

New Testament Writings

15

The New Testament

striking feature recognized by New Testament scholars is that the literature reflects an internal Jewish debate pinning down the two leading characters or literary "heroes," Jesus and Paul, against the Jerusalemite leadership of the time. It is that tension that accounts for both the Gospel stories and the Pauline argumentation. The Gentiles are merely outsiders with no voice of their own. They are not a party to the debate, however, they function as part of the argument. The two main foci of the debate, circumcision and the rules concerning table fellowship between Jew and Gentile, have them in view. Those two issues have the lion's share in the showdown stories of Jesus and Paul with the Jerusalemite leaders. Still there are two more matters that are paramount. The first is whether Jesus of Nazareth is the Messiah, Son of David, the King of peace of the latter days, as his followers claim against the Jerusalemite leadership. This issue is exacerbated since he is presented as having been crucified, which is a sign of outright curse according to Deuteronomy 21:23.[1] Actually, the Pauline gospel word is coined as being "the word concerning the cross" (1 Cor 1:18; 2:2). The other matter, which is usually overlooked in scholarship, is how a "Jew" is defined. We all assume that Jesus and Paul were "of course" Jews since both were circumcised on the eighth day (Lk 2:21; Phil 3:5). This assumption is so pervading that the overwhelming majority of modern day scholars mock those who even dare to bring up the question of whether Paul was a Jew or a Christian. However, such mocking eschews the issue raised in 1 Corinthians concerning Paul's "Jewishness" or at least the definition of a "Jew": "To the Jews I became as a Jew, in order to win Jews; to those under the law I became as one under the law—though

---

[1] See also Josh 8:29.

not being myself under the law—that I might win those under the law." (9:20) In this regard one can safely add what we hear in Romans:

> You who boast in the law, do you dishonor God by breaking the law? For, as it is written, "The name of God is blasphemed among the Gentiles because of you." Circumcision indeed is of value if you obey the law; but if you break the law, your circumcision becomes uncircumcision. So, if a man who is uncircumcised keeps the precepts of the law, will not his uncircumcision be regarded as circumcision? Then those who are physically uncircumcised but keep the law will condemn you who have the written code and circumcision but break the law. For he is not a real Jew who is one outwardly, nor is true circumcision something external and physical. He is a Jew who is one inwardly, and real circumcision is a matter of the heart, spiritual and not literal. His praise is not from men but from God. (2:23-29)

Since this is the obvious teaching throughout the Old Testament, the question for us to deal with is when, where, why, and how the prominence of fleshly circumcision came about. What were the circumstances that triggered such a non-scriptural phenomenon?

To recapitulate, in order for us to fathom the reason behind the rise of the New Testament literature, one is to figure out the interplay between the four ingredients of the debate between Paul and the Jerusalemite leadership: circumcision, Jewishness, table fellowship, and the messiahship of Jesus. Of the four topics, and although its understanding is as hotly debated as the other three in the New Testament writings, still Jewishness is essentially linked to geography. As we saw, the language *yehudit* pertains to *yehudah* ([the kingdom of] Judah) in scripture, so also the appellative *yehudi* (Jew)—plural *yehudim*—essentially refers, by definition, to someone pertaining to that same *yehudah*. Thus it would behoove us to start our discussion with the area known as *yehud* in New Testament times in order to figure out if and to which extent it affected the tension between the two parties at odds, especially since, in the debate, it is coupled with "being circumcised on the eighth day" (Phil 3:5).

The Province yehud in Palestine

The province *yehud* was in the southwestern part of Persia "beyond the (Euphrates) River" satrapy covering the Syrian Wilderness. The Seleucids inherited it as such and tried to Hellenize it both socially and religiously. In mid-second century B.C. a priestly family of Modein, under the leadership of their elder, Mattathias the Hasmonean, spearheaded a revolt originally aimed at their peers who succumbed under pressure. Taking advantage of the weakening grip of the Seleucids after their loss to the rising power of the Roman Republic, Mattathias and his followers, surnamed Maccabees (Hebrew "hammerlike") after their battle hero Judas, son of Mattathias, managed to rule de facto over *yehud*. Being of a priestly family, they established an ethnarchy that soon turned into a kingly sovereignty aimed at "resurrecting" the Davidic dynasty. With the control of both religious and political life, the Hasmonean kings became the omnipotent rulers of *yehud*, yet as clients of Rome. Aristobulus II who ruled from 67-63 B.C. was both king and high priest. Upon conquering Jerusalem in 63 B.C., the Roman general Pompeius deposed Aristobulus and took him along with his son Antigonus to Rome as hostages, and named Hyrcanus II, Aristobulus' brother, as high priest in his stead. As if that was not insult enough to the Hasmonean house, soon enough and with the approval of Rome, to boot, the ruler of *yehud* over more than thirty years (37-4 B.C.) was none other than Herod the Idumean (Edomite), a "descendant" of Esau the ultimate nemesis of Jacob who should have ruled over Edom.[2] And to add insult to injury,

---

[2] See Ezek 25:12-14; Joel 3:19 and Am 9:11-12. See also Is 34; Jer 49:7-22; Ob 1; Mal 1:1-5, where Edom is punished because of its mishandling of Israel.

in 23 B.C. Herod's kingdom of *yehud* is expanded to include the southern part of modern Syria.

In order to placate the Hasmoneans and their followers, Herod embarked on the construction of a monumental temple at Jerusalem.[3] The Judahite leadership of Jerusalem was obviously elated and, in order to support the project, instituted the scriptural didrachma levy[4] for those living in the province *yehud*, and vied to impose such a levy on all their circumcised brethren throughout the Roman empire. Without such help the temple project would have suffered, and Herod would have blamed the Jerusalemite religious leadership for the lack of support.[5] The only practical and sure way of controlling as well as unifying such support was for that same leadership to export its own understanding of the definition of a "follower of the scriptural teaching" over the entire expanse of the Roman empire. All such followers were to be *yehudim*, and their identifying sign (*sēmeion*)[6] or mark (*stigma*)[7] was fleshly circumcision. Put otherwise, being a *yehudi* in those times was de facto being controlled by the Hasmoneans and later their heirs in Jerusalem and Herod's kingdom. The matter was more of a political rather than a religious nature. The religious aspect of circumcision was only a medium of control to secure support for the interests and aims of the "followers of the dictates of scripture" in *yehud*.[8]

---

[3] The Jews then said, "It has taken forty-six years to build this temple, and will you raise it up in three days?" (Jn 2:20)

[4] Each who is numbered in the census shall give this: half a shekel according to the shekel of the sanctuary (the shekel is twenty gerahs), half a shekel as an offering to the Lord. (Ex 30:13)

[5] The epitome of irony is that this matter needed the approval of Rome, the result of which was that, after the sack of Jerusalem in 70 A.D., the Romans took over the administration of the tax and used the funds to support the temple of Jupiter *Capitolinus* in Rome.

[6] Gen 1:11; Rom 4:11.

[7] Gal 6:18 within the larger context of vv.12-18 where Paul is extensively counteracting fleshly circumcision.

[8] A similar counterpart in our own times is the way the leaders of the State of Israel try to "impose" on the worldwide Jews their view of the matter in order to secure the

16

Circumcision and its Function

Even a cursory look at a concordance will show that the reference to circumcision is not only scarce, but also it is virtually consigned to the Pentateuch and Joshua; thereafter one hears of it only twice in Jeremiah 4:4 and 9:25. It is nowhere to be found in the Writings (*ketubim*). Rather than circumcision, it is the abiding by or disobedience to the Law that is the crimson thread that holds together the entire span of the scriptural epic, beginning with Abraham. Immediately after the lengthy chapter Genesis 17 detailing the institution of the covenant of circumcision, which underscores the apparent sufficiency of Abraham's "trust" in the divine promise (Gen 15:16),[1] one hears:

> The Lord said, "Shall I hide from Abraham what I am about to do, seeing that Abraham shall become a great and mighty nation, and all the nations of the earth shall bless themselves by him? No, for I have chosen him, that he may charge his children and his household after him to keep the way of the Lord by doing righteousness and justice; so that the Lord may bring to Abraham what he has promised him." (18:17-19)[2]

Lest the hearers assume that it is a passing thought on the author's part, they are hit with the same message, and in no uncertain terms, at the passing of the torch to Isaac, where we are specifically and unequivocally told that the promise made to Abraham carries onto his son *because of* Abraham's obedience to the laws of God:

> Now there was a famine in the land, besides the former famine that was in the days of Abraham. And Isaac went to Gerar, to

---

[1] The two instances are clearly linked through the mention of covenant in Gen 15:19-21 where reference to the surrounding nations is made, which nations will be, as "foreigners," invited to undergo circumcision and be part of the Abrahamic family and its blessing, as already intimated in Gen 12:1-3.

[2] Notice how these verses specifically refer to Gen 12:1-3.

Abimelech king of the Philistines. And the Lord appeared to him, and said, "Do not go down to Egypt; dwell in the land of which I shall tell you. Sojourn in this land, and I will be with you, and will bless you; for to you and to your descendants I will give all these lands, and I will fulfil the oath which I swore to Abraham your father. I will multiply your descendants as the stars of heaven, and will give to your descendants all these lands; and by your descendants all the nations of the earth shall bless themselves: *because* Abraham obeyed my voice and kept my charge, my commandments, my statutes, and my laws." (26:1-5)

This teaching goes hand in hand with the move from circumcision of the flesh to circumcision of the heart that appears in Deuteronomy and is picked up in the Prophets:

Circumcise therefore the foreskin of your heart, and be no longer stubborn. For the Lord your God is God of gods and Lord of lords, the great, the mighty, and the terrible God, who is not partial and takes no bribe. He executes justice for the fatherless and the widow, and loves the sojourner, giving him food and clothing. Love the sojourner therefore; for you were sojourners in the land of Egypt. You shall fear the Lord your God; you shall serve him and cleave to him, and by his name you shall swear. He is your praise; he is your God, who has done for you these great and terrible things which your eyes have seen. Your fathers went down to Egypt seventy persons; and now the Lord your God has made you as the stars of heaven for multitude. (Deut 10:16-22)

If your outcasts are in the uttermost parts of heaven, from there the Lord your God will gather you, and from there he will fetch you; and the Lord your God will bring you into the land which your fathers possessed, that you may possess it; and he will make you more prosperous and numerous than your fathers. And the Lord your God will circumcise your heart and the heart of your offspring, so that you will love the Lord your God with all your heart and with all your soul, that you may live. (30:4-6)

Behold, the days are coming, says the Lord, when I will make a new covenant with the house of Israel and the house of Judah, not like the covenant which I made with their fathers when I took them by the hand to bring them out of the land of Egypt, my covenant which they broke, though I was their husband, says the Lord. But this is the covenant which I will make with the house of Israel after those days, says the Lord: I will put my law within them, and I will write it upon their hearts; and I will be their God, and they shall be my people. And no longer shall each man teach his neighbor and each his brother, saying, 'Know the Lord,' for they shall all know me, from the least of them to the greatest, says the Lord; for I will forgive their iniquity, and I will remember their sin no more. (Jer 31:31-34)

Therefore say, "Thus says the Lord God: I will gather you from the peoples, and assemble you out of the countries where you have been scattered, and I will give you the land of Israel." And when they come there, they will remove from it all its detestable things and all its abominations. And I will give them one heart, and put a new spirit within them; I will take the stony heart out of their flesh and give them a heart of flesh, that they may walk in my statutes and keep my ordinances and obey them; and they shall be my people, and I will be their God. But as for those whose heart goes after their detestable things and their abominations, I will requite their deeds upon their own heads, says the Lord God. (Ezek 11:17-21)

For I will take you from the nations, and gather you from all the countries, and bring you into your own land. I will sprinkle clean water upon you, and you shall be clean from all your uncleannesses, and from all your idols I will cleanse you. A new heart I will give you, and a new spirit I will put within you; and I will take out of your flesh the heart of stone and give you a heart of flesh. And I will put my spirit within you, and cause you to walk in my statutes and be careful to observe my ordinances. You shall dwell in the land which I gave to your fathers; and you shall be my people, and I will be your God. (36:24-28)

In both Jeremiah and Ezekiel, fleshly circumcision plays no role whatsoever in the new covenant that is binding upon those returning from exile. Furthermore, what seals the practical non-value of circumcision is that there is no mention of it at all in the *ketubim*, the scriptural literature whose main point is belittling Greek wisdom with the aim of inviting the Hellenized

nations of the area to endorse the *torah* as the expression of true
wisdom. The authors could have at least brought circumcision
into the picture as the tangible sign for someone's endorsement
of the Law, but they did not. The same view of circumcision is
expressed in Romans 2:23-29.

Those who accepted the challenge of the scriptural message
gathered in congregations where scripture was read to them
and, in conformity with Genesis 17, circumcised their male
children at the age of eight days. This custom in and of itself was
not a distinctive mark, since it was part of the Hamite and
Semite cultures:

> Thus says the Lord: "Let not the wise man glory in his wisdom,
> let not the mighty man glory in his might, let not the rich man
> glory in his riches; but let him who glories glory in this, that he
> understands and knows me, that I am the Lord who practice
> steadfast love, justice, and righteousness in the earth; for in these
> things I delight, says the Lord. Behold, the days are coming, says
> the Lord, when I will punish all those who are *circumcised but yet
> uncircumcised*—Egypt, Judah, Edom, the sons of Ammon, Moab,
> and all who dwell in the desert that cut the corners of their hair;
> for all these nations are uncircumcised, and all the house of Israel
> is uncircumcised in heart." (Jer 9:23-26)

The Reason behind Scriptural Circumcision

Still, if circumcision is not a big deal, why introduce it as
necessary in the first place, only to relegate it soon enough to a
position of non-relevance? At the time scripture was essentially
conceived, one of the basic features of the Greek culture was
reverence of the human body. In the philosophical Greek
worldview, humans shared the same features and mores as the
deities.[3] A corollary was that the human body was viewed as
perfect and should not be mutilated in any way, shape or form.
It stands to reason that in their program to denigrate the culture

---

[3] In my estimation this is the basis behind *theosis* (becoming god or divinization) in
Christian theological lingo.

of their foreign oppressor, the scriptural authors would make out of circumcision—a common practice in their culture that was abhorred by the Greeks—a central piece in their message. It would behoove us to briefly review how scripture presents the matter.

It is to Abram, of the progeny of Shem (11:10, 29), that the promise of God is addressed:

> Now the Lord said to Abram, "Go from your country and your kindred and your father's house to the land that I will show you. And I will make of you a great nation, and I will bless you, and make your name great (*'agaddelah* [from the root *gaddel*] *šemeka*), so that *you will be a blessing* (Greek: you will be blessed). I will bless those who bless you, and him who curses (*meqallel* from the root *qallel*) you I will curse (*'a'or* from the root *'arar*); and by you all the families of the earth shall bless themselves." (Gen 12:1-3)

Notice the close link to Genesis 9:25-27:

> he [Noah] said, "Cursed (*'arur*) be Canaan; a slave of slaves shall he be to his brothers." He also said, "Blessed (*baruk*) by the Lord my God be Shem; and let Canaan be his slave." God enlarge Japheth, and let him dwell in the tents of Shem; and let Canaan be his slave."[4]

In both cases, the blessing is mentioned with its counterpart, the curse. The original is more overarching because it links Genesis 12 further back to Genesis 8 where God promises not to repeat again the curse of the flood:

> And when the Lord smelled the pleasing odor, the Lord said in his heart, "I will never again curse (*qallel*) the ground because of man, for the imagination of man's heart is evil from his youth; neither will I ever again destroy every living creature as I have done. While the earth remains, seedtime and harvest, cold and heat, summer and winter, day and night, shall not cease." (8:21-22)

---

[4] Circumcision becomes the medium through which Japheth would share in the blessing bestowed upon Shem.

Genesis 12:1-3 is more encompassing than it appears since (1) it is the "name" of Abram that will be made great and (2) belittlement is introduced in opposition to aggrandizement. The combination of these two themes is intentional: it functions as the enactment of the belittling of the kings, 'anše haššem (the men of the "name" [renown]), and of the bringing down of the nephilim, those about to fall (6:1-4). Phraseology wise, Genesis 12 harks back to the use of the roots 'arar (curse) and qallel (despise; belittle): 'arar in 9:25 and qallel in chapter 8. Further, it is through Sarai, Abram's barren wife (11:30), and not through Abram himself, that God's blessing to make Abram the father of a multitude of nations will be accomplished. This, in turn, functions as the realization of 6:4 where one hears that it is women who beget children to (and thus for)[5] the "men of renown." Kings will issue from Abraham (17:6), but more importantly specifically from Sarah (v.16) since Abraham "was ninety-nine years old" (v.1) and thus, as Paul rightly commented, "he [Abraham] considered his own body ... as good as dead" (Rom 4:19). God counters Abraham's doubtfulness with the words, "Sarah your wife shall bear (yoledet [active feminine participle of yalad]) you a son" (Gen 17:19; see also vv.17 and 21); whereas, of Abraham not even the hiphil form holid (from yalad) is used. This omission is all the more striking given that, in the same context, Ishmael is said to be "the father of (yolid; hiphil of yalad) twelve princes" (v.20). More pertinent to our discussion is that the ultimate enactment of this blessing of all families of the earth and their members, foreigners as well as indigenous people, takes place through circumcision, the epitome of belittlement in the eyes of the Greeks:

> When Abram was ninety-nine years old the Lord appeared to Abram, and said to him, "I am God Almighty; walk before me, and be blameless. And I will make my covenant between me and you, and will multiply you exceedingly." Then Abram fell on his face; and God said to him, "Behold, my covenant is with you, and

---

5 The Hebrew preposition be carries both connotations.

you shall be the father of a multitude of nations. No longer shall your name be Abram, but your name shall be Abraham; for I have made you the father of a multitude of nations. I will make you exceedingly fruitful; and I will make nations of you, and kings shall come forth from you. And I will establish my covenant between me and you and your descendants after you throughout their generations for an everlasting covenant, to be God to you and to your descendants after you. And I will give to you, and to your descendants after you, the land of your sojournings, all the land of Canaan, for an everlasting possession; and I will be their God." And God said to Abraham, "As for you, you shall keep my covenant, you and your descendants after you throughout their generations. This is my covenant, which you shall keep, between me and you and your descendants after you: Every male among you shall be circumcised. You shall be circumcised in the flesh of your foreskins, and it shall be a sign of the covenant between me and you. He that is eight days old among you shall be circumcised; every male throughout your generations, whether born in your house, or bought with your money from any foreigner who is not of your offspring, both he that is born in your house and he that is bought with your money, shall be circumcised. So shall my covenant be in your flesh an everlasting covenant. Any uncircumcised male who is not circumcised in the flesh of his foreskin shall be cut off from his people; he has broken my covenant." And God said to Abraham, "As for Sarai your wife, you shall not call her name Sarai, but Sarah shall be her name. I will bless her, and moreover I will give you a son by her; I will bless her, and she shall be a mother of nations; kings of peoples shall come from her." Then Abraham fell on his face and laughed, and said to himself, "Shall a child be born to a man who is a hundred years old? Shall Sarah, who is ninety years old, bear a child?" And Abraham said to God, "O that Ishmael might live in thy sight!" God said, "No, but Sarah your wife shall bear you a son, and you shall call his name Isaac. I will establish my covenant with him as an everlasting covenant for his descendants after him. As for Ishmael, I have heard you; behold, I will bless him and make him fruitful and multiply him exceedingly; he shall be the father of twelve princes, and I will make him a great nation. But I will establish my covenant with Isaac, whom Sarah shall bear to you at this season next year." When he had finished talking with him, God went up from Abraham. Then Abraham took Ishmael his son and all the slaves born in his house or bought with his money, every male among the men of Abraham's house, and he circumcised the flesh of their foreskins that very day, as God had said to him. Abraham was ninety-nine years old when he was circumcised in the flesh of his foreskin. And Ishmael his son was thirteen years old when he was circumcised in the flesh of his foreskin. That very day Abraham and his son Ishmael were circumcised; and all the men of his house, those born in the house and those bought with money from a foreigner, were circumcised with him. (Gen 17)

Genesis 17 is axial to the entire scriptural premise, as is evident from the following features:

- In it one hears of circumcision for the first time in scripture, and then it is mentioned no less than ten times.

- The circumcision covenant is as much everlasting as that made with Noah and his sons and the animals (9:16). Both are all encompassing given that the circumcision covenant is offered to the outsider as well as the insider (17:12-13). It is interesting to note that not only Ishmael was circumcised, but also "those bought with money from a foreigner" were circumcised (vv.26-27), and that this happened before Isaac the chosen was even born (18:3), let alone circumcised (v.4).

- The inclusiveness of the circumcision covenant is reflected in the change of names of Abram and Sarai in conjunction with the promise to be "the father of a multitude of nations" (v.5) and "a mother of nations" (v.16), respectively. However—and this is precisely where the literary device of belittlement is at its extreme— the new names reflect a demeaning or lessening compared to the original ones. While Sarai means "my princes" and Abram "a great (highly positioned) father," Sarah means "princess," that is to say, still unmarried and thus without children and Abraham means "the father of the weakling/sickling lamb."[6] This corroborates my thesis that scripture is written "against the grain" of world literatures: the protagonists are belittled no less than the outsiders.

Circumcision, which was underscored against the Greek mores, was not glorified per se. Its value was not magical. The covenant of circumcision was an invitation to submit to the covenant of the Law, which is the medium through which God reigns and rules. It is God who issues the Law with his own finger (Ex 31:18). Nowhere are we told that he performs the act of circumcision, save for the circumcision of the heart so that his statutes be obeyed: "And the Lord your God will circumcise your heart and the heart of your offspring, so that you will love the Lord your God with all your heart and with all your soul, that you may live." (Deut 30:6) In the Mosaic statutes, fleshly circumcision is mentioned once and then only obliquely in conjunction with a woman's giving birth to a male child:

The Lord said to Moses, "Say to the people of Israel, If a woman conceives, and bears a male child, then she shall be unclean seven days; as at the time of her menstruation, she shall be unclean. And on the eighth day the flesh of his foreskin shall be circumcised. Then she shall continue for thirty-three days in the blood of her purifying; she shall not touch any hallowed thing,

---

[6] See article by Iskandar Abou-Chaar, "Rereading Isaiah 40-55 as "Project Launcher" for the Books of the Law and the Prophets," *Festschrift in Honor of Professor Paul Nadim Tarazi, Volume 1, Studies in the Old Testament,* (New York: Peter Lang Publishing, Inc., 2013), pp.114. See also Iskandar Abou-Chaar, "Analytical Reading of Isaiah 40-55 as the Parable of Abraham and Sarah and its Reenactment in Genesis 32," The Journal of the Orthodox Center for the Advancement of Biblical Studies (JOCABS) Vol. 6, No 1 (2013), p. 34.

nor come into the sanctuary, until the days of her purifying are
completed." (Lev 12:1-4)

Circumcision, Passover, and the "Foreigners"

In view of the primacy of the circumcision of the heart over that
of the flesh in the Old Testament, one can understand how, at
no point, do we hear that "foreigners" actually submitted to or
were forced into being circumcised in the flesh.[7] The reason that
is given is that such circumcision was a condition expressly in
view of the celebration of the passover:

And the Lord said to Moses and Aaron, "This is the ordinance of
the passover: no foreigner shall eat of it; but every slave that is
bought for money may eat of it after you have circumcised him.
No sojourner or hired servant may eat of it. In one house shall it
be eaten; you shall not carry forth any of the flesh outside the
house; and you shall not break a bone of it. All the congregation
of Israel shall keep it. And when a stranger shall sojourn with you
and would keep the passover to the Lord, let all his males be
circumcised, then he may come near and keep it; he shall be as a
native of the land. But no uncircumcised person shall eat of it."
(Ex 12:43-48)

At that time the Lord said to Joshua, "Make flint knives and
circumcise the people of Israel again the second time." So Joshua
made flint knives, and circumcised the people of Israel at
Gibeathhaaraloth. And this is the reason why Joshua circumcised
them: all the males of the people who came out of Egypt, all the
men of war, had died on the way in the wilderness after they had
come out of Egypt. Though all the people who came out had
been circumcised, yet all the people that were born on the way in
the wilderness after they had come out of Egypt had not been
circumcised. For the people of Israel walked forty years in the
wilderness, till all the nation, the men of war that came forth out
of Egypt, perished, because they did not hearken to the voice of

---

[7] See my earlier comments regarding circumcision in conjunction with the rape of
Dinah where I show that the story revolves around the betrayal of the covenant of
circumcision by Jacob's children; p.118. See also my comments in *C-Gen* 170-172.

the Lord; to them the Lord swore that he would not let them see the land which the Lord had sworn to their fathers to give us, a land flowing with milk and honey. So it was their children, whom he raised up in their stead, that Joshua circumcised; for they were uncircumcised, because they had not been circumcised on the way. When the circumcising of all the nation was done, they remained in their places in the camp till they were healed. And the Lord said to Joshua, "This day I have rolled away the reproach of Egypt from you." And so the name of that place is called Gilgal to this day. While the people of Israel were encamped in Gilgal they kept the passover on the fourteenth day of the month at evening in the plains of Jericho. And on the morrow after the passover, on that very day, they ate of the produce of the land, unleavened cakes and parched grain. (Josh 5:2-11)

Although a few chapters later we hear that Joshua subjected the "sojourners" (foreigners) to hear in detail the law of Moses together with the people of Israel (8:30-35), at no point in chapter 5 are we told that any one of those "foreigners" was circumcised. This oddity can be explained by looking at the only other references to circumcision between Exodus 12 and Joshua 5, which reveal the authors' understanding of fleshly circumcision:[8]

And the Lord said to me, "Arise, go on your journey at the head of the people, that they may go in and possess the land, which I swore to their fathers to give them.' "And now, Israel, what does the Lord your God require of you, but to fear the Lord your God, to walk in all his ways, to love him, to serve the Lord your God with all your heart and with all your soul, and to keep the commandments and statutes of the Lord, which I command you this day for your good? Behold, to the Lord your God belong heaven and the heaven of heavens, the earth with all that is in it; yet the Lord set his heart in love upon your fathers and chose their descendants after them, you above all peoples, as at this day. Circumcise therefore the foreskin of your heart, and be no longer stubborn. For the Lord your God is God of gods and Lord of

---

[8] Except for the oblique reference in Lev 12:3.

lords, the great, the mighty, and the terrible God, who is not partial and takes no bribe. He executes justice for the fatherless and the widow, and loves the sojourner, giving him food and clothing. Love the sojourner therefore; for you were sojourners in the land of Egypt. You shall fear the Lord your God; you shall serve him and cleave to him, and by his name you shall swear. He is your praise; he is your God, who has done for you these great and terrible things which your eyes have seen. Your fathers went down to Egypt seventy persons; and now the Lord your God has made you as the stars of heaven for multitude." (Deut 10:11-22)

And when all these things come upon you, the blessing and the curse, which I have set before you, and you call them to mind among all the nations where the Lord your God has driven you, and return to the Lord your God, you and your children, and obey his voice in all that I command you this day, with all your heart and with all your soul; then the Lord your God will restore your fortunes, and have compassion upon you, and he will gather you again from all the peoples where the Lord your God has scattered you. If your outcasts are in the uttermost parts of heaven, from there the Lord your God will gather you, and from there he will fetch you; and the Lord your God will bring you into the land which your fathers possessed, that you may possess it; and he will make you more prosperous and numerous than your fathers. And the Lord your God will circumcise your heart and the heart of your offspring, so that you will love the Lord your God with all your heart and with all your soul, that you may live. And the Lord your God will put all these curses upon your foes and enemies who persecuted you. And you shall again obey the voice of the Lord, and keep all his commandments which I command you this day. (30:1-8)

Notice how the circumcision of the heart applies to the new covenant after the exile (Deut 30) as well as to the original covenant (ch.10). Notice also how the original covenant includes reference to the "sojourners," making the Israelite's attitude to them as a condition of the Law itself by comparing the "sojourners" in the earth of the promise to the Israelites in the earth of Pharaoh. God brought the Israelites out of Egypt *in order to* give them his law, which requires that they extend the same kind of mercy toward the "foreigners," which God extended toward the Israelites when they were the *foreigners* in Egypt. The passover was precisely the feast that was supposed to remind Israel of God's beneficence, yet it was not celebrated in the earth of the promise after Joshua: "For no such passover had been kept since the days of the judges who judged Israel, or during all the days of the kings of Israel or of the kings of Judah." (2 Kg 23:22) Further, at its reinstatement under Josiah, it is not fleshly circumcision that takes central stage—actually it is not mentioned at all. What we hear are the (actual words of) Law, that is, the circumcision of the heart:

> Then the king sent, and all the elders of Judah and Jerusalem were gathered to him. And the king went up to the house of the Lord, and with him all the men of Judah and all the inhabitants of Jerusalem, and the priests and the prophets, all the people, both small and great; and he read in their hearing all the words of the book of the covenant which had been found in the house of the Lord. And the king stood by the pillar and made a covenant before the Lord, to walk after the Lord and to keep his commandments and his testimonies and his statutes, with all his heart and all his soul, to perform the words of this covenant that were written in this book; and all the people joined in the covenant. (2 Kg 23:1-3)

What is stunning is that scripture unequivocally underscores the fact that the celebration of Passover did not occur between Joshua 5 and 2 Kings 23. The importance of the reinstatement of Passover under Josiah is evident in its detailed mention in 1 Esdras (1:1-22), a book contemporary with the Maccabean literature. One can understand why, during all that time, circumcision was not mentioned: it was non-functional and thus one can surmise that no "foreigner" had the need to undergo it. It was simply not on the horizon of the authors; the entire epic covering Joshua through 2 Kings centered on the disobedience to the Law. The only one who abided by that Law and, therefore, during whose lifetime Israel resided in the earth of the

promise at peace with the "strangers," was Joshua son of Nun.
Add to this that during that same time Caleb, whose name
means "dog" and thus functions as an oblique stand-in for the
"outsiders," was given prominence in that he inherited Hebron,
the city of Abraham, "because he wholly followed the Lord, the
God of Israel" (Josh 14:14b) resulting in Joshua's blessing:
"Then Joshua blessed him; and he gave Hebron to Caleb the
son of Jephunneh for an inheritance." (v.13) The importance of
this is evident in that the authors twice recounted Caleb's
inheriting Hebron in Judah (Josh 14:13-15 and 15:13-14), and
that it was referenced in the Maccabean literature: "Joshua,
because he fulfilled the command, became a judge in Israel.
Caleb, because he testified in the assembly, received an
inheritance in the land." (1 Macc 2:55-56) The conclusion is
unavoidable: the message of the Book of Joshua is that it is
obedience to the Law, the expression of God's will, that is
required of both Israelite and Gentile, regardless of
circumcision.

Prominence of Circumcision

The "dormant" circumcision becomes "alive" and even steals
the show in the Maccabean literature that deals with the revolt
of the Palestinian followers of scripture against the Seleucids,
heirs of Alexander of Macedon, against whose hegemony
scripture was conceived:

> And after Alexander had reigned twelve years, he died. Then his
> officers began to rule, each in his own place. They all put on
> crowns after his death, and so did their sons after them for many
> years; and they caused many evils on the earth. From them came
> forth a sinful root, Antiochus Epiphanes, son of Antiochus the
> king; he had been a hostage in Rome. He began to reign in the
> one hundred and thirty-seventh year of the kingdom of the
> Greeks. In those days lawless men came forth from Israel, and
> misled many, saying, "Let us go and make a covenant with the
> Gentiles round about us, for since we separated from them many
> evils have come upon us." This proposal pleased them, and some

of the people eagerly went to the king. He authorized them to observe the ordinances of the Gentiles. So they built a gymnasium in Jerusalem, according to Gentile custom, and removed the marks of circumcision, and abandoned the holy covenant. They joined with the Gentiles and sold themselves to do evil. (1 Macc 1:7-15)

After subduing Egypt, Antiochus returned in the one hundred and forty-third year. He went up against Israel and came to Jerusalem with a strong force. He arrogantly entered the sanctuary and took the golden altar, the lampstand for the light, and all its utensils. (1:20-21)

Now on the fifteenth day of Chislev, in the one hundred and forty-fifth year, they erected a desolating sacrilege upon the altar of burnt offering. They also built altars in the surrounding cities of Judah, and burned incense at the doors of the houses and in the streets. The books of the law which they found they tore to pieces and burned with fire. Where the book of the covenant was found in the possession of any one, or if any one adhered to the law, the decree of the king condemned him to death. They kept using violence against Israel, against those found month after month in the cities. And on the twenty-fifth day of the month they offered sacrifice on the altar which was upon the altar of burnt offering. According to the decree, they put to death the women who had their children circumcised, and their families and those who circumcised them; and they hung the infants from their mothers' necks. (1:54-61)

In those days Mattathias the son of John, son of Simeon, a priest of the sons of Joarib, moved from Jerusalem and settled in Modein. (2:1)

Then Mattathias cried out in the city with a loud voice, saying: "Let every one who is zealous for the law and supports the covenant come out with me!" (2:27)

And Mattathias and his friends went about and tore down the altars; they forcibly circumcised all the uncircumcised boys that they found within the borders of Israel. (2:45-46)

At the suggestion of Ptolemy a decree was issued to the neighboring Greek cities, that they should adopt the same policy toward the Jews and make them partake of the sacrifices, and should slay those who did not choose to change over to Greek customs. One could see, therefore, the misery that had come upon them. For example, two women were brought in for having circumcised their children. These women they publicly paraded about the city, with their babies hung at their breasts, then hurled them down headlong from the wall. (2 Macc 6:8-10; see also the parallel account in 4 Macc 4:23-25)

The Maccabees and their followers were using circumcision as a "national flag," a "standard," around which they would easily rally their followers for their own agenda.

Still the issue of circumcision does not explain the total range of reactions against the Jerusalemite leadership by the Pauline contingent living in the "dispersion" (*diaspora*; Jn 7:35; Jas 1:1; 1 Pet 1:1). Scripture's attitude toward circumcision is so clear that Paul simply needed to refer to it in order to silence his opponents: "For neither circumcision counts for anything nor uncircumcision, but keeping the commandments of God." (1 Cor 7:19) The points of contention, in addition to the issue of circumcision, were the defining lines of Jewry, table fellowship, and the crucifixion of the Davidic Messiah. In order to understand what was going on in the Roman empire during the first century A.D. among those who subscribed to the scriptural teaching, one is to take into consideration the situation prevailing "on the ground" in all its ramifications.

17

Common Table Fellowship

Circumcision would not have been a problem for the Pauline contingent living outside *yehud*. Actually, at the Jerusalem meeting detailed in Galatians 2 and Acts 15, the Gentile Titus, who accompanied Paul, was not forced to submit to circumcision. An agreement was reached at the Jerusalem meeting, and upon giving his right hand to the "pillars," Paul promised to "remember the poor, which very thing I was eager to do" (Gal 2:10). Paul kept this promise in spite of the subsequent rift at Antioch, as is evident from his writings:

> Now concerning the contribution for the saints: as I directed the churches of Galatia, so you also are to do. On the first day of every week, each of you is to put something aside and store it up, as he may prosper, so that contributions need not be made when I come. And when I arrive, I will send those whom you accredit by letter to carry your gift to Jerusalem. (1 Cor 16:1-3)

> For Macedonia and Achaia have been pleased to make some contribution for the poor among the saints at Jerusalem; they were pleased to do it, and indeed they are in debt to them, for if the Gentiles have come to share in their spiritual blessings, they ought also to be of service to them in material blessings. (Rom 15:26-27)

Yet James (*Iakōbos*; Jacob) and his followers, that is, the Jerusalemite leadership, pressured the Gentiles, who were willing to submit to the Law and thus behave as circumcised in their hearts, to abide by the food restrictions upheld by the *yehudim* (Gal 2:11-14). Abiding by food restrictions would have jeopardized the Pauline mission among the Gentiles on two levels. The first was scriptural in that it contradicted Isaiah's description of the eschatological Zion:

For I know their works and their thoughts, and I am coming to
gather all nations and tongues; and they shall come and shall see
my glory, and I will set a sign among them. And from them I will
send survivors to the nations, to Tarshish, Put, and Lud, who
draw the bow, to Tubal and Javan, to the coastlands afar off, that
have not heard my fame or seen my glory; and they shall declare
my glory among the nations. And they shall bring all your
brethren from all the nations as an offering to the Lord, upon
horses, and in chariots, and in litters, and upon mules, and upon
dromedaries, to my holy mountain Jerusalem, says the Lord, just
as the Israelites bring their cereal offering in a clean vessel to the
house of the Lord. *And some of them also I will take for priests and for
Levites, says the Lord.* (66:18-21)

Secondly, and more importantly, was the situation "on the
ground." There was a basic difference between the Greek and
the Roman polities. As I detailed earlier the Greek polity
revolved around cities that constituted the basic societal units:
Sparta, Athens, Corinth, Troy. Roman society was
fundamentally tribal, the basic societal unit being not so much
the city but the "household"[1] whose head was the "father"
(Latin *paterfamilias*). The *paterfamilias* had as full and
incontrovertible authority as the *'ab* of Bedouin shepherd
society. In the Old Testament the authors frontally attacked the
Greeks and offered them a society patterned after shepherdism.
In the New Testament the strategy changed. It opted for
"taming," "harnessing" the opponent by using the Roman
traditions against the imperial power, which was the real
nemesis of the power of God and his anointed. The Pauline
school used the Roman household as the *ekklēsia* (*kat' oikon
ekklēsia*; house church), the scriptural *qahal* that is summoned by
the father's voice according to his pleasure. The *familia* was as
ad hoc as the *qahal*, basically a reality produced or created[2] by
the father's will (*thelēma*) as uttered through his lips. In other
words, the New Testament was still anti-Greek, and although

---

[1] Hebrew *bet-'ab* (house of the father) corresponding to the Latin *familia*.
[2] The Latin *creare* literally means "to call [out]."

pro-Roman (*senatus* [elders] *populusque* [and the people] *Romanus*), it was not pro-emperor in its post-Caesar connotation.[3] Hence, just as in the LXX, the New Testament *hoi Hellēnes* (the Hellenes, the Greeks) has a negative connotation, but not so *hoi Rōmaioi* (the Romans). So it was of the essence that the apostle to the nations be presented not only as a Jew, but also and repeatedly as a "Roman" citizen (Acts 16:37-38; 22:25-29; 23:27).

The house church was not just a convenience on the practical level. The house meal was a central feature of Roman societal fabric in the same way it was in shepherd culture. It was the forum where Roman patricians and even slaves in positions of authority, such as the *oikonomos* (house manager), could voice their opinions concerning the *res publica* (the public matter) and thus the Republic, later even the empire. So someone like Paul, a follower of the Law and a Roman citizen, would be welcomed in a Roman household (*oikos*) and would even be on friendly terms with the head of the household, the like of Lydia[4] (Acts 16:14-15) or the jailer[5] in Philippi (vv.27-36). Paul would have the opportunity to voice his teaching while the attendees, Jews

---

[3] Originally *imperator* meant simply "commander."

[4] One who heard us was a woman named Lydia, from the city of Thyatira, a seller of purple goods, who was a worshiper of God. The Lord opened her heart to give heed to what was said by Paul. And when she was baptized, with her household, she besought us, saying, "If you have judged me to be faithful to the Lord, come to my **house** and stay." And she prevailed upon us. (Acts 16:14-15)

[5] When the jailer woke and saw that the prison doors were open, he drew his sword and was about to kill himself, supposing that the prisoners had escaped. But Paul cried with a loud voice, "Do not harm yourself, for we are all here." And he called for lights and rushed in, and trembling with fear he fell down before Paul and Silas, and brought them out and said, "Men, what must I do to be saved?" And they said, "Believe in the Lord Jesus, and you will be saved, you and your **household**." And they spoke the word of the Lord to him and to all that were in his **house**. And he took them the same hour of the night, and washed their wounds, and he was baptized at once, with all his family. Then he brought them up into his **house**, and set food before them; and he rejoiced with all his **household** that he had believed in God. But when it was day, the magistrates sent the police, saying, "Let those men go." And the jailer reported the words to Paul, saying, "The magistrates have sent to let you go; now therefore come out and go in peace." (Acts 16:27-36)

as well as Gentiles, would listen. In this manner, someone the like of Paul would be acting under the "protection" of a paterfamilias or materfamilias. Thus the scriptural message could spread unhindered for anyone interested in endorsing and following it. That this was the Pauline school's policy is reflected in the following two stories where the non-reception by the synagogue and its *yehudim* would not put an end to the spreading of the gospel—it would proceed in a "house" next door:

> Now when they had passed through Amphipolis and Apollonia, they came to Thessalonica, where there was a synagogue of the Jews. And Paul went in, as was his custom, and for three weeks he argued with them from the scriptures, explaining and proving that it was necessary for the Christ to suffer and to rise from the dead, and saying, "This Jesus, whom I proclaim to you, is the Christ." And some of them were persuaded, and joined Paul and Silas; as did great many of the devout Greeks and not a few of the leading women. But the Jews were jealous, and taking some wicked fellows of the rabble, they gathered a crowd, set the city in an uproar, and attacked *the house (oikia) of Jason*, seeking to bring them out to the people. And when they could not find them, they dragged Jason and some of the brethren before the city authorities, crying, "These men who have turned the world upside down have come here also, and *Jason has received them*; and they are all acting against the decrees of Caesar, saying that there is another king, Jesus." And the people and the city authorities were disturbed when they heard this. And *when they had taken security from Jason and the rest, they let them go.* (Acts 17:1-9)

After this Paul left Athens and went to Corinth:

> And he found a Jew named Aquila, a native of Pontus, lately come from Italy with his wife Priscilla, because Claudius had commanded all the Jews to leave Rome. And he went to see them; and because he was of the same trade he stayed with them, and they worked, for by trade they were tentmakers. And he argued in the synagogue every sabbath, and persuaded Jews and Greeks. When Silas and Timothy arrived from Macedonia, Paul was occupied with preaching, testifying to the Jews that the Christ was

Jesus. And when they opposed and reviled him, he shook out his garments and said to them, "Your blood be upon your heads! I am innocent. From now on I will go to the Gentiles." And he left there and went to *the house (oikian) of a man named Titius Justus*, a worshiper of God; *his house (oikia) was next door (synomorousa)*[6] *to the synagogue.* Crispus, the ruler of the synagogue, believed in the Lord, together with all his household; and many of the Corinthians hearing Paul believed and were baptized. (18:1-8)

The ending of Acts corroborates that this manner of proceeding was the rule:

When they had appointed a day for him, they came to him at his lodging in great numbers. And he expounded the matter to them from morning till evening, testifying to the kingdom of God and trying to convince them about Jesus both from the law of Moses and from the prophets. And some were convinced by what he said, while others disbelieved. So, as they disagreed among themselves, they departed, after Paul had made one statement: "The Holy Spirit was right in saying to your fathers through Isaiah the prophet: 'Go to this people, and say, You shall indeed hear but never understand, and you shall indeed see but never perceive. For this people's heart has grown dull, and their ears are heavy of hearing, and their eyes they have closed; lest they should perceive with their eyes, and hear with their ears, and understand with their heart, and turn for me to heal them.' Let it be known to you then that this salvation of God has been sent to the Gentiles; they will listen." And he lived there two whole years at his own expense, and welcomed all who came to him, preaching the kingdom of God and teaching about the Lord Jesus Christ quite openly and unhindered. (28:23-31)

It is in such households, transformed into scriptural "congregations," that everybody partook at the same table while listening to Paul and his colleagues (16:34; 20:11; 1 Cor

---

[6] Connoting that both residences were adjacent in the sense of sharing the one wall, as in our townhouses. This unique Greek adjective, which was coined by Luke, reflects Paul's intention not to be the one to break the relation with the Jerusalemite leadership. Even if the synagogue broke with him, "Jews" were still welcome in his "house churches."

11:17-34). As Paul insisted, at those common tables, not everybody ate the same kind of food and no one had to right to impose one's kind of food on the others (Rom 14)[7] just as no one was allowed to impose circumcision or uncircumcision on the other (1 Cor 7:18-19), but everyone partook of the teaching which was the bread of life. However, the "content" of the teaching was none other than the correct and unadulterated teaching of the Old Testament as we hear in the Pastorals as well as the other Pauline letters where the Gentiles are "sucked" into becoming an integral part of the scriptural story (see especially 1 Cor 10:1-11).

Given the reality of the adage *verba volant, scripta manent* (spoken words fly away, written words remain), and in its effort to salvage the Old Testament from distortion by the Jerusalem leadership in the "absence" of the leaders of the Pauline school,[8] that is, after their demise, the Pauline school *scripturalized* the Apostle's teaching in his letters. These letters were to be read aloud along with the Old Testament at the congregational meetings of his churches: "And when this letter has been read among you, have it read also in the church of the Laodiceans; and see that you read also the letter from Laodicea." (Col 4:16)[9] The Pauline literature is thus canonized as scripture in the strictest manner:

> Now concerning the coming of our Lord Jesus Christ and our assembling to meet him, we beg you, brethren, not to be quickly shaken in mind or excited, either by spirit or by word, or *by letter purporting to be from us*, to the effect that the day of the Lord has come. (2 Thess 2:1-2)

---

[7] Such an attitude would actually have been an outright insult to the Roman host.

[8] Paul prepared his followers by referring to his eventual demise as "absence" (*apousia*) as either opposed to his "presence" (*parousia*) among them or as leading to the Lord's *parousia* (coming, presence). See 2 Cor 13:1-10; Phil 1:25-27; 2:12-13.

[9] Notice also in Revelation that each of the seven individual letters addressed to the churches of the Roman province Asia, whose capital is Ephesus, the headquarters of the Pauline school, is intended for all seven of them: "He who has an ear, let him hear what the Spirit says *to the churches*." (Rev 2:7, 11, 17, 29; 2:6, 13, 22)

Therefore, beloved, since you wait for these, be zealous to be
found by him without spot or blemish, and at peace. And count
the forbearance of our Lord as salvation. So also our beloved
brother Paul wrote to you according to the wisdom given him,
speaking of this as he does in all his letters. There are some things
in them hard to understand, which the ignorant and unstable
twist to their own destruction, *as they do the other scriptures.* (2
Pet 3:14-16)

18

Paul as Moses

C an one say more as to how and in which sense the Pauline writings are canonized? I am convinced one can. Time and again in my commentaries on the Pauline epistles I have argued that Galatians functions as a blue print for all of them.[1] I will mention here just two features, one material and the other formal to confirm this. As is clear from the entire Pauline corpus, the Apostle's perpetual bone of contention concerns table fellowship, dietary rules (Rom 14; 1 Cor 8; 10:25-31; Gal 2:11-14) and circumcision (Rom 2-4; 1 Cor 7:18-19; Gal 2:1-9, 12; 5:1-11; 6:12-15; Eph 2:11; Phil 3:3-5; Col 2:11; 3:11; 4:11). These issues are paralleled in sharpness in Paul's continuous showdown with the Judahite leadership of Jerusalem (1 Cor 3:16-23; 9:1-7; 2 Cor 11; Gal 2). All three elements are combined in Galatians 2:1-14. Also, Galatians is the only epistle that is addressed to multiple churches of the same province (1:2), which gives it a taste of universality and thus an aspect of incontrovertible authority. Note its beginning and ending:

> I am astonished that you are so quickly deserting him who called you in the grace of Christ and turning to a different gospel—not that there is another gospel, but there are some who trouble you and want to pervert the gospel of Christ. But even if we, or an angel from heaven, should preach to you a gospel contrary to that which we preached to you, let him be accursed. As we have said before, so now I say again, If any one is preaching to you a gospel contrary to that which you received, let him be accursed. (1:6-9)

> Henceforth let no man trouble me; for I bear on my body the marks of Jesus. (6:17)

---

[1] See my article "Paul's Letter to the Churches of Galatia," The Journal of the Orthodox Center for the Advancement of Biblical Studies (JOCABS) Vol. 9, No 1 (2016).

THE RISE OF SCRIPTURE

Such authority as well as universality brings to mind Moses of the Old Testament, and this is precisely how Paul presents himself in Galatians, that is, as a new Moses. Speaking of the Law Paul writes: "Why then the law? It was added because of transgressions, till the offspring should come to whom the promise had been made; and it was ordained by angels through (*en kheiri*; at the hand of) an intermediary." (3:19) Later he autographs the letter in the following terms: "See with what large letters I am writing to you with my own hand (*en kheiri mou*; at my hand)." (6:11) The fact that this "Mosaic" signature comes up as a refrain throughout his entire corpus cannot be but intentional.[2] At the end of the second and the fourth major epistles we read:

I, Paul, write this greeting with my own hand. (1Cor 16:21)

See with what large letters I am writing to you with my own hand. (Gal 6:11)

At the end of the three captivity epistles we read:

I, Paul, write this greeting with my own hand. (Col 4:18)

At the end of the epistles to the Thessalonians we read:

I, Paul, write this greeting with my own hand. *This is the mark in every letter of mine; it is the way I write.* (2 Thess 3:17)

At the end of the four letters to individuals we read:

I, Paul, write this with my own hand. (Philem 1:19)

As I mentioned earlier, this is done to insure that Paul's interpretation of scripture be preserved in his absence, that is, after his demise. The casting of the leader of the Pauline school as a new, or another, Moses serves another purpose. The invitation to the Gentiles is not to undergo fleshly circumcision, but rather circumcision of the heart, that is to say, for them to become a *bar* or *bat miṣwah*[3] intimated in the two passages

---

[2] At hearing it, one is forced to agree with 2 Peter 3:14-16 that the Pauline letters were conceived as authoritative scripture.

[3] Son or daughter of the commandment.

concerning the new covenant in Jeremiah and Ezekiel. In other words, the bottom line is "keeping the commandments of God" (1 Cor 7:19), and since love for the neighbor is the epitome of the entire Law (Gal 5:14; Rom 13:8-10), "neither circumcision nor uncircumcision is of any avail, but faith working through love" (Gal 5:6). The most tangible test for such love is full table fellowship with the others regardless of the food one consumes (Rom 14). The true bread of life *for all* is the teaching that the scriptural God is the deity of all *equally* and that he will ultimately judge each of us as to whether we shall have implemented in deed his bidding for us to care for our needy neighbors (Mt 25:31-46). Caring for the needy is what the scriptural God requires from us; he does not require sacrificial offerings or observance of appointed feasts:

> Hear the word of the Lord, you rulers of Sodom! Give ear to the teaching of our God, you people of Gomorrah! "What to me is the multitude of your sacrifices? says the Lord; I have had enough of burnt offerings of rams and the fat of fed beasts; I do not delight in the blood of bulls, or of lambs, or of he-goats. When you come to appear before me, who requires of you this trampling of my courts? Bring no more vain offerings; incense is an abomination to me. New moon and sabbath and the calling of assemblies—I cannot endure iniquity and solemn assembly. Your new moons and your appointed feasts my soul hates; they have become a burden to me, I am weary of bearing them. When you spread forth your hands, I will hide my eyes from you; even though you make many prayers, I will not listen; your hands are full of blood. Wash yourselves; make yourselves clean; remove the evil of your doings from before my eyes; cease to do evil, learn to do good; seek justice, correct oppression; defend the fatherless, plead for the widow. Come now, let us reason together, says the Lord: though your sins are like scarlet, they shall be as white as snow; though they are red like crimson, they shall become like wool. If you are willing and obedient, you shall eat the good of the land; but if you refuse and rebel, you shall be devoured by the sword; for the mouth of the Lord has spoken." (Is 1:10-20)

Thus says the Lord: "Heaven is my throne and the earth is my footstool; what is the house which you would build for me, and what is the place of my rest? All these things my hand has made, and so all these things are mine, says the Lord. But this is the man to whom I will look, he that is humble and contrite in spirit, and trembles at my word. He who slaughters an ox is like him who kills a man; he who sacrifices a lamb, like him who breaks a dog's neck; he who presents a cereal offering, like him who offers swine's blood; he who makes a memorial offering of frankincense, like him who blesses an idol. These have chosen their own ways, and their soul delights in their abominations; I also will choose affliction for them, and bring their fears upon them; because, when I called, no one answered, when I spoke they did not listen; but they did what was evil in my eyes, and chose that in which I did not delight." (66:1-4)

The Epistolary Corpus

In order to ensure that the legacy of Paul's "house churches" would remain open to the *yehudim* and their followers, the writers of the New Testament included in the canon four letters addressed to leaders of house churches (1 and 2 Timothy, Titus, and Philemon)[4] whose intentional clustering is sealed with an ending similar to that found at the closure of each cluster of the epistles addressed to churches: the writing is with Paul's own hand.[5] They further conceived the letter to the Hebrews followed by seven epistles attributed to Paul's nemeses at the Jerusalem meeting: James, Peter, and John. In so doing, all authoritative voices were presented as being in unison with that of *the Apostle*. This is sealed by the assertion of Peter—the "other" apostle (Gal 2:7-8)—at the closure of his writings: "And count the forbearance of our Lord as salvation. So also our beloved brother Paul wrote to you according to the wisdom given him, speaking of this as he does in all his letters. There are some things in them hard to understand, which the ignorant

---

[4] Here again the numeral four is reflective of universality.
[5] See above.

and unstable twist to their own destruction, as they do the other scriptures." (2 Pet 3:15-16)

The letter to the Hebrews functions as a straddle that closes the Pauline corpus and presages the seven "catholic" epistles. The hearer can only suppose that its assumed literary author is Paul from the reference to Timothy at the end of the letter, which brings to mind Paul's request from his adjutant at the end of 2 Timothy:

> You should understand that our brother Timothy has been released, with whom I shall see you if he comes soon. (Heb 13:23)

> Do your best to come to me soon. (2 Tim 4:9)

Still, the absence of the name of the addressees as well as the writer is intentional in order to give the impression that it is a magisterial treatise on the Old Testament and, more specifically, on the temple priesthood. It is, to say the least, a tour de force that expands on the thesis of Galatians, the Pauline letter that purports that the three leaders, James, Peter, and John, the "pillars" of Jerusalem, accepted the authenticity of the Pauline gospel message (2:1-10), and in which Paul pins down the Jerusalem "above" against the "present" Jerusalem (4:25-26). On the other hand, the letter to the Hebrews presents the "new" Joshua as the Jesus of the Gospels.[6] Unlike the previous Pauline epistles that are specifically aimed at the Gentiles, this fourteenth epistle assumes a thorough knowledge of the Old Testament data, and thus gives the distinct impression that it is addressed to the leaders of the *yehudim* and their followers. This explains its very early title "to the Hebrews" in the New Testament manuscripts in spite of the fact that neither the term "Hebrew/s" nor even the term "Jew/s" is to be found therein.

My understanding of the function of this letter, both content wise and canonical position wise, is corroborated by the fact that, on the one hand, it is the last chapter of Paul's voice and,

---

[6] In the next chapters, I shall discuss in detail Jesus, the other New Testament "hero" besides Paul.

348 THE RISE OF SCRIPTURE

on the other hand, it opens the door for the leaders of the *yedudim* to express with their own voice the same teaching in the next seven letters. The number "seven" is clearly intentional since it reflects the divine *imprimatur.*[7] James, the top leader, is given the place of honor. His letter is addressed "to the twelve tribes in the Dispersion" (Jas 1:1) in which he endorses the primacy of the love for the needy neighbor championed not only in Galatians but in all other Pauline epistles:

What does it profit, my brethren, if a man says he has faith but has not works? Can his faith save him? If a brother or sister is ill-clad and in lack of daily food, and one of you says to them, "Go in peace, be warmed and filled," without giving them the things needed for the body, what does it profit? So faith by itself, if it has no works, is dead. But some one will say, "You have faith and I have works." Show me your faith apart from your works, and I by my works will show you my faith. (Jas 2:14-18)

For through the Spirit, by faith, we wait for the hope of righteousness. For in Christ Jesus neither circumcision nor uncircumcision is of any avail, but faith working through love. (Gal 5:5-6)

Do not be deceived; God is not mocked, for whatever a man sows, that he will also reap. For he who sows to his own flesh will from the flesh reap corruption; but he who sows to the Spirit will from the Spirit reap eternal life. And let us not grow weary in well-doing, for in due season we shall reap, if we do not lose heart. So then, as we have opportunity, let us do good to all men, and especially to those who are of the household of faith. (Gal 6:7-10)

We give thanks to God always for you all, constantly mentioning you in our prayers, remembering before our God and Father your work of faith and labor of love and steadfastness of hope in our Lord Jesus Christ. (1 Thess 1:2-3)[8]

Then after Peter, the other "pillar," who in his own voice "canonizes" as scripture the letters of Paul (2 Pet 3:15-16), we

[7] For the value of the numerical 7, see the Excursus on Number Symbolism in *NTI3* 22-28.
[8] See also, e.g., Eph 1:15-16; Col 1:3-4.

hear from the third "pillar," John, who immortalizes in his three letters[9] the centrality of love as being not a "new," but actually the "old" commandment from the beginning (2 Jn 1:5). He even asserts that: "If any one says, 'I love God,' and hates his brother, he is a liar; for he who does not love his brother whom he has seen, cannot love God whom he has not seen. And this commandment we have from him, that he who loves God should love his brother also." (1 Jn 4:20-21) Taken together these two statements echo what we hear in Galatians: "For the whole law is fulfilled in one word, 'You shall love your neighbor as yourself.' ... But the fruit of the Spirit is love, joy, peace, patience, kindness, goodness, faithfulness, gentleness, self-control; against such there is no law." (Gal 5:14, 22-23)

At the other end of the seven "catholic" epistles stands Jude. It is a short epistle of 25 verses and yet its functional importance cannot be overlooked. Just as the English "James" and its French counterpart *Jacques* are made up names for the original *Iakōbos* that is the Grecicized version of the LXX *Iakōb* (Jacob), the English and French "Jude" is equally a fabricated name for the original *Ioudas* that is none other than Judah (Heb *yehudah*), both the forefather, son of Jacob, and the tribe and, later, kingdom, bearing his name. In other words, *Ioudas* and *Iakōbos* are the two sides of the same coin, stand-ins, respectively for the *yehud* and *yehudim*[10] of New Testament times.[11] The intended close relation between the two names is borne out in that Jude—more accurately Judah—is introduced as "the brother of James (more accurately Jacob)" (Jude 1:1). On the other hand, biblical scholars and others have noticed that 2 Peter and the letter of Jude are very close content wise, to the extent that the hearer is under the impression that Jude is a "repeat" of 2 Peter. From

---

[9] My readers are reminded that the numeral three reflects the "indeed-ness" of a matter.

[10] Represented by their leader (forefather) Jacob whose other name is "Israel."

[11] The English and French translations betray the unwarranted scholarship tendency toward historicizing and individualizing the scriptural accounts that are essentially parabolic.

the perspective of literature, this is intended as the endorsement by *yehud*, centered around the "pillars" of Jerusalem, of the teaching heard in 2 Peter which, in turn, endorses outspokenly the Pauline gospel as "scripture" on the same level as the Old Testament writings (2 Pet 3:15-16).

The outcome of this masterly structure of the New Testament canon is unmissable. Paul's "hope" that Jerusalem and its leadership would one day endorse his gospel to the Gentiles (1 Cor 16:1-3; Rom 15:25-29; Acts 20:18-23) is fully realized after his demise at the end of his race in the service of that gospel (2 Tim 4:6-8). His "scriptures" (letters) will be read aloud and heard alongside the "scriptures" in his household churches throughout the Roman empire, all the way to its westernmost region beyond Rome (Rom 15:24-28) which is, in turn, a realization of the hope he expressed during his house arrest in that city (Acts 28:30-31).

The Book of Revelation

At this point, when the hearers of both the Old Testament scriptures and the Pauline scriptures are filled with that message of the realization[12] of the scriptural hope, they are ready for the concluding Book of Revelation which consists of a divine "prophecy" (1:3) that is realized on and in its own terms. This control over the events can be seen in that the words, and thus terms, of the prophecy (1:3) are consigned in a "book" (22:7, 10, 18, 19) that is already "sealed" (5:1). The vacillation of RSV between using two different terms, "book" and "scroll," to render the original Greek *biblion*[13] is completely misleading. KJV uses "book" faithfully throughout except where "scroll" (a rolled manuscript) fits the context: "And the heaven departed as a scroll (*biblion*) when it is rolled together." (6:14a) The utter

---

[12] In both senses of both the implementation of that hope and their own realization thereof.

[13] Technically speaking, a small book. The Greek noun *biblos* (book) is found only twice in the phrase "the book of life" (3:5; 20:15).

control over the world events is further evident in that the "book," an obvious stand-in for scripture, ends by restoring the "world" to its pristine condition only when "the one seated on the throne" is in total control. The "one seated on the throne" in 4:2 is addressed by both the four living creatures and the twenty four elders surrounding him in terms reminiscent of Genesis 1: "Worthy art thou, our Lord and God, to receive glory and honor and power, for thou didst create (*ektisas*) all things, and by thy will they existed and were created (*ektisthēsan*)." (Rev 4:11) Although the verb *ktizō* is not found in LXX Genesis 1, it is heard twice in Genesis 14: "And he [Melchizedek] blessed him [Abram] and said, 'Blessed be Abram by God Most High, maker of (*hos ektisen*) heaven and earth' ... But Abram said to the king of Sodom, 'I have sworn to the Lord God Most High, maker of (*hos ektisen*) heaven and earth.'" (Gen 14:19, 22) The closing chapter of the prophecy inscribed in that same book (Rev 22:7, 10, 18, 19) is cast in a vocabulary reminiscent of Genesis 2, the other facet of Genesis 1:

> Then he showed me the river of the water of life, bright as crystal, flowing from the throne of God and of the Lamb through the middle of the street of the city; also, on either side of the river, the tree of life with its twelve kinds of fruit, yielding its fruit each month; and the leaves of the tree were for the healing of the nations" (Rev 22:1-2)

> I warn every one who hears the words of the prophecy of this book: if any one adds to them, God will add to him the plagues described (*tas gegrammenas*; which are scripturalized) in this book, and if any one takes away from the words of the book of this prophecy, God will take away his share in the tree of life and in the holy city, which are described (*tōn gegrammenōn*; which are scripturalized) *in this book.* (vv.18-19)

> And out of the ground the Lord God made to grow every tree that is pleasant to the sight and good for food, the tree of life also in the midst of the garden, and the tree of the knowledge of good

and evil. A river flowed out of Eden to water the garden, and there it divided and became four rivers. (Gen 2:9-10)

Put otherwise, in spite of all the efforts of the "children of Adam" (ha'adam) to thwart God's original intent and plan, God will restore everything to the way it was when he found "everything he had made" to be "very good" (Gen 1:31). There is no doubt as to who is control, at least within the realm of scripture. And that should be sufficient for "the hearers of the words of this prophecy" since all other literature—including the "lost" Annals of the Kings of Judah and Israel—is *immaterial,* per scripture whose "words are faithful (trustworthy) and true" (*pistoi kai alēthinoi*; Rev 21:5; 22:6)"[14]:

> Now Jesus did many other signs in the presence of the disciples, which are not written in this book; but these are written that you may believe that Jesus is the Christ, the Son of God, and that believing you may have life in his name. (Jn 20:30-31)

> This is the disciple who is bearing witness to these things, and who has written these things; and we know that his testimony is true. But there are also many other things which Jesus did; were every one of them to be written, I suppose that the world itself could not contain the books that would be written. (21:24-25)

Still, it is noteworthy that this "prophecy," inscribed in a "book," is handed down by God in and around Ephesus (chapters 2 and 3),[15] the headquarters of the Pauline school, which school is the only legitimate heir of the Ezekelian school that had earlier conceived that "heavenly" God in and around the river Chebar in the region of the Two Rivers. It is of note to point out that both localities—Chebar and Ephesus—lie as far

---

[14] See also 1 Tim 1:15; 3:1; 4:10; 2 Tim 2:11; Tit 3:8 where the Greek is *pistos ho logos* (faithful is the word). RSV has "The saying is sure" while KJV, closer to the original, has "This *is* a faithful saying."

[15] The seven churches that are addressed by the same Spirit are all located in cities of the Roman province Asia whose capital was Ephesus. The number of churches, seven, is the divine numeral that reflects that the message is both divine in its origin and universal in its purview. This aspect of the Book of Revelation militates for its building upon the "gospel" outlined in Paul's letter to the churches of Galatia, a position I defended in *NTI₄* 18-19.

away as can be from both the earthly Jerusalem and the city of Rome, the two backbones of the *yehudim*,[16] which are simultaneously referred to obliquely in the statement "*the great city* which is allegorically called Sodom and Egypt, *where their Lord was crucified* " (Rev 11:8). The hearers already know that, according to the Gospels, the Lord was crucified at Jerusalem by the orders of the Roman governor Pontius Pilate, representing the "great city" Rome. They are also aware that Jerusalem was expressly dubbed "Sodom" by Isaiah:

> And the daughter of Zion is left like a booth in a vineyard, like a lodge in a cucumber field, like a besieged city. If the Lord of hosts had not left us a few survivors, we should have been like Sodom, and become like Gomorrah. Hear the word of the Lord, you rulers of Sodom! Give ear to the teaching of our God, you people of Gomorrah! (1:8-10)

Ephesus must have been chosen for other considerations, symbolic as well as geographical. It was the capital city of the Roman province Asia, one the largest and, more importantly, the westernmost in Asia Minor (Turkey). So Ephesus, which lies on the coast facing Greece and Macedonia and, beyond them, Italy, was situated, so to speak, at the border between East and West, between the "Jews" and the "Gentiles (Hellenes; nations)." The importance, if not centrality, of this matter in the eyes of the New Testament authors can be seen in the lengthy episode of Acts 17. There Paul is depicted as having shown the power (according to the Spirit; Rom 1:4) of his gospel to both Jews and Hellenes *at the same time*, just as he presented it in Romans 1:16 (For I am not ashamed of the gospel: it is the power of God for salvation to every one who has faith, to the Jew first and also to the Greek [Hellene]):

> While Apollos was at Corinth, Paul passed through the upper country and came to Ephesus. There he found some disciples. And he said to them, "Did you receive the Holy Spirit when you

---

[16] See later my comments on Josephus and the Jerusalemite leaders of the first century.

believed?" And they said, "No, we have never even heard that there is a Holy Spirit." And he said, "Into what then were you baptized?" They said, "Into John's baptism." And Paul said, "John baptized with the baptism of repentance, telling the people to believe in the one who was to come after him, that is, Jesus." On hearing this, they were baptized in the name of the Lord Jesus. And when Paul had laid his hands upon them, the Holy Spirit came on them; and they spoke with tongues and prophesied. There were about twelve of them in all. And he entered the synagogue and for three months spoke boldly, arguing and pleading about the kingdom of God; but when some were stubborn and disbelieved, speaking evil of the Way before the congregation, he withdrew from them, taking the disciples with him, and argued daily in the hall of Tyrannus. This continued for two years, so that all the residents of Asia heard the word of the Lord, *both Jews and Greeks*. And God did extraordinary miracles by the hands of Paul, so that handkerchiefs or aprons were carried away from his body to the sick, and diseases left them and the evil spirits came out of them. Then some of the itinerant Jewish exorcists undertook to pronounce the name of the Lord Jesus over those who had evil spirits, saying, "I adjure you by the Jesus whom Paul preaches." Seven sons of a Jewish high priest named Sceva were doing this. But the evil spirit answered them, "Jesus I know, and Paul I know; but who are you?" And the man in whom the evil spirit was leaped on them, mastered all of them, and overpowered them, so that they fled out of that house naked and wounded. And this became known to *all residents of Ephesus, both Jews and Greeks*; and fear fell upon them all; and the name of the Lord Jesus was extolled. Many also of those who were now believers came, confessing and divulging their practices. And a number of those who practiced magic arts brought their books together and burned them in the sight of all; and they counted the value of them and found it came to fifty thousand pieces of silver. So the word of the Lord grew and *prevailed mightily (ischyen)*.[17] (Acts 19:1-20)

---

[17] The same root *ischy—* is commonly coupled with the root *dynam—* especially in Ephesians where the coupling occurs at both ends of the epistle: "having the eyes of your hearts enlightened, that you may know what is the hope to which he has called you, what are the riches of his glorious inheritance in the saints, and what is the

Consequently, Paul's followers residing in Ephesus in the Roman province Asia, "saints" and, more importantly, "faithful" (*pistois*) (Eph 1:1) to God's "faithful word" —Jews as well as Hellenes (2:11-22) as "one" (v.14)—can boldly as well as safely put on the all-defensive "armor of God" (6:11,[18] 14-17) in order to "be able to *withstand* (*antistēnai*; stand against) in the evil day, and having done all, to *stand* (*stēnai*)" (v.13) while awaiting the "coming" (*parousia*) of "Jesus Christ the faithful (*pistos*) witness (*martys*; martyr), the first-born of the dead, and the ruler of kings on earth" (Rev 1:5) and crying out to him "Come, Lord Jesus!" (22:20b). And what applies to the Ephesians applies by extension to all Paul's followers throughout the Roman empire, that is to say, the entire *oikoumenē* (inhabited world), since the Roman empire was inhabited by people from all the surrounding "nations." That the Letter to the Ephesians was meant to be universal is reflected in the fact that the phrase "in Ephesus" (*en Ephesō*; Eph 1:1) is absent from that epistle's earliest manuscripts. It as though the omission was intended to be filled mentally with the name of any locality. In other words, Ephesus functioned as the (scriptural) center of the orb in lieu of Rome. Thus the famous Roman *urbi et orbi* (to the city and the entire orb) would apply, scripturally, to Ephesus, and not to Rome, let alone Jerusalem. In other words, Ephesus, *as the Pauline headquarters*, functioned de facto as the "Jerusalem above," Zion "our mother" (Gal 4:26), not so much due to its inhabitants or even the believers residing in it, but rather due to the fact that God's word, *now as writ*, is heard unadulterated in the "house churches" within its confines through the reading out of the

---

immeasurable greatness of his power (*dynameōs*) in us who believe, according to the working of his great might (*ischyos*)" (1:18-19); Finally, be strong (*endynamousthe*) in the Lord and in the strength of his might (*ischyos*)" (6:10).

[18] Noteworthy is the fact that this verse (Put on the whole armor of God, that you may be able to stand against the wiles of the devil) immediately follows "Finally, be strong in the Lord and in the strength of his might" (v.10) referred to in the previous footnote where I discuss the occurrence of the root *ischy*— in Acts 19:20.

content of the Pauline epistles (Col 4:16) and by extension the entire New Testament (vv.10 and 14).[19]

---

[19] See my comments in *C-Col* 97-103.

19

The Value of Joshua

The scriptural Joshua presented the Pauline school with very valuable features that corresponded to their situation "on the ground" and thus proved to be prized as the main name of their literary protagonist. First and foremost was that the securing of the earth of the promise for Israel was directly linked to *his own personal obedience to the requirements of the Law*. This feature of Joshua is of the essence in the author's mind as is evident in its repetition twice over three subsequent verses right at the opening of the book:

> Be strong and of good courage; for you shall cause this people to inherit the land which I swore to their fathers to give them. Only be strong and very courageous, being careful to do according to all the law which Moses my servant commanded you; turn not from it to the right hand or to the left, that you may have good success wherever you go. This book of the law shall not depart out of your mouth, but you shall meditate on it day and night, that you may be careful to do according to all that is written in it; for then you shall make your way prosperous, and then you shall have good success. Have I not commanded you? Be strong and of good courage; be not frightened, neither be dismayed; for the Lord your God is with you wherever you go. (Josh 1:6-9)[1]

What made Joshua even more appealing to the Pauline school lies in that the Maccabean literature itself points out to Joshua's obedience as his essential feature in a passage that typifies each of the main scriptural figures with one characteristic:

> Was not Abraham found faithful when tested, and it was reckoned to him as righteousness? Joseph in the time of his distress kept the commandment, and became lord of Egypt. Phinehas our father, because he was deeply zealous, received the covenant of everlasting priesthood. Joshua, because he fulfilled the command, became a judge in Israel. Caleb, because he

---

[1] See my comments on these verses in *C-Josh* 65-78.

testified in the assembly, received an inheritance in the land. David, because he was merciful, inherited the throne of the kingdom for ever. Elijah because of great zeal for the law was taken up into heaven. Hannaniah, Azariah, and Mishael believed and were saved from the flame. Daniel because of his innocence was delivered from the mouth of the lions. (1 Macc 2:52-60)

In turn, this respect on the part of the Hasmoneans, heirs of the Maccabees, toward Joshua allowed the Pauline school to use it against the Jerusalemite leadership as "circumcision party." As we saw earlier Joshua never imposed circumcision on the "foreigners" living together with his followers in the same cities and towns.[2] So both Joshua's championing the primacy of the Law over insiders and outsiders and his relegating circumcision to a secondary status *according to the teaching of scripture* made him a prime prototype for the literary champion of the epic produced by the Pauline school. However, in spite of Joshua's faithfulness to all the commandments of the Law (Josh 1:6-9) the people forsook the Lord at his demise (Judg 2:7-13), which provoked disastrous results:

So the anger of the Lord was kindled against Israel, and he gave them over to plunderers, who plundered them; and he sold them into the power of their enemies round about, so that they could no longer withstand their enemies. (v.14).

Israel's attitude persisted constantly over the generations of multiple "judges":

But whenever the judge died, they turned back and behaved worse than their fathers, going after other gods, serving them and bowing down to them; they did not drop any of their practices or their stubborn ways. (v.19)

In order to remedy this situation the New Testament authors appealed to another scriptural figure that was cast along the lines of success in spite of apparent failure, the "servant" of whom Isaiah spoke. That that servant was paramount on the

---

[2] *See earlier Co-inheritance with the Nations.*

authors' mind is evident from the manner in which Luke and then Matthew handle the original Gospel of Mark in conjunction with the "beginning" of Jesus' ministry. Luke moves the pericope of Jesus' rejection at Nazareth (Mk 6:1-6) to the start of his Galilean ministry and expands it into fifteen verses (Lk 4:16-30). However and more importantly, he puts the entire episode under the aegis of a verbatim quotation from Isaiah (61:1-2) that "happened" to be the reading of the day:

> And he came to Nazareth, where he had been brought up; and he went to the synagogue, as his custom was, on the sabbath day. And he stood up to read; and there was given to him the book of the prophet Isaiah. He opened the book and found the place where it was written, "The Spirit of the Lord is upon me, because he has anointed me to preach good news to the poor. He has sent me to proclaim release to the captives and recovering of sight to the blind, to set at liberty those who are oppressed, to proclaim the acceptable year of the Lord." And he closed the book, and gave it back to the attendant, and sat down; and the eyes of all in the synagogue were fixed on him. And he began to say to them, "Today this scripture has been fulfilled in your hearing." And all spoke well of him, and wondered at the gracious words which proceeded out of his mouth; and they said, "Is not this Joseph's son?" And he said to them, "Doubtless you will quote to me this proverb, 'Physician, heal yourself; what we have heard you did at Capernaum, do here also in your own country.'" And he said, "Truly, I say to you, no prophet is acceptable in his own country. But in truth, I tell you, there were many widows in Israel in the days of Elijah, when the heaven was shut up three years and six months, when there came a great famine over all the land; and Elijah was sent to none of them but only to Zarephath, in the land of Sidon, to a woman who was a widow. And there were many lepers in Israel in the time of the prophet Elisha; and none of them was cleansed, but only Naaman the Syrian." When they heard this, all in the synagogue were filled with wrath. And they rose up and put him out of the city, and led him to the brow of the hill on which their city was built, that they might throw him down headlong. But passing through the midst of them he went away. (Lk 4:16-30)

The expansion concerning Elijah and Elisha is thoroughly
Lukan since it holds the only reference to Elisha in the New
Testament.[3] This interest in the "nations" as well as "Israel" is
clearly taken from the parallel passage speaking about the
"servant" as chosen through God's spirit:

> Behold my servant, whom I uphold, my chosen, in whom my soul
> delights; I have put my Spirit upon him, he will bring forth justice
> to the nations. He will not cry or lift up his voice, or make it heard
> in the street; a bruised reed he will not break, and a dimly burning
> wick he will not quench; he will faithfully bring forth justice. He
> will not fail or be discouraged till he has established justice in the
> earth; and the coastlands wait for his law. Thus says God, the
> Lord, who created the heavens and stretched them out, who
> spread forth the earth and what comes from it, who gives breath
> to the people upon it and spirit to those who walk in it: "I am the
> Lord, I have called you in righteousness, I have taken you by the
> hand and kept you; I have given you as a covenant to the people,
> a light to the nations, to open the eyes that are blind, to bring out
> the prisoners from the dungeon, from the prison those who sit in
> darkness." (Is 42:1-7)

That the one school that produced the New Testament had this
in mind is corroborated by Matthew's equally extensive
quotation from the same prophet Isaiah referred to also by
name in Luke:

> Jesus, aware of this, withdrew from there. And many followed
> him, and he healed them all, and ordered them not to make him
> known. This was to fulfil what was spoken by the prophet Isaiah:
> "Behold, my servant whom I have chosen, my beloved with
> whom my soul is well pleased. I will put my Spirit upon him, and
> he shall proclaim justice to the Gentiles. He will not wrangle or
> cry aloud, nor will any one hear his voice in the streets; he will
> not break a bruised reed or quench a smoldering wick, till he
> brings justice to victory; and in his name will the Gentiles hope."
> (Mt 12:15-21)

---

[3] See earlier my comments concerning those two prophets' beneficent activity among
the "outsiders."

The close parallelism between the Lukan and Matthean pericopes is secured through two features. In both cases the opponents decide to be rid of Jesus, and in both cases we are told that Isaiah's scripture was "fulfilled."

What is of import is the mention of "anointing" in the quotation from Isaiah 61:1 used by Luke. The verb *ekhrisen* (anointed; from the verb *khriō*) is from the same root as the passive participle *Khristos* (Christ, Anointed). This is precisely the other most frequent "name" of Jesus in the New Testament. These two "names"—Jesus and Christ—are independent since they function as often separately as they do as a pair. Considering Jesus as a proper name and Christ as a "functional" appellation or a title is a fictitious dichotomy for the following reasons:

1. Such differentiation does not exist in Semitic languages where proper names are a figment of a non-Semite's imagination. In Semitic languages the same referenced word functions differently in different phrases or sentences, and it is only in the literary setting that the hearer figures out whether the same noun refers to an actual person or a function. That is why the Hebrew *yehošuaʿ* (Joshua) has a "meaning" (the Lord saves) as it is actually written in Matthew: "she will bear a son, and you shall call his name Jesus, for he will save his people from their sins." (1:21). Consequently it functions as the parallel name Emmanuel does: "All this took place to fulfil what the Lord had spoken by the prophet: 'Behold, a virgin shall conceive and bear a son, and his name shall be called Emmanuel' (which means, God with us)." (vv.22-23)

2. Very often *Khristos* is used on its own—without the definite article *ho* (the) or even independently

from Jesus—and all of us take it as a proper noun
as we do in our English language.

On the other hand, Christ is very often used in parallel with
Son of God or Son of David or even simply David. This is
understandable since kings, who were considered as "sons of
God" or even "gods"[4] were anointed into that function.[5] Of
import for us in this regard is the portrayal of Jesus, the new
Joshua (the Lord saves), as also and even primarily a new David,
in conjunction with the gospel (*evangelion*). Consider, for
instance, the following:

> And the angel said to her, "Do not be afraid, Mary, for you have
> found favor with God. And behold, you will conceive in your
> womb and bear a son, and you shall call his name Jesus. He will
> be great, and will be called the *Son of the Most High*; and the Lord
> God will give to him the throne of his father *David*, and he will
> reign over the house of Jacob for ever; and of his kingdom there
> will be no end." (Lk 1:30-33)

> And the angel said to them, "Be not afraid; for behold, I bring
> you good news (*evangelizomai*) of a great joy which will come to all
> the people; for to you is born this day in the city of *David* a *Savior*,
> who is *Christ* the Lord. (2:10-11)

> So the woman left her water jar, and went away into the city, and
> said to the people, "Come, see a man who told me all that I ever
> did. Can this be the *Christ*?" (Jn 4:28-29)

> They said to the woman, "It is no longer because of your words
> that we believe, for we have heard for ourselves, and we know
> that this is indeed the *Savior* of the world." (4:42)

> Paul, a servant of Jesus Christ, called to be an apostle, set apart
> for the *gospel* of God which he promised beforehand through his
> prophets in the holy scriptures, the gospel concerning his Son,
> who was descended from *David* according to the flesh and

---

[4] "For to us a child is born, to us a son is given; and the government will be upon his
shoulder, and his name will be called 'Wonderful Counselor, Mighty God,
Everlasting Father, Prince of Peace.'" (Is 9:6 RSV) "Thy throne, O God, *is* for ever
and ever: the sceptre of thy kingdom *is* a right scepter." (Ps 45:6 KJV)
[5] See, e.g., Judg 9:8; 1 Sam 9:16; 15:1; 16:3, 12; 2 Sam 2:4, 7; 5:3, 17.

designated *Son of God* in power according to the Spirit of holiness by his resurrection from the dead, Jesus *Christ* our Lord. (Rom 1:1-4)

For I am not ashamed of the gospel: it is the power of God for *salvation* to every one who has faith, to the Jew first and also to the Greek. (1:16)

Joshua, Isaiah, and Hosea

In order to unlock the way the Pauline school went about creating a literature aimed at invalidating the false allegations of the Jerusalemite *yehudim*, the "circumcision party," one is to take seriously the opening of the Pauline corpus written "by the hand" of the new Moses, Paul. The gospel he preached in the New Testament is nothing else save "the gospel God promised beforehand through his prophets in the holy scriptures" (Rom 1:1-2). The specific reference to the "prophets" is not fortuitous. One is to look closely at the Prophets, the second part of the Old Testament, to find the solution as to how the Pauline contingent conceived an epic "on the ground"—common to them and to the leadership of *yehud*—around their protagonist, Jesus, the new Joshua. The reason is evident. The Old Testament epic of the scriptural Israel and Judah (*yehudah*) is contained extensively and only in the books of the Prophets, both Prior and Latter. In those scrolls one finds all the basic elements of the Jesus Christ epic and their interconnectivity as well. In other words the epic of the Gospels was conceived literally "according to the scriptures (of the Prophets)."

The first book of the Prior Prophets, the first book of the Latter Prophets, and the first book of the Scroll of the Twelve are under three names that are from the verbal root *yaša'*, which obviously cannot be happenstance but rather is intentional. The work of Joshua, which was undone by his followers after his death, was given new hope and even assuredness in Isaiah. In turn this message of hope was reiterated in Hosea (3:5) at the beginning of the repeated story of disobedience overarching the

Twelve Prophets in preparation for the concluding caveat (Mal 4:1-6) that harks back to the Law and the Prophets (in the person of Elijah).

Joshua accedes to the title of "servant of the Lord," which was reserved to Moses,[6] only at the end of the book (Josh 24:29) after he has proven his total submission to God's law (as for me and my house, we will serve the Lord; v.15). However, the bliss did not survive him. Even Caleb, the one who was blessed by Joshua to inherit Abraham's Hebron of Judah, is linked early on with the tribe of Judah (Num 13:6) that is slated to become the leader of the tribes (Judg 1:1-2) obviously with an eye on David who will succeed Saul the Benjaminite and with whom the Lord will conclude a covenant of steadfast love forever (2 Sam 7:25-29). The "everlastingness" of the Davidic covenant is clearly aimed toward the future beyond the repeated misbehavior of David's progeny. The success of this covenant is referred to in Isaiah 55 (v.3) which is the last chapter of the Book of the Consolation (Is 40-55) whose main protagonist is the "servant" who fulfills to a T the divine will and brings the good news (gospel) of liberation (61:1) to the nations as well as Israel (42:1-7; 49:1-6). In this sense he realizes forever what the first "servant" Joshua accomplished only during his lifetime. However, it is not the inherent value of the servant, as the new David, that ensures the success of his mission. Rather it God's spirit which abides upon the servant that guarantees his success:

> Behold my servant, whom I uphold, my chosen, in whom my soul delights; I have put my Spirit upon him, he will bring forth justice to the nations. (Is 42:1)

> The Spirit of the Lord God is upon me, because the Lord has anointed me to bring good tidings to the afflicted; he has sent me to bind up the brokenhearted, to proclaim liberty to the captives, and the opening of the prison to those who are bound. (61:1)

---

[6] No less than 18 times.

This scenario is picked up in the stories of Jesus' commission at his baptism in the Jordan:

> And when he came up out of the water, immediately he saw the heavens opened and the Spirit descending upon him like a dove; and a voice came from heaven, "Thou art my beloved Son; with thee I am well pleased." (Mk 1:10-11; see also Mt 3:16-17 and Lk 3:21-22)

Opting for the crucifixion as the culmination of the mission of the anointed (Christ) servant has a double aim. Firstly, it is a counter-blow to the leadership of the *yehudim* by overbidding a greater shame in the eyes of the Roman authorities than the shame of circumcision in the eyes of the Greeks who, by that time, were no longer rulers of the surrounding world. Secondly, and perhaps more importantly, it was a blow against imperial power: if the crucified chosen by God, and not Caesar, is the "lord" (*kyrios*) then, as a corollary, even the slaves of the empire are not their lords' slaves, but God's: "Masters (*hoi kyrioi*, lords), treat your slaves justly and fairly, knowing that you also have a Master (*kyrion*, lord) in heaven." (Col 4:1) Isaiah foresaw this literally stunning blow to the Roman emperor in his depiction of the "servant":

> Behold, my servant shall prosper, he shall be exalted and lifted up, and shall be very high. As many were astonished at him—his appearance was so marred, beyond human semblance, and his form beyond that of the sons of men—so shall he startle many nations; *kings shall shut their mouths because of him; for that which has not been told them they shall see, and that which they have not heard they shall understand.* (Is 52:13-15)

Still, what is truly startling and unheard of in the matter is that it was at the express "will" of his God that the servant was put to suffer that utter shame before the eyes of "many nations": "Yet it was the will of the Lord to bruise him; he has put him to grief." (53:10a) This unconditional obedience to God's will is unequivocally picked up in the Gospels:

And going a little farther he fell on his face and prayed, "My Father, if it be possible, let this cup pass from me; nevertheless, not as I will, but as thou wilt." (Mt 26:39)

And he said, "Abba, Father, all things are possible to thee; remove this cup from me; yet not what I will, but what thou wilt." (Mk 14:36)

Father, if thou art willing, remove this cup from me; nevertheless not my will, but thine, be done. (Lk 22:42)

20

Jesus of Nazareth

If the authors of the Pauline corpus presented their
protagonist as the new Moses of the Gentiles and those
writings touched on all the matters pertaining to the tension
between him and the Jerusalemite leadership concerning the
Gentiles, why was that corpus deemed insufficient to be read in
the Pauline churches alongside the Old Testament? Why did
the Pauline school produce the more massive literature of the
four Gospels whose main protagonist is not Paul, but another
leader, Jesus the Christ?

In order to answer this question one is to realize that until
Paul, scripture was not only read in the synagogues to the
hearing of "Israel," but was addressed to that Israel. The
Gentiles were only spoken of, but were never the addressees.
This is the case even in the *ketubim* whose function is to
encourage the Gentiles to renege on the false wisdom of their
sophia and to endorse the *torah* as the true wisdom. The "novelty"
regarding the Pauline corpus—the writings of the new Moses—
is that it is specifically and primarily, if not exclusively, *addressed*
to the nations. The letters, starting with Galatians, contain the
gospel to the (uncircumcised) Gentiles by their apostle (Gal 2:7-
8). But, in order for this message to be authoritative when read,
it not only had to be "according to scripture" materially (content
wise), but also had to be "scriptural" formally, that is, cast as
"scripture," especially since it was read in conjunction with the
Old Testament that defines scripture. Whenever Paul refers to
"scripture" or "scriptures" he is unequivocally intending the
Old Testament. Even Peter's imprimatur that canonizes Paul's
letters as scripture does so by comparing them to the "other"
scriptures: "And count the forbearance of our Lord as salvation.
So also our beloved brother Paul wrote to you according to the
wisdom given him, speaking of this as he does in all his letters.
There are some things in them hard to understand, which the

ignorant and unstable twist to their own destruction, as they do the other scriptures." (2 Pet 3:15-16) It is important to remember that this imprimatur, which is the product of the Pauline school, is cast as proceeding from the mouth of Peter, "the apostle to the circumcision," who was Paul's counterpart at the Jerusalem meeting. Peter carried to those circumcised the *same* gospel that Paul was carrying to the Gentiles (Gal 2:7-8) as a result of the *one* (source of) apostolate.[1] Consequently, the Pauline writings had to "sound" scriptural, that is, à la Moses and the Prophets. If that condition was not fulfilled, then Paul's gatherings would not have been house churches/*qehalim* (plural of *qahal*), and his table fellowships would not have been true fellowships where Peter's and James' Jews would partake as equals with Paul's Gentiles (Gal 2:11-14) in order for all to hear *together and in unison* the same "teaching" as was done early on under Joshua (Josh 8:32-35). Such gatherings had to be "by definition" *qehalim* as Paul makes unequivocally clear to his Gentiles elsewhere: "For God is not a God of confusion but of peace. As in all the churches of the saints … What! Did the word of God originate (*exēlthen*; came out, proceeded) with (*apo*; on the part of) you, or are you the only ones it has reached?" (1 Cor 14:33, 36) After all, in the Pauline Gentile churches, it is the "oracles of God" entrusted to the *yehudim* (Rom 3:2) that were heard. Paul had no choice regarding the priority of the *yehudim* over the Gentiles (1:16; 2:9-10) since it was already firmly established at the outset of the Prologue to Sirach:

> Whereas many great teachings have been given to us through the law and the prophets and the others that followed them, on account of which *we should praise Israel for instruction and wisdom*; and since it is necessary not only that the readers themselves should acquire understanding but also that *those who love learning should be able to help the outsiders* by both speaking and writing.

---

[1] See my comments in *Gal* 69-70 where I point out that, in the original Greek, the nouns "gospel" (*evangelion*) in v.7 and "mission" (*apostolēn*; apostolate) in v.8 are not repeated when speaking of Paul and then Peter or of Peter and then Paul.

A side-effect of this reality can be seen in that, unlike the synagogue *('edah, synagōgē)* that was exclusively comprised of *yehudim*, the Pauline church *(qahal, ekklēsia)*, primarily comprised of Gentiles, was *necessarily* inclusive of the *yehudim*. This necessary aspect of the church was actually imposed upon it by the Apostle even in the "absence" of *yehudim*. Their "presence" was always insured by the "collection" for the "saints" of Jerusalem and Judah that Paul instituted in all his churches, just as he had promised to do at the Jerusalem meeting:

> ... and when they perceived the grace that was given to me, James and Cephas and John, who were reputed to be pillars, gave to me and Barnabas the right hand of fellowship, that we should go to the Gentiles and they to the circumcised; only they would have us remember the poor, which very thing I was eager to do. (Gal 2:9-10)

> Now concerning the contribution for the saints: as I directed the churches of Galatia, so you also are to do. On the first day of every week, each of you is to put something aside and store it up, as he may prosper, so that contributions need not be made when I come. And when I arrive, I will send those whom you accredit by letter to carry your gift to Jerusalem. If it seems advisable that I should go also, they will accompany me. (1 Cor 16:1-4)

> At present, however, I am going to Jerusalem with aid for the saints. For Macedonia and Achaia have been pleased to make some contribution for the poor among the saints at Jerusalem; they were pleased to do it, and indeed they are in debt to them, for if the Gentiles have come to share in their spiritual blessings, they ought also to be of service to them in material blessings. (Rom 15:25-27)

How did the Pauline school go about making its writings "sound" scriptural, that is, à la Moses and the Prophets? In the Old Testament the critical teaching of the Latter Prophets aimed against the leaders of Jerusalem and Samaria, religious as well as political, was "retrojected" to the times before the establishment of the Kingdoms of Israel and Judah whose "story" was the concern of the Prior Prophets. The "presence" of the Latter Prophets within that "story" is made explicit through the express reference to Isaiah in 2 Kings 19-20[2] and to Jonah in 2 Kings 14:25.[3] If one adds the extensive literature dealing with the activities of Elijah and Elisha, which spans nineteen chapters (1 Kg 17-2 Kg 13), then one will readily conclude that the story of the kingdoms (1 and 2 Kings) is more appropriately the story of the prophetic critique of those kingdoms, that is, a literature similar to Isaiah 1-39 and the Book of Jeremiah. Still, and more importantly, the entire span of 1 and 2 Kings is not only bracketed with the mention of "the law of Moses" (1 Kg 2:3 and 2 Kg 23:25), but also underscores the perennial disobedience to its statutes and commandments "since the days of the judges who judged Israel, or during all the days of the kings of Israel or of the kings of Judah":

> And the king commanded all the people, "Keep the passover to the Lord your God, as it is written in this book of the covenant." For no such passover had been kept since the days of the judges who judged Israel, or during all the days of the kings of Israel or of the kings of Judah; but in the eighteenth year of King Josiah this passover was kept to the Lord in Jerusalem. Moreover Josiah put away the mediums and the wizards and the teraphim and the idols and all the abominations that were seen in the land of Judah and in Jerusalem, that he might establish the words of the law which were written in the book that Hilkiah the priest found in the house of the Lord. Before him there was no king like him, who turned to the Lord with all his heart and with all his soul and with all his might, according to all the law of Moses; nor did any like him arise after him. (2 Kg 23:21-25)

The centrality of the law of Moses for the scriptural purview as well as story is corroborated in that it also overarches the entire second part of scripture, the Prophets:

---

[2] In this case the intention is unmissable in that the content of these chapters are found virtually verbatim in Is 37-38.

[3] 1 Kg 13:31-32 may well be an oblique reference to the message of the prophet Amos and 2 Kg 22:13-28 that speaks of the prophet Micaiah (*mikayehu*) seems to refer to the prophet Micah (*mikah*), a short form of *mikayehu*, except that the former was active in the Kingdom of Israel while the latter in the Kingdom of Judah.

After the death of Moses the servant of the Lord, the Lord said to Joshua the son of Nun, Moses' minister, "Moses my servant is dead; now therefore arise, go over this Jordan, you and all this people, into the land which I am giving to them, to the people of Israel. Every place that the sole of your foot will tread upon I have given to you, as I promised to Moses. From the wilderness and this Lebanon as far as the great river, the river Euphrates, all the land of the Hittites to the Great Sea toward the going down of the sun shall be your territory. No man shall be able to stand before you all the days of your life; as I was with Moses, so I will be with you; I will not fail you or forsake you. Be strong and of good courage; for you shall cause this people to inherit the land which I swore to their fathers to give them. Only be strong and very courageous, being careful to do according to all the law which Moses my servant commanded you; turn not from it to the right hand or to the left, that you may have good success wherever you go. This book of the law shall not depart out of your mouth, but you shall meditate on it day and night, that you may be careful to do according to all that is written in it; for then you shall make your way prosperous, and then you shall have good success. Have I not commanded you? Be strong and of good courage; be not frightened, neither be dismayed; for the Lord your God is with you wherever you go." (Josh 1:1-9)

For behold, the day comes, burning like an oven, when all the arrogant and all evildoers will be stubble; the day that comes shall burn them up, says the Lord of hosts, so that it will leave them neither root nor branch. But for you who fear my name the sun of righteousness shall rise, with healing in its wings. You shall go forth leaping like calves from the stall. And you shall tread down the wicked, for they will be ashes under the soles of your feet, on the day when I act, says the Lord of hosts. Remember the law of my servant Moses, the statutes and ordinances that I commanded him at Horeb for all Israel. Behold, I will send you Elijah the prophet before the great and terrible day of the Lord comes. And he will turn the hearts of fathers to their children and the hearts of children to their fathers, lest I come and smite the land with a curse. (Mal 4:1-6)

To top it all off, this centrality of the Law extends over the third part of scripture, the *ketubim*, and is sealed in the Prologue of Sirach which, for my readers' benefit, would be worthwhile to quote again in full:

> Whereas many great teachings have been given to us through the law and the prophets and the others that followed them, on account of which we should praise Israel for instruction and wisdom; and since it is necessary not only that the readers themselves should acquire understanding but also that those who love learning should be able to help the outsiders by both speaking and writing, my grandfather Jesus, after devoting himself especially to the reading of the law and the prophets and the other books of our fathers, and after acquiring considerable proficiency in them, was himself also led to write something pertaining to instruction and wisdom, in order that, by becoming conversant with this also, those who love learning should make even greater progress in living according to the law.

> You are urged therefore to read with good will and attention, and to be indulgent in cases where, despite our diligent labor in translating, we may seem to have rendered some phrases imperfectly. For what was originally expressed in Hebrew does not have exactly the same sense when translated into another language. Not only this work, but even the law itself, the prophecies, and the rest of the books differ not a little as originally expressed.

> When I came to Egypt in the thirty-eighth year of the reign of Euergetes and stayed for some time, I found opportunity for no little instruction. It seemed highly necessary that I should myself devote some pains and labor to the translation of the following book, using in that period of time great watchfulness and skill in order to complete and publish the book for those living abroad who wished to gain learning, being prepared in character to live according to the law.

Even a first time hearer of this Prologue will not miss that the entire tripartite Old Testament scripture not only starts with and is anchored in the Law, but also through the Prophets and the Writings (*ketubim*), it invites the hearers to "walk according to that Law." Thus, following Moses does not translate into following in his footsteps, but rather following his teaching. Put otherwise Moses is a "teaching." That is why it was necessary for the Law to *precede* the epic whose protagonists are consequently presented as "forewarned" and thus accountable on judgment day (Mal 4:1-6). In turn, the "outsiders" are indirectly also forewarned as evident from Sirach.

However, *in scripture*, Moses has, for all intents and purposes, failed. Not only did neither he nor his followers who left Egypt enter into the earth of the promise, but the following generations of those who resided in that earth ended in an exile similar to that of Egypt with no apparent assuredness of deliverance except for the sheer benevolence of the scriptural God. If the earlier benevolence was in view of the promulgation of the Law (Ex 3:12; ch.19), then the new benevolence was in view of abiding by that same Law (Ezek 20:9-26). A new Moses was not enough. Paul, the new Moses, needed to offer to the Gentiles a sure guarantee[4] of redemption from their servitude to Caesar, the new Pharoah, and also offer such to the *yehudim* who were subjugated to and humiliated by Rome. This guarantee was readily available in scripture itself. Joshua was the post-Moses leader who insured, at least in his lifetime, the peaceful residence of the tribes of Israel in the scriptural Canaan that overlapped with the *yehud* of Paul's opponents. So it was understandable for the Pauline school to opt for a new Joshua who would implement forever what Joshua of old was able to secure only in his lifetime. This "second chance" offered by the new Joshua is precisely what one hears in chapter four of the epistle "to the Hebrews," a mini-treatise on the Old Testament teaching:

> Therefore, while the promise of entering his rest remains, let us fear lest any of you be judged to have failed to reach it. For good

---

[4] Notice the centrality of *asphaleia* (assuredness) and its cognates *asphales* and *asphalōs* in Luke-Acts and Paul: Lk 1:4; Acts 2:36; 5:23; 16:23; 21:34; 22:30; 25:26; Phil 3:1; 1 Thess 5:3; Heb 6:19.

news came to us (*esmen evēngelismenoi*; we were evangelized) just as
to them; but the message (*ho logos*; the word) which they heard did
not benefit them, because it did not meet with faith in the hearers.
For we who have believed enter that rest, as he has said, "As I
swore in my wrath, 'They shall never enter my rest,'" although
his works were finished from the foundation of the world. For he
has somewhere spoken of the seventh day in this way, "And God
rested on the seventh day from all his works." And again in this
place he said, "They shall never enter my rest." Since therefore
it remains for some to enter it, and those who formerly received
the good news failed to enter because of disobedience, again he
sets a certain day, "Today," saying through David so long
afterward, in the words already quoted, "Today, when you hear
his voice, do not harden your hearts." For if Joshua (*Iēsous*[5]
[Jesus]) had given them rest, God would not speak later of
another day. So then, there remains a sabbath rest for the people
of God; for whoever enters God's rest also ceases from his labors
as God did from his. Let us therefore strive to enter that rest, that
no one fall by the same sort of disobedience. For the word of God
is living and active, sharper than any two-edged sword, piercing
to the division of soul and spirit, of joints and marrow, and
discerning the thoughts and intentions of the heart. And before
him no creature is hidden, but all are open and laid bare to the
eyes of him with whom we have to do. Since then we have a great
high priest who has passed through the heavens, Jesus, the Son of
God, let us hold fast our confession. For we have not a high priest
who is unable to sympathize with our weaknesses, but one who
in every respect has been tempted as we are, yet without sin. Let
us then with confidence draw near to the throne of grace, that we
may receive mercy and find grace to help in time of need.
(Heb 4:1-16)

Still for the new Joshua to function properly, that is,
scripturally, he had to be cast by the New Testament authors
similarly to how the Old Testament authors cast their Moses. In
practical terms, he had to fulfill all the following conditions at
the same time:

---

[5] Which is the LXX rendering of the Hebrew *yehošua'*.

1. Just as the teaching of Moses was a retrojection of that of the Prophets, so also the teaching of Jesus was cast as a retrojection of that of the gospel of Paul, the apostle to the nations.[6] Suffice it to mention here that the teacher Jesus is introduced as coming from Galilee (Mk 1:9) and the "gospel of God" he was heralding (v.14) is cast in a terminology taken right out of Paul's "hand." The phrase "beginning of the gospel" occurs exclusively in Philippians 4:15 and Mark 1:1.

2. Just as Moses was, as issuer of the Law (instruction; teaching), the "instructor" or "teacher" so also Jesus was to be *the teacher*. This was accomplished on at least two levels. On the one hand, consulting any concordance will readily show that "teacher" or "master" is the highest incidence for a term of address toward Jesus in the Gospels. On the other hand and more importantly, at their first encounter with Jesus, those who listened reacted in the following terms: "And they were all amazed, so that they questioned among themselves, saying, "What is this? A new teaching! With authority he commands even the unclean spirits, and they obey him" (Mk 1:27); "And they were all amazed and said to one another "What is this word? For with authority and power he commands the unclean spirits, and they come out." (Lk 4:36)

3. It is the teaching of Jesus that is primary as will be sealed at the closing of Matthew: "And Jesus came and said to them, 'All authority in heaven

---

[6] I have discussed this matter in detail in my tetralogy of New Testament Introduction.

and on earth has been given to me. Go therefore and make disciples of all nations, baptizing them in the name of the Father and of the Son and of the Holy Spirit, teaching them to observe all that I have commanded you; and lo, I am with you always, to the close of the age.'" (28:18-20)

4. As corollary of the preceding, just as the Latter Prophets become prophets as Moses and, by extension, his representatives, so also Paul is portrayed as the emissary (apostle) of Jesus and bearer of his gospel (message).

5. Just as the teaching of Moses would become the muster for the final judgment for the wicked and the righteous (Mal 4:1-6), so also that of Jesus will be the measure for the ultimate judgment for Gentiles as well as the *yehudim* (Mt 25:31-46).

The Old Testament addressed to the scriptural Israel was already sealed in its tripartite structure. Since the New Testament is addressed expressly to the scriptural Gentiles, it had to sound in their ears as containing the entire message of the Old Testament. So the "teaching" of the new "teacher" had to reflect the entire teaching of the Old Testament. That was not insurmountable since the Old Testament itself makes such connections. See, for example, how in Galatians Paul appeals to Isaiah while speaking of Sarah in Genesis in conjunction with her barrenness (Gal 4:21-28). That the entire Old Testament was in the New Testament authors' purview is at clearest in Luke:

Then he said to them, "These are my words which I spoke to you, while I was still with you, that everything written about me in the law of Moses and the prophets and the psalms must be fulfilled." (24:44)

Besides, Psalms, which is the representative book of the *ketubim* in the Lukan quotation, is referenced extensively in the New

Testament and so is Job twice,[7] outside the numerous allusions to the other books of that literature. Even Matthew and Luke, who use the phrase "the law and the prophets," allude obliquely to the *ketubim* in Jesus' saying: "Yet wisdom is justified by all her children." (Mt 11:19/Lk 7:35)[8] Notice, last yet not least, how Matthew casts the three kinds of "apostles" Jesus sends out along the lines of the Old Testament tripartite division:

> Therefore I send (*apostellō*; send as apostles) you prophets and wise men and scribes,[9] some of whom you will kill and crucify, and some you will scourge in your synagogues and persecute from town to town, that upon you may come all the righteous blood shed on earth, from the blood of innocent Abel to the blood of Zechariah the son of Barachiah, whom you murdered between the sanctuary and the altar. (23:34-35)

Notice also how Jesus' messengers are cast in order to reflect total conformity of the New Testament literature to that of the Old Testament: the two martyrdoms mentioned in Matthew overarch the entire Old Testament in that the mention of the first occurs in Genesis 4 whereas the second is referred to in 2 Chronicles, the last book of the *ketubim*, in its twenty fourth chapter (vv.20-21).

Jesus' Resurrection from the Dead

The assuredness of the success of the divine plan through the new Joshua, the Isaianic "servant of the Lord," especially in the matter of joining "outsider" and "insider" into one *familia*, *bet-'ab*, house church, was expressed in the New Testament epic as his "having been raised from (among) the dead." Starting with the garden of Eden, the natural end of one's life was a given. It was not an issue that needed to be discussed as it is done in

---

[7] Job 5:13 in 1 Cor 3:19 and Job 41:11 in Rom 11:35.

[8] I have often alluded to the *ketubim*'s main thesis as being to present the law as the true wisdom. Hence the scholarly reference of the third part of the Old Testament as "Wisdom Literature."

[9] Scribes (*grammateis*) are the professionals in matters of the (alphabetical) "letters" (*grammata*) of the Law.

philosophical and religious debates. "Death" in scripture is a matter of punishment and condemnation: for his sin of disobedience, Adam's punishment was his not being allowed to eat from the "tree of life" and so he was condemned to die exiled outside the garden. On the level of a people living in a city, the condemnation would be to take them away from their city and earth and put them into someone else's domain. So the central point in the epic is not that Jesus died—all human beings are bound to die—but that he was "condemned" to death and by crucifixion, to boot. The importance of that matter is evident in the painstakingly detailed accounts not only of his trial in all four Gospels but also of the events leading to it. In other words, he was found guilty and everyone, Romans as well as *yehudim*, wanted to damn his memory unto oblivion. In order to redress such wrong, Jesus had to be exonerated by a higher court, namely, the court of the scriptural God who had to intervene and turn around the verdict from "guilty" to "righteous" given that, per Isaiah, the servant would not only be righteous, but also make many to be accounted righteous (53:11), and that he "was numbered among the transgressors" (v.12) by a human court:

> Yet it was the will of the Lord to bruise him; he has put him to grief; when he makes himself an offering for sin, he shall see his offspring, he shall prolong his days; the will of the Lord shall prosper in his hand; he shall see the fruit of the travail of his soul and be satisfied; by his knowledge shall the righteous one, my servant, make many to be accounted righteous; and he shall bear their iniquities. Therefore I will divide him a portion with the great, and he shall divide the spoil with the strong; because he poured out his soul to death, and was numbered with the transgressors; yet he bore the sin of many, and made intercession for the transgressors. (Is 53:10-12)

In legal terminology, to exonerate is tantamount to "make someone stand, raise someone" as is clear from Romans: "Let not him who eats despise him who abstains, and let not him who abstains pass judgment on him who eats; for God has welcomed him. Who are you to pass judgment on the servant of another? It is before his own master that he *stands* or falls. And he will *be upheld*, for the Master is able to *make him stand*." (14:3-4)[10] And if so, this is in order to accomplish the mission assigned to him by the same Isaiah, that is, to evangelize (bring the good news of the gospel message to) both the restored of Israel and the nations (42:1-7; 49:1-12; 61:1-2). This *function* of Jesus' "scriptural" resurrection is evident in the way in which all four Gospels deal with it:

1. In Mark, the earliest Gospel and the blue print for the other three, one does not hear of how Jesus' resurrection took place except in the additional pericope (16:9-16) comprising elements from the other Gospels.[11] In the original ending (vv.1-8) we have just the invitation to Peter and his colleagues to meet Jesus in (the) Galilee (of the nations) where he had preceded them (v.7) as he had told them (14:28).

2. Mark's intention is elaborated upon in the Gospel of Matthew (28:10-20). The message that the disciples are supposed to carry is Jesus' teaching "word for word" to all nations (v.20).

3. In turn, Matthew's understanding is corroborated in the Gospel of John where in chapter 21 Jesus is said to have invited Peter to throw himself into the Sea of Tiberias[12] (named after the emperor Tiberius [Lk 3:1] and thus a stand-in for the Mediterranean [Roman] Sea) without fear to "feed my sheep" (Jn 21:17) with

---

[10] The Greek original for the English "be upheld" and "make (him) stand" is the same *histēmi* that is used in the phrase "Christ is risen (*anestē*)."

[11] See *NTI₄* 105-6.

[12] Its other, more common name, in the Gospels is "Sea of Galilee" again a pointer to the "Galilee of the nations" (Is 9:1).

his teaching already consigned in "this book" (20:30) which is none other than the Gospel of John.

4. Unlike the other three Gospels the gospel of Luke has the resurrected Jesus appear to his disciples at Bethany, in the neighborhood of Jerusalem (24:50), whence he sends them to preach the gospel to "all nations beginning with Jerusalem" (v.47) and "to the end of the earth" (Acts 1:11) which will be realized when Paul reaches Rome, the capital "of the whole earth," and preaches there the gospel to the Gentiles (28:28-31).[13]

Our Raising by God compared to that of Jesus

First and foremost the traditional view held in both Roman Catholicism and Eastern Orthodoxy concerning the "saints" having *already* experienced a resurrection similar to Christ's after their death is non-tenable according to scripture:

> Do you not know that all of us who have been baptized into Christ Jesus were baptized into his death? We were buried therefore with him by baptism into death, so that as Christ *was raised* from the dead by the glory of the Father, we too might walk in newness of life. For if we have been united with him in a death like his, we *shall* certainly *be united* with him in a resurrection like his. We know that our old self was crucified with him so that the sinful body might be destroyed, and we might no longer be enslaved to sin. For he who has died is freed from sin. (Rom 6:3-7)

> But in fact Christ has been raised from the dead, the first fruits of those who have fallen asleep. For as by a man came death, by a man has come also the resurrection of the dead. For as in Adam all die, so also in Christ shall all be made alive. But each in his

---

[13] Notice the play on the "two years' in view of the "third day" of the resurrection.

own order: Christ the first fruits, *then at his coming* those who belong to Christ. (1 Cor 15:20-23)

> For since we believe that Jesus died and rose again, even so, through Jesus, God will bring with him those who have fallen asleep. For this we declare to you by the word of the Lord, that we who are alive, who are left until the coming of the Lord, shall not precede those who have fallen asleep. For the Lord himself will descend from heaven with a cry of command, with the archangel's call, and with the sound of the trumpet of God. And the dead in Christ will rise first. (1 Thess 4:14-16)

Appealing to Matthew 27:52-53 (the tombs also were opened, and many bodies of the saints who had fallen asleep were raised, and coming out of the tombs after his resurrection they went into the holy city and appeared to many) does not turn the tables in this matter. This is clearly a case of literary prolepsis where a future event is cast in the past in order to underscore the assuredness of such. Firstly, the "saints" is a term that applies to all believers in the New Testament. Secondly, not all the saints but only "some" are said to have been raised. Thirdly, even if one takes the statement literally, this is presented as a one time event related to Jesus' time of death.

On the other hand, even if according to both Romans 6 and 1 Corinthians 15 our raising will be like Christ's, that does not mean that we shall be in a similar "position" as he, since he is exalted "at the right hand" of God (Acts 2:33-34; 5:31), that is, in a position of "power": "Then comes the end, when he delivers the kingdom to God the Father after destroying every rule and every authority and power." (1 Cor 15:24) As for our raising, it will be simply unto "life," and in no way unto "power." While Jesus is the *Lord* we shall always be, even after our raising, his *slaves*. And whenever we share in his ruling,[14] it will still be as his slaves just as an *oikonomos* in a Roman household. Scripture has prepared us for this "painful" reality when it insisted that God liberated the Israelites from being

---

[14] E.g., Mt 19:28; 1 Cor 6:2-3; Rev 20:4-6.

slaves in Egypt to becoming his—God's—slaves, a teaching that is reiterated by Paul in the remainder of Romans 6 in conjunction with his having mentioned our future raising in the likeness of that of Christ who remains our Lord:

> But now that you have been set free from sin and have become slaves of God (*doulōthentes*; have been enslaved by/unto God), the return you get is sanctification and its end, eternal life. For the wages of sin is death, but the free gift of God is eternal life in Christ Jesus our Lord. (vv. 22-23)

And lest we forget, Paul will make it clear that, even as "lords," we still have one "Lord" in heaven:

> Masters (*Hoi kyrioi*; Lords), treat your slaves justly and fairly, knowing that you also have a Master (*kyrion*; Lord) in heaven. (Col 4:1)

21

The Gospel Epic in Five Books

Since the Pauline corpus corresponds to the prophetic literature, then the teaching of Jesus Christ had to function as the Law communicated to the Gentiles. Its production had to be ingenious. On the one hand it had to correspond to the Old Testament Law and thus cast in five books. On the other hand, it had to reflect the universality of all the nations and thus cast in four books.[1] This task was accomplished by splitting one of the Gospels—Luke—into two volumes. Put otherwise, the *same* total gospel message was handed, at the same time, in five volumes and in four "works." An example of such ingenuity can be found in the Gospel story of the multiplication of the bread and fishes. At the first round five thousand people were fed and, on the second turn, four thousand. That is to say, the first recipients of the feeding were Israel and the second recipients were the nations.[2] However, both were fed with bread and fish, that is, the same food.

A closer look at the Gospels will reveal two more striking features. The one message is nothing other than the Pauline gospel. Just as the Pauline letters were conceived as scripture, so too the Gospels were cast as "books" or "writings" to which nothing further could be added, that is, they were cast as a "canon" (rule) as originally intended by Paul himself:

> But far be it from me to glory except in the cross of our Lord Jesus Christ, by which the world has been crucified to me, and I to the world. For neither circumcision counts for anything, nor uncircumcision, but a new creation. Peace and mercy be upon all

---

[1] I have consistently indicated in my Commentaries as well as multi-volume Introduction that the numeral four, reflecting the four geographical directions or the four sides of a building, was indicative of universality.

[2] See my comments in *NTI*₁ 175-6 and 182-3.

who walk by this rule (*kanoni*), upon the Israel of God. (Gal 6:14-16).

The earliest Gospel, Mark, was entitled "gospel" (*evangelion*) using a Pauline expression "the beginning of the gospel" (1:1; Phil 4:15). The second, Luke, a double volume work was split into two "words": "In the first book (*logon*; word), O Theophilus, I have dealt with all that Jesus began to do and teach" (Act 1:1). *logos* is another term Paul uses to refer to his gospel preaching. Had Luke followed Mark in using *evangelion* (gospel), he would have ended with two "gospels," which would have contradicted Paul's statement in Galatians: "I am astonished that you are so quickly deserting him who called you in the grace of Christ and turning to a different gospel—not that there is another gospel, but there are some who trouble you and want to pervert the gospel of Christ." (1:6-7) So the choice was ingenious as well as intended. The third Gospel, John, starts with the gospel message as *logos* (1:1) and ends by expressly scripturalizing itself into a "book," "this book" *exclusive of any additions*:

> Now Jesus did many other signs in the presence of the disciples, which are not written in this book; but these are written that you may believe that Jesus is the Christ, the Son of God, and that believing you may have life in his name. (20:30-31)

> But there are also many other things which Jesus did; were every one of them to be written, I suppose that the world itself could not contain the books that would be written. (21:25)

Matthew, the last Gospel to be written, at the outset assumes the reality of the gospel as "book" by calling itself "the Book of Genesis" (1:1).[3] The reference to "genesis" accomplishes two things. On the one hand, it presents Matthew as the definitive book just as Genesis functioned in the Old Testament, that is, having been produced last it was put first in order to have its thesis set the tone for the rest of the literature. In this sense Genesis is the institutional, constitutional book of the entire Old

---

[3] The intentionality is evident in that the original Greek of Mt 1:18 refers to the "genesis" (*genesis*)—and not the "birth" (*gennēsis*)—of Jesus Christ.

Testament in that it contains all the essential terminology of that literature.[4] In the same way Matthew functions as "*this* gospel of the Kingdom" (24:14). On the other hand, by entitling itself as "the book of *Genesis*" Matthew intimates to the hearers that it functions similarly to the first book of the Law and thus should be read as the first in a series of five, the four Gospels and the Book of Acts.[5]

The Canonical Sequence Luke, John, and Acts

Considering the programmatic sequence of the gospel "word" settling into a "book," the canonical sequence Mark-Luke-John seems logical. Doing so separates the Book of Acts from Luke thus allowing Acts to function as an Introduction to the Pauline corpus. By the same token, the separation of Acts from Luke secured that the "image" of Jesus in the hearer's mind would not be monopolized by the "Lukan" image of him, which in turn would have idolized Jesus into one representation. By devising the canon the way they did, the authors secured that Jesus would be "gathered" out of the four Gospels, similar to the scriptural Moses who has always to be "gathered" out of four books,[6] and that Paul would be "gathered" out of fourteen letters or even fifteen books if one factors in the Book of Acts. The multiplicity of "sources" in the case of the central scriptural characters made sure the hearers would never conceptualize them as a Platonic self-standing "idea" or "person," that is, they would never be able to "historicize" them into controllable "statues" to which one can point. To the contrary, as many Christians witness—more often against their will than willingly—that Jesus Christ *is* the Book of the four Gospels or, more accurately, the Book of the four Gospels is "confessed" by

---

[4] Such as creation, sin, covenant, circumcision, salvation.
[5] For more details regarding the redaction of the four Gospels, see my article "The Gospel of Matthew within the New Testament Canon," The Journal of the Orthodox Center for the Advancement of Biblical Studies (JOCABS) Vol. 9, No 1 (2016).
[6] Exodus, Leviticus, Numbers, Deuteronomy.

them as being Jesus the Christ whom they worship and to whom they bow down.[7]

The Use of Greek instead of Latin

An oblique jab against Roman authority as impersonated in the emperor can be found in the decision of the Pauline school to follow in the footsteps of its predecessors regarding the language of the written text. The authors of the Old Testament did not write in Greek, the language of the conqueror, but in a Semitic tongue. The authors of the New Testament did the same; they wrote not in Latin but in the language of the conquered Greece and Macedonia. Although one cannot prove unequivocally that the authors knew enough Latin to produce a literature as substantial as the New Testament, it is very clear that they wanted to give that impression to their readers. Note the following:

1. Their main apostle was a Roman citizen (Acts 16:37-38; 22:25-29; 23:27).

2. Occasionally they used the original Latin *centurio*, transliterated and Grecized as *kenturiōn*[8] instead of its Greek counterpart *ekatontarkhos*[9] or *ekatontarkhēs*[10] (chief over one hundred), especially when such use was done on purpose in the case of Mark 15:39 (*kenturiōn*) and its parallel Luke 23:47 (*ekatontarkhēs*).

3. An oblique allusion to, at least, their interest in Latin is found in John 19:20: "Many of the Jews read this title, for the place where Jesus was

---

[7] Orthodox Christians should give this matter utmost importance and kiss in reverence that Book instead of the Icon of Christ—made by the hands of a human iconographer and not "written by the finger of God" (Ex 31:18)—which was not "deified" until as late as the Seventh Ecumenical Council in 787.

[8] Mk 15:39, 44, 45.

[9] See, e.g., Mt 8:5, 8; 27:54.

[10] See, e.g., Mt 8:13; Lk 7:6; 23:47.

crucified was near the city; and it was written in Hebrew, in Latin (*Rōmaisti*), and in Greek."

4. The names of three of the main New Testament "writers" are Latin: Paulus, Marcus, and Luc(i)a(nu)s.

Part Four

Post New Testament

22
Mishandling of Scripture

If Ezekiel's assumption is that the addressed children of the rebellious fathers are themselves charged with rebellion, then what is the use of the already written scroll, and in which sense that scroll is Israel's scripture? Unfortunately, both Jews and Christians have eschewed these pertinent questions that are essential for the understanding of scripture. Instead, preference is given to theological subject matters dealing with the "nature" of the deity, the "meaning" of the human being, and the relation(ship) between God and man. Such matters ultimately revolve around the "value" of the human being—more specifically of our kind of human being (Hellene versus barbarian)—which was the common denominator in ancient Greek philosophical writings and literature. It is no wonder then that the Platonic soul was conceived as divine, and that the Iliad and the Odyssey are filled with gods and semi-gods realistically intermingling with humans. This "realism" can be quintessentially seen in Virgil's Aeneid, the aim of which was to link the emerging imperial Rome to the Hellenes via Troy, and thus make of the Romans the descendants of the Iliad's Trojans who are essentially a "literary" reality.

That same mood pervaded Roman Judea under the Hasmonean leadership that considered itself the "heir" of the scriptural kings of Israel and Judah, just as Virgil's Roman leaders were presented as the biological heirs of Greece. This same tendency found its apex among the Jerusalemite leadership under King Herod, Rome's client, who transformed Palestine into a major Greco-Roman entity. However, while Herod's Jerusalem and its temple ultimately ended in rubble at the hand of the Romans in 70 A.D., the factually lasting outcome of that period were the writings of Josephus Flavius that established a Greco-Roman style Judaism, which remained dormant for centuries until it resurfaced in the 20th century with the establishment of the state of Israel as a "Jewish state" and no less "foreseen by scripture itself." Josephus Flavius was in a unique position to do what he did. He was, through his mother, a descendant of the Hasmoneans and thus a priest by right and, by the same token, a member of the Jerusalemite aristocracy that was by and large sympathetic to Herod and his pro-Roman stance. After all, Herod was the builder of the Jerusalem temple that secured steady and sure income to its servers. In spite of his earlier anti-Roman stand in Galilee where he led Jewish insurgents against Rome, once captured, Josephus very readily became a zealous client of Rome. As such, he first wrote his *Jewish War* as an apologia to his fellow Jews as to why he changed his mind.

Still, Josephus' more valuable work is his later *Jewish Antiquities*. While in Rome he must have realized that beyond the Aeneid, it was the works of Virgil's contemporaries, *Roman Antiquities* by Dionysius of Halicarnassus and *History of Rome* by Livy, he had to emulate.[1] These writings conveyed the story of the Romans over the centuries until their own times. The function of such "histories" was to legitimize the newly emerging Roman empire in the eyes of the world and even its own citizens by showing that the "Romans" were not recent come-abouts, but rather an age-long and continuous reality that spanned centuries. This is precisely what Josephus embarked to do in order to legitimize Judaism. However—and there lies the calamity—to do so Josephus used scripture as though it were the "pre-history" of the Jews such as Josephus himself. In actuality scripture was conceived as merely a *mashal*, that is, a story upholding the instructional divine word for all times and ages as to how to behave uprightly in the eyes of God, the judge of all. In Josephus' *Jewish Antiquities* the scriptural "instructional story" was handled as though it were a prequel to his *Jewish War* and, by extension, to the subsequent sociological history of the

---

[1] Josephus emulates Dionysius' work not only in the title but also in the number of books (20).

"Jews" through the centuries. The Jews of his time did not give too much attention to Josephus' writings. "His writings, while generally ignored by fellow Jews, were preserved by Christians not only because they chronicled generally and so well the 'time between the testaments,' but also because they contained specific references to John the Baptist, Jesus of Nazareth, and Jesus' brother James."[2] So this utter mishandling if not outright misreading of scripture was in fact perpetrated by Christians. Jewish apologetes used the stratagem of "antiquity" by pointing out that Moses the lawgiver and the scriptural prophets were more ancient than Plato and even Solon. They contended that much of Greek wisdom was borrowed from the Law and the Prophets. Such a stratagem proved most appealing to the Christians since they were, by all standards, newcomers in the arena of history when compared to the Greeks and Romans. This approach allowed the Christians to legitimize themselves over and against the Greco-Romans, especially since these were perceived as the scriptural "nations." The Christians viewed themselves as the ("heirs" of) scriptural Israel. The Achilles' heel in this process was that it used scripture to legitimize a human community in the eyes of, if not outright over and against, those holding the upper hand, rather than considering the message of scripture with which that community was "entrusted" of higher value than any other messages, as Paul taught. Paul's argument is potent since he begins by equalizing the Jews and the non-Jews using the intrinsic value of circumcised in the flesh versus uncircumcised in the flesh:[3]

> Circumcision indeed is of value if you obey the law; but if you break the law, your circumcision becomes uncircumcision. So, if a man who is uncircumcised keeps the precepts of the law, will not his uncircumcision be regarded as circumcision? Then those who are physically uncircumcised but keep the law will condemn you who have the written code and circumcision but break the law. For he is not a real Jew who is one outwardly, nor is true

[2] Louis H. Feldman, "Josephus" in *Anchor Bible Dictionary*, vol.3, 982.
[3] See my comments in *C-Rom* 71-74.

circumcision something external and physical. He is a Jew who is
one inwardly, and real circumcision is a matter of the heart,
spiritual and not literal. His praise is not from men but from God.
(Rom 2:25-29)

At hearing this, the impatient addressee may rush to conclude
that there is no functional difference between the Jews and the
non-Jews. Not so, retorts Paul:

> Then what advantage has the Jew? Or what is the value of
> circumcision? Much in every way. To begin with, the Jews are
> entrusted with the *oracles (logia) of God*. What if some were
> unfaithful? Does their faithlessness nullify the faithfulness of God?
> By no means! Let God be true though every man be false, as it is
> written, "That thou mayest be justified in *thy words (logois)*, and
> prevail when thou art judged." (3:1-4)

Thus, against Josephus Flavius and the early Christian
apologetes and "theologians," Paul underscored the value of
God's message *as embedded* in the scriptural words over the
teachings of the Gentiles and also over those of the Jews who
were obstinate in their disobedience to God's words as delivered
in his Law and Prophets (Rom 3:5-20). In other words, Paul
correctly captured the teaching of Ezekiel and Psalm 78:

> A Maskil of Asaph. Give ear, O my people, to my teaching;
> incline your ears to the words of my mouth! I will open my mouth
> in a parable; I will utter dark sayings from of old, things that we
> have heard and known, that our fathers have told us. We will not
> hide them from their children, but tell to the coming generation
> the glorious deeds of the Lord, and his might, and the wonders
> which he has wrought. He established a testimony in Jacob, and
> appointed a law in Israel, which he commanded our fathers to
> teach to their children; that the next generation might know
> them, the children yet unborn, and arise and tell them to their
> children, so that they should set their hope in God, and not forget
> the works of God, but keep his commandments; and that they
> should not be like their fathers, a stubborn and rebellious
> generation, a generation whose heart was not steadfast, whose
> spirit was not faithful to God. (Ps 78:1-8)

In 1 Corinthians, Paul speaks against the tendency pervading Christian and Jewish thought to present their constituency through the centuries as being the actual fleshly heirs of God's scriptural congregation (*qahal/ekklēsia*).[4] The Apostle writes to his *Gentile* Corinthians:

> I want you to know, brethren, that our fathers were all under the cloud, and all passed through the sea, and all were baptized into Moses in the cloud and in the sea, and all ate the same supernatural food and all drank the same supernatural drink. For they drank from the supernatural Rock which followed them, and the Rock was Christ. Nevertheless with most of them God was not pleased; for they were overthrown in the wilderness. Now these things are warnings (*typoi*) for us, not to desire evil as they did. Do not be idolaters as some of them were; as it is written, "The people sat down to eat and drink and rose up to dance." We must not indulge in immorality as some of them did, and twenty-three thousand fell in a single day. We must not put the Lord to the test, as some of them did and were destroyed by serpents; nor grumble, as some of them did and were destroyed by the Destroyer. Now these things happened to them as a warning (*typikōs*), but they were written down (*egraphē*) for our instruction (*nouthesian*), upon whom the end of the ages has come. (1 Cor 10:1-11)

Paul's approach is clearly a far cry from the traditional Christian and Jewish thought. The scriptural story is a "type," a "parable" as Ezekiel and Psalm 78 would say. Accordingly, it is a scripted (consigned as a writ) *instructional story* for all upcoming generations of children,[5] not a "history" or a sequence of historical human events. That is why, instead of pinning the Jew and the Christian against one another, both of whom claim to be God's scriptural people, Paul reads the scriptural fathers as "our fathers," that is to say, the Corinthians' fathers as well as his. In so doing, he is not cajoling or glorifying

---

[4] The "outsiders" would be termed as *goyim/ethnē* (nations; Gentiles; heathens).
[5] As Psalm 78:5-8 insists.

the Corinthians,[6] rather he is belittling them by making them the progeny of "adulterous" forebears (1 Cor 10:5-11). Put otherwise, instead of inflating their hubris as citizens of the capital of Achaia, the Roman province covering ancient Greece, he scripturalizes them, rendering these proud descendants of the ancient Hellenes viler than the barbarians they despise. Indeed, if they are the progeny of the scriptural "fathers," then the words of Ezekiel and Jeremiah apply to them as well:

> For you are not sent to a people of foreign speech and a hard language, but to the house of Israel—not to many peoples of foreign speech and a hard language, whose words you cannot understand. Surely, if I sent you to such, they would listen to you. (Ezek 3:5-6)

> Has a nation changed its gods, even though they are no gods? But my people have changed their glory for that which does not profit. (Jer 2:11)

Instead of extending the scriptural story into a subsequent "history of the Jewish people" or "history of the church," Paul "sucks" the Corinthians "into the scriptural story," thus forcing upon them the rebellion of the scriptural Israel and making it their own. He is essentially reading scripture as it stands, as he explicitly states elsewhere:

> But the scripture consigned all things[7] to sin (*hypo hamartian*), that what was promised to faith in Jesus Christ might be given to those who believe. (Gal 3:22)

> For God has consigned all men to disobedience, that he may have mercy upon all.[8] (Rom 11:32)

---

[6] This is precisely what Paul accuses his opponents of doing, counting circumcision "scalps" for their own glory: "It is those who want to make a good showing in the flesh that would compel you to be circumcised, and only in order that they may not be persecuted for the cross of Christ. For even those who receive circumcision do not themselves keep the law, but they desire to have you circumcised that they may glory in your flesh." (Gal 6:12-13)

[7] That is, both Jews and Gentiles; see my comments in *Gal* 157-9 and *C-Rom* 222.

[8] See previous note.

There is no place for hubris in the scriptural story since, as the Apostle asserts, "What then? Are we Jews any better off? No, not at all; for I have already charged that all men, both Jews and Greeks, are under (the power of) sin (*hyph' hamartian*)." (Rom 3:9)

Returning to 1 Corinthians 10 one finds the reason behind the impossibility of extending the scriptural story into subsequent history. Whenever the hearers are addressed by that story, they are not only instructed, but they are posited at "the end of the ages" (v.10) and thus under divine final judgment, which is precisely what Paul explicitly says in the passage (vv.7-10) that is bracketed by his statements regarding the scriptural story of disobedience being a "warning" for the Corinthians as well as himself (vv.6 and 11).

The handling of scripture as it truly is, an instructional story, was masterly accomplished by Luke in his two-volume work, Luke-Acts. The subject matter of his mini-epic "story" is the gospel message as carried sequentially by two heroes, Jesus and Paul. Jesus offers the gospel message to the Jews of his time who end up, scripture style, refusing it. The message is offered in turn to the Gentiles by Paul, the second hero, in hope they would accept it. This follows the pattern presented in Romans 9-11, first the Jews, then the Gentiles. Unlike Virgil's *Aeneid*, Dionysius' *Roman Antiquities*, and Livy's *History of Rome* that charted the establishment of the Roman empire after a long and tortuous odyssey, the Lukan dyptich does not end on an assured positive note, but rather it has an open-ended finale of *hope* that the seed refused by the Jews and planted by Paul among the Gentiles in Rome and elsewhere would someday produce the desired fruits (Acts 28:17-31), thus fleshing out in a story-like manner the teaching of Romans 11. Luke built upon the Markan premise that Jerusalem would be destroyed by the Romans should the Jews opt for an armed revolt against their oppressors instead of following the admonition to the scriptural Israel to "repent" of its revolt against God's message of peace for both Israel and the nations (Is 2). As Paul insisted in his letter

to the Romans, the Romans would have to willingly submit to
that same scriptural message in order to secure the true peace
that comes from God alone and is heralded not through human
sword, but rather through "the sword of the Spirit, which is the
word of God" (Eph 6:17) and is none other than "the gospel of
peace" (v.15).

My contention is that Josephus Flavius was unhappy with the
Lukan approach whereby the assuredness (*asphaleia*) of the
teaching lies in the *hope* it entails, so he wrote his *Jewish Antiquities*
to counteract Luke-Acts that presented Jesus and Paul as the
"heirs" of the scriptural Moses and Prophets. Josephus was a
Hasmonean at heart. Having first tried the path of revolt, which
proved unsuccessful, he could not resign himself to the defeat,
as an expression of God's punishment of the hubris of the
Hasmonean style Jews of the times. So he followed the path of
Herod the Idumean and became a "client" of Rome. And since
Rome understood the language of power and human greatness,
Josephus painted the Jewish past in a grandiose manner rather
than in dismal terms after the manner of Ezekiel 16, 20, and 23,
Hosea 1-2, and Psalm 78. In other words, against God's express
teaching in the Prophets, especially Isaiah and Ezekiel, he sided
with the Romans the same way Isaiah's Judahites sided with
Egypt (Is 20:1-6), and Ezekiel's exiles were contemplating
becoming "clients" of Babylon (Ezek 20:32).[9]

This non-scriptural, if not outright anti-scriptural, mood
pervaded subsequent Christian tradition much more than it did
Jewish tradition. The reason for the discrepancy is that the
"definition" of a Jew relied more on being bound by the Torah
rather than on being circumcised, as Paul correctly taught in
Romans 2:25-3:2. Traditionally, circumcision is not undertaken
by one's choice, whereas becoming a *bar-miṣwah* or *bat-miṣwah*

---

[9] Josephus proved to be the forerunner of Eusebius of Caesarea who, in his *History of
the Church*, was acting as the "client" of the Roman emperor Constantine after two
and a half centuries of martyrs who fell under the Roman sword in order to witness
for their Lord against the "beast" of the Apocalypse.

(son or, respectively, daughter of the commandment) does happen by one's choice after much preparation and deliberation.[10] It is a personal commitment to have one's life ruled by the divine commandments that entail blessing as well as curse (Lev 26; Deut 28). It is a personal choice between two paths:

> See, I have set before you this day life and good, death and evil. If you obey the commandments of the Lord your God which I command you this day, by loving the Lord your God, by walking in his ways, and by keeping his commandments and his statutes and his ordinances, then you shall live and multiply, and the Lord your God will bless you in the land which you are entering to take possession of it. But if your heart turns away, and you will not hear, but are drawn away to worship other gods and serve them, I declare to you this day, that you shall perish; you shall not live long in the land which you are going over the Jordan to enter and possess. I call heaven and earth to witness against you this day, that I have set before you life and death, blessing and curse; therefore choose life, that you and your descendants may live, loving the Lord your God, obeying his voice, and cleaving to him; for that means life to you and length of days, that you may dwell in the land which the Lord swore to your fathers, to Abraham, to Isaac, and to Jacob, to give them. (Deut 30:15-20)

The early Christian thinkers, being overwhelmingly Greco-Romans, were prone to go either the Platonic-Plotinic way or that of Virgil, Dionysius of Halicarnassus, and Ovid. The earliest promoter of the theology that revolved around "Christology" or the "person of Christ,"[11] is Justin. He introduced the Platonic understanding of *logos* into the scriptural *dabar*, when in fact that *dabar* is essentially a "parabolic story" rather than a "notion" or "eternal idea." It is understandable

---

[10] The same approach can be seen in the Roman Catholic tradition, whereby confirmation is not only post-baptism but also post-communion. On the other hand, in the Orthodox "mystical" tradition, all three sacraments—baptism, chrismation, communion—take place during the same service where the infant is "mystically" transformed into a "new being."

[11] As corroborated by the debates of the ecumenical councils.

then that he is traditionally known not only as "Justin the Martyr," but also as "Justin the Philosopher." His quest was essentially a philosophical one as is clear from his writings. Such an approach pervaded the writings of others, including Irenaeus, and later the Alexandrian Christian school which controlled classical theology through the teachings of the Cappadocians who endorsed and developed the teachings of the school of Alexandria.[12] It is quite amazing that the scriptural text would end up—according to that theology—speaking of its "word" (parabolically instructional story) in terms of "person" or "being."

On the other hand, Eusebius of Caesarea's *Ecclesiastical History* followed in the footsteps of Josephus' *Jewish Antiquities*. Although he begins his work with the life of Jesus Christ, rather than with the Old Testament story that Josephus used, his real "hero" is not Christ, but Constantine. This is evident in his dedication to Constantine the end of Book IX and the entirety of Book X, in addition to his "Life of Constantine," "the Oration of Constantine," and "The Oration of Eusebius" at the thirteenth anniversary of Constantine's reign. What is striking in Eusebius' handling of Constantine is that he used Old Testament precedents to describe the emperor's feats, making Constantine a new or another Moses and, ultimately, another "Christ" who was able to realize the *pax Romana* as though it were the universal peace predicted/depicted in Isaiah 2:1-4. Subsequent theological endeavors, whether Middle Ages efforts, East or West theologies, or critical, modern or self-aggrandizing post-modern writings, are all self-perpetrating "traditions of men."[13]

The problem with all theologies is that they speak about God, thus creating an idol. What, after all, is essentially the difference between expressing words about God and creating a statue of God? Theologians say that they are continuing the tradition

---

[12] Gregory the Theologian refers to Origen as being "the whetstone of us all."
[13] Orthodox theology, both classical and more so self-naming post-modern, consistently extolls the "fathers" while Psalm 78 denigrates them.

initiated by the prophets and Paul, yet how could that be when scripture expressly says that God himself put his *own* words in Jeremiah's mouth (chapter 1), which words were then re-issued to Baruch who committed them to a writ (chapter 36), which writ was cast "into the midst of the Euphrates" (51:63) to be picked up by Ezekiel as an already written scroll (chapter 2)? Paul upheld this intra-scriptural movement from oral to final and canonized writ. When one hears his letters canonically, one encounters this movement:

- Like Ezekiel before him, at the outset of his letters Paul states that he is not bringing anything new, but is restating for the Gentiles what his predecessors conveyed to Israel: "Paul, a servant of Jesus Christ, called to be an apostle, set apart for the gospel of God which he promised beforehand through his prophets in the holy scriptures ... to bring about the obedience of faith for the sake of his name among all the nations, including yourselves." (Rom 1:1-2, 5-6)

- After iterating the same message to the Greeks in 1 Corinthians, he concludes this diptych with the phrase "The salutation of *me* Paul with mine own hand." (1 Cor 16:21 KJV)

My contention is that one should listen to scripture as it stands in the Hebrew canon.[14] The Law and the Prophets witnessed to in the New Testament[15] support my contention that both

---

[14] The contention is still valid even in the LXX canon, since it basically hinges on the sequence Pentateuch followed by Joshua and Judges. That this sequence was kept in both canons militates for an essential aspect of another contention of mine, that the authors of the Hebrew text were themselves the translators of the LXX Greek text.

[15] Think not that I have come to abolish the law and the prophets; I have come not to abolish them but to fulfil them. (Mt 5:17) So whatever you wish that men would do to you, do so to them; for this is the law and the prophets. (7:12) For all the prophets and the law prophesied until John (11:13). On these two commandments depend all the law and the prophets. (Mt 22:40) Then he said to them, "These are

Testaments were written much closer in time than it is usually assumed, and that the New Testament followed as a necessary sequel to the Old Testament.

---

my words which I spoke to you, while I was still with you, that everything written about me in the law of Moses and the prophets and the psalms must be fulfilled." (Lk 24:44) And on the sabbath day they went into the synagogue and sat down. After the reading of the law and the prophets, the rulers of the synagogue sent to them, saying, "Brethren, if you have any word of exhortation for the people, say it." (Acts 13:14-15)

23
The Saga Continues

Philo and Josephus submitted to the philosophy and socio-polity against which scripture was conceived. Philo's proximity to Jerusalem and Judah would explain his endorsement of the "Judahites" (Jews). Alexandria with its expansive library functioned as a second Rome, actually the intellectual Rome.[1] The Judahites of Jerusalem prided themselves on being "special" by historicizing scripture. The Judahites of Alexandria did the same on the philosophical level contending that Moses and his Law preceded by centuries the philosophers of Greece and their wisdom. Greek philosophers are presented as having appropriated the Mosaic teaching and turning it into their wisdom. In support of this theory, the Alexandrian Judahites devised the legend of scripture being officially translated from Hebrew into Greek in Alexandria, at the behest of the Greek Ptolemy II of Egypt in the third century B.C., in order for the Greeks to recognize the superiority of the scriptural wisdom reflected in the Five Books of Moses. The naming of those books in Greek, especially the first one—Genesis—betrays that interest. The Greek thinkers were always interested in the natural world and its origins. However, therein lies the trap: whenever one uses the opponent's terminology in order to subdue that opponent, in reality one has already surrendered and thus lost the battle. That was the deadly error of both the Jerusalemite and Alexandrian Judahites. The Jerusalemites read the scriptural "epic" as an (anti)Greek saga to aggrandize themselves and ironically fell prey to Rome, the new Babylon, as aptly described in the Book of Revelation. By historicizing the teaching handed to them to save them from succumbing to the fate of the scriptural Israel, they actualized the "exile" in their own times. The Alexandrians, de facto, gave

---

[1] Constantinople was not yet on the horizon.

primacy to the LXX over the Hebrew original, thus perverting the original intention of the scriptural authors.[2] In so doing, the scriptural *dabar* was subjugated to the Platonic *logos*, thus creating an avalanche of perversions of the "gospel of God" contained in the prophetic teachings of the Old Testament (Rom 1:1-2), and a jargon of "falseness" instead of truth, just perverting the original Pauline *logos* (gospel word) into *paralogia* (deceiving speech; Col 2:4), *pithanologia* (beguiling speech; Col 2:4), *mataiologia* (vain discussion; 1 Tim 1:6; Tit 1:10), all from the same root *log—* as *logos* and all strictly forbidden by Paul. The epitome of perversion is that they hid their "tradition of men" (Col 2:8) under the revered term *theologia*,[3] thus paving the way for the later Alexandrian Christian "theology" that took hold of all subsequent Christian doctrines. It is no wonder then that Greek has the upper hand over Hebrew[4] in all Christian denominations, to the extent that a substantial number of so-called "theologians"[5] do not even read Hebrew, let alone understand it.

---

[2] It is interesting that Paul uses this imagery of "perversion" to describe the actions of his opponents: "I am astonished that you are so quickly deserting him who called you in the grace of Christ and turning to a different gospel—not that there is another gospel, but there are some who trouble you and want to pervert the gospel of Christ." (Gal 1:6-7) For Paul the gospel is nothing more nor less than the teaching of the Old Testament: "Paul, a servant of Jesus Christ, called to be an apostle, set apart for the gospel of God which he promised beforehand through his prophets in the holy scriptures." (Rom 1:1-2) Yet, he writes a lengthy epistle to explain his statement. The same does the "Pauline" John: "Beloved, I am writing you no new commandment, but an old commandment which you had from the beginning; the old commandment is the word which you have heard. Yet I am writing you a new commandment, which is true in him and in you, because the darkness is passing away and the true light is already shining." (1 Jn 2:7-8)

[3] A term not found in scripture.

[4] In spite of claims to the contrary.

[5] I say "so-called" since neither "theology" nor "theologian" is to be found in scripture. Notice how, in order to justify their presumption, those same "theologians" bestowed the title of "theologian" to the Apostle John! In so doing, they indirectly considered the title "theologian" as higher in value than "apostle," making of Matthew, Mark, Luke, and even Paul as *mere* apostles when compared to the presumed author of the fourth Gospel, which they further dubbed as the "spiritual" Gospel, making of the other three non-spiritual, or less spiritual, productions. This

In Judea, the legacy of the "Judahites" was sealed by Josephus Flavius and impacted to a great extent all subsequent Judaism. Josephus joined the "Judahites" in their armed revolt against Rome (66-70 A.D.) while he was the military governor of Galilee. Eventually he was captured and taken to Rome as captive. There he realized the odds were against the "Judahites" and defected to the Roman camp by offering his services as an interpreter to the Emperor Vespasian who granted him freedom and even adopted him into his Flavian clan; hence the surname "Flavius." Josephus' first major work, "The Jewish War," had an understandably a pro-Roman tilt. It is, however, his later opus, "Antiquities of the Jews," that is of importance for our discussion. In it he "historicized" the data of scripture *in order to* justify his stand that his contemporary Judahites were the flesh and blood heirs of the scriptural Israel and Judah. He even explains their submission to Rome as the result of (the scriptural) God's will to grant Rome universal power.[6] Such a position can be justified on the basis of Isaiah 44:24-45:6 where God chooses Cyrus to be his locum tenens. Paul even endorsed this view in Romans and Titus:

> Let every person be subject to the governing authorities. For there is no authority except from God, and those that exist have been instituted by God. Therefore he who resists the authorities resists what God has appointed, and those who resist will incur judgment. For rulers are not a terror to good conduct, but to bad. Would you have no fear of him who is in authority? Then do what is good, and you will receive his approval, for he is God's servant for your good. But if you do wrong, be afraid, for he does not bear the sword in vain; he is the servant of God to execute his wrath on the wrongdoer. Therefore one must be subject, not only to avoid God's wrath but also for the sake of conscience. For the same reason you also pay taxes, for the authorities are ministers of God, attending to this very thing. Pay all of them their dues,

reminds me of the ongoing debate between Christian theologians as to which of the titles, "professor" or "doctor," is of higher value before the name of the individual concerned.

[6] This position he upheld in "The Jewish War."

taxes to whom taxes are due, revenue to whom revenue is due, respect to whom respect is due, honor to whom honor is due. (Rom 13:1-7)

Remind them to be submissive to rulers and authorities, to be obedient, to be ready for any honest work, to speak evil of no one, to avoid quarreling, to be gentle, and to show perfect courtesy toward all men. (Tit 3:1-2)

However, there is a far cry between the approaches of Josephus and Paul. Instead of selling himself to the Romans, as Josephus did, Paul challenged them by positing the "power" (*dynamis*) and "salvation" (*sōtēria*), which are imperial prerogatives and even "titles,"[7] as attributes of the gospel he is preaching to the Romans in order that they submit to it:

Paul, a servant of Jesus Christ, called to be an apostle, set apart for the gospel of God which he promised beforehand through his prophets in the holy scriptures, the gospel concerning his Son, who was descended from David according to the flesh and designated Son of God in power according to the Spirit of holiness by his resurrection from the dead, Jesus Christ our Lord, through whom we have received grace and apostleship to bring about the obedience (*hypakoēn*; submission) of faith for the sake of his name among all the nations, including yourselves who are called to belong to Jesus Christ; (Rom 1:1-6)

For I am not ashamed of the gospel: it is the power of God for salvation to every one who has faith, to the Jew first and also to the Greek. (1:16)

His gospel even entails righteousness (*dikaiosynē*), the pride of the Roman legal system:

For in it the righteousness of God is revealed through faith for faith; as it is written, "He who through faith is righteous shall live." (1:17)

It is precisely this teaching that is the extended parabolic story in Ezekiel (chapters 16, 20, 23).

---

[7] The Roman emperor is the "power" of the gods and the "savior" (*sōtēr*) of the people.

Taking his lead from Romans 9-11, the Lukan "narrative" (*diēgēsin*; Lk 1:1) purports the itinerary of the preaching of the Pauline gospel. First it was offered by the scriptural Jesus to the Judahites in the Gospel of Luke, and it was then shared with the nations by the scriptural Paul in the Book of Acts. The unity of those two volumes is sealed in that both are addressed to the same Theophilus (Lk 1:3; Acts 1:1) and that Acts is introduced as a second "word" (*logon*; Acts 1:1; KJV "treatise"; RSV "book"). Consequently, they are to be read in tandem. At the end of Acts, Paul, although under house arrest in Rome, "lived there two whole years at his own expense, and welcomed all who came to him, preaching the kingdom of God and teaching about the Lord Jesus Christ quite openly and unhindered" (Acts 28:30-31). Whether intended or not, this last statement sounds as an indictment of the attitude of Josephus, the consummate "Judahite" who "bought" his freedom by submitting to the Roman cause. The scriptural Paul, on the other hand, was a free Roman citizen and yet chose to be "living as a citizen would (*politevesthe*) in a manner worthy of the gospel" (Phil 1:27), that is to say as "a citizen of the commonwealth (*politevma*; citizenry) in heaven awaiting as savior the Lord Jesus Christ" (3:20).[8] It is in this same letter that Paul wields a heavy blow to the "circumcision party" and their self-righteousness:

> For we are the true circumcision, who worship God in spirit, and glory in Christ Jesus, and put no confidence in the flesh. Though I myself have reason for confidence in the flesh also. If any other man thinks he has reason for confidence in the flesh, I have more: circumcised on the eighth day, of the people of Israel, of the tribe of Benjamin, a Hebrew born of Hebrews; as to the law a Pharisee, as to zeal a persecutor of the church, as to righteousness under the law blameless. But whatever gain I had, I counted as loss for the sake of Christ. Indeed I count everything as loss because of the surpassing worth of knowing Christ Jesus my Lord. For his sake I have suffered the loss of all things, and count them as refuse, in order that I may gain Christ and be found in him, not

---

[8] This fits perfectly the Lukan description of his behavior at the closure of Acts.

THE RISE OF SCRIPTURE

having a righteousness of my own, based on law, but that which
is through faith in Christ, the righteousness from God that
depends on faith; that I may know him and the power of his
resurrection, and may share his sufferings, becoming like him in
his death, that if possible I may attain the resurrection from the
dead. Not that I have already obtained this or am already perfect;
but I press on to make it my own, because Christ Jesus has made
me his own. Brethren, I do not consider that I have made it my
own; but one thing I do, forgetting what lies behind and straining
forward to what lies ahead, I press on toward the goal for the
prize of the upward call of God in Christ Jesus. (Phil 3:3-14)

It is no wonder then that Josephus decided to undermine the
Lukan opus in his "Antiquities of the Jews." There is no need to
discuss here the different opinions concerning the
authenticity—whether full or partial—of the three passages
concerning Jesus, John the Baptist, and James "the brother of
Jesus." Suffice it to point out that, although information about
Jesus and the Baptist is found in all four Gospels, reference to
James' demise occurs exclusively in Acts 12:1-2. More
importantly for our case is to ask why Josephus would be
interested in the aforementioned three to the exclusion of Paul
and even Peter. To answer this question one should begin with
Josephus' interest in historicizing the Old Testament, which
went hand in hand with the overall interest of the Judahites. In
order to dynamite the efforts of the followers of the Old
Testament outside Palestine who produced a literature of
similar (scriptural) fabric,[9] Josephus historicized three of the
main characters in that literature, Jesus,[10] John the Baptist,[11]
and James,[12] and made them "martyrs" for his cause when
covering his contemporary period. His choice was obviously

---

[9] "So also our beloved brother Paul wrote to you according to the wisdom given him,
speaking of this as he does in all his letters. There are some things in them hard to
understand, which the ignorant and unstable twist to their own destruction, as they
do the other scriptures." (2 Pet 3:15-16)

[10] *Antiquities of the Jews* (Book 18, Chapter 3, 3).

[11] *Antiquities of the Jews* (Book 18, Chapter 5, 2).

[12] *Antiquities of the Jews* (Book 20, Chapter 9, 1).

dictated by the fact that all three were presented as having been active in Palestine and thus were viewed as "Judahites." Paul obviously was not. As for Peter, it was risky to include him since he is presented in Galatians as "apostle" to the circumcision, that is, as someone who was "sent out" and thus was active among the diaspora outside Palestine that was under the aegis of James (Jacob) and his "party." More importantly, in Acts 10, 11, and 15, Peter is portrayed as a champion of the Pauline gospel.

The Flavian trend of historicizing scripture and individualizing its characters as "hero figures" smacks of Greco-Roman Hellenism where the aggrandizing of gods, demi-gods, and macho warriors held sway against the scriptural twist of belittlement of one's ancestry.[13] This trend re-emerged in the twentieth century among both Jewish and Christian scholars. Scores of books are dedicated to the "Jewishness" of Jesus and that of Paul.[14] In the case of Paul, one even speaks of his upholding the value, if not necessity, of the temple, mistakenly applying his temple and sacrifice terminology (Rom 12:1-2; 15:15-16; Phil 2:17) to the Herodian temple of Jerusalem rather than to the temple of the new Zion, not made by the hand of man, that descends from heaven (Rev 21:2), and where priests taken from among the nations will be serving (Is 66:18-21). The Pauline spiritual temple is made out of "human" stones (1 Cor 3:16) and the mother of Paul's followers is the "Jerusalem above" (Gal 4:26).

---

[13] In scripture, solely the God without temple is depicted as "great" in his having appeared "at the beginning" along the river Chebar whose original Hebrew root *kbr* connotes greatness (see *C-Ezek* 32). All his works, including the "mighty upon earth," praise only him (Ps 148). The so-called "success" of the scriptural Israel is due exclusively to his steadfast love (*hesed*), to which an entire psalm (136) is dedicated.

[14] John P. Meier, in his "A Marginal Jew: Rethinking the Historical Jesus" stresses so much the outstanding intellectual features of Jesus that, to justify himself, adds a footnote in which he refers to other intellectually "outstanding Jews" throughout history, pointing out that such seems to be a typical characteristic of that "nation"!

The interest among Jews and Christians alike in the Jewishness of a "historical" Jesus is best exemplified in the ever-increasing number of Jewish Professors of New Testament in Christian religious institutions. Of course, among the Jews, there is also a resurgence in reinstating "James the Righteous" as the leader of so-called Palestinian or Judean Christianity—a view launched by early Christian thinkers—with the obvious intention of lessening the central value of the scriptural Paul, even though Luke unequivocally states that it was "in Antioch [that] the disciples were for the first time called Christians" (Acts 11:26). The repeated phenomenon by followers of scripture to misuse and abuse it is obviously intended to give the so-called "heirs" of the scriptural Israel the upper hand in deciding the meaning of the original text. In so doing, one speaks of a "living tradition" under the aegis of the spirit of the scriptural God, which voids the "life-giving words," if not "letters" (*grammata*),[15] of scripture of their inherent authority. In the first centuries A.D., the authority of scripture was upheld exclusively by John Chrysostom who spoke more than once of "scripture being its own interpreter." He stressed in the preface of his homilies the utmost importance of abiding by the scriptural narrative *as it stands*:

> It were indeed meet for us not at all to require the aid of the written Word, but to exhibit a life so pure, that the grace of the Spirit should be instead of books to our souls, and that as these are inscribed with ink, even so should our hearts be with the Spirit. But, since we have utterly put away from us this grace, come, *let us at any rate embrace the second best course.*

> For that the former was better, God has made manifest, both by His words, and by His doings. Since unto Noah, and unto Abraham, and unto his offspring, and unto Job, and unto Moses too, He discoursed not by writings, but Himself by Himself, finding their mind pure. But after the whole people of the Hebrews had fallen into the very pit of wickedness, then and

---

[15] See 2 Tim 3:15 for the Old Testament and Gal 6:11 for the New Testament.

thereafter was *a written word, and tables,* and the admonition which is given by these.

And this one may perceive was the case, not of the saints in the Old Testament only, but also of those in the New. For neither to the apostles did God give anything in writing, but instead of written words He promised that He would give them the grace of the Spirit: for He, says our Lord, shall bring all things to your remembrance. And that you may learn that this was far better, hear what He says by the Prophet: I will make a new covenant with you, putting my laws into their mind, and in their heart I will write them, and, they shall be all taught of God. And Paul too, pointing out the same superiority, said, that they had received a law not in tables of stone, but in fleshy tables of the heart.

But since in process of time they made shipwreck, some with regard to doctrines, others as to life and manners, there was again need that they should be put in remembrance by *the written word.*

Reflect then how great an evil it is for us, who ought to live so purely as not even to need written words, but to yield up our hearts, as books, to the Spirit; now that we have lost that honor, *and have come to have need of these, to fail again in duly employing even this second remedy.* For if it be a blame to stand in need of written words, and not to have brought down on ourselves the grace of the Spirit; *consider how heavy the charge of not choosing to profit even after this assistance, but rather treating what is written with neglect, as if it were cast forth without purpose, and at random, and so bringing down upon ourselves our punishment with increase.*

But that no such effect may ensue, *let us give strict heed unto the things that are written*; and let us learn how the Old Law was given on the one hand, how on the other the New Covenant.[16]

Yet historicizing scripture to make it relevant to one's own time is a universal phenomenon. In the words of scripture itself, it is the "tradition of men" (*paradosis anthrōpōn*) that is strictly

---

[16] Italics are mine.

prohibited by both Paul (Col 2:8) and his Lord Jesus (Mk 7:8).
Let me mention a few examples of historicizing:

- In order to root his new imperial religion in
  history so as to compete with and overcome "old
  Rome," Constantine, followed by his successors,
  the Byzantine Christian Emperors, started
  building monuments on the supposedly Judeo-
  Christian "sites." The Byzantines decided that
  the mountain of Transfiguration was Mount
  Tabor even though no mention of such is found
  in the New Testament. They decided to build a
  church in Jerusalem where wood of the
  scriptural cross of the scriptural Jesus was
  "found." They decided where the scriptural
  Jesus was born in Bethlehem and the place
  where the scriptural Gabriel appeared to the
  scriptural Mary in Nazareth. In both places a
  monumental church was erected.

- The cross, the "banner" of Jesus, the "slave"
  (*doulos*) of God (Phil 2:5-9), whose gospel Paul
  used to "teach" the "barbarians" (Rom 1:14-15;
  1 Cor 14:11; Col 3:11), was made into a banner
  for the armies who claimed "victories" over
  those same barbarians.[17]

- European Christians established the *Holy*
  Roman Empire and devised their own *holy*
  "crusades" that, ironically, were aimed at the
  territories of the Byzantine Empire.

---

[17] In the Orthodox Church we hear this hymn: "O Lord, save thy people and bless
thy inheritance, granting victories (*nikas*) to the kings (*basilevsi*; Byzantine emperors)
over the barbarians (*kata barbarōn*; against the barbarians) and, by the power of thy
cross, preserving thy polity (*politevma*; Roman [Byzantine] commonwealth
[citizenry])."

- The Dutch in South Africa and the English in North America went the whole nine yards by considering themselves part of the scriptural Israel and the aborigines the scriptural Canaan. The result of this was that they decimated entire populations with impunity since they considered that God himself sanctioned their actions. It is then no wonder that the Netherlands, the United States of America, and the United Kingdom wholeheartedly supported the State of Israel in spite of its mistreatment of the indigenous Palestinians.

- The Latter-Day Saints (Mormons) retrojected the American continent, a non-biblical geography, into the scriptural story. They posited that the North American Indians were descendants of one of the ten lost tribes of the scriptural Israel.[18] The ethnically non-Semitic Ashkenazi Jews did the same in the 20th century through political Zionism: the Jews, wherever they were, were entitled to the land of their scriptural "ancestors." In order to implement their myth they created another myth: *a land without people* (thus denying even the existence of the autochthonous Palestinians) for a people without a land (the Jews).

- Many contemporary Christian Palestinians adhere to and promote the teaching that the Palestinians are the *'am ha'aretz* (the people of the land [earth]) of Palestine and, as such, are the actual descendants of the "original" scriptural Israelites. The "people of the land" is

---

[18] The traditional Christians can only blame themselves for having planted the seeds of stretching forward the already canonized scriptural parabolic story.

encountered in scripture and seems to refer to those who remained in Palestine during the Babylonian exile. The most pertinent passage in this regard is in Ezra:

> Now when the adversaries of Judah and Benjamin heard that the returned exiles were building a temple to the Lord, the God of Israel, they approached Zerubbabel and the heads of fathers' houses and said to them, "Let us build with you; for we worship your God as you do, and we have been sacrificing to him ever since the days of Esarhaddon king of Assyria who brought us here." But Zerubbabel, Jeshua, and the rest of the heads of fathers' houses in Israel said to them, "You have nothing to do with us in building a house to our God; but we alone will build to the Lord, the God of Israel, as King Cyrus the king of Persia has commanded us." Then the people of the land discouraged the people of Judah, and made them afraid to build, and hired counselors against them to frustrate their purpose, all the days of Cyrus king of Persia, even until the reign of Darius king of Persia. (4:1-5)

Taken with the other references to "the people of the land" before the exile in 2 Kings and 2 Chronicles, one concludes that those people never left Palestine and contemporary Palestinians are their descendants, that is to say, the descendants of the scriptural Hebrews.

The real calamity, if not disaster, in all this is that all these people view themselves as the scriptural God's "chosen community" or, more accurately, the descendants thereof, and thus consider themselves entitled to act "in his name" or on his behalf in the same way as the citizens of a country would act.[19] They assume that they are the "obedient" servants of God in spite of the scriptural "datum" reiterated ad nauseam that their scriptural "forebears," generation after generation, were not obedient. Let me give two examples of my own tradition, the Orthodox Church. The Greek Orthodox in today's Corinth proudly point out that they kept the uninterrupted legacy of the church founded by Paul there in that they are the children of the Corinthians who were evangelized by Paul. If what they are actually stressing is the "living tradition" that was handed through the generations in Corinth, then they obviously assume that the original Corinthians repented at one point of the "harlotry" against God which Paul accused them of, and then lived according to his teaching which they communicated to the subsequent generations of Corinthians. But is there any indication that the original Corinthians repented? Should one assume the historical factuality of the scriptural data, then the mere fact of a second letter to the Corinthians at the end of which Paul threatens them (chapter 13) is proof to the contrary. The same argument applies in the case of the residents of Thessaloniki whose city was supposedly graced with the "actual" presence and the "live" preaching of the Apostle. Whenever the contemporary Corinthians and Thessalonians speak of the "living tradition" that was maintained through the centuries in their cities, they are de facto referring to Paul's teaching. But where does one find that teaching save in his four letters to those cities? To speak of an additional "oral" tradition is something the Apostle himself categorically forbade: "Now concerning the coming of our Lord Jesus Christ and our assembling to meet him, we beg you, brethren, not to be quickly shaken in mind or excited, either by spirit or *by word,* or by letter *purporting to be from us,* to the effect that the day of the Lord has come." (2 Thess 2:1-2) To use the following, "Do you not

---

[19] The notion of country is actually mythical since it is always "imposed" on a given geography through artificial borders by a "fait accompli" policy. Borders are artificial and/or by agreement, and thus many remain the object of disputes.

remember that when I was still with you I told you this?" (v.5)
as a counterargument is nonsensical since there is no indication,
let alone proof, as to what was said and, much less, as to how
that material was communicated to the universal church. It is
the *written* teaching of Paul to both the Corinthians and the
Thessalonians that is read aloud authoritatively[20] to the ears of
all Orthodox throughout the world. Moreover, one never hears
of the "response" or "reaction" of the Corinthians and
Thessalonians in Paul's letters. Their response is as immaterial
as that of the doubly "foolish" (*anoētoi*; mindless, brainless)
Galatians (Gal 2:1, 3) to whom Paul had to "say again" *in writing*
what he had originally taught them and against which they
turned their deaf ears, just as the scriptural Israel did time and
again: "As we have said before, so *now I say* (*legō*) *again*, If any
one is preaching to you a gospel contrary to that which you
received, let him be accursed." (Gal 1:9) That what he "said"
again was in writing with his own hand,[21] using alphabetical
letters, is sealed at the end of the epistle: "See with what large
letters (*grammasin*; alphabetical letters) I am writing (*egrapsa*; I
already wrote [in this epistle]) to you with my own hand." (6:11)
Thus, it is too late to be changed, it is etched in written letters
forever.[22]

The other example pertains to the children of the Greek
(Arabic *rum*; Roman) Orthodox Patriarchate of Antioch of
whom I am one. They pride themselves of their "Antiochian"

---

[20] The summons for being *orthoi* (standing aright attentively) is always heard in
conjunction with the Gospel Book or the readings from it or from the Book of the
Apostle comprising readings from the epistles and Acts.

[21] That is to say as authoritatively as the teaching of God "with (through) the hand of
Moses" (Gal 3:19).

[22] The aorist *egrapsa* is known as the literary aorist and functions as a seal that what
has just been written cannot be changed. The same rule applies to the perfect tense
as in the following story: "Pilate also wrote a title and put it on the cross; it read, 'Jesus
of Nazareth, the King of the Jews.' Many of the Jews read this title, for the place
where Jesus was crucified was near the city; and it was written in Hebrew, in Latin,
and in Greek. The chief priests of the Jews then said to Pilate, 'Do not write, The
King of the Jews, but, This man said, I am King of the Jews.' Pilate answered, 'What
I have written (*gegrapha* [perfect tense]) I have written (*gegrapha*).'" (Jn 19:19-22)

heritage on two counts. On the one hand, "in Antioch the disciples were for the first time called Christians" (Acts 11:26). On the other hand, they have kept alive the "living tradition" of Chrysostom's Antioch down to their days. The irony, however, is that, if one takes seriously the homilies of that same Chrysostom, his Antioch was, scripturally speaking, as "harlot" as the Corinth and Thessalonica of Paul. If they actually mean that they are keeping the *teaching* of Chrysostom—as I hope my brethren of the Greek Patriarchate of Jerusalem are keeping the teachings of Cyril of Jerusalem rather than the heritage of their forebears—then they will be hopefully *his* "children." This is why we refer to Chrysostom and Cyril and their peers as "fathers" of the church. It is their "life-giving" teaching—to the extent as it conforms to the apostolic teaching[23]—that we, hopefully, tend to keep and abide by, and not a "living Orthodox tradition." We should not even try to follow their "example"—not that it is necessarily bad, but because it is potentially detrimental[24]—since "Why do you call me good? No one is good but God alone" (Mk 10:18; Lk 18:19; see also Mt 19:17).

Whether they are aware of it or not, theology, which is nothing other than the canonized "tradition of men," has held sway over all Christian communities since the times of Justin the Martyr and Philosopher. Theology is a euphemism for Christianism (*Khristianismos*) which is as much a socio-political

[23] So we ought to assess their teaching in the light of scripture and not vice versa as is commonly done in the Orthodox Church, and all other Christian communities for that matter. One speaks of the Orthodox faith, the Roman Catholic doctrine, the Anglican tradition, the Lutheran theology, the Calvinist way, and the like. Martin Luther and Calvin are as revered by their followers as Basil the Great and Gregory the Theologian are by the Orthodox, and Augustine and Thomas Aquinas by the Catholics, and as Joseph Smith and Brigham Young are by the Church of Jesus Christ of Latter-Day Saints (Mormons). In the case of the Lutheran and Calvinist churches, their appellations themselves betray their allegiances.
[24] This caveat becomes the more pertinent in light of how scripture systematically describes the behavior of the "forefathers."

construct as the Judaism (*Ioudaismos*) condemned by Paul in
Galatians 1:13.

24

Scripture versus Theology

Just a few decades after the caveat Paul had issued against all Greco-Romans, "Do not boast over the branches. If you do boast, remember it is not you that support the root, but the root that supports you" (Rom 11:18), Justin the Martyr (100-165 A.D.), more à propos Justin the Philosopher, wrote apologies and dialogues at the expense of the scriptural word. In trying to counteract the Judaism of Trypho, Justin became the "founder of theology" and the father of "Christianism" that have since plagued the world. Justin made his arguments on the premise that in each of us there is a spark of the eternal *logos*. Consequently, the Greek philosophers from old were privy, albeit partially, to the *logos* that appeared in its fullness in Christ. Justin planted the seed of the ill-conceived misconception that Greek philosophy prepared the nations for Christ, just as the Old Testament did for the Jews, hence equating in value the scriptural *torah* with the Greek *sophia*, an abhorrence from the perspective of the Old Testament Writings (*ketubim*). His view was championed by the Christian school of Alexandria, and by his heirs, Clement, Origen, Athanasius, and Cyril of Alexandria, and the Cappadocians, especially Gregory of Nazianzus, who elaborated on this premise. The Greek philosophers such as Plotinus, Origen's contemporary, had a free hand to develop Plato's philosophy into religious mysticism operating exclusively in the realm of the "divine" and "eternal."

The philosophical approach to scripture distorted the original meaning of the Hebrew *'aman* and its correspondent Greek *pistevō* from the connotation of "trust; be faithful" into that of "belief" in the sense of a creed entailing both mental comprehension and expression in words formulated by us. Put otherwise, the key theological perversion of the gospel lies in using the original *pistevō* in the sense of *homologeō* (confess). The original meaning of *pistis* (usually translated as faith) is to "trust

in someone's words." The corollary of that trust is to act
according to those words, especially when they concern
behavior, as clearly asserted by Paul:

> For through the Spirit, by faith (*pisteōs*), we wait for the hope of
> righteousness. For in Christ Jesus neither circumcision nor
> uncircumcision is of any avail, but faith (*pistis*) working
> (*energoumenē*; actualizing itself; practicing the work of) through
> love. You were running well; who hindered you from obeying
> (*peithesthai*) the truth? This persuasion (*peismonē* from the same root
> as the verb *peithesthai*) is not from him who calls you. (Gal 5:5-8)[1]

Although the Greek *pistevō* and *homologeō* are distinguishable to
the ear, their Latin counterparts *confido*, whence confidence, and
confiteor (confess; avow), whence *confessio* (confession), are audibly
closer. Just as its Greek counterpart *homologeō* (confess), whence
homologēsis (confession), [2] the Latin *confiteor* is exclusively an
action of the "believer" (one who puts his confidence in) and
never of God. In other words, all "confessions of faith" are the
product of humans and are, at best, questionable and, at worst,
erroneous from the authoritative purview of scripture. Rather
than the apostolic gospel word (Gal 1:8-9) that the Apostle
received directly from God (Gal 1:1, 12; see also Jer 1:1-2, 9)
and that was handed down in the prophetic and apostolic
writings,[3] the ultimate reference that one trusts in is a confession
of belief formulated in words and ideas non-existent in
scripture. Such confessions of belief become "living oral
tradition" that is handed down through the centuries.[4] *Exposition
(Hexēgēsis; Exegesis) of the Sayings of the Lord*, a five-book opus
written by Papias, Bishop of Hierapolis (ca. 60—130 A.D.), is an
early example of oral tradition. In his preface, Papias states that

---

[1] In my discussion of these verses I have shown that the verb *peithomai* (be persuaded;
[thus] put one's trust; [thus] obey), from the verb *peithō* (persuade), occurs as synonym
of the verb *pistevō* (trust) (see *Gal* 277-81).

[2] Notice that the root of *homologeō* is from the noun *logos* (word, speech) and the verb
legein (speak, say).

[3] See Jer 36:4, 32; Gal 6:11; Lk 1:3; Jn 20:30-31; 21:24-25. See also Chrysostom's
first Homily on Matthew.

[4] See my extensive comments on this matter and its fallacy in *The Saga Continues*.

rather than relying on written texts, he relied on the memory of those he questioned who may have had some sort of connection to the apostles or elders of the early church. The scriptural criticism against the "tradition of men" expressed in their *own* non-scriptural words is evident in the endless series of negative terms based on the Greek root *log—* that pervades the Pauline literature and describes the human pervert and perverting production: *paralogia, pithanologia, genealogia, mataiologia, dialogismos, dilogia, psevdologia* (all from the same root *log—* as *logos*).

Theology, which is the lingo of every Christian group, whether church or denomination, is by definition a "perversion" (*metastrephein*; turn around, pervert; Gal 1:7) of God's gospel teaching found *in* the Old Testament *writings* propounded by God's apostle Paul (Rom 1:1-2) *in his writings*. The original Greek verb *metastrephein* used in Galatians is found only twice more in the New Testament, once in Acts, which is a quotation from Joel 3:4 (2:31 RSV), and the other in James:

> The sun shall be turned into (*metastraphēsetai*) darkness and the moon into blood, before the day of the Lord comes, the great and manifest day. (Acts 2:20)

> Be wretched and mourn and weep. Let your laughter be turned to (*metastraphētō*) mourning and your joy to dejection.[5] (Jas 4:9)

The connotation is unmistakably intended to convey a total change to the opposite. What Paul continually stresses is that the only gospel is the one formulated by him in his letters. Any other gospel is not simply another melody of the same tune, but is outright anti-gospel:

> But even if we, or an angel from heaven, should preach to you a gospel contrary to (*par' ho*)[6] that which we preached to you, let

---

[5] Even if one follows the alternate reading of *metatrapētō* from *metatrepein*, one ends up with the same result since this verb means "change mode, form, aspect."

[6] The Greek *par' ho* means "off track (to the side of)" and not necessarily "contrary." Vulgate translates it into *praeter[quam]* (to the side of, beyond), KJV translates it into "other" and JB translates into "different."

him be accursed. As we have said before, so now I say again, If any one is preaching to you a gospel contrary to (*par' ho*) that which you received, let him be accursed. (Gal 1:8-9)

To explain their endorsement of the "historical" Jesus as being the reflection, if not incarnation, of the eternal *logos*, Christian thinkers were forced to resort to the highest levels of intellectual acrobatics. In doing so, they had to coin and explain new terminology and morphology totally foreign to the scriptural world, which then became premises that were imposed unnaturally on the scriptural text and the subject of endless controversies.[7] We Christians rush to conclude that the true gospel was preserved, albeit in "other words," in the express formulation of our respective "confessions." We even go so far as to contend that our "other words" are more appropriate, if not more accurate, than the scriptural "words."[8] Below are a few examples.

- "Theology" (Greek *theologia*) and the related verb "theologize" (*theologein*) are not found in the Septuagint for the simple reason that the original Semitic does not support such a premise. In scripture God is the *subject* of the action of speaking, whereas in theology he is, willy-nilly— and in spite of all acrobatic justifications—the *object*, the subject matter talked about. In this sense, "theology" was the earliest human activity in scripture as attested to in the wordy debate about God's "word" of command among man, woman, and the serpent,[9] and the ensuing

---

[7] In this regard comes to mind the words of the Psalmist: "He who sits in the heavens laughs; the Lord has them in derision." (Ps 2:4)

[8] The argument given is that the "barbarian" Semitic language could not fully encompass the "reality of the matter" (Latin *res*).

[9] For those knowledgeable of the original scriptural language, the noun *naḥaš* translated as "serpent" has the connotation of (bad) omen, which would be the American "bad news." Such, in my conviction, is theology!

twisting thereof.[10] The epitome of theological irreverence, if not outright blasphemy, is that theology was raised to a higher level than *oikonomia* (management; [divine] plan of [salvation]).[11] Put otherwise, the main concern of scripture, which is God's dealing with us, is relegated to a "fleshly" or, at best the "soul-ly" (*psykhikon*; psychic) level, while "true" theology is reserved to the "spiritual" (*pnevmatikon*). According to Paul this is the epitome of self-deceit (1 Cor 1-3; 2 Cor 11). Put bluntly, theology as it is practiced is no better than Plotinus' fantasizing mysticism that pervaded Jewish and Christian thought throughout the centuries.

* "Trinity" (Greek *trias*) is not to be found in the LXX and yet was turned into an essential "mystery." Most of my readers are aware of the endless controversies concerning the relation between the three "persons" of the trinity, the Father, the Son, and the Holy Spirit. "Triune" is a most recent contemporary jargon that is being debated.

---

[10] So in spite of Origen's insistence that he was the "spiritual" being par excellence, in reality he was merely the "son of (the soul-ly [psychic]) Adam" par excellence. The LXX *psykhē* is the rendering of the Semitic *nepheš* (passing breath): "then the Lord God formed man of dust from the ground, and breathed into his nostrils the breath of life; and man became a living being (*nepheš*; Greek *psykhē*)." (Gen 2:7)

[11] Actually the Semitic root *dbr* whence *dabar* reflects the understanding of "leading" a flock and thus "managing" it. This meaning is evident in the Arabic verb *dabbara* (manage) and the noun *tadbir* ([factual, practical] management), the latter being the commonly accepted translation of the scriptural divine "plan" (*oikonomia*; economy). Thus the scriptural *logos*, which renders *dabar*, has nothing to do with the Greek "philosophical" *logos*. The scriptural God is, before and after all, a wise *shepherd*.

- "Becoming man"[12] (Greek *enanthrōpēsis*), referring to the second person of the Trinity, also not found in the LXX, was coined to accommodate the belief in Christ's divine "nature." Here one can see the use of not only Greek philosophy but also Greek non-LXX terminology taking precedence and imposing its exotic connotations on the scriptural text. These connotations dismiss the meaning of the actual *grammata* of scripture and replace it with a "spiritual" meaning.[13] A corollary of God's "becoming man" (Greek *enanthrōpēsis*) is man's "becoming God" or more accurately "becoming (a) god" (*theosis*), again a term not found in the LXX, let alone in the original Hebrew. In a nutshell, what was reserved for the Roman emperors, one at a time, now becomes accessible to each and every one of us through the one "emperor" Jesus Christ.

- The early Greco-Roman fathers' distortion of the original connotation of faith into a "belief" as in a "creed" culminated in the Nicene Creed:

  I believe in one God, the Father Almighty, maker of heaven and earth, and of all things visible and invisible. And in one Lord Jesus Christ, the Son of God, the only begotten, begotten of the father before all worlds. Light of Light, Very God of Very God, Begotten not made of one essence (*homoousios*; of the same essence) with the Father, by whom all things were made. Who for us men and for our salvation came down from heaven, and was incarnate of the Holy Spirit and the

---

[12] I opted for this translation over "incarnation" since the latter literally means "becoming (taking on) flesh" rather than "human being" (*anthrōpos*).

[13] See my comments on 2 Cor 3:1-3 in *C-2 Cor* 69-73 regarding the fallacy of that view.

Virgin Mary, and was made man; And was crucified also for us under Pontius Pilate, and suffered and was buried; and the third day he rose again according to the scriptures; and ascended into heaven, and sitteth at the right hand of the Father; and He shall come again with glory to judge the quick and the dead, whose kingdom shall have no end. And I believe in the Holy Spirit, the Lord and giver of life, who proceedeth from the Father, who with the Father and the Son together is worshipped and glorified, Who spake by the prophets; and I believe in One Holy Catholic and Apostolic Church, I acknowledge one baptism for the remission of sins. I look for the resurrection of the dead, and the life of the word to come.

• The introduction of *homoousios* is undeniably non-scriptural, if not outrightly anti-scriptural. The sheer impossibility of that term in any way, shape, or form being scriptural is borne out by the fact that there is no correspondent to it in the original Hebrew. The majority of the attendees at the first ecumenical Council of Nicea (325 A.D.) originally rejected *homoousios*. It was included in the Nicene Creed with the proviso that it be enveloped by an extended introduction where the Lord Jesus Christ is presented *not as God* who is exclusively the Father and the *one God* according to the preceding article, but unequivocally as the "Son of God," who is "begotten *from* (*ek*) the Father," "God *from* (*ek*) God." Subsequent theology assumes, for all intents and purposes, that the reality of the matter lies in the term *homoousios* and proceeds to explain it. Even though the entire article[14] clearly stresses the subordination of the son Jesus Christ to God the Father, for the most part, this is dealt with as simply a footnote to the non-scriptural *homoousios*.

- This infatuation with the philosophical term *ousia* in the sense of "(essential) nature" (*physis*)[15] led to the discussion of the two "natures" in (of) Christ and to the coining of the four (in)famous adverbs, *synkhytōs* (without confusion), *atreptōs* (without change), *adiaiphetōs* (without division), *akhōristōs* (without separation) to speak of those two "natures" at the Council of Chalcedon (451 A.D.), which adverbs are in turn nowhere to be found in scripture.[16] It is thus a dispute over the meaning of these words (*logomakhia*)[17] that resulted in splitting Eastern Christendom, a split that is still plaguing us in spite of many conferences that acquiesce that the difference is merely verbal and in no way material.[18] So within less than five centuries, the Pauline "gospel of obedience" (Rom 1:5; 15:18)[19] was

---

[14] "And in one Lord Jesus Christ, the Son of God, the only begotten, begotten of the father before all worlds. Light of Light, Very God of Very God, Begotten not made of one essence with the Father, by whom all things were made."

[15] The original non-philosophical connotation of *physis* is that of "nature" in the sense of comportment, which is reflected in the Arabic where the same noun *ṭabi'at* is used to speak of the character of a person as well as of the creation in the sense of the total physical nature.

[16] Besides, how many Christians are even aware of them or can pronounce them, and how many can explain, let alone justify, their functionality in their daily lives?

[17] 1 Tim 3:4.

[18] I am referring to the serious and yet non-ending attempts of Eastern Orthodox (Chalcedonian or Dyophysite [holding the belief in the two natures in Christ]) Christians and Oriental Orthodox (non-Chalcedonian or Monophysite [holding to the belief in the one divine nature of Christ]) Christians at unification.

[19] The *scriptural* (inscribed in scripture) teachings of *God* that are to be "obeyed."

metamorphosed and was "transfigured" into a creed of human words and ideas.

- In spite of all the ado regarding the contemporary adjective "ecumenical" (*oikoumenik-os*; fem. *-ē*), its original meaning is incontrovertible: pertaining to the Roman *oikoumenē*. Being Greco-Roman entailed endorsing the ethos of the Greco-Roman world, besides being impacted with Greek philosophy. The Roman *oikoumenē* (habitation) with the special place held by its emperor as social and religious figure, and its infatuation with buildings and city life, is completely the opposite of shepherd life and is criticized as anti-God in scripture. Whatever Constantine's intentions were regarding his endorsement of the Christianism of his time, that Christianism and its theology submitted totally to the Roman emperor, the quintessential nemesis of the followers of the gospel teaching in the Apocalypse. Consequently, as repeatedly upheld by many theologians, particularly the Greek Orthodox, a council or synod cannot possibly be ecumenical unless it is convened by the Roman emperor. What makes this matter pertinent is that Constantine, the not yet baptized Christian, convened the first ecumenical council in 325. That is to say, arguably the most momentous council in Christianism was convened and presided over by a pagan emperor who acted as the referee, if not judge, in matters of Christian "theology." This submission to the "God-protected" imperial authority became a staple of the Orthodox Church in its life and theology although it tried to conceal this behind a superimposed *symphonia* between the church and the empire, between the celestial and the terrestrial. The empire, we are told, was "baptized" into becoming a Christian empire. The official religion of the empire was the emperor's: *cujus regio, hujus religio* (Whose is the realm, his is the religion). The emperor even appointed the Patriarch of Constantinople who could be exiled by that same palatial authority.[20] So can one really speak of "symphony?" Even after the fall of Constantinople, the specter of the emperor persisted in the person of the Patriarch of Constantinople who donned the imperial-like garb during church services and was the recipient of the *polykhronion* (unto many years) hymn. Up to this day the Greek Orthodox and the Greek Catholic are still known as the "people of the Roman emperor": the official appellation of the Orthodox is *rum* (Romans) and that of the Catholics is "Melkites" (the kingly ones).

• This imperial prerogative of *cujus regio, hujus religio* is detectable in the case of the conversion of *Rus'* (the Russians). It was the decision of Vladimir of Kiev to endorse the religion of the Byzantine emperor that led to the baptism of all Russians to the extent that, in Orthodox tradition, Vladimir is viewed as the "evangelizer" of Russia and is honored with the title of "Equal-to-the-Apostles." The same applies to Boris I, Prince and Baptizer of Bulgaria, also "Equal-to-the-Apostles," whose baptismal name was Michael after his godfather the Byzantine emperor Michael III.

---

[20] As in the case of John Chrysostom.

Christianity did not fare better in the West. By the eighth century, Charlemagne devised the "*Holy* Roman empire" with the obvious blessing of the church. Seven centuries later, in the Iberian Peninsula, one hears of the "Catholic monarchs" Isabella I of Castille and Ferdinand II of Aragon, and of their grandson Charles V, the "*holy* Roman emperor." Ironically, this situation prevailed until the times of Luther who, in spite of his sweeping reformation, had to bow down to the rule *cujus regio, hujus religio* in order to avoid the mayhem his reformation would have produced among and within the principalities of his Germany.[21] All the ado about *sola scriptura* is mere lip service and in reality self-servicing for the reformers to assert their own views in order to justify their split from the Vatican. While trumpeting the *sola scriptura* slogan, Luther managed to write his 95 (theological) theses and his colleague Philipp Melanchthon penned his theological treatise (*loci communes*) and the "Augsburg Confession," thus imitating the Golden Age of the Byzantine Eastern Church. John Calvin, the "prince of exegetes," having engaged in many commentaries on the biblical books, could not resist writing the "Institutes of the Christian religion" which is considered by many of his followers to be his "seminal work of Protestant systematic theology." Karl Barth beat everyone else by coming up with his "Church Dogmatics," a fourteen-volume magnum opus that was published in stages from 1932 to 1967, thus making the "reformed" Barth an actual "theologian." In fact, the history of the Protestant movement has produced more "branches" than the early church and its own array of "confessions" and "assemblies," "conferences," and "conventions."

The endless and repeated efforts of theology, since the earliest centuries of Christian Alexandria, has been to justify itself on the basis of *theo-logein* (speaking divinely; uttering God) being

---

[21] This ethos still prevails in many European countries. In England the monarch is considered as the head of the "national" church and the prime minister is to be a member of the Anglican community.

equivalent to, if not the same as, *logos Theou* (word of God). The impossibility of such lies in that God is the agent and speaks his own words, whereas in theology the speaker is the human being who speaks *about* God or God's word as is evident in the phrase "Patristic theology" or "the theology of so and so." Thus all theology is human opinion as reflected in the term *dogma* (doctrine), which is from the verb *dokei* (it seems [to so and so]). In scripture, God does not "reveal" himself or a "truth" regarding himself,[22] rather he issues a command to be followed so that we would live according to his "good will" (*evdokia*; from the same root as *dokei*). The correct response of the believer to the prophetic and apostolic *written words* of God should be one of obedience since these words are essentially a *torah*, an instruction to be followed. God speaks words to the hearing of the people so that the hearers would "do" those words, and not "debate" their meaning:

> Keep my statutes, and do them; I am the Lord who sanctify you. (Lev 20:8)

> You shall therefore keep all my statutes and all my ordinances, and do them. (20:22)

> So you shall keep my commandments and do them: I am the Lord. (22:31)

> Therefore you shall do my statutes, and keep my ordinances and perform them; so you will dwell in the land securely. (25:18)

> If you walk in my statutes and observe my commandments and do them. (26:3)

> But if you will not hearken to me, and will not do all these commandments. (26:14)

> If you spurn my statutes, and if your soul abhors my ordinances, so that you will not do all my commandments, but break my covenant, I will do this to you. (26:15-16)

---

[22] See my earlier and repeated comments concerning the scriptural God's not being or having a "self" (*nepheš*; *psykhē*; soul)

All the theological acrobatics, whether mental or mystical, have nothing to do with the scriptural God who did not ask *ha'adam* (the human being) to comprehend him, but to obey his will *without contention*—as sheep would a shepherd— (Gen 2:16-17). That will is subsumed in God's own *words*: "... man (*ha'adam*) does not live by bread alone, but ... man (*ha'adam*) lives by everything that proceeds out of the mouth of the Lord." (Deut 8:3) And God's "good will" (*evdokia*; good pleasure) is unequivocal:

> Will the Lord *be pleased* with thousands of rams, with ten thousands of rivers of oil? Shall I give my first-born for my transgression, the fruit of my body for the sin of my soul?' He has showed you, O man (*'adam*), what is good; and what does the Lord require of you but to do justice, and to love kindness, and to walk humbly with your God? (Mic 6:7-8)

How could it be otherwise when it is, through God's same "will" that he decided to bruise his lamb (ewe) for the sake of us all:

> Yet it was the *will* of the Lord to bruise him; he has put him to grief; when he makes himself an offering for sin, he shall see his offspring, he shall prolong his days; the will of the Lord shall prosper in his hand; he shall see the fruit of the travail of his soul and be satisfied; by his knowledge shall the righteous one, my servant, make many to be accounted righteous; and he shall bear their iniquities. Therefore I will divide him a portion with the great, and he shall divide the spoil with the strong; because he poured out his soul to death, and was numbered with the transgressors; yet he bore the sin of many, and made intercession for the transgressors. (Is 53:10-12)

Scripture is by definition a canonized, that is, closed off, writ. It was not the church that closed this canon. It was the original authors who scripturalized their writ: Jeremiah in chapter 36, Paul in Galatians 6:11, John in 20:30-31 and 21:24-25, and Revelation in 22:18-19, all of whom followed the lead of Moses who sealed God's words into a "book."[23] This was done

---

[23] Deut 17:18; 28:58, 61; 29:20, 21, 27; 30:10; 31:24, 26; Josh 1:8.

precisely in order that it not be at the mercy of the recipients. Unfortunately historical theology, in all denominations, Christian as well as Jewish,[24] supplanted scripture with its own comments intending to sacralize tradition and thus give it a binding value equal to that of scripture. Put otherwise the "traditions of man" supplanted the "words of God." What is really sad concerning "theological ruminations" is that their concern is essentially theoretical, dealing with God or more precisely the "godhead" both in its eternal reality and its human aspect. Consider the amount of ink used to tackle immaterial issues the like of eternity, trinity, distinction between essence and energies in God, consubstantiality, the *filioque*, incarnation of the divine, relation between soul and body, what "salvation" is all about, how one is "saved," what "heaven" is, the "theology" of the icons, the difference between the icon of Christ and those of the saints, not to speak of "apophatic theology."[25] Consider Maximus the Confessor who brought Justin the Philosopher's view of the *logos*[26] to its logical end by advocating "natural theology" and thus the non-necessity of scripture. Then consider the number of hungry people who could have been fed with the cost of that ink, not to mention the expenses of national and international conferences and symposia held to debate those subjects.

Scripture is neither about God who, in scripture, is "inexistent"[27] *by design* so that we, the human beings, would not contradict with our thoughts and ways the one who unambiguously declared "my thoughts are not your thoughts, neither are your ways my ways" (Is 55:8), which are expressed through "my word that goes forth from my mouth" (v.11). This

---

[24] Just consider the place of high honor the medieval philosopher Moses Maimonides holds in Judaism. He was unequalled according to the adage "From Moses to Moses there arose none like Moses."

[25] A kind of theologizing that speaks of God in "negations"—what he is not or cannot be—because he remains beyond whatever the human being can say of him. It is mysticism brought to its extreme.

[26] Each of us has a spark of the eternal divine *logos*.

[27] In the sense of "non-egregious."

is not, even with the broadest stretch of imagination, an invitation to imitate the divine activity by appropriating God's word in order to give it an updated twist in every new generation, as though the scriptural God had an academy, as Plato did, where he would train his disciples as "theologians." Scripture does not allow any such conclusion; it prohibits it:

6Seek the Lord while he may be found, call upon him while he is near; 7let the wicked forsake his way (Heb *derek*; Gr *hodous* [ways]), and the unrighteous man his thoughts (Heb *maḥšebot* [calculations, designs]; Gr *boulas* [plans, purposes]); let him *return* (Heb *šub* [turn around, change one's behavior] Gr *epistrephō* [turn around, change direction]) to the Lord, that he may have mercy on him, and to our God, for he will abundantly pardon. 8For my thoughts (Heb *maḥšebot* [calculations, designs]; Gr *boulai* [plans, purposes]) are not your thoughts (Heb *maḥšebot* [calculations, designs]; Gr *boulai* [plans, purposes]), neither are your ways (Heb *derakim* [paths]; Gr *hodoi* [*paths*]) my ways (Heb *derakim* [paths]; Gr *hodoi* [*paths*]), says the Lord. 9For as the heavens are higher than the earth, so are my ways (Heb *derakim* [paths]; Gr *hodos* [*path*]) higher than your ways (Heb *derakim* [paths]; Gr *hodōn* [*paths*]) and my thoughts (Heb *maḥšebot* [calculations, designs]; Gr *dianoēmata* [thoughts]) than your thoughts (Heb *maḥšebot* [calculations, designs]; Gr *dianoias* [mind, understanding]). 10For as the rain and the snow come down from heaven, and return not thither but water the earth, making it bring forth and sprout, giving seed to the sower and bread to the eater, 11so shall my word be that goes forth from my mouth; it shall not return to me empty, but it shall accomplish that which I purpose (Heb *haphaṣ* Gr *thelō*), and *prosper* (Heb *hiṣliaḥ*; make correct) *in the thing for which I sent it* (Gr *evodōsō tas hodous sou kai entalmata mou*; I shall set on the path of success your paths and my commandments). 12For you shall go out in joy, and be led forth in peace; the mountains and the hills before you shall break forth into singing, and all the trees of the field shall clap their hands. 13Instead of the thorn shall come up the cypress; instead of the brier shall come up the myrtle; and it shall be to the Lord for a memorial (Heb *šem* [name, fame], Gr *onoma* [name]), for an everlasting sign which shall not be cut off. (Is 55)

Except for the inveterate theologians who read their respective
"theologies" into the original, the intention of the above passage
is plain: God expects his followers to walk the path that is willed
by him, regardless of their mental (philosophical) perception of
that will.[28] It is precisely Adam's mental perception of God's
direct commandment that got him and us in trouble. The bias
against Greek philosophy is evident in the phrasing of v.11b *by
the same authors of both the original and the LXX* where (1) the paths
of the hearers and the commandments of the Lord are one and
the same reality and (2) they are both the result of the divine
action that is expressed through the verb *ev[h]odoō* coined from
the same root as *hodos* (path) underscoring that the divine
commandments pertain not to theological teaching, but rather
are aimed at behavior. The subordination of the Greek to the
scriptural Hebrew is detectable even in the New Testament that
was originally written in Greek. Paul's teaching to his Gentiles
about "walking" according to the dictates of the Spirit, rather
than doing the desires of the flesh in Galatians, are recast in
Romans in a phraseology that betrays his teaching developed in
the Corinthian correspondence against Greek philosophy that
gives the upper hand to mental cogitation over action:[29]

> But I say, walk (*peripateite*) by the Spirit, and do not gratify the
> desire (*epithymian*) of the flesh. For the flesh desires (*epithymei*)
> against the Spirit, and the Spirit (is) against the flesh; for these are

---

[28] This is confirmed in Ezekiel where the gathering of the scattered is aimed at their
following God's commandments that they had broken, which disobedience resulted
in their being scattered (11:17-20; 36:24-27).

[29] In this regard it is worth pointing out that the Romans' taking over Greek
philosophy by translating it into Latin proved to be a smart move, since it allowed
them to concentrate on constructing roads and aqueducts and on developing a legal
system that dealt with action rather than cogitation. My readers are reminded that
Paul upheld his Roman heritage while heavily criticizing the Hellenes. He attacked
Caesar and the imperial power but never the Roman way of life, In writing to
residents of the Roman colony Philippi, he actually gave it as an example to follow:
"Finally, brethren, whatever is true, whatever is honorable, whatever is just, whatever
is pure, whatever is lovely, whatever is gracious, if there is any excellence, if there is
anything worthy of praise, think about these things." (4:8).

opposed to each other, to prevent you from doing (*poiēte*) what you would.[30] (Gal 5:16-17)

> For God has done what the law, weakened by the flesh, could not do: sending his own Son in the likeness of sinful flesh and for sin, he condemned sin in the flesh, in order that the just requirement of the law might be fulfilled in us, who walk (*peripatousin*) not according to the flesh but according to the Spirit. For those who live (*ontes*; are) according to the flesh set their minds on (*phronousin*; are mindful of) the things of the flesh, but those (who live)[31] according to the Spirit (set their minds)[32] on the things of the Spirit. (For)[33] To set the mind on (*to phronēma*; the way of thinking of) the flesh is death, but to set the mind on (*to phronēma*; the way of thinking of) the Spirit is life and peace. For the mind that is set on (*to phronēma*; the way of thinking of) the flesh is hostile to God; *it does not submit to God's law*, indeed it cannot; and those who are (*ontes*) in the flesh cannot please God. (Rom 8:3-8)

It is immediately noticeable that the (manner of) "being," reflected in the original *ontes* (from the verb *einai* [be]) points to two different actions: "walking" according to a set of precepts[34] or "thinking, cogitating" (in order to decide which way to follow). However, just as in Galatians, by starting with the scriptural verb *peripateō*—the LXX rendering of the original scriptural Hebrew *halak*, the classic verb used with "way/s" (*derek/derakim*; *hodos/hodoi*) in the Old Testament—Paul is subordinating human thought, with which we choose, to the

---

[30] My translation. RSV's rendering is one of its most disastrous perversions, leveling the Spirit of God with the human flesh by describing both as having "desires;" whereas, Paul is linking the element "desire" (*epithymia*), which is negative in scripture, exclusively with the flesh in v.16: "But I say, walk by the Spirit, and do not gratify the desires of the flesh. For the desires of the flesh are against the Spirit, and the desires of the Spirit are against the flesh; for these are opposed to each other, to prevent you from doing what you would." (Gal 5:16-17 RSV)

[31] Not in the original.

[32] Not in the original.

[33] In the original (*gar*).

[34] Which fits both scriptural law and Roman law, however in this case it is the scriptural divine law, that is to say, the law of the one under whose aegis Roman authorities govern (Rom 13:1-7).

divine thought that is expressed in terms of dictates showing the path for us to follow which does not allow any option.

But one may ask, "Have we not been granted by God the *liberum arbitrium* (freedom of choice)? Are we to be submissive sheep and not "reasonable" sheep as the text of the baptismal service says?" First of all, *liberum arbitirum* is nowhere to be found in scripture, let alone condoned by God. Second of all, sheep are by definition submissive precisely because they are dumb; the only sound they can utter is "baa" and even then they have no choice but to follow the "voice" of the shepherd who alone has a say in matters concerning the flock. That is why, *in scripture*, the humans, including Israel, are not the "free" people of God. They have remained all along the wandering and thus lost sheep until the end of the scriptural story when the obedient sheep, that is to say, *as (dumb) flock*, will *become* God's people and he *becomes* their God:

> And I will give them one heart, and put a new spirit within them; I will take the stony heart out of their flesh and give them a heart of flesh, that they may walk in my statutes and keep my ordinances and obey them; and they shall be my people, and I will be their God. (Ezek 11:19-20)

> And they shall bear their punishment—the punishment of the prophet and the punishment of the inquirer shall be alike—that the house of Israel may go no more astray from me, nor defile themselves any more with all their transgressions, but that they may be my people and I may be their God, says the Lord God. (14:10-11)

> And I will provide for them prosperous plantations so that they shall no more be consumed with hunger in the land, and no longer suffer the reproach of the nations. And they shall know that I, the Lord their God, am with them, and that they, the house of Israel, are my people, says the Lord God. And you are my sheep, the sheep of my pasture, and I am your God, says the Lord God. (34:29-31)

> They shall not defile themselves any more with their idols and their detestable things, or with any of their transgressions; but I

will save them from all the backslidings in which they have
sinned, and will cleanse them; and they shall be my people, and
I will be their God. My servant David shall be king over them;
and they shall all have one shepherd. They shall follow my
ordinances and be careful to observe my statutes. They shall
dwell in the land where your fathers dwelt that I gave to my
servant Jacob; they and their children and their children's
children shall dwell there for ever; and David my servant shall be
their prince for ever. I will make a covenant of peace with them;
it shall be an everlasting covenant with them; and I will bless them
and multiply them, and will set my sanctuary in the midst of them
for evermore. My dwelling place shall be with them; and I will be
their God, and they shall be my people. Then the nations will
know that I the Lord sanctify Israel, when my sanctuary is in the
midst of them for evermore. (37:23-28)

In spite of the *plain* meaning of scripture that can be both
heard and understood by all, Christians and Jews have been,
still are, and will forever remain debating who God's people
are,[35] thus indicting themselves under Ezekiel's judgment:

And he said to me, "Son of man, I send you to the people of
Israel, to a nation of rebels, who have rebelled against me; they

---

[35] As for us Orthodox, we shall continue to approach scripture from the sacred
theology of the "tradition of man" established by our church fathers, and the closer
to our own times the "father" is, the more authoritative he is. We hail Maximus the
Confessor and his *logos* theology as the "updated" voice of Justin and Origen. We hail
Symeon the New[er] Theologian and his mysticism as the "more recent" voice of
Gregory the Theologian and even of John the (Evangelist) Theologian. We hail
Gregory Palamas with his distinction between the essence and the energies of God as
the master of Orthodox theological symphony of all the "fathers." It is no wonder
that Orthodox seminary students take a short cut by reading as authoritative
Vladimir Lossky's twentieth century "the Mystical Theology of the Eastern Church"
and live in the mystical clouds of their imaginations instead of listening repeatedly
until the end of days—and teaching others to do so (Mt 5:17-20)—to the words of
the scroll written by the hand of the One who alone speaks out of his scriptural, not
mystical, cloud (Ezek 1-2). However, here again the mystic Orthodox will retort with
their *merkabah* "theology," insisting that it is shared by Jewish scholars. And the cycle
will go on and on in spite of my repeated insistence that mysticism is a (fourth
monotheistic) religion of its own, besides Judaism, Christianity, and Islam, the proof
thereof being that Jewish, Christian, and Muslim mystics speak the *exact same*
language and even refer to, if not even quote, one another.

and their fathers have transgressed against me to this very day."
(2:3)

And he said to me, "Son of man, go, get you to the house of Israel,
and speak with my words to them. For you are not sent to a
people of foreign speech and a hard language, but to the house of
Israel -- not to many peoples of foreign speech and a hard
language, whose words you cannot understand. Surely, if I sent
you to such, they would listen to you. But the house of Israel will
not listen to you; for they are not willing to listen to me; because
all the house of Israel are of a hard forehead and of a stubborn
heart." (3:4-7)

Congregations and Churches

Both Jews and Christians have applied the two scriptural terms
reflecting human congregations—synagogue (Hebrew *'edah*;
Greek *synagōgē*) and church (Hebrew *qahal*; Greek *ekklēsia*)—to
two kinds of man-made buildings. The disciples of Christ have
produced, developed, and maintained a so-called "Christian"
architecture[36] of which they feel proud and unabashedly
advertise it as being "for God's great glory," while this same
God has unequivocally stated for the ages:

> Heaven is my throne and the earth is my footstool; what is the
> house which you would build for me, and what is the place of my
> rest? All things my hand has made, and so all these things
> are mine, says the Lord. But this is the man to whom I will look,
> he that is humble and contrite in spirit, and trembles at my word.
> (Is 66:1-2)

Paul's communities gathered in Roman households that were
referred to as "house churches" (*kat' oikon ekklēsiai*). Granted
some of those houses were ornate, but they were there and
Paul's followers did not build them; they, as "church," just used
them. Their gatherings were meals of "gratitude" (*evkharistia*) for
the "grace" (*kharis*) bestowed on them through the scriptural

---

[36] I recall having taken at seminary a full semester course on Christian architecture
as part of the Masters in Theology program.

"words" as "bread of life," and in no way mysterious religious meals where the flesh and blood of the deity were consumed. At the occasion of the gathering, what took place was the "remembrance" (*anamnēsis*) that God's messenger gave his life for the cause of spreading those words of life among the Gentiles.[37] It was not his death that gave the congregants life, but his words of teaching that are the "bread for life" (Jn 6:68).[38] It is sad that the Pauline tradition that upheld the centrality of the Roman households while criticizing the "deification" (*apotheosis*) of the emperor was reversed. In the stone churches of his empire that are built with his permission and blessing, the "Christian" leader/emperor is honored on a special seat.[39] As for the contemporary Christian *oikoumenē* (ecumenicalism) just consider the non-ending list of meetings of the World Council of Churches whose aim, it is said, is to show the rest of the world the essential unity among the Christians. There is no need to comment or even criticize its endeavors especially in this age where every tiny parish has its own website that is used essentially to "show off" under the guise of propagating "the faith." This is evident from the mere and understandable fact that no website speaks ill of itself. The smallest website puts to shame the pride of emperor Justinian who built a most impressive shrine, Hagia Sophia, in honor of God's eternal wisdom—wisdom that built for itself a house in the scriptural heavens once and for all. Compare the approach of contemporary Christian websites to the 1500 page "scriptural

---

[37] See my comments on 1 Cor 11:23-26 in *C-Cor* 204-12.

[38] That is why, in the Orthodox church even crosses and icons are blessed with the Gospel Book, whereas the Gospel Book itself is never blessed or consecrated: it is the bestower of blessings. All sacramental services start with the words "Blessed is the Kingdom of the Father and the Son and the Holy Spirit" while the celebrant is holding the Gospel Book with which he performs the blessing of the "fellowship table."

[39] The now "Christian" emperor still lives after 1543 not only in the person of the Patriarch of Constantinople but also in that of every Orthodox bishop during church ceremonies.

website" that incessantly speaks *ill* about its own people and their buildings, and does so in divine statements, to boot.

Scripture is about walking correctly (*orthopodoun*; Gal 2:14) while on the "way" (path; Hebrew *derek*; Greek *hodos*) by correctly practicing (*orthopraxis*, from the verb *prassein* [practicing]) and doing (*poiein*; Rom 1:32-2:3) what is defined and delineated in the Law. "Membership" in God's people will be assessed against such practice on judgment day. Much ado about *orthodoxy* (correct opinion), which by definition is creedal formulations of the human mind, is immaterial at best and blasphemous at its worse. Put otherwise, while God is imposing upon us a way of living, we spend time assessing him and giving our opinion of him, that is, giving a true (definition of the) godhead. Unfortunately, this view stamped the Eastern churches, especially the Orthodox church to which I pertain. In spite of the tendency of its constituent autocephalous communities to be national,[40] the liturgical and the monastic life of the church are, by and large, if not in detail, uniform. An Orthodox monastic would feel at home anywhere in the Orthodox world in the same way an Orthodox believer would feel at ease in any liturgy in the Orthodox world in spite of the difference in language.[41]

A striking feature of the Orthodox church is that its theology and ethos (way of living) are impacted by mysticism. The ethos of Orthodox monastic life revolves around the "rich" and multi-faceted liturgical cycle of services through and in which human life is sanctified. This ethos itself is superseded with a higher

---

[40] Witness the chasm between theory and practice. The Orthodox maintain that a church may not be national; *phyletism* (nationalism) was even condemned at a synod convened at Constantinople in 1872. Still, while the older Patriarchates are known by the name of a city (Constantinople, Alexandria, Antioch, Jerusalem), as in the New Testament, the more recent Patriarchates use the national appellation: Russian Orthodox Church (despite the fact that its official title is Patriarchate of Moscow), Romanian Orthodox Church, Serbian Orthodox Church, Bulgarian Orthodox Church, Greek Orthodox Church.

[41] Orthodox believers cognizant of their services can "guess" where the service is at and what the rubrics are saying.

level of introversion whereby the individual leaves the monastic communal life and seeks union with the "intangible divine" in isolation and thus does not even partake of the Eucharist, which pertains after all to the "tangible" realm in that it needs bread and wine, whereas the ultimate aim of "theosis" does not. This monastic ethos pervaded the life of the Orthodox parishes where the main "business," if not "order of business," revolves around the celebration of and participation in the church "services" above all other kind of "services."[42] Its theology and liturgical life is often recalled with statements that are basically unscriptural. We frequently hear statements similar to the following:

- The "living" tradition of the Orthodox church preserves the "spirit" of scripture. The Orthodox church is (the extension of) Christ (through the centuries) if not Christ is the church.

- The church is the Kingdom of heaven here and now.

- One experiences salvation in the liturgical life of the church.[43]

---

[42] This, by the way, opened wide the door for commerce on the back of holy things as prohibited by the prophets. I am aware that, in the Old World, many have made their "business' to build up such businesses. But none of them topped the endeavor in the "New World" where, in order to promote the business, a confectioner of priestly garments wrote a book about the "theology" of the material used in such confections and how the more expensive material reflects the higher level of sanctity. In a way this was to be expected in a tradition where the bishop dons the imperial garb of the Roman-Byzantine emperor in no less of a lengthy "service" before the beginning of the liturgy!

[43] Our Lord, who will judge all nations (Mt 25:31-46), commands: "And in praying do not heap up empty phrases (*battalogēsēte*; use vain repetitions) as the Gentiles do; for they think that they will be heard for their many words. Do not be like them, for your Father knows what you need before you ask him." (6:7-8) One wonders how a pious Orthodox who attends all the services during Great Lent would still find time to feed the hungry and visit the sick, especially after working 40 hours or more at a full-time job.

- It is the recitation of the Nicene Creed, the expression of true faith, which entitles one for communion.[44]

- The aim of life is to experience "theosis," which is to become (like) God.[45]

Similar to the mission of other religious dominations, the mission in the Orthodox church is to have the others "join" or—more diplomatically put—be received into it, or— more sophisticatedly put—be received into the Orthodox faith.[46] The success of the mission is measured against the number of converts. However, such an approach falls under Paul's harsh criticism in Galatians.[47] One does not express one's faith through the adoption of a creed or a confession of belief, but rather through a life "lived" as an expression of the one "fruit" of the Spirit (Gal 5:22). Actually, leaving one's church or denomination for another church or denomination is often pointless since leaving is usually done for reasons that have nothing to do with the will of God.[48]

My hope is that some of my readers will engage directly with scripture without referring to the "tradition of men." The ultimate challenge is living one's life according to the rules of the scriptural judgment detailed not only in Matthew 25 and Paul's letters, but also detailed repeatedly throughout the Law and the Prophets.

---

[44] It is not so much the Lord's prayer that was recited before table fellowship more than 250 years before Nicaea.

[45] Scripturally, we should be doing God's will expressed in his *commandment* words and inviting others, all others, to abide by them.

[46] It often uses theological statements mentioned previously to extol its exaltedness.

[47] "It is those who want to make a good showing in the flesh that would compel you to be circumcised, and only in order that they may not be persecuted for the cross of Christ. For even those who receive circumcision do not themselves keep the law, but they desire to have you circumcised that they may glory in your flesh." (Gal 6:12-13)

[48] To be convinced, just read and re-read Ezekiel 16, 20 and 23 once a week during the year and once a day during Great Lent.

25

Toward a Solution to the Dilemma

Civilizations, East, West, Far East and Far West (the Americas)—with the exception of Mongolia—revolved around cities and especially its buildings. Although these were a staple of the scriptural authors' world, the scripture they wrote harshly criticized anything built by the human beings, especially majestic structures. Majestic buildings are meant to be "writings" in stone, extolling human beings to quasi-divine, if not outright divine, stature. All major edifices erected by humans have texts explaining the reason behind and the function of such structures. The superiority of writing over building is evident in that writing is lasting without the need of a building. Although libraries are helpful to preserve the literary works, still they are not necessary per se.[1] This explains the uniquely scriptural "self-destruct mode" twist. Not only does scripture "level down" temples and palaces, but also, and most unexpectedly, the value of any "human" literature. A first time reader of scripture will be struck by the repetitiously boring insistence that the worldly deeds and accomplishments of any and all monarchs of Israel and Judah are of no concern to the scriptural authors and are relegated to the "Annals" or "(Books of the) Chronicles" of those kings.[2] The only matter the authors are concerned with is those kings' "sin of disobedience" against God's will inscribed in the Law of Moses. What is literally over the top and an intentional setup is the authors' *damnatio memoriae* (total damning of the memory unto oblivion) stance since the palaces of Samaria and Jerusalem, together with their libraries that housed the Kingly Chronicles, were either destroyed or looted; at any rate, the so-called Kingly Annals mentioned—yet never quoted—in scripture are nowhere to be found outside it.

---

[1] Contemporary electronics have shown this, although they can be viewed as electronic buildings since they are made by the hands of man.
[2] No less than thirty three times in 1 and 2 Kings.

This scriptural feature in and of itself stands as a condemning sword of Damocles over the heads of theologians and biblical archaeologists. Both look for an actuality or an artifact when, intentionally, the scriptural authors relegate all such realities to oblivion, even if they existed.[3] Millions, if not billions, of dollars have been spent trying to resurrect a past the scriptural authors were aware of and yet condemned to oblivion. My readers are reminded of what I stressed before: the authors were the elite of the heirs of the most impressive multi-millennial civilization of the time, and yet they were dynamiting that civilization at its roots when they lumped under the same divine judgment not only Israel and Judah but Nineveh and Babylon as well. Scripture unequivocally describes to us the scenario of the (last) judgment of *all* nations (Mt 25:31-46) where knowledge of any kind as well as prayer and fasting will not even be in the picture. What will be in the picture is how one cared for the sick and needy. Those millions of dollars spent trying to resurrect the past would have been better used to take care of those millions who are hungry, thirsty, strangers, naked, sick and in prison (v.44-45).

Since the scriptural story or narrative is sui generis it stands on its own ground regardless of its value. It presents itself as incontrovertibly absolutely authoritative:

---

[3] I would not be surprised if someone unearthed the remains of Aesop's hare and tortoise in Greece. Actually my comment is not as facetious as it sounds given the reception among scholars of the work of the "world renowned" archaeologist and New Testament scholar Sir William Ramsay on the historical "veracity" of Paul's letters and Luke's Acts. I am taking Sir Ramsay's assertions with a grain of salt assuming that he is referring to the authors of that fictional "literature." That those authors were cognizant of the geography of Asia Minor and its then history cannot possibly be debated. However, to take the leap and assert that what they wrote was a factual rendering of actual events is equivalent to saying that given the accuracy with which Mark Twain described the mores of Henry VIII's London, his "the Prince and the Pauper" is relating factual events down to the look-alikes using the seal of the monarchy as a nut cracker!

- It purports that the exclusively sole functional deity that judges not only humans but also all other deities (Ps 82) issued its detailed will on a wilderness mountain, away from both Egypt with its fortress cities and the scriptural Canaan with its temples and palaces in the region of the Two Rivers.

- Furthermore it purports that in addition to Israel and Judah God's will is to be heeded by citizens of all kingdoms (Am 1-2) including Assyria and Babylonia and the nations of the far away coastlands, i.e., Greece (Gen 10; Is 42:4-10; 49:1; 51:5; 60:9; 66:19).

- In the Prophets—Latter as well as Prior—it purports (1) that the divine law issued in the wilderness was systematically contravened in Israel and Judah to whom that law was entrusted, and (2) because they contravened the law Israel and Judah were doomed by the scriptural deity.

- In the Writings (*ketubim*), that same scripture is inviting the remnant of Israel and Judah, scattered among the nations, to gather in congregations to hear the Law of Moses in order that it be followed by all, since it contains the true wisdom sought after by those nations "to the close of the age" (Mt 28:20).

Put otherwise, this canonized—that is, totally closed off— narrative is *not* to be continued or stretched out through human writings and examples generation after generation.[4] Rather it is to be proclaimed **as is** time and again. By "as is" I mean without chapters and verses, let alone comments on oral

---

[4] Doing so would be contravening Psalm 78:1-8 and Ezekiel 2:3.

tradition.[5] This matter was—and thus should have been—
settled once for all by John Chrysostom in his preamble to his
first homily on Matthew and the entire New Testament.
Scripture is the granter of the life spoken of *in it* for those who
are interested—not in "life" but—*in that life* described *in it* (Rev
22:17-19). The scriptural future is already contained and sealed
in scripture itself and does not lie somewhere ahead. Neither does
the scriptural "coming" kingdom lie somewhere up there or
ahead. Rather this kingdom is contained in the "parables of the
kingdom" as laid down in the Gospels. The Christian Orthodox
hear at every liturgy:

> *Remembering (Memnēmenoi*; Having in remembrance), therefore this
> saving commandment and *all those things (pantōn) which have come to
> pass (gegenēmenōn)* for us: the Cross, the Grave, the Resurrection on
> the third day, the Ascension into heaven, the Session at the right
> hand, *and the second and glorious Advent (parousias*; coming again)…

How could one possibly remember Christ's Parousia, which
Paul insists has not come yet, as purported "by spirit, word, or
letter" (2 Thess 2:2), unless that Parousia has been spoken of—
written about—in scripture and thus heard of by the believers,
along with all the other events consigned therein? The same
applies to the so-called person of Jesus Christ. In the Orthodox
Church during the "entrance," the Gospel Book is held high by
the deacon proclaiming, "This is (the) wisdom (of God), let all
stand aright and be attentive (to its teaching)." The
congregation then replies: "Come let us worship and bow down
before Christ." In other words, the Book and (the "person" of)
Christ—conversely Christ *as person*—are functionally
equivalent, just as are the teaching and the teacher. If you
reminisce anything else besides your teacher's *teaching*, then you
are not reminiscing that person, but rather at best *your*

---

[5] This is precisely what is done during our services regardless of whether those
readings are followed by sermons and comments or not. Often the reading itself is so
clear in its condemnation that the congregation leaders try to soften the blow in order
to outbid God with their own "compassion" and "righteousness," that is, in doing
exactly what Jesus Christ said they would do in Matthew 23.

relationship and at worst *your* infatuation with that person. In scripture when told his family was asking to see him, Jesus pointed out his *actual* "family":

> While he was still speaking to the people, behold, his mother and his brothers stood outside, asking to speak to him. But he replied to the man who told him, "Who is my mother, and who are my brothers?" And stretching out his hand toward his disciples, he said, "Here are my mother and my brothers! For whoever does the will of my Father in heaven is my brother, and sister, and mother." (Mt 12:46-50)

> And his mother and his brothers came; and standing outside they sent to him and called him. And a crowd was sitting about him; and they said to him, "Your mother and your brothers are outside, asking for you." And he replied, "Who are my mother and my brothers?" And looking around on those who sat about him, he said, "Here are my mother and my brothers! Whoever does the will of God is my brother, and sister, and mother." (Mk 3:31-35)

> Then his mother and his brothers came to him, but they could not reach him for the crowd. And he was told, "Your mother and your brothers are standing outside, desiring to see you." But he said to them, "My mother and my brothers are those who hear the word of God and do it." (Lk 8:19-21)

In other words, according to Jesus, those who are his "family" are those—whoever they might be—who hear his *teaching*, which is God's word wherein lies his *will*. That is precisely why hearing is not enough, but *doing* what the divine will requires is of the essence. Theologians err whenever they hear Jesus in order to formulate their own confessional creeds concerning him. Instead of holding in esteem his authoritative teaching and recognizing him as their master and doing his bidding, they view him as their servant. So instead of sitting at the feet of "the teacher" in order to listen to him, as Mary did (Lk 10:39; Jn 11:28-29), and then relaying his *teaching as inscribed in scripture* to others, they pontificate about his "person" in order that the hearers praise *their* teaching, if not their mind and even their *person*.

The personification of the self and, by extension, the personification of the characters in the scriptural story pervaded theological endeavors across Christendom to the extent that the original words of scripture were rephrased, using the justification "to make it more understandable" to the reader/hearer. Doing so rendered the scriptural God in need of an interpreter, just as the Greek and Roman deities needed Hermes or Mercury to convey their thoughts to humans.[6] A classic example of such rephrasing is found in the RSV translation of Romans 2:17-23 that contravenes not only the original Greek, but also the Latin and even KJV translations:

> But if you call yourself a Jew and rely upon the law and *boast in God* (RSV changes this to *"boast of your relation to God"*) and know his will and approve what is excellent, because you are instructed in the law, and if you are sure that you are a guide to the blind, a light to those who are in darkness, a corrector of the foolish, a teacher of children, having in the law the embodiment of knowledge and truth—you then who teach others, will you not teach yourself? While you preach against stealing, do you steal? You who say that one must not commit adultery, do you commit adultery? You who abhor idols, do you rob temples? You who *boast in the law*, do you dishonor God by breaking the law? (Rom 2:17-23)

Verses 17 and 23 that bracket the passage are clearly intended to underscore the fact that, for a Jew, the non-iconic deity is co-extensive, if not equivalent, with the Law. This intention is evident in the original where in both cases one hears *kavkhasai en* (boast in).[7] However, RSV personalized God by presenting him as one with whom the Jew has a *relationship* when compared with

---

[6] Notice how the theological field or concern called "hermeneutics" is coined after Hermes.

[7] See Vulgate (*gloriaris in*, in both cases), KJV (boast of, in both cases) and JB (*te glorifies en Dieu; te glorifies dans la Loi*—the prepositions *"en"* and *"dans"* have the same value in that both mean "in").

the *soullessness* of the Law. This obviously appeals to Christians whose "soul" has been programmed to imagine that there is a spark of the divine within it when, in fact, scripturally speaking, the human "soul" is of the same consistency as that of the animal (Gen 1). The scriptural Paul, however, is concerned with God's judgment of *all,* and it is the Law that is the instrument of divine judgment unto blessing as well as curse (Lev 26; Deut 28) for both Jews and Gentiles. This is precisely what he said in Romans:

> Therefore you have no excuse, O man, whoever you are, when you judge another; for in passing judgment upon him you condemn yourself, because you, the judge, are doing the very same things. We know that the judgment of God rightly falls upon those who do such things. Do you suppose, O man, that when you judge those who do such things and yet do them yourself, you will escape the judgment of God? Or do you presume upon the riches of his kindness and forbearance and patience? Do you not know that God's kindness is meant to lead you to repentance? But by your hard and impenitent heart you are storing up wrath for yourself on the day of wrath when God's righteous judgment will be revealed. For he will render to every man according to his works: to those who by patience in well-doing seek for glory and honor and immortality, he will give eternal life; but for those who are factious and do not obey the truth, but obey wickedness, there will be wrath and fury. There will be tribulation and distress for every human being who does evil, the Jew first and also the Greek, but glory and honor and peace for every one who does good, the Jew first and also the Greek. For (*gar*) God shows no partiality. (2:1-11)

Notice how Paul *justifies,* through the conjunction "for" (*gar*) at the end of verse 11, God's impartiality in his judgment of all (vv.1-10). Still what is most important in this regard is that Paul explains, through the same conjunction "for" (*gar*)[8] at the start of the following section (vv.12-16), how God goes about his impartial judgment:

---

[8] Unfortunately omitted in RSV.

(For) All who have sinned without the law will also perish without the law, and all who have sinned under the law will be judged by the law. For it is not the hearers of the law who are righteous before God, but the doers of the law who will be justified. When Gentiles who have not the law do by nature what the law requires, they are a law to themselves, even though they do not have the law. They show that what the law requires is written on their hearts, while their conscience also bears witness and their conflicting thoughts accuse or perhaps excuse them on that day when, according to my gospel, God judges the secrets of men by Christ Jesus. (Rom 2:12-16)

Paul clearly appeals to the legal principle *ignorantia juris non excusat* (ignorance of the law excuses not) after having stressed earlier that mere knowledge of the Law, without its practice, is insufficient as well (1:32-2:5). So the bottom line is that the key feature at judgment is whether or not one *has done* God's will embedded in the text of the Law, and through the gospel (of God) that Paul is preaching (1:1-2), it has become applicable to "all men" (2:16). This is precisely why he made it his "ambition to preach the gospel where Christ has *not* been named already" (15:20) so that "They shall see who have never been told of him, and they shall understand who have never heard of him" (v.21). He was assigned "to bring about the obedience of faith for the sake of his name among all the nations" (1:5), with an "obligation both to Greeks and to barbarians, both to the wise and to the foolish" (v.14).

Scripture was conceived as self-sufficient and authoritative over and above the minds and the hearts of humans. According to Matthew, the humans do not know the secrets of their own hearts, and it is God who will reveal those secrets on judgment day. Even when both the sheep and the goats will confess—per scripture—that they were not "aware" of their actions, they will still be accountable for those actions. The reason behind the accountability is that the scriptural God is *the* righteous judge:[9]

---

[9] The defining aspect of God is neither his eternity nor his fatherhood, as is usually stressed in Orthodox as well as other theologies, but that he is the righteous judge.

"The Lord reigns; let the earth rejoice; let the many coastlands be glad! Clouds and thick darkness are round about him; *righteousness and justice are the foundation of his throne.*" (Ps 97:1-2; see also Ps 82 and Gen 3[10]) That divine feature is so much of the essence that Paul is forced to unequivocally declare that without it there would be no hope for the world (Rom 3:1-5). The primary intent of scripture is to lead the hearers to the path of righteousness and have them *walk* on that path by listening and submitting to scripture's instruction. The bottom line in and from the scriptural perspective is not so much hearing the Law as it is doing its commands.[11] Notice how teaching comes second to doing in Jesus' Sermon on the Mount:

> For truly, I say to you, till heaven and earth pass away, not an iota, not a dot, will pass from the law until all is accomplished. Whoever then relaxes one of the least of these commandments and teaches men so, shall be called least in the kingdom of heaven; but he who does them and teaches them shall be called great in the kingdom of heaven. For I tell you, unless your righteousness exceeds that of the scribes and Pharisees,[12] you will never enter the kingdom of heaven. (Mt 5:18-20)

Paul carried that same scriptural message to the Gentiles when he totally discarded the understanding of faith as a creed to be boastfully recited instead of understanding it as divine instruction to be followed. At the outset of 1 Thessalonians Paul equates faith with love in that both have to be shown through action: "We give thanks to God always for you all, constantly mentioning you in our prayers, remembering before our God

---

[10] See earlier my comments on that chapter.

[11] During a debate between two former students of mine one asked, "If at the judgment someone who was never cognizant of scripture and, moreover, 'does not believe in God,' is found having done what the 'sheep' did in Matthew 25, would that person pass muster and be welcomed into the kingdom?" The other answered, "Absolutely. How else could it be?" The retort was, "So what is your problem with Father Paul's take on scripture that it is presenting us with the instruction of the—scripturally speaking—'inexistent' God? And why would you insist that belief in his existence is necessary?"

[12] That is, those assigned to "teach."

and Father your *work* (*ergou*) of faith and *labor* (*kopou*) of love and steadfastness of hope in our Lord Jesus Christ."[13] (1:2-3) Elsewhere he says the same thing, intrinsically linking faith and love as two sides of the same coin: "For in Christ Jesus neither circumcision nor uncircumcision is of any avail, but faith working through love." (Gal 5:6) In the following verse he uses the verb "running" (the race) which corresponds to the "walking" in the way of the Law which is to be obeyed: "You were running well; who hindered you from obeying the truth?" (v.7). A few verses later he refers to the expression of love as "walking" according to God's spirit: "For the whole law is fulfilled in one word, 'You shall love your neighbor as yourself.' But if you bite and devour one another take heed that you are not consumed by one another. But I say, walk by the Spirit, and do not gratify the desires of the flesh." (vv.14-16) Put otherwise, at the last judgment God will not inquire about how correctly we intellectually fathomed him with our own words and thoughts. Rather he will check on the microchip he had, unbeknown to us, inserted in our feet to check on the miles we shall have "walked" to visit the hungry, thirsty, strangers, naked, sick and those in prison.

Even a cursive hearing of scripture will reveal that its teaching keeps in check the arrogance and the self-righteousness of the recipients of that teaching who are systematically portrayed as rebellious and disobedient. In Matthew we hear Jesus saying: "The scribes and the Pharisees sit on Moses' seat; so practice and observe whatever they tell you, but not what they do; for they preach, but do not practice." (23:2-3) Most of us look for a cheap way out of complying with that teaching, and end up behaving like the Pharisee of the parable (Lk 18:10-14). We Orthodox Christians love the Feast of Pascha, and are proud of our fasting and prayer during Great Lent. Yet each year the

---

[13] Both work and labor qualify Paul's own activity as apostle (see 1 Cor 4:12, e.g.). See below on the equalization between the apostle and his "children" when it comes to God's gift and calling.

words of the Paschal sermon put the toilers from the first hour on par with those who come just for Easter at the eleventh hour:

If any be a devout lover of God, let him partake with gladness from this fair and radiant feast. If any be a faithful servant, let him enter rejoicing into the joy of his Lord. If any have wearied himself with fasting, let him now enjoy his reward. If any have labored from the first hour, let him receive today his rightful due. If any have come after the third, let him celebrate the feast with thankfulness. If any have come after the sixth, let him not be in doubt, for he will suffer no loss. If any have delayed until the ninth, let him not hesitate but draw near. If any have arrived only at the eleventh, let him not be afraid because he comes so late. For the Master is generous and accepts the last even as the first. He gives rest to him who comes at the eleventh hour in the same way as him who has labored from the first. He accepts the deed, and commends the intention.

This intentional belittling to the extreme of the recipients of the message is nothing new since it was already planted by Ezekiel, the "father" of scripture:

And he said to me, "Son of man, I send you to the people of Israel, to a nation[14] of rebels, who have rebelled against me; they and their fathers have transgressed against me to this very day. The people also are impudent and stubborn: I send you to them; and you shall say to them, 'Thus says the Lord God.' And whether they hear or refuse to hear (for they are a rebellious house) they will know that there has been a prophet among them. And you, son of man, be not afraid of them, nor be afraid of their words, though briers and thorns are with you and you sit upon scorpions; be not afraid of their words, nor be dismayed at their looks, for they are a rebellious house. And you shall speak my words to them, whether they hear or refuse to hear; for they are a rebellious house." (2:3-7)

And he said to me, "Son of man, go, get you to the house of Israel, and speak with my words to them. For you are not sent to a

---

[14] In the original it is "nations" with the intent of totally equalizing between Israel and the "nations" in God's purview when it comes to sin, as already underscored in Genesis 1-11.

people of foreign speech and a hard language, but to the house of
Israel -- not to many peoples of foreign speech and a hard
language, whose words you cannot understand. Surely, if I sent
you to such, they would listen to you. But the house of Israel will
not listen to you; for they are not willing to listen to me; because
all the house of Israel are of a hard forehead and of a stubborn
heart." (3:4-7)

In the second passage one hears that the nations who hear the
word of instruction addressed to Israel have a better chance of
accepting it. Moreover, the messenger himself is belittled to the
extreme in that he is handed an already written scroll. It is as
though God found him even more untrustworthy than
Jeremiah. Whereas God put his words into Jeremiah's mouth
(Jer 1:9) and trusted him to dictate them to Baruch who
committed them to a scroll (36:6, 17, 32), the same God handed
Ezekiel a scroll already written on both sides (Ezek 2:9-10)
which the prophet had to swallow as such (3:2-3) and,
consequently, just regurgitate it *as is*. The intentionality of these
hyperbolic statements is corroborated in 3:17: "Son of man, I
have made you a watchman for the house of Israel; whenever
you hear a word from my mouth, you shall give them warning *from
me*." Yet this prophet who was "sent out" shall not only be "shut
in," but also "dumb" when the people approach him:

But the Spirit entered into me, and set me upon my feet; and he
spoke with me and said to me, "Go, *shut yourself within your house*.
And you, O son of man, behold, cords will be placed upon you,
and you shall be bound with them, so that *you cannot go out among
the people*; and I will make your tongue cleave to the roof of your
mouth, so that *you shall be dumb and unable to reprove them*; for they
are a rebellious house. But *when I speak with you, I will open your
mouth*, and you shall say to them, 'Thus says the Lord God'; he
that will hear, let him hear; and he that will refuse to hear, let him
refuse; for they are a rebellious house." (3:24-27)

Put otherwise, God will be reading out of the scroll the words he has already committed to writing.[15] It is as though God himself decided to recite his own written words lest, for whatever reason, his words would be contradicted by his prophet. Even Paul did not fare better than Ezekiel since what he preached to the Gentiles was the content of "the holy scriptures (writings, scrolls)" of "God's prophets" among whom was Ezekiel (Rom 1:2).[16]

Scripture is the consummate equalizer. Not only is Israel leveled with the nations under God's thumb, but Israel's prophets are also locked under that same thumb. Even Balaam, a prophet from the nations, was forced to utter the words God dictated to him (Num 22-24). It is the "scriptural story" *as it is written and sealed* within the binds of a scroll that is to be read aloud to the hearers, whomever they might be. The hearers are "sucked into" the story as either Israel or the nations. We, Jews and Christians, under the influence, or rather curse, of "identity" are used to thinking in terms of insider and outsider. However in the scriptural story, the first reference to the *toledot* of Shem, the "forefather" of the scriptural Israel through Abraham, is lumped into one *toledot* with those of his brothers (Gen 10:1) precisely because they were locked together into the one ark and thus into the one destiny.[17] Their destiny is described within the confines of the scriptural story up to its end that includes the coming judgment that is "remembered" as part of that "sealed" story. That is why the "future" is already

---

[15] This in and of itself should force those who still uphold the so-called "living oral tradition" to rethink this matter.

[16] In other words, in order to understand scripture, we have to learn scriptural Hebrew, and not ask God to learn English. I have no doubt that when they preached the Slavs, the two brothers, Cyril and Methodius, devised the new alphabet by following the blue print of Greek, that is to say, they baptized the new alphabet into the original. Cyril is recognized as having had knowledge of both Arabic and Hebrew.

[17] Only later, after the flood and the sin of arrogance by all the nations (Gen 11:1-9) is Shem's *toledot* singled out (v.10).

written and thus cannot be but remembered.[18] Put otherwise, there is "no way out" of the scriptural story. Once one begins to hear it, one is already entrapped in it. The only possible way out is to ignore it. However, ignoring it is not equivalent to eliminating or erasing it. It is you who are eliminated or erased out of its perspective. As for it, it will proceed to the following potential recipients who lend their ears to hear it and hopefully do its bidding:

> And whatever town or village you enter, find out who is worthy in it, and stay with him until you depart. As you enter the house, salute it. And if the house is worthy, let your peace come upon it; but if it is not worthy, let your peace return to you. And if any one will not receive you or listen to your words, shake off the dust from your feet as you leave that house or town. (Mt 10:11-14)

> And he called the twelve together and gave them power and authority over all demons and to cure diseases, and he sent them out to preach the kingdom of God and to heal. And he said to them, "Take nothing for your journey, no staff, nor bag, nor bread, nor money; and do not have two tunics. And whatever house you enter, stay there, and from there depart. And wherever they do not receive you, when you leave that town shake off the dust from your feet as a testimony against them." And they departed and went through the villages, preaching the gospel and healing everywhere. (Lk 9:1-6)

> Whatever house you enter, first say, 'Peace be to this house!' And if a son of peace is there, your peace shall rest upon him; but if not, it shall return to you. And remain in the same house, eating and drinking what they provide, for the laborer deserves his wages; do not go from house to house. Whenever you enter a town and they receive you, eat what is set before you; heal the sick in it and say to them, 'The kingdom of God has come near to you.' But whenever you enter a town and they do not receive you, go into its streets and say, 'Even the dust of your town that

---

[18] I keep stressing this fact that is strange for Western ears that were formatted by Greek philosophy.

clings to our feet, we wipe off against you; nevertheless know this, that the kingdom of God has come near. (Lk 10:5-11)

But when the Jews saw the multitudes, they were filled with jealousy, and contradicted what was spoken by Paul, and reviled him. And Paul and Barnabas spoke out boldly, saying, "It was necessary that the word of God should be spoken first to you. Since you thrust it from you, and judge yourselves unworthy of eternal life, behold, we turn to the Gentiles. For so the Lord has commanded us, saying, 'I have set you to be a light for the Gentiles, that you may bring salvation to the uttermost parts of the earth.'" And when the Gentiles heard this, they were glad and glorified the word of God; and as many as were ordained to eternal life believed. And the word of the Lord spread throughout all the region. (Acts 13:45-49)

When they had appointed a day for him, they came to him at his lodging in great numbers. And he expounded the matter to them from morning till evening, testifying to the kingdom of God and trying to convince them about Jesus both from the law of Moses and from the prophets. And some were convinced by what he said, while others disbelieved. So, as they disagreed among themselves, they departed, after Paul had made one statement: "The Holy Spirit was right in saying to your fathers through Isaiah the prophet: 'Go to this people, and say, You shall indeed hear but never understand, and you shall indeed see but never perceive. For this people's heart has grown dull, and their ears are heavy of hearing, and their eyes they have closed; lest they should perceive with their eyes, and hear with their ears, and understand with their heart, and turn for me to heal them.' Let it be known to you then that this salvation of God has been sent to the Gentiles; they will listen." And he lived there two whole years at his own expense, and welcomed all who came to him, preaching the kingdom of God and teaching about the Lord Jesus Christ quite openly and unhindered. (Acts 28:23-31)

26

Paradigms for Living

The impressive and challenging paradigms for implementing the scriptural teaching is found in the many and multifaceted brotherly and sisterly "orders" and "congregations" that developed within Roman Catholicism. To preempt any misunderstanding, I am not referring to, let alone endorsing, the correctness of the Roman Catholic church in its organization, theology, teaching, view of the sacraments, and the like. In this sense it is a church as any other church. What is impressive though is the many and varied "orders" or "congregations" or "societies" that blossomed and developed within the confines of Roman Catholicism, all of which have a high level of independence and autonomy. Most of these were conceived from the beginning as universal, that is to say, the area of their commitment covers the entire globe or, scripturally speaking, "their field is the world" where each member plants the specific "seed" the congregation or order is committed to (Mt 13:38). The earliest such congregations revolved around the classic monastic pattern (Carmelites in ca. 1206; Franciscans in 1209) or were dedicated to preaching the gospel in order to oppose heresy (Dominicans [the Order of Preachers] in 1216).

Orders, Societies, and Congregations within the Roman Catholic Church

In 1534, the Jesuits (Society of Jesus) opened the door for the rise of "outwardly" orders where the main concern were the needs of the others on both the intellectual level—not merely religion and theology[1]—and on the practical level of down-to-

---

[1] The Jesuits are renowned for their full-fledged universities where, included in the student body, are persons of all colors and creeds, not just Christians. Arts and

earth needs the like of which are described in Matthew 25:31-
46. This "out one goes to *serve* others" attitude proved to be the
major force behind the rise of the many and diverse
congregations of the seventeenth, nineteenth, and twentieth
centuries, which were unconventional in their boldness. These
include:

- Sisters of the Child Jesus (1676)

- Brothers of the Christian Schools—de Lasallians
  (1680)

- Christian Brothers (1802)

- Marist Brothers (1817)

- Little Brothers of Jesus (1933)

- Little Sisters of Jesus (1939)[2]

- Missionaries of Charity (1950)

The boldness lies not only in the non-religiosity of their fields of
endeavors—educating and care for the physical needs of
others—but also in the non-churchliness of their congregants in
that members of these orders are not necessarily priests or
official members of the clergy, but rather simply "brothers" or
"sisters," that is, members of the "society." Although other
religious affiliations, including the churches that arose from the
Reformation, have tried to copy or follow suit in similar
undertakings, none has been able to come close to the impact
of the Roman Catholic orders. What is amazing in this regard
is that while those brothers and sisters are under the papacy,
they are doing what they set out to do regardless of papacy,
except for making sure to change the picture of the pope when
necessary in the buildings and rooms of their institutions. They

sciences, after all, are for all to benefit from and do not require a "creedal" stand as
precondition.
[2] Notice that the last two "orders" were prompted by the aftermath of World War I
which brought about the Great Depression.

do not even preach Catholicism; they just simply do what they *individually* set out to do *for others*, any others, knowing that they will be held personally accountable (Mt 25:14-30) on the day of which Jesus speaks in Matthew 25:31-46.[3] Irrelevant to my argument is the immoral behavior of certain brothers and sisters and even institutions, universities or hospitals under the aegis of a given order. Other religious affiliations are not exempt of similar cases of such behavior among their leadership, be they bishops, priests, pastors, elders, monks, nuns, and the like. What I am pointing out is the trend of those orders that allows the individual to commit oneself to a certain "kind of service" (1 Cor 12:4-6)[4] until the reckoning day of everyone's "secret(s)" according to Paul's gospel (Rom 2:16), which is nothing else than the scenario described in Matthew 25:31-46.

Médecins Sans Frontières (Doctors Without Borders)

The total irrelevance of church affiliation or religious creed is corroborated by the organization *Médecins Sans Frontières* (Doctors Without Borders), an international humanitarian non-governmental organization established in France in 1971, in response to the aftermath of war in Biafra. This group was founded by a small group of French doctors and journalists who believed that all people have the right to medical care,

---

[3] As for the church leaders they are taken care of in Mt 24:45-51 and the church communities in Mt 25:1-13. See my comments in *NTI₄* 257-9.

[4] To say that Paul's admonition applies to the "church" as understood theologically and not to the open society, especially among the Orthodox, is untenable on two counts. On the one hand, in Paul's time his "churches" were "(Roman) house churches" where the membership included *all* the members of the Roman household family, whether "baptized" or not (e.g., Philem 1:1-2). On the other hand, the church Paul is talking about is co-extensive with God's "people" that shall be defined only at the end (Jer; Ezek); that is why the church is not fully "defined" until that day (Eph 2:11-22). Only those super-Orthodox stamped by their theological preconception believe that the church Paul is referring to is the One Holy Catholic Apostolic—understand Orthodox—church in any which way each one of them perceives it. Witness the debate still raging among Orthodox "theologians" as to whether *their* "Church" was at Crete this past June 2016 or not!

regardless of race, religion, or political affiliation, and that the
needs of people outweigh respect for national borders.[5]
Although this last statement is noble and inspiring, from my
perspective what is as impressive is the fact that the founders are
French. Beginning in the thirteenth century, we see a
prevalence of Orders being founded or established in France.
Excluding the Carmelites of Palestine, the Franciscans of Italy,
and the Dominicans,[6] all Catholic orders and societies,
including even the contemplative Cistercians (end of the twelfth
century) and Trappists (1664), up to and including the twentieth
century were founded in France. The Irish Christian Brothers
(1802) are a copy of the de-Lasallian Brothers of the Christian
Schools founded in France in 1694, and the Calcutta
Missionaries of Charity (1950) are a copy of the Little Brothers
and Sisters of Jesus orders founded in France in the 1930s.[7] It
stands to reason that *Doctors Without Borders* would be founded
by Frenchmen in the "Roman Catholic minded" France,[8] and
implements to a T the will of the scriptural God. The only
condition the organization imposes on its volunteers is that they
serve the physical needs of those who require such care. These
volunteers indeed serve *in deed* the scriptural God. What is even
more impressive is that the majority of its members, and those
who work alongside them, are married with families that they
leave for lengthy stretches of time to serve the unknown
stranger. This makes them obedient, to an extreme, to the
divine scriptural command by virtually abiding literally to the
equally extreme lordly statements:

---

[5] This information was copied here from the basic information found in Wikipedia
(*Médecins Sans Frontières*).
[6] Actually founded in Toulouse in Southern France by the Spanish Priest Dominic
of Caleruega in 1216.
[7] The Little Sisters of Jesus originated in French Algeria at the hands of a French
nun; the order is a copy of that of the Little Brothers of Jesus in that they were
founded three years apart under the impetus and auspices of Charles de Foucault.
[8] What I am stressing here is the "roman" mentality regardless of religion and
theology.

You shall not wrong a stranger or oppress him, for you were strangers in the land of Egypt. (Ex 22:21)

You shall not oppress a stranger; you know the heart of a stranger, for you were strangers in the land of Egypt. (Ex 23:9)

When a stranger sojourns with you in your land, you shall not do him wrong. The stranger who sojourns with you shall be to you as the native among you, and you shall love him as yourself; for you were strangers in the land of Egypt: I am the Lord your God. (Lev 19:33-34)

He who loves father or mother more than me is not worthy of me; and he who loves son or daughter more than me is not worthy of me; (Mt 10:37)

From the scriptural viewpoint *Doctors Without Borders* is the culmination of the movement of "orders" dedicated to serving the real needs of others that punctuated the history of Roman Catholicism.[9]

William Penn

One denomination that rose from the Reformation movement was "The Religious Society of Friends" or "Quakers." One of America's most famous Quaker is William Penn, who was granted the land that became the colony of Pennsylvania, and whose history is forever linked to Philadelphia,[10] the city of brotherhood. It is within such a city that Penn envisioned Indians, Jews, Catholics, and Protestants of all affiliations would live, and actually did live in brotherly harmony, as much as is humanly possible, *on this earth*. Penn and his city of Philadelphia[11] function as God and "his" scripture do: each of

---

[9] So many, if not the majority of, clergy are "needful to be needed" and thus, as someone once put it, are not fit for "real" jobs. Like the church they serve they plant in the minds of people the "need" for a deity, by definition fabricated, in order for them to fill that need with their "fabricated" theology and spirituality around a ritual that ensure their own livelihood.

[10] The closest "sister city" of Penn's creation would be Philadelphia of the Book of Revelation (Rev 3:7-13).

[11] Just as Pennsylvania is Penn's "woods."

the two pairs reflects the same "reality." Just as scripture is co-extensive and co-equivalent with God, so is Philadelphia with William Penn: their "stories" are intertwined into one functional "reality."[12] In the beginning was William Penn, then came about Philadelphia out of his own mind and heart, both shaped by the scripture of the scriptural God. Still, William Penn would not have been who he was and did what he did were he not imbued with the Friends' "mentality." Instead of yearning for "union" with the "divine," they harnessed the divine spark which they believe is in each of us—which others refer to as soul or image or spirit—into obedience to the divine "dictates" rather than to "being." The most impressive outcome of such an attitude is the large number of primary and secondary schools the Friends founded in many countries, two of which are the Friends Girls School and Friends Boys School in Ramallah, Palestine. Since their founding in 1869 and 1918 respectively, these schools are still functioning despite the miserable situation surrounding Ramallah since 1967.[13]

Xavier Plassat

A striking contemporary example of individual commitment to the scriptural teaching is the French Dominican friar (brother) Xavier Plassat. Plassat has dedicated his life to eradicating human slavery in the Brazilian Amazon.[14] What is of the essence in this example is that someone is toiling not for the sake of his own faith or to propagate the creed of his own church,

---

[12] In this regard, the Philadelphians sought to "honor" him by instituting a gentleman's agreement that no new construction would rise higher than the statue of Penn's atop the City Hall. According to scripture, it is always the senior who honors a junior and never a junior the senior. According to me, it is William Penn who honors Philadelphia in spite of his "little stature," and regardless of the height of skyscrapers that dot the city's skyline.

[13] Those interested readers can find more information and details at the following links https:// en.wikipedia. org/ wiki/ List_of_Friends_schools and https:// en. wikipedia.org /wiki /Ramallah_Friends_Schools.

[14] See for more details http://www.vanityfair.com/news/2015/11/modern-day-slave-trade.

but merely for the sake of others.[15] Let me quote the end of the *Vanity Fair* magazine article describing his efforts:

> The public's awareness of slavery will not soon disappear. International commerce, banks, and the powerful corporations that have joined the National Pact may demand a Dirty List that continues to be credible. Plassat understands that the situation is very serious. I spoke with him about the possibility that much of his work in Brazil could be undone. If that happens, I said, his strategy may still endure as a legacy affecting the lives of millions around the world. He replied that "legacy" does not matter to him. Direct action in the present time does. He says he will never return to France: his opponents had better know that about him. Whatever happens, Plassat will not be deterred. I remember how once, in his speeding car, Plassat cut across a pasture, following the merest trace of a track through high grass. I asked, "Is this a footpath or a road?" He said, "It's a road, of course!" He laughed. He looked over at me. He said, "It's a question of faith."[16]

Icelanders and the Syrian Refugees

Both the citizenry and the government of Iceland are opening the doors of their country to welcome refugees from war-torn Syria. This undertaking is not sponsored by a church or by a religious group within the community; it is simply an endeavor of people. In essence what these Icelanders are doing is living out the teaching of the scriptural God. The following is taken from an article by Christine Hauser in the September 1, 2015 issue of the *New York Times* entitled, "Icelanders Use Facebook to Open Door to Refugees."

> Responding to a growing international crisis, thousands of Iceland's residents have taken to social media to put pressure on

---

[15] Actually, we do not know the reason behind Plassat's commitment, which may well be proven on judgment day to have been for his own personal glory.

[16] Just imagine if Plassat would have had to have the approval of his Dominican Order or be backed and supported by a Mission Center. See also the facetious article http://www.acts17-11.com/snip_rejected.html relating how the Apostle Paul would have been denied his misssion. Thank God he did what he said he did in Gal 1:16b-17.

their government to take in more migrants. The island nation has already said it will take in 50 migrants, but officials said on Tuesday that the country would consider raising that number. A newly formed Facebook group, Syria is Calling, which has more than 13,000 members, is urging the government to take in 5,000.

"The idea is to show the government that there exists a will to receive even more refugees from Syria than the 50 that have already been discussed. We want to push the government—show them that we can do better, and do so immediately!" a group post said in English and Icelandic.

The group said some of its members have offered to open their houses to migrants and others have volunteered to donate money, clothes, furniture and other items, or to help the new arrivals assimilate. The Facebook page also said: "Refugees are our future spouses, best friends, our next soul mate, the drummer in our children's band, our next colleague, Miss Iceland 2022, the carpenter who finally fixes our bathroom, the chef in the cafeteria, the fireman, the hacker and the television host. People who we'll never be able to say to: 'Your life is worth less than mine.'

"Open the gates."

Thousands of migrants, many of them from the Middle East and North Africa, are escaping war and strife in their homelands, with some of them taking a perilous journey across the sea in an effort to reach safe harbor in Europe. Iceland, which has a population of 320,000, was hard hit by the financial crisis seven years ago, but there have been recent signs that its economy is improving, with tourism booming and 4.1 percent growth in the gross domestic product predicted for this year.

Iceland Review quoted Eyglo Hardardottir, the social affairs minister as saying in a televised interview that there were plans for municipalities to estimate how many refugees they would be able to accept. Responding to concerns that an influx might strain Iceland's resources, Ms. Hardardottir said migrants have historically paid taxes and contributed to society. "We are one of the richest nations in the world, and we can accept many more than we have been accepting in the past," she said.

The Syria is Calling Facebook page mentioned that the country's people banded together to help in 1973, when 4,000 people fled to Iceland from a volcanic eruption in the Westmand Islands off Iceland's southern coast.

In the current refugee crisis, some citizens have offered rooms in their homes, or suggested housing migrants in a former army base.

"It is evident that it is immoral to have it standing empty while people are dying," one Icelander, Oli Gneisti Soleyjarson, wrote in a Facebook comment.

The reasoning and the phraseology of these Icelanders does not reflect either the already long lost Lutheran background of the country, or its democratic form of government. Nor does it mention "mercy," let alone "God." In this regard it would behoove us to remember the Lord's injunction, "Not every one who says to me, 'Lord, Lord,' shall enter the kingdom of heaven, but he who does the will of my Father who is in heaven" (Mt 7:21). The movement in Iceland started with its citizens. The government was actually pressured by the people. What is impressive from the perspective of scripture is that there is no condescension, and thus no Pharisaic attitude *à la* Luke 18:11-12, but rather a simple and matter-of-fact attitude *à la* the Samaritan:

> But a Samaritan, as he journeyed, came to where he was; and when he saw him, he had compassion, and went to him and bound up his wounds, pouring on oil and wine; then he set him on his own beast and brought him to an inn, and took care of him. And the next day he took out two denarii and gave them to the innkeeper, saying, "Take care of him; and whatever more you spend, I will repay you when I come back." (Lk 10:33-35)

So the citizens of the farthest land in the realm of the nations assigned to Paul the Apostle acted according to his gospel. It is irrelevant whether the Icelanders were aware of that gospel. That gospel is not mentioned as a reason behind the way they acted. The sparsity of the island population—less than 400,000

inhabitants on a little over 100,000 square kilometers of land—
is also irrelevant since populating their island was not in the
purview of those same Icelanders, especially that they were on
the wake of a major economic crisis. In scriptural terms, the
Icelanders, residents of a quasi-desert island, extended the
scriptural world, the Syrian Desert, into their own world or
rather transformed their world into a scriptural one. While the
majority of the Europeans were busy protecting their
"Christian" civilizations, with their majestic monuments and
cathedrals[17] against the perceived invasion of Muslim refugees,
the Icelanders decided to welcome these needy strangers and
even "take them into marriage." The majority of Europeans
followed the example of the scriptural Israel that opted for
building a temple and a city with its ramparts as a protective
fence. Iceland, which has no standing army to protect itself,
opened the doors of its ramparts to the fledglings of a country
torn by an "international" war, and invited them into a society
that is, by the assessment of the Global Peace Index, the most
peaceful in the world.

Albanian Besa

A little over one year after Hauser's article appeared in the *New
York Times*, a similar article about Albania appeared on
http://www.bbc.com entitled, "What can Albania teach us
about trust?"[18] In it Quinn Hargitai wrote:[19]

> "My [Muka's, an Albanian] grandmother actually took in a
> family.
>
> "Didn't that ever get difficult?" I asked.

---

[17] Presumably built unto God's great glory.
[18] It is of note, in my eyes, that the author used the noun "trust" that corresponds to
the original meaning of the scriptural Hebrew root *'aman* and LXX Greek *pistis*,
usually translated as "faith."
[19] http://www.bbc.com/travel /story/20160909-what-can-albania-teach-us-about-trust.

"Not really for us, we were okay. But for many families it was a struggle, a lot of them didn't have the money to support the Kosovars. Many people went into debt doing it, but they would never turn anyone away."

When I asked her why, she shrugged. "It's the Albanian way. It's besa."

I had heard the word besa before, and knew that it meant something akin to belief, trust or faith, but I hadn't heard it in this context before. Muka explained that it's like a code for Albanians, one that dictates their generous hospitality. If someone comes to you looking for help, you give them a place to stay. It's that simple.

After our discussion, I was fascinated by the concept of besa and wanted to learn more, so I contacted Orgest Beqiri, an Albanian university student and history buff I had met during my time in the country. I knew that if anyone knew more detail about besa, it would be him. When we met, he explained that the tradition has been passed down for centuries as part of the Kanun of Lekë Dukagjini, a set of customary laws created in the 15th Century to govern the tribes of northern Albania. Though the Kanun is often considered to be the original source of besa, many argue that the tradition is in fact even older and that the Kanun merely put words to the tribal traditions that had existed long before.

"There's an old proverb written in the Kanun,"[20] he said. "'*Shpija para se me qenë e Shqiptarit, asht e Zotit dhe e mikut*', which means 'Before the house belongs to the owner, it first belongs to God and the guest.' It's a strong tradition, and in the older times, if you were a traveller or seeking refuge, you could knock on the door of the first house you found and ask 'Head of the house, do you want guests?' and the owner would have to take you in. The Kanun says that the master of the house should always have a spare bed ready at any time of day or night, in case a guest arrives unexpectedly."

---

[20] Which is the Arabic for "law" or "code." A transliteration of the Greek *kanōn* (rule; ruler), Arabic *qanun* reached Albania through Turkish, the language of the Ottoman empire.

"So it was a duty, then?" I asked him. "Even if you didn't want to host someone, you were bound by besa to do it?"

"Not exactly. Yes it's a duty, but honestly most Albanians really enjoy hosting guests. It's a point of pride for them. In fact, there's an old story about a town in the north somewhere that rebelled when a hotel was going to be built there. All the people went to the town hall and complained, saying people who needed a place to stay could just come and knock on their doors."

More recently, Albania has again found itself offering *besa*, this time to those travelling from the Middle East. Hundreds of Iranian exiles are currently residing within the country after having been relocated from Camp Liberty in Iraq. Albanian Prime Minister Edi Rama has also expressed an intent to aid Syrian refugees, provided a collaborative agreement is reached with other European nations, saying that Albania will not ignore its duty… The truth remains that this Balkan nation is small and poor, and as such, it hardly receives international attention for its exploits. Yet, at a time when refugees are being turned away at borders all over the world, it seems that there is a lot to learn from Albania's penchant for hospitality.

As in the case of Iceland there is absolutely nothing in the Albanian report that reflects either the religious background of the country, Muslim or otherwise, or its democratic form of government. Since Albania lies at the opposite end of Europe compared to Iceland, it is as though these two tiny and insignificant countries on the geo-political map of Europe, joined hands to encompass that continent into a scriptural "Syrian Wilderness" where all the sheep are part of the *one* flock of the *one* "non-egregious" shepherd. In Iceland and Albania the scriptural message *was* implemented, and these nations will remain, as scripture itself, a shaming proposition to both the "Nimrods" of Europe and elsewhere and the "Babels" (Gen 10:8-10) throughout our planet.

If you love those who love you, what credit is that to you? For even sinners love those who love them. And if you do good to those who do good to you, what credit is that to you? For even sinners do the same. And if you lend to those from whom you hope to receive, what credit is that to you? Even sinners lend to sinners, to receive as much again. But love your enemies, and do good, and lend, expecting nothing in return; and your reward will be great, and you will be sons of the Most High; for *he is kind to the ungrateful and the selfish. Be merciful, even as your Father is merciful.* (Lk 6:32-36)

But I say to you, Love your enemies and pray for those who persecute you, so that you may be sons of your Father who is in heaven; for he makes his sun rise on the evil and on the good, and sends rain on the just and on the unjust. For if you love those who love you, what reward have you? Do not even the tax collectors do the same? And if you salute only your brethren, what more are you doing than others? Do not even the Gentiles do the same? *You, therefore, must be perfect, as your heavenly Father is perfect.* (Mt 5:44-48)

27

The Faithfulness of God's Word

Our response to God's calling through our faith expressed in creeds is, according to scripture, literarily and literally immaterial. It is solely God's faithfulness to his scripturalized[1] word (Is 55:8-13) that is the subject matter:

> Then what advantage has the Jew? Or what is the value of circumcision? Much in every way. To begin with, the Jews are entrusted with (*epistevthēsan*) the oracles of God. What if some were unfaithful (*ēpistēsan*)? Does their faithlessness (*apistia*) nullify the faithfulness (*pistēn*)[2] of God? By no means! Let God be true though every man be false, as it is written, "That thou mayest be justified in thy words, and prevail when thou art judged." But if our wickedness serves to show the justice of God, what shall we say? That God is unjust to inflict wrath on us? (I speak in a human way.) By no means! For then how could God judge the world? … What then? Are we Jews any better off? No, not at all; for I have already charged that all men, both Jews and Greeks, are under the power of sin, as it is written: "None is righteous, no, not one; no one understands, no one seeks for God." (Rom 3:1-6, 9-11)

It is *solely* the "scripturalized" (divine) *logos* (word) that is *pistos* (faithful; sure), and not our assessments of it. Paul asserts this for the ages in his letters to the leaders of his churches (1 Tim 1:15; 3:1; 4:9; 2 Tim 2:11; Tit 3:8).[3] This is why the Gospel Book itself is never "blessed" since it is the bestower of blessings as much as God himself.[4] In other words, scripture is co-extensive and co-equivalent with God and, for all practical purposes, "is" God

---

[1] See Jn 20:30-31; 21:24-25 and 2 Pet 3:15-16, and my comments on them earlier.

[2] Which is usually translated as "faith." Besides, all the highlighted Greek words are from that same root.

[3] See my *C-Past*.

[4] The opening statement of all Orthodox sacramental liturgies is "Blessed is the Kingdom of the Father, and of the Son, and of the Holy Spirit" while the celebrant is holding high the Gospel Book and blesses with it the holy table or the baptismal font.

functionally in this world. It sanctifies (renders holy [hallows]; Hebrew *qaddeš*; Greek *hagiazei*; Latin *sanctificit*) *all things* including us or, at least, it is intended to do so. Scripture is the presence of the non-iconic God among us in his totality: eyes, ears, and especially "right hand" with which he bestows on us either his blessing or curse (Lev 26; Deut 28; Rev 22:18-19). The "throne" where he resides is nothing else save the "praises (*tehillot*) of Israel" (Ps 22:3 RSV; 22:4 Hebrew),[5] which is the Book of Psalms (*sepher tehillim*) itself. The God of whom scripture speaks is totally contained within the scriptural story, and so are his "promises." As we hear in the last words of scripture itself: "if any one takes away from the words of the book of this prophecy, God will take away his share in the tree of life and in the holy city, which are written (*gegrammenōn*; scripturalized)[6] in this book." (Rev 22:19)

Scripture is a propositional tightly knit literature that is not meant to be imposed on us or on others, but is offered as an option. However, this option may not to be tampered with à la Plato or debated, reworded, and expanded upon à la theology. The scriptural option is total submission to its content and premises as having come from the one who will judge us all *according to the rules inscribed in it.* The freedom we have is not for us to interpret its contents to fit either our "logic" or "illogic" as the case may be; its contents are "plain" to those who have ears to hear. Still we are not free to block the dissemination of its teachings to those who would like to receive them *as they are*, that is, *literarily and thus literally*. Literality in literature comes out of the word interplay and puns that do not exist save in the

---

[5] "Yet thou art holy, enthroned on the praises of Israel."

[6] The RSV calamitous translation "described" gives the impression that the authors were referring to something that already "is" out there, somewhere and is inviting their hearers to accede to that place at their death. That is the calamity, if not catastrophe, of theological lingo that produces a "religion" that is controlled by its human "protectors" according to the principle *cujus regio, ejus religio* (whose realm, his religion; that translates in practice: the religion of the ruler was to dictate the religion of those ruled) to which even Martin Luther submitted after he shed off himself and his followers the "rule" of the pope!

original. In other words, its meaning cannot be imposed from other sources. With all due respect to twenty-first century Jews, it is important to understand that the scriptural language is not the Hebrew they speak and write today, but rather it is a Semitic Hebrew language concocted by the authors themselves. With all due respect to my fellow Greeks, understanding contemporary Greek does not give them an edge over the others since the New Testament Greek is the LXX Old Testament Greek that the authors, themselves the translators,[7] intentionally subordinated to *their* Hebrew.[8] Scripture and its language—and by the same token its message—are to be approached the way we had to approach the Ugaritic literature unearthed at Ras Shamra (Ugarit). Ugaritic did not exist somewhere "out there" but had to be learned *out of* the discovered literature—if the texts say that the Ugaritic deities spoke Ugaritic, then it is so. Similarly, if in scripture the scriptural God spoke scriptural Hebrew, then it is so. The corollary is that in order to address that God and pray to him, one is to use the prayers he taught us through his emissaries, and not bombard him with unending "theological" hymns[9] we concocted to embellish "*our*" services.

Scripture *itself* is to be preserved for the following generations since ours is already disobedient, if not condemned, according to Psalm 78 and Ezekiel 2-3. Yet the psalm is inviting us to relay the scriptural "teachings" and *not* our example, be it good or bad since only God is good. To be able to do so, one should download the "app" of the Bible in one's own maternal

---

[7] Unless one subscribes to the legend of the Letter of Aristeas to Philocrates.

[8] One example should suffice. The very important *pistis* cannot possibly be fathomed unless one has mastered the unmatched versatility of the original Hebrew root *'aman*. In this regard one should not make "excuses in sins" but learn from the Muslim tradition whereby it is not required from all Muslims—Indonesia is the most populous Muslim country—to know Arabic, however their Imams *must* know very well Qur'anic Arabic.

[9] The people hardly understand such even in the translations. They simply nod in order not to be subjected to an extra session of explanations in an even more complicated lingo.

language and listen to it once a year and, whenever one is asked as to what scripture is saying, one should replay it or recite it by heart to the inquirer without any extra comments. Those who are "brave of heart" (*gibborim*) should learn Latin vocabulary and grammar and then listen to the Vulgate, and do likewise when inquired of. Those who venture to be "kingly" should learn scriptural Greek vocabulary and grammar and then listen to the LXX, and do likewise when inquired of. Those who desire to be "perfect"[10] must learn scriptural Hebrew vocabulary and grammar, and then listen to the Old Testament in scriptural Hebrew, and do likewise when inquired of. This is the only way that we—dust of the ground who are destined to return to that dust when our "breathing" leaves us—will perpetrate the presence of the scriptural God among our progeny. This will offer them real hope in the sole one who is "the living One," residing in the words of the scroll handed down to Ezekiel. Let the "call" of the Entrance of the Gospel in Orthodox rubrics resonate "ages without end" in our—and more so our childrens'—world: "This is (scriptural and consequently divine) wisdom, let us be (fully) attentive to its teaching."

Whenever we are prone to action, let us recite in unison in the words of Psalm 119, the ode to the *torah*: "It is time *for the Lord* to act, for *thy law has been broken*." (v.126) His teaching summons us to act according to his will through our *feet* and not our grey cells:

> When I think of thy ways, I turn my feet to thy testimonies; I hasten and do not delay to keep thy commandments (vv.59-60)

> I hold back my feet from every evil way, in order to keep thy word. I do not turn aside from thy ordinances, for thou hast taught me. (101-102)

---

[10] I do not mean that à la Origen.

Thy word is a lamp to my feet and a light to my path. I have sworn an oath and confirmed it, to observe thy righteous ordinances. (vv.105-106)

Let me live, that I may praise thee, and let thy ordinances help me. I have gone astray like a lost sheep; seek thy servant, for I do not forget thy commandments. (vv.175-176)

The scriptural God's fold is all-encompassing since it includes all humankind as the *one* flock of the *one* shepherd:

"Truly, truly, I say to you, he who does not enter the sheepfold by the door but climbs in by another way, that man is a thief and a robber; but he who enters by the door is the shepherd of the sheep. To him the gatekeeper opens; the sheep hear his voice, and he calls his own sheep by name and leads them out. When he has brought out all his own, he goes before them, and the sheep follow him, for they know his voice. A stranger they will not follow, but they will flee from him, for they do not know the voice of strangers." This figure[11] Jesus used with them, but they did not understand what he was saying to them. So Jesus again said to them, "Truly, truly, I say to you, I am the door of the sheep. All who came before me are thieves and robbers; but the sheep did not heed them. I am the door; if any one enters by me, he will be saved, and will go in and out and find pasture. The thief comes only to steal and kill and destroy; I came that they may have life, and have it abundantly. I am the good shepherd. The good shepherd lays down his life for the sheep. He who is a hireling and not a shepherd, whose own the sheep are not, sees the wolf coming and leaves the sheep and flees; and the wolf snatches them and scatters them. He flees because he is a hireling and cares nothing for the sheep. I am the good shepherd; I know my own and my own know me, as the Father knows me and I know the Father; and I lay down my life for the sheep. And I have other sheep, that are not of this fold; I must bring them also, and they will heed my voice. So there shall be one flock, one shepherd." (Jn 10:1-16)

---

[11] *paroimia*, another term for *parabolē* (parable; Hebrew *mashal* [instructional story]). The LXX title for the Book of the "Proverbs (*meshalim*) of Solomon" is *Paroimiai Salōmōntos*.

About the Author

The V. Rev. Dr. Paul Nadim Tarazi has been teaching Scripture for well over forty years. His teaching ministry has included a full-time professorship at St Vladimir's Orthodox Theological Seminary in Crestwood, New York, as well as adjunct positions at Holy Cross Greek Orthodox School of Theology in Brookline, Massachusetts, and the St. John of Damascus Institute of Theology in Balamand, Lebanon. His work covers the full range of scriptural studies in Old and New Testaments, Biblical Hebrew and Greek, Academic Arabic, and Homiletics. He has been a guest lecturer at numerous universities and institutions in the United States and Canada, as well as Australia, Chile, Estonia, Finland, Greece, Israel, Jordan, Palestine, Romania, Serbia, and Syria, and has represented the Antiochian Orthodox Church at various ecumenical gatherings.

Fr. Paul is the author of a three volume Introduction to the Old Testament, a four volume Introduction to the New Testament, Galatians: A Commentary, I Thessalonians: A Commentary, and Land and Covenant. His work in the Chrysostom Bible series includes Genesis: A Commentary, Philippians: A Commentary, Romans: A Commentary, Colossians & Philemon: A Commentary, 1 Corinthians: A Commentary, 2 Corinthians: A Commentary, Ezekiel: A Commentary, Joshua: A Commentary, Isaiah: A Commentary, Jeremiah: A Commentary, Hebrews: A Commentary and The Pastorals: A Commentary. His Audio Bible Commentaries on the books of the Old and New Testament are available online through the Orthodox Center for the Advancement of Biblical Studies (OCABS).

Fr. Paul was born in Jaffa, Palestine, moved to Cairo, Egypt and then to Beirut, Lebanon, where he studied at the Christian Brothers French School prior to attending the Jesuit University School of Medicine in Beirut. He pursued theological studies at

the Orthodox Theological Institute in Bucharest, Romania
where he received his Th.D. degree in New Testament in 1975.
He was ordained to the holy priesthood in the United States in
1976 and served as pastor of parishes in Connecticut and New
York. He currently lives in Leland, North Carolina.